UnAustralian Art

Ten Essays on Transnational Art History

Butler &
Donaldson

Contents

Foreword

The first sentences of Ernst Gombrich's monumental *The Story of Art*, originally published in 1950, are 'There is really no such thing as Art. There are only artists'. A few sentences later, Gombrich cautions us to remember that 'Art with a capital A has no existence'. We in the writing of this book have taken from Gombrich here. There is the obvious self-contradiction of his stating that there is no Art at the beginning of a 600-page book on just that subject. And we too are aware of the implicit self-contradiction of calling our history one of UnAustralian art when it is a history of Australian art, the story of how we came to be who we are today. But we wanted to use the qualifier 'UnAustralian' to make the point that Australian art has always been, at least as much, UnAustralian: not about the formation of some national ideal or character, not about the distance and isolation of us living here, but about what we have in common with other people and other cultures, about how Australia is part of, and belongs to, the rest of the world.

This brings us to the other piece of Gombrich's advice: that there is no such thing as Art but only artists. For our history is not so much of Australian art as of UnAustralian artists. It is they and not so much their work who come to live in Australia, they and not so much their work who leave Australia and continue their lives overseas. Our UnAustralian history is at least as much social as it is artistic, as much concerned with the personal relations and connections between artists, gallerists, critics and curators as it is with the stylistic development of art. Our history is therefore a history of cities and scenes and not countries and landscapes. Indeed, it is arguable that our artists have *always* had an UnAustralian conception of art, and it is only our historians and art institutions who have imposed a specific nationalism upon them. This UnAustralian history might be nothing more than a history of Australian art told from the point of view of artists, and it is perhaps not coincidental that one of us is a practising artist.

For the most part, the essays are reprinted here in the form in which they were originally published or delivered as lectures. In a way, we wanted to make clear or at least be faithful to the scenes—the particular times and places—in which they came about and the 'artistic'—open-ended, experimental, provisional—spirit in which they were written. In some cases, however, fresh research has led to some of the essays being expanded and to corrections being made when mistakes were discovered. (Australian art history has been littered with errors and misunderstandings, mistakes that have been repeated by our art historians, including by us.) Now considered as chapters in a book, the texts have undergone some editing to provide greater depth to existing lines of argument and to avoid repetition. On rare occasions, too, we have added notes to refer to events that have taken place after the paper in question was published or delivered. Indeed, these chapters, each of which connects Australia to another place, to artists or to a wider artistic movement, might be understood collectively as a preliminary version of a longer and larger project—perhaps a more conventionally art-historical one—to write a new history of Australian art in the twentieth century.

Undoubtedly, there has been something of a progression or development in our thinking since the idea for a new history of Australian art first came to us some fifteen years ago. As revealed by the list of our other writings on UnAustralian art at the back of the book, we began with an essay that outlined an alternative history of twentieth-century Australian art, of the kind we hope one day to return to ('A Short History of UnAustralian Art'). We then wrote drafts or preliminary versions of a number of the proposed chapters or periods of this history ('French, Floral and Female: A History of UnAustralian Art, 1900–1930', 'Stay, Go, or Come: A History of Australian Art, 1920–40'). We subsequently wrote a series of more synoptic essays connecting Australian art to that of other countries or cultures, a number of which are reprinted in this book ('Ten Rooms: The Real Spaces of Asian–Australian Artistic Interaction', 'Another Australia: British–Australian Art 1880–1970', 'War and Peace: 150 Years of Germany and Australia'). Finally, as the implications of this effectively 'globalist' conception of art became clearer to us, we began experimenting with the idea of including not just Australian immigrants and emigrants in our Australian story, but all those who have made art about 'Australia' in some way, whether or not they had ever actually visited the country ('I Am, You Are, We Are All Australian', 'All The World's Australias').

Here again, in something of the spirit of Gombrich, there is another potential self-contradiction in a question to which we return several times in what follows: from where do we write and for whom do we write if Australian art can effectively be made by anyone? What boundary do we seek to draw around what counts as Australian art? As we hope these essays show, this hypothesis of thinking about the art of this country more broadly opens up so much more to be seen that we believe is properly 'Australian'. The history that we seek to write is the history that informs our present, the history of the contemporary reality of Australia as a colonised country of mass immigration and many cultures, and of the increased acknowledgement overseas of the contributions of Australian artists (maybe movie stars and directors in particular, but visual artists too). However, as we emphasise throughout, if we write from the point of view of our present, this present also allows us to re-see and recast the past. It is not only to think, for example, that provincialism never really characterised the story of Australian art despite its prevalance in art-historical discourse, but that any number of Australian art historians had the same intuition as we have about the real nature of Australian art, which is that the national was only ever one part of the narrative of our art and, indeed, in many ways arose in reaction to international art.

On the one hand, then, we suggest that these essays propose something of a new conception of Australian art and introduce a whole series of hitherto unknown artists and art-historical incidents into a revised and expanded conception of Australian art. On the other hand, perhaps in light of this new historical designation itself, we can see that much of this UnAustralian history has already been told, not only by a series of revisionist accounts written since the 1970s, but also by a number of Australian art historians, critics and curators since at least the 1920s. Moreover, there has been, especially in the last twenty years, a whole series of art exhibitions—a number of which we list in our introduction—that have sought to bring to our attention and record for history the contributions of immigrant and expatriate artists, which we also take up here. But again, as another way of conceiving Australian art, the designation 'UnAustralian' amalgamates these often disparate undertakings, which have largely lacked a sense of what they share with so many others. What we seek to do in the essays that follow is to generalise, sometimes almost to the point of universality, various immigrant and emigrant artistic experiences, to see each as part of a wider phenomenon, as pointing beyond itself to a different conception of Australian art altogether.

Over the years since the idea of a possible history of UnAustralian art first came to us, any number of people have helped and encouraged us. First of all, we thank the Power Institute Foundation for Art and Visual Culture at the University of Sydney, in particular Mark Ledbury and Marni Williams, and our copyeditor Belinda Nemec. We also thank the editors of the various magazines and journals that originally published these essays, and the academics, museum curators and directors of cultural institutions who asked us to speak and thus gave us the occasion (and necessity) to gather and publicly present our thoughts: Ian North (Contemporary Art Centre of South Australia), Michael Fitzgerald (*Art &*

Australia), Ryan Johnson and Amelia Barikin (*emaj*), Anthony White and Richard Woodfield (*Journal of Art Historiography*), Melissa Harper and Marguerite Nolan (*Journal of Australian Studies*), Alan Cruickshank (*Broadsheet*), Tansy Curtin and Karen Quinlan (Bendigo Regional Art Gallery), Arpad Sölter and Jochen Gutsch (Goethe-Institut), Kalli Rolfe (Kalli Rolfe Contemporary Art), Helen Hughes and Nicholas Croggon (*Discipline*), Campbell Grey and Michele Helmrich (University of Queensland Art Museum), Charles Green and Ian McLean (University of Melbourne) and Catherine Chevalier (*May*). We thank as well Sophie Berckelaers, the granddaughter of Michel Seuphor; Emmanuel Jaeger of the gallery Jeanne Bucher Jaeger, Paris; Raymond Creuze of Galerie Creuze, Paris; Christophe Michel of the Galerie Suzanne Michel; Isabelle van Ongeval of the AMVC-Letterenhuis, Antwerp; the art historian Domitille d'Orgeval; the archivists at l'Institut mémoires de l'édition contemporaine, Caen, in particular Yves Chevrefils Desbiolles; the archivists at the Bibliothèque Kandinsky, Paris; the archivists at the Smithsonian's Archive of American Art, New York; the staff of the Provincetown Art Association and Museum, Massachusetts; the archivists of the National Library of Australia, the National Gallery of Australia, the State Library of New South Wales, the State Library Victoria and the Museum of Applied Arts and Sciences, Sydney; as well as Steven Miller at the Research Library and Archive of the Art Gallery of New South Wales, Harriet McAtee of the University of Queensland and Jessica Neath of Monash University. Finally, we thank those colleagues who offered advice, insight and on occasion criticism, including Janet Burchill, Juan Davila, Robert Dixon, Matthys Gerber, Jeff Gibson, Alison Inglis, Darren Jorgensen, Tom Melick, Mark Ray, Naomi Riddle, Isabelle Scherer, Laurence Simmons, Nika Span, Ann Stephen, Krunoslav Stipešević and Elena Taylor, as well as the two anonymous reviewers of the manuscript that was submitted to Power Publications.

But especially we thank our partners and families: Anne Wallace, Nathaniel and Sylvie Butler, and Lotte Donaldson, Elena and Emily Taylor, Margaret and Alan Donaldson and the late Margaret Balding.

Rex Butler and ADS Donaldson

—

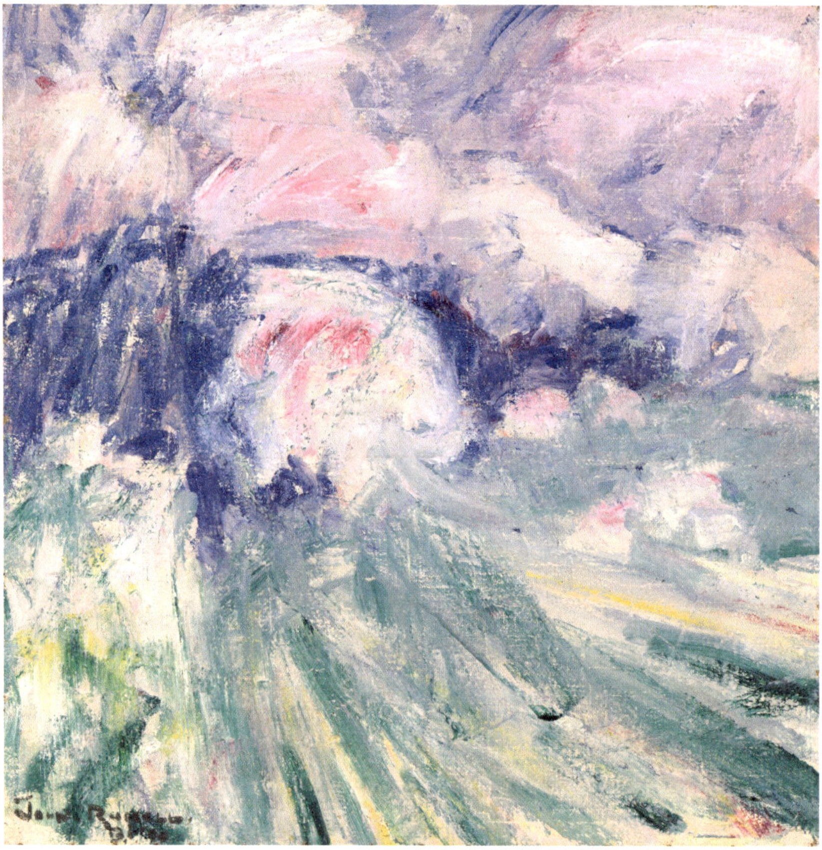

0.1 John Russell
Rough sea, Belle-Île, 1900

Introduction

The genesis of this collection of essays is a painting, John Russell's *Rough sea, Belle-Île* (1900), which we encountered again at the National Gallery of Victoria in 2004. It is a small, square painting, some 63 × 63 centimetres, depicting the land, sea and sky around Belle-Île, off the coast of Brittany, which Russell had first visited in 1886 before moving there in 1888. With its smeared passages of green, pink and white, the painting is unable to maintain the distinction between the various elements of the landscape it otherwise wants to represent. Almost violent, the canvas seems in constant movement, with its endless dashing of waves and turbulent atmosphere challenging the then conventional demand made of painting to picture the world. When we look at it closely, it is as though we are somehow inside both the landscape and the painting at the same time. Indeed, Russell's depiction is undoubtedly a provocation of sorts. We can certainly think of no comparable work made by any other artist anywhere at the time. Are we not struck by how abstract expressionist mid-century modern it is, how despite its size it is so physically and materially overwhelming, how in a sense it is nothing less than painting against painting?

Russell was, until his art-historical revival in the 1970s, our lost impressionist.[1] He had learned the art of unmixed colour from Claude Monet, beside whom he painted on the coast of Belle-Île during the summer of 1886. Such was Russell's reputation as a friend of both Vincent van Gogh and Auguste Rodin that when the young Henri Matisse was at a crossroads in the late 1890s he sought Russell out to help him break from his dull academic palette. Over two trips to Russell's Château de l'Anglais on Belle-Île, Matisse learned from Russell vital lessons in the liberation of colour that were to be foundational for his later work.[2] The debt Matisse felt he owed Russell was so great that it seems no coincidence that he named his first son Jean and his second son Pierre after the Sydney painter (Russell's middle name was Peter). In fact, the great self-portraitist van Gogh's favourite portrait of himself was done by Russell—the two had become friends during their student days at the Académie Cormon in Paris in 1886—and it has hung inside the entrance of the Van Gogh Museum in Amsterdam since its opening. The strength of the two artists' relationship was such that in a letter to Russell at the beginning of 1890 Van Gogh, a matter of months before his suicide, confirmed his willingness to give one of his paintings to Russell for a future national collection in Australia:

> If you should go to Paris, please go and take a canvas of mine at my brother's, if you still stick to the idea of some day getting together a collection for your native country.[3]

The offer was never taken up, but for us it points towards another possible Australian art history. It is a history that would be built not on our belated adaptations of other cultures but on our contemporaneous exchanges with them. A history in which we do not receive art from elsewhere and at a distance, but are instead part of that history we usually understand ourselves to be standing outside. Australian art history was inward-looking, so for much of the twentieth century Russell was a marginal figure, his expatriatism precluding his inclusion in the

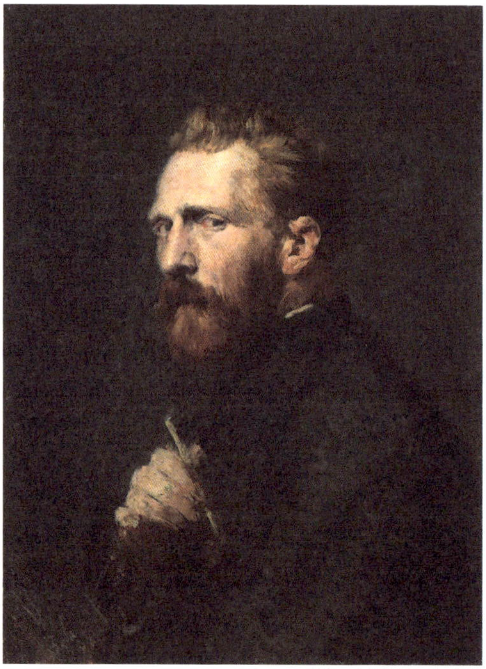

0.2 John Russell
Portrait of Vincent van Gogh, 1886

dominant narratives of a national art still focused on impressionistic depictions of Australia's 'harsh' landscape.[4] And this exclusion was categorical, because these isolationist histories of Australian art have always sought the distinctiveness and separation of our art and not its commonalities and belonging—the wildness of the bush; the 'youth' of the country; the uniqueness of the light; the distance from Western influences. Our dominant art histories from the early twentieth century on have endeavoured, almost without exception, to draw a geographic frame or wall around what would count as Australian art. In his 1966 *The Art of Australia*, Robert Hughes excludes, for instance, the pioneering linocut artist Horace Brodzky, who, 'though Australian, lived in England since Edwardian times and never exhibited in Australia'.[5] In his 1997 *Art in Australia*, Christopher Allen frankly acknowledges that his book concerns 'art made by Europeans in Australia'.[6] And even though Andrew Sayers attempts to correct this by including work by Indigenous artists in his 2001 *Australian Art*, he contends that, 'in order to create a new shape for the history of Australian art, I have confined this book to works created in Australia'.[7] But this is, in fact, the old shape.

The first gesture of our new UnAustralian history is simply to open the aperture more widely onto what counts as Australian art. It is to capture all those artists who were born and educated here or trained or worked here for some period of time. The effect of this is, obviously, to include more in the definition of what counts as Australian. After Ernst Gombrich, we also focus on the history of artists over art because we are concerned with the real experiences of those connected to art in the twentieth century, and not with the supposed national character of Australian art as exemplified by the schools of painting located here, such as those at Heidelberg and Heide, that dealt with Australian landscapes, mythologies or the character of its people.[8] As these essays will reveal, Australians throughout the twentieth century did not necessarily feel that when they went overseas they were no longer Australian. Even though they often stayed away for long periods, and sometimes forever, they nearly always maintained connections with where they came from, as with Russell's near invisible return to Watson's Bay in Sydney after some forty years in Europe. And Australians overseas continued to identify with each other, forming networks of mutual support and training in classes taught by Australians, often beside other Australians. Early critics and historians of Australian art living overseas did not automatically exclude fellow expatriates from their histories of Australian art. As we will make clear, they even formed groups with and organised exhibitions of the work of Australians living overseas, pointedly counting their work as Australian.

In understanding these artists' work as Australian, these critics were not looking for some putative national quality, as the subsequent generation of Australian art historians would have us believe. Indeed, the case was almost the opposite, with the defining quality of Australian art being its very cosmopolitanism or non-nationalism. Consider, for instance, the Sydney-educated art critic, activist and writer Edith Fry, who founded the group Australian Artists in Europe while living in London, piqued by their exclusion from the *Exhibition of Australian Art* organised by Sydney Ure Smith at Burlington House in London in 1923. Fry, our foremost contemporary historian of Australian expatriatism before and after World War I, observed of the painting by Daylesford-born Ambrose Patterson in Ure Smith's show:

> *Collins Street, Melbourne* … has true luminosity—but Patterson worked for years in Paris. Was it there that he learnt the truth of vision that makes him more Australian than the Australians?[9]

Or as Wellington-born (and the Australasian is an important perspective for our history) artist and critic Raymond McIntyre, who also lived and worked in London, asked of the second of the two exhibitions that Fry curated featuring Australian artists in Europe: 'When is an Australian not an Australian?' To which he answered with a similar paradox:

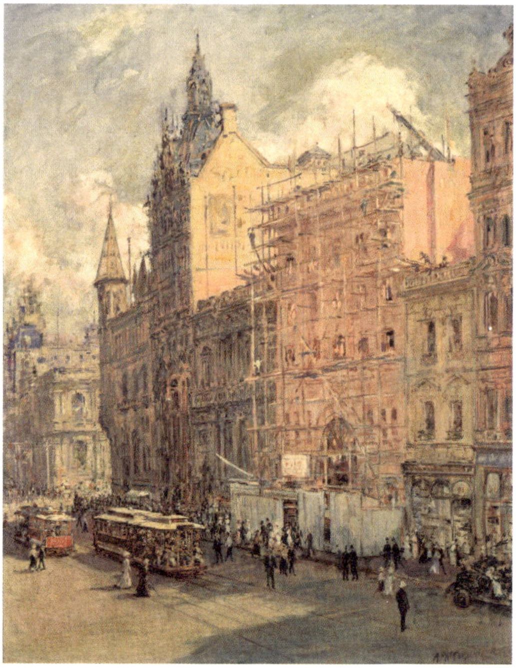

0.3 Ambrose Patterson
Collins Street, Melbourne, 1911

> We might even say that, in proportion as they cease to be Australians, their work becomes more interesting, viewed from the standpoint of modern artistic developments in Europe.[10]

In other words, early in the twentieth century, and certainly in the nineteenth century, before the nationalist histories of Australian art started being written, artists and critics found no necessary disparity between being Australian and being part of the world. It is to capture something of this impulse that we have decided to call our history that of UnAustralian art. It is precisely to take a distance from the necessity that the art of this country express something of a national character, assumed to be some combination of the landscape, light and people. And it is to point to this other, hitherto excluded part of our history in which the 'Australian' is not obvious and is not even something striven for by art. We believe that our prevailing national histories cannot be understood without this excluded part, and that those nationalist histories are even a reaction to it. As much as this UnAustralian history is an extension of and complement to the existing Australian art histories, it is also an inversion and overturning of those histories, the revealing of their hidden condition: that 'outside' without which they would not be possible.

This fork in the road can be seen as early on as an incident that took place in 1906 in London. As related by William Moore in his first national history of Australian art, *The Story of Australian Art* (1934), Tom Roberts had been in the habit for a number of years of holding an annual dinner at the restaurant Au Petit Riche in Soho for Australian artists living in England at which gum leaves were ceremonially burned. Regular attendees included John Longstaff, James Quinn, Fred Leist, BE Minns and, of course, Roberts himself. Moore writes:

> One night Charles Conder appeared. He had been away from the group for some time and for some reason or other was left rather alone. 'Anyone going my way?' he asked as the party broke up. As no one moved, he went out alone.[11]

From this time on, Conder was increasingly afflicted by alcoholism and venereal disease, often spending time in a sanatorium, until dying of a 'general paralysis of the insane' three years later in Surrey, where he is buried. The most successful artist at that dinner, Conder had exhibited with the New English Art Club and the New Salon in Paris, before being invited to participate in art dealer Samuel Bing's ground-breaking first and second exhibitions at his la Maison de l'Art Nouveau in 1895 and 1896. Indeed, Conder's friend and drinking partner in Paris was Henri de Toulouse-Lautrec, in whose work he occasionally featured. Another of Conder's great friends, the French post-impressionist Jacques-Émile Blanche, once described him sitting in his home on Cheyne Walk, Chelsea:

> Swathed in a cloud of cigarette smoke [he smoked more than sixty cigarettes a day], Conder had the distant expression of one who would get drunk on port from morning to night, and who in an opium smoker's delirium believed that from his Chelsea window he looked out not only on the Thames but also on India and Australia.[12]

This view from Conder's window looks out upon another Australian art history. It would be an alternative to the familiar and by now exhausted story of Australian art heralded by the publication in 1962 of Bernard Smith's *Australian Painting*, which has not been displaced by any of the subsequent accounts of Australian art. For us this story is as tired as it is blinkered, and cannot account for the actual conditions of art, the way we got to where we are today.

We write this at the present moment fully aware that the academic study of Australian art has been in decline for the first two decades of the twenty-first century. Students today in universities and art schools are increasingly taking courses in contemporary art, understood to be a separate subject from that of Australian art. This decline in the study of Australian art is mirrored in the diminution of the authority of the specialist curator of Australian art in our state and national galleries. Theirs is a position whose influence is being undermined by the event status that art exhibitions are increasingly being required to achieve. Instead of generating scholarship and extending and strengthening collections, the curator of Australian art today is often at the whim of those gallery directors whose primary motivation is an increase in audience numbers and not a better understanding of Australian art. In some ways, however, these curators have been the architects of their own downfall. Like the art historians, their senior members have largely been unable to re-imagine a new history for the exhibition-going public. The default curatorial model over the past thirty years has centred around a periodic re-examination of the canonical national artists, which in practice has meant the regular remounting of Roberts, Sidney Nolan, Margaret Preston, Arthur Boyd, Albert Tucker, Russell Drysdale, Albert Namatjira, the Heidelberg School, and more recently William Robinson and Margaret Olley, in a cycle that has its obverse in the neglect of such artists as Ralph Balson, Moya Dyring and Stan Ostoja-Kotkowski, and many others who have never been given a retrospective at a state gallery. And all of this is to overlook the fact that a whole generation of Australian expatriate artists has not yet received a survey, or has had one only in very recent times. We have been waiting too long already for state gallery exhibitions of the work, for example, of Derwent Lees, Roy de Maistre and Margaret Cilento, let alone Ambrose Patterson, Richard Hayley Lever and Iso Rae. Indeed, it was only in 2014 that Dorrit Black and Mortimer Menpes received long-overdue recognition, with important exhibitions at the Art Gallery of South Australia, and not until 2018 that Russell's life and work were acknowledged at the Art Gallery of New South Wales with only his second retrospective, the first having been held in Amsterdam some forty years earlier.[13]

So, tired, even bored, with the old story of Australian art, and in the context of a lack of compelling academic accounts and a frequently absent curatorial direction, we seek to present here another history of who we are and, indeed, always have been. If a new past is available, it is perhaps because we can do art history differently in a digital age; and these essays rely for their evidence on the digitisation of innumerable artworks, archives, collections, photographs, magazines, journals, periodicals and newspapers, both here and around the world. The immediate accessibility of so much new information, we suggest, leads not merely to a revisionist inclusion of new and hitherto overlooked figures, but to a whole new kind of 'horizontal' history, putting together long sequences of these figures to produce a different historical pattern. But if this new digital era has allowed new figures to emerge, new events to be seen, new information to be gleaned and new tendencies to appear, these essays also rely on situated archival research in libraries and art museums in, among other places, Belgium, the Americas, Italy, New Zealand and France. Moreover, this digitisation, if it introduces a revolution in scholarly method, also allows us to realise that the transmission of academic information was almost as rapid in the past. Once we were surprised to discover that Duchamp's painting *Nude descending a staircase* (1912) was reproduced in Australian newspapers the same year it was the *succès de scandale* of the 1913 Armory Show in New York, but today we think nothing of knowing that Kandinsky's book *Concerning the Spiritual in Art* was available in Australia the year it was translated into English, and was even reviewed in Melbourne's *Argus* newspaper the year it was published in its original German.[14]

Indeed, it is remarkable to consider that there were no fewer than four Australians in that famous Armory Show, which we in Australia have always looked upon as an outbreak of European modernism in faraway America that came before ours and did not ultimately concern us. They were Charles Conder, Derwent Lees, Frank Nankivell and Francis McComas. The first two are recognisable to us, but the latter two are nearly unknown artists. Nankivell was a member of the Association of American Painters and Sculptors and on the committee behind the show; but the least well known of them all, McComas, was included in the exhibition as a representative of Californian art, and it was in that State that he made his reputation as a leader of the Monterey School, the West Coast's tonal post-impressionism. That is to say, Australians were intimately involved in impressionism and its immediate aftermath not only in France, but also in America. There were Australians making contributions to impressionism in France, America and Australia, and this internationalism of impressionism, the observation that it occurs not only in France, widens our understanding of the Australian involvement in a global movement. If the 2013 exhibition *Australian Impressionists in France* at the National Gallery of Victoria introduces us to the idea of an Australian impressionism without gumtrees, then McComas's watercolours remind us that American impressionism involved Monterey cypresses, which in turn reminds us that the eucalyptus was also a subject of the art of Matisse, Paul Signac, Piet Mondrian and Giacomo Balla.[15] Or, to widen our focus still further, the possibility of not merely a national but also an international gumtree school reminds us of Frenchman Félix Delahaye's garden established at Recherche Bay, Tasmania, as part of Bruni d'Entrecasteaux's expedition that visited Van Diemen's Land in 1792 and 1793, and the appointment in 1857 of German Ferdinand von Mueller to the newly created position of director of the Botanic Gardens in Melbourne. And these have their obverse in Napoleon's wife Josephine's collection of emus, kangaroos and black swans at the Château de Malmaison on the River Seine on the outskirts of Paris in the early nineteenth century.

But if in our history of UnAustralian art we have so far emphasised the story of Australian expatriates, we should not forget the story of our immigrants, who have likewise largely been excluded from our national histories. Their art has been seen as not originating in this country or exhibiting elements of our national culture, with their stories belonging only to each artists' place of origin. And, again, to point to a path not taken, as part of the influx of postwar migrants from eastern, central and southern Europe, of artists, curators and art historians whose names Australians would have to learn how to pronounce and spell, the case of the Hungarian Margit Pogány is instructive. Pogány was nearly seventy years old when she arrived in Melbourne as a refugee in 1948. An artist herself, she later held exhibitions in Melbourne in 1951 and 1955. She had been Constantin Brâncuşi's great muse in Paris and, when she arrived from war-torn Europe, among her few possessions was a bust of herself by the renowned School of Paris sculptor. In dire personal circumstances, in 1952 she offered to sell *Mlle Pogány* (1913) to the National Gallery of Victoria, an offer the institution felt able to refuse. However, when the possibility of acquiring the work came to the attention of James Johnson Sweeney, director of the Museum of Modern Art in New York, he quickly manoeuvred to make it part of his own museum's collection. This story invites us to think that in his bust Brâncuşi was showing us an image in advance of the postwar

Australian migrant, as well as presenting us with a work of Australian art. It is a face and a sculpture that we can see now only in New York, where it is often on display, tantalising us with the possibility of another kind of Australian art history.[16]

Here again with the story of our immigrants we open the aperture, and by not closing off the borders of our history, we see not only how Australia is in the world but also how the world is in Australia. It is to realise that so much of what we count as distinctively Australian is the result of other cultures. (Indeed, much of the look and even the collection of the National Gallery of Australia is thanks to the input of Sweeney.) But for all of that, perhaps not everything is included in this newly expanded history. Even our inclusiveness ultimately has its limits. There is no place in our story, for instance, for the Bacchus Marsh–born Scottish painter and associate of the Glasgow Boys EA Hornel, or the Sydney-born School of Paris figurative painter Édouard Goerg, not only because they grew up, studied and lived elsewhere, but more importantly because they did not identify as Australians. Equally, the sculptor Heinz Henghes, the renowned photographer, collector and historian of photography Helmut Gernsheim, and the eminent art historian Ernst Kitzinger are not included, although they were all aboard the transport ship HMT *Dunera* that arrived in Australia in 1940, because they were interned only

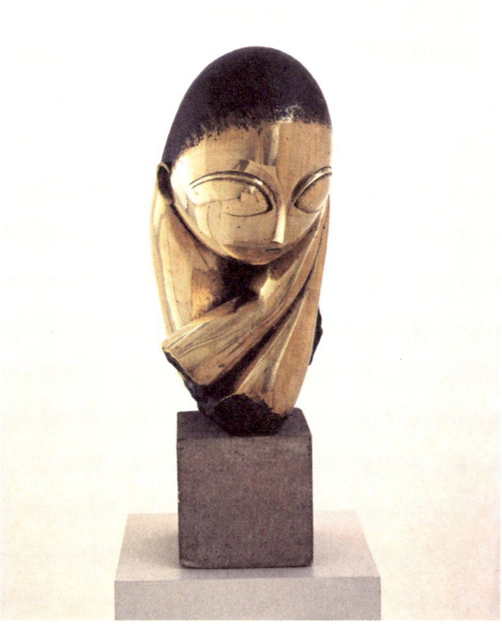

0.4 Constantin Brâncuși
Mlle Pogány, 1913

briefly and left soon afterwards to make careers in America. However, such figures as Mortimer Menpes, 'Australia's Whistler' as he was known, and the abstract and surrealist painter of the 1930s JW Power, who never returned to Australia after leaving as a young doctor in 1908, are included because they departed here Australian and, although their careers kept them away permanently, continued to identify as Australian. For his part, Menpes presented his thirty-eight copies of historical European paintings (including Frans Hals's *The laughing cavalier* of 1624 and Diego Velázquez's *Portrait of Princess Maria Margarita* of 1659) to the nation before it had a collection, and Power bequeathed his fortune to the University of Sydney to:

> make available to the people of Australia the latest ideas and theories in the plastic arts by means of lectures and teaching and by the purchase of the most recent contemporary art of the world.[17]

Here too with Power we are reminded of the path not taken. The opportunity to acquire Power's substantial collection of the inter-war Parisian avant-garde, which included works by Juan Gris, Fernand Léger, Otto Freundlich and Diego

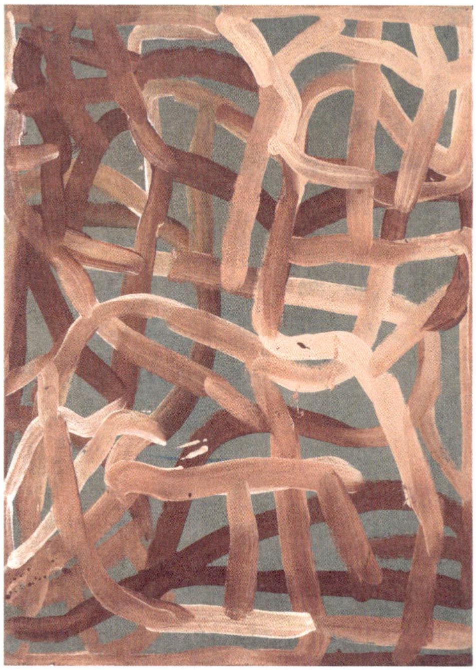

0.5 Emily Kngwarreye
Yam dreaming, 1995

Rivera, when it came up for auction in 1962 following the death of his widow, was unfortunately not seized. Nevertheless, it is an opportunity that, as with van Gogh's offer of a picture, Conder's of a walk home and Pogány's of her sculpture, we can hold in our minds and use to think about ourselves differently.

Perhaps the only real equivalent to John Russell at the beginning of our history is Emily Kngwarreye at the end. Certainly, we can find no comparison to that explosion of paint in Russell's *Rough sea* in 1900 until we get to the dragged stringy lines in Kngwarreye's *Yam dreamings* of the 1990s. And in both of their works we want to find a kind of utopia, *Erewhon* or crossing of space: in Russell an Australia in the world; in Kngwarreye a world in Australia. For if our encounter with Russell was one inspiration for this UnAustralian history, it is equally true that the encounter with Kngwarreye was the other. Indeed, we even feel that we would not have been struck by one without the other, that we would not have truly understood what was at stake in Russell's work without Kngwarreye, and would not have understood what was at stake in Kngwarreye's work without Russell. Our UnAustralian art history is absolutely a post-Aboriginal-art history because it is Aboriginal art that has always shown us how to be local and universal without being national.

Aboriginal art certainly forces us to re-read Australian art, although our real point is that it also disaggregates the category of Australian art; that, against all of the undoubtedly well-meaning efforts to write a history of Australian art that includes Aboriginal art, the real effect of Aboriginal art is to do away with the very possibility of a national art history. That is to say, if we are to consider together the art done by Indigenous and non-Indigenous Australians—and we must—it is exactly not in terms of some overarching category of the 'Australian' that we would do so. Put simply, Indigenous Australians—even Michael Nelson Jagamara creating the mosaic in 1988 for the forecourt of the new Parliament House—do not make 'Australian' art. Rather, as a recent exhibition at the Art Gallery of New South Wales that hung the work of Kngwarreye alongside that of her admirer and collector the American conceptual painter Sol LeWitt reveals, there are larger and longer-lasting narratives at play than that of nationhood: just as Kngwarreye must be considered a post-conceptual painter, so LeWitt must be understood as a desert artist.[18] (It is in this way that Matisse and Mondrian when they paint gumtrees can be considered Australian.)

Ultimately, we are not claiming any great originality with our UnAustralian art history here. For all of our criticism of Australian art historians for writing nationalist accounts of Australian art, and our chastening of a generation of museum curators for representing the same canonical figures, it is also reasonable to think that not only are things changing today but a different past altogether is coming into view. Although the idea for this history came to us as something of a sudden insight or inspiration, it is exactly in light of it that we can see that we are not unique in proposing such an alternative vision of Australian art. As we make clear throughout what follows, there have been any number of important 'UnAustralian' writers, critics and art historians, stretching back almost to the beginning of Australian art history itself (Edith Fry, Raymond McIntyre, Alleyne Zander, Jack Lindsay and even William Moore). We can equally find a number of catalogues and exhibitions in both state and regional galleries that have taken up our immigrant and expatriate artists. To mention here just five examples: *New Influences Exhibition: A Tribute to Artists Who Have Come From Other Countries to Live in Australia* at the Newcastle Art Gallery in 1962, *Swiss Artists in Australia 1771–1991* at the Art Gallery of New South Wales in 1991, *Intensely Dutch: Image, Abstraction and the Word Post-War and Beyond* at the Art Gallery of New South Wales in 2009, *The Europeans: Emigré Artists in Australia, 1930–60* at the National Gallery of Australia in 1997, and the books *Australian Latvian Artists* (1979) and *Lithuanian Artists in Australia, 1950–1990* (2003).[19]

But again, what the hypothesis of an 'UnAustralian' art allows us to do is amalgamate and generalise such incidents, to see their commonality and what wider tendencies they point to. And, indeed, it has enabled us to situate our own particular 'Australian' art-historical enquiry within a still larger 'globalist' context. For, as we will point out several times, with the advent of 'contemporary' art the twentieth-century story of a modernism that originated in Europe, moved to America and then spread around the world is now being rethought and rewritten via connections and conversations between countries and cultures that were thought to be separate and the discovery and recording of multiple modernisms that were unmediated by more dominant cultures. We are, of course, aware—to start with the largest intellectual currents first—of attempts to consider 'multiple modernities' by such postcolonial art scholars as Geeta Kapur, Kobena Mercer and Salah Hassan.[20] Their writings are followed or accompanied by a number of important art exhibitions, most notably *Modernités plurielles 1905–1970* (*Plural modernities*), curated by Catherine Grenier for the Centre Pompidou in Paris in 2013; *Postwar: Art Between the Pacific and the Atlantic, 1945–1965*, curated by Okwui Enwezor for the Haus der Kunst in Munich in 2017; the revisionist or at least ironically titled *Paris: Capital of the Arts, 1900–1968*, held at the Royal Academy of Arts in London in 2002; and *Cubism in Asia: Unbounded Dialogues*, organised by the Japan Foundation in 2005.

At times, in such essays as 'Trans-Pacific: Abstract Painting in Australia, New Zealand and America 1930–1960' and in an essay we recently wrote for a Gordon Walters retrospective, we can be seen to follow certain recent 'convergence' theories of art, which, risking the art-historical sin of isomorphism, suggest that visual similarities between works of art from places that do not appear to be connected can be understood to be meaningful. Here we note the work of David Singh Grewal in sociology and Piotr Piotrowski in art history, but also the collection *Crossing Cultures: Conflicts, Migration and Convergence,* edited by Jaynie Anderson.[21] (And undoubtedly lying behind all of this, at least as it takes place in art history, is the recently revived Aby Warburg and his notion of *pathosformel*.)[22] Perhaps more conventionally, in a series of essays published here ('Cities within Cities: Australian and New Zealand Art in the Twentieth Century', 'Against Provincialism: Australian–American Connections 1900–2000', 'Madí and Mary Webb: Australia and South America' and 'Alice and Taos: Two Sides of the Same Coin') and elsewhere (see our bibliography on p. 251), we were inspired by or at least felt a commonality with a number of books and exhibitions tracing the connections between two places, one of which was regarded as 'central' and the other as 'marginal'. This would precisely not be that series of shows putting together such metropolises as New York and Paris, Paris and Berlin and Paris and Moscow, held at the Pompidou from the mid-1980s onwards, or *Berlin-Tokyo/Tokyo-Berlin*, held at Berlin's Neue Nationalgalerie in 2006.[23] Rather, we would begin with something like Darcy Grimaldo Grigsby's 2002 book *Extremities: Painting Empire in Post-Revolutionary France* on the role of the French colonies in the development of French art.[24] But closer to home we can also think of the work of Jean-Claude Lesage on the colonies of Australian and New Zealand artists at Étaples on the northern coast of France and Anne Gérard-Austin on Australians in the French Salons in the late nineteenth and early twentieth centuries, both of which we refer to in what follows.[25] However, this internationalising project is itself international, with such scholars as Nina Lübbren writing on the exchanges between artists in the artist colonies around Europe; Scott A Shields on the same kinds of exchanges occurring on the West Coast around Monterey; and Tim Barringer chronicling the even wider movements of dispersed material objects around postcolonial spaces.[26] There is equally a whole series of important American shows from the 2000s on that have sought not only to 'deprovincialise' American art by showing the real-time artistic exchanges between the West Coast and the East Coast and between California and Latin America (the continuing *Pacific Standard Time* exhibitions initiated by the Getty Foundation), but also the connections between North and South America altogether occurring throughout the twentieth century (*Constructive Spirit: Abstract Art in North and South America* at the Newark Museum in 2010, *Under the Same Sun: Art from Latin America Today* at the Guggenheim Museum, New York, in 2014).

As we continued to work on our UnAustralian project, we increasingly became aware of the similarities between our work and other projects around the world. As with the artists, critics and curators we look at here, the question might be asked: what is our relationship to this work? It is not simply provincial, either in subject matter or impulse. Rather, as Geeta Kapur writes in 'When Was Modernism in Indian Art?': 'We should see our trajectories crisscrossing the Western mainstream and, in their very disalignment from it, making up the ground that restructures the international'.[27] And, in truth, much of what we point to here is retrospective in realisation, effectively connections that we have noticed or have had our attention drawn to after we began. Indeed, we have increasingly begun to think of what we are doing here in terms of coincidence: that being subject to the same artistic and intellectual pressures as many others around the globe we have responded in approximately similar ways. But there always remains a certain specificity, and perhaps even incommensurability, about our and those other projects. For all of our pointing towards the UnAustralian—the incessant and long-term connections between Australia and other cultures and other places—this remains a story of Australian art. The universal, as the philosophers keep on telling us, can only ever be grasped and narrated from a particular place. There are always boundaries around what we can see, what we can speak of, what counts as UnAustralian.[28]

Nevertheless, if this is the story of the presence and influence of many other places and cultures in the story of Australian art, we also hope to show the presence of Australia in those other places and cultures. If it is a rewriting of Australia on the basis of the international, it is also a rewriting of the international (New Zealand, Asia, America, Europe, and South America) on the basis of Australia. In many ways, this is the fundamental argument of Bernard Smith's *European Vision and the South Pacific, 1768–1850*; and if there is any suggestion that we in undertaking this project come from an intellectually provincial culture, let this one simple reference—which comes before all of that other thinking about 'convergence' and 'alternative modernities'—put that to rest. The relationship we point to is always two-way, deeply undermining (while in reaction also making possible) the claims of any singular national culture. To put it in terms of the oceans that connect us—again, a theme that runs through this book—if it is true that the bronzed Australian of Max Dupain's iconic nationalist photograph *Sunbaker* (1937) was actually a British labourer on holiday, then it is equally the case that the suspended tiger shark in Damien Hirst's foundational work of Young British Art, *The impossibility of death in the mind of someone living* (1991), was caught off the coast of Queensland.[29]

—

1 Elizabeth Salter, *The Lost Impressionist: A Biography of John Peter Russell*, Angus and Robertson, London, 1976.
2 See on this Hilary Spurling, *The Unknown Matisse: A Life of Henri Matisse, Volume One, 1869–1908*, Alfred A Knopf, New York, 2005, pp. 117–36.
3 Cited in Ann Galbally, *A Remarkable Friendship: Vincent van Gogh and John Peter Russell*, Miegunyah Press, Melbourne, 2008, p. 212.
4 It is only thanks to Russell's cousin Thea Proctor, for instance, that Russell is included in Bernard Smith's *Australian Painting, 1788–1960*, Oxford University Press, London, 1962, p. 166, fn. 21. Smith would earlier write 'John Russell: Australia's Unknown Artist', *Meanjin*, vol. 15, no. 4, Summer 1956, pp. 352–6, also acknowledging the influence of Proctor.
5 Robert Hughes, *The Art of Australia*, Penguin, UK, 1966, p. 24.
6 Christopher Allen, *Art in Australia: From Colonization to Postmodernism*, Thames & Hudson, London, 1997, p. 8. Hughes also excludes the work of such artists as the German-born Peter Kaiser, 'since their work clearly belongs to a European and not an Australian context' (p. 24). This would be despite Kaiser living some eleven years in Australia, from 1940 until 1951, and exhibiting regularly at Macquarie Galleries, thereafter being part of the Merioola set and a member of the Sydney Group, along with such artists as Jean Bellette, James Cant and Paul Haefliger.
7 Andrew Sayers, *Australian Art*, Oxford University Press, 2001, pp. 5–6.
8 Ernst Gombrich, *The Story of Art*, Phaidon, New York, 1962, p. 5.
9 Edith M Fry, 'Australian Artists at Burlington House', *Sydney Morning Herald*, 1 January 1924, p. 2.
10 Raymond McIntyre, 'Exhibitions', *Architectural Review*, vol. 57, January/June 1925, p. 214.
11 William Moore, *The Story of Australian Art: From the Earliest Known Art of the Continent to the Art of Today*, vol. 2, Angus & Robertson, Sydney, 1934, p. 10.
12 Cited in Jane Roberts, *Jacques-Émile Blanche*, Gourcuff Gradenigo, Paris, 2012, p. 92.
13 *Dorrit Black: Unseen Forces*, ed. Tracey Lock-Weir, exhibition catalogue, Art Gallery of South Australia, Adelaide, 2014; *The World of Mortimer Menpes: Painter, Etcher, Raconteur*, ed. Julie Robinson, exhibition catalogue, Art Gallery of South Australia, Adelaide, 2014; and Wayne Tunnicliffe, *John Russell: Australia's French Impressionist*, Art Gallery of New South Wales, Sydney, 2018.
14 'Art for a Purpose', *Argus*, 31 July 1914, p. 4.
15 See on this Rex Butler and ADS Donaldson, 'I Am, You Are, We Are All Australian', *Broadsheet*, vol. 44, no. 1, 2015, pp. 72–4. See also Helen Hughes, 'Tom Nicholson's Comparative Monument: Conjoining the Politics and Histories of Australia and Israel Through the Trope of the Eucalyptus', in the same issue (pp. 62–5).
16 We might recall here another episode similar to this. Tim Bonyhady in his *Good Living Street: The Fortunes of My Viennese Family* (Allen & Unwin, Crows Nest, 2011) recalls the story of his great-aunt who in the early 1960s felt so grateful for her and her family's lives in Australia having emigrated as refugees from Vienna just before World War II that she sought to gift Gustav Klimt's portrait of her mother to the Art Gallery of New South Wales, only to be refused. Today Klimt's *Portrait of Hermine Gallia* (1904) hangs permanently in Room 41 of the National Portrait Gallery in London.
17 See website of the Power Institute Foundation for Art and Visual Culture, https://sydney.edu.au/arts/our-research/centres-institutes-and-groups/power-institute.html.
18 We are referring here to the Sol LeWitt exhibition *Your Mind Is Exactly at That Line*, Art Gallery of New South Wales, 20 February – 3 August 2014.
19 *New Influences Exhibition: A Tribute to Artists Who Have Come From Other Countries to Live in Australia*, ed. Newcastle Branch of the Good Neighbour Council, exhibition catalogue, Newcastle Regional Art Gallery, New South Wales, 1962; *Swiss Artists in Australia 1777–1991*, ed. Barry Pearce, exhibition catalogue, Art Gallery of New South Wales, Sydney, 1991; *Intensely Dutch: Image, Abstraction and the Word, Post-War and Beyond*, ed. Hendrik Kolenberg, exhibition catalogue, Art Gallery of New South Wales, Sydney, 2009; *The Europeans: Emigré Artists in Australia, 1930–1960*, ed. Roger Butler, exhibition catalogue, Australian National Gallery, Canberra, 1999; *Australian Latvian Artists*, exhibition catalogue, Society of Latvian Artists in Australia, Strathfield, 1979; and *Lithuanian Artists in Australia, 1950–1990*, ed. Genovaite Elena Kazokas, exhibition catalogue, Europe–Australia Institute, Melbourne, 2003.
20 See, for example, Geeta Kapur, *When Was Modernism: Essays on Contemporary Cultural*

Practice in India, Tulika Books, New Delhi, 2000; Kobena Mercer, *Exiles, Diasporas and Strangers*, MIT Press, Cambridge, MA, 2008; and Salah Hassan, 'The Modernist Experience in African Art: Visual Expressions of the Self and Cross-Cultural Aesthetics', *Nka: Journal of Contemporary African Art*, vol. 2, Spring–Summer 1995. We might also think here of John Clark, 'Doing World Art History with Modern and Contemporary Asian Art', *World Art*, vol. 1, 2011, pp. 93–9; Kobena Mercer's edited collection *Cosmopolitan Modernisms*, MIT Press, Cambridge, MA, 2005; and Arjun Appadurai's edited collection, *Modernity at Large: Cultural Dimensions of Globalization*, University of Minnesota Press, Minneapolis, 1996.

21 See David Singh Grewal, *Network Power: The Social Dynamics of Globalization*, Yale University Press, New Haven, 2009, especially the chapter 'Network Power and Cultural Convergence'; Piotr Piotrowski, 'From Global to Alter-Globalist Art History', *Teksty Drugie*, vol. 1, 2015, pp. 112–34; and *Crossing Cultures: Conflicts, Migration and Convergence*, ed. Jaynie Anderson, Melbourne University Publishing, 2009. See also Catherine De Lorenzo, 'Bernard Smith: "Cultural Convergence" and Art History', in eds. Jaynie Anderson, Christopher R. Marshall and Andrew Yip, *The Legacies of Bernard Smith: Essays on Australian Art, History and Cultural Politics*, Power Publications, Sydney, 2016, pp. 325–7; and Terry Smith, 'World Picturing in Contemporary Art: The Iconogeographic Turn', *Australian and New Zealand Journal of Art*, vol. 7, no. 1, 2006, pp. 24–46. For a dissenting view see Jonathan Harris, 'Academic Difficulties with "Convergence": Globalization and Contemporary Art', in eds. James Elkins, Zhivka Valiavicharska and Alice Kim, *Art and Globalization* Pennsylvania State University Press, Pennsylvania, 2010.

22 On Warburg's *pathosformel*, see Georges Didi-Huberman, *The Surviving Image: Phantoms of Time and Time of Phantoms; Aby Warburg's History of Art*, Pennsylvania State University Press, Pennsylvania, 2016; and it is perhaps no surprise that Didi-Huberman curated an art exhibition based on Warburg's ideas, entitled *Atlas: How to Carry the World on One's Back?* at the Museo Nacional Centro de Arte Reina Sofía in Madrid in 2010.

23 We refer to Pontus Hulten's landmark series of Centre Pompidou exhibitions *Paris–New York* (1977), *Paris–Berlin* (1978) and *Paris–Moscow* (1979).

24 Darcy Grimaldo Grigsby, *Extremities: Painting Empire in Post-Revolutionary France*, Yale University Press, New Haven, 2002.

25 Jean-Claude Lesage, *Peintres Australiens à Étaples*, Amis du Musée de la Marine d'Étaples, Étaples-sur-mer, 2000; and Anne Gérard-Austin, 'The Australian Painters in Parisian Salons Between 1886 and 1914', MA thesis, University of Sydney, 2006.

26 *Call of the Coast: Art Colonies of New England*, eds. Thomas Denenberg, Amy Kurtz Lansing and Susan Danly, exhibition catalogue, Portland Museum of Art, Oregon, 2009; *Artists at Continent's End: The Monterey Peninsula Art Colony, 1875–1907*, ed. Scott A. Shields, exhibition catalogue, University of California Press, Berkeley, 2006; eds. Tim Barringer and Tom Flynn, *Colonialism and the Object: Empire*, Material Culture and the Museum, Routledge, London, 1998; and eds. Tim Barringer, Douglas Fordham and Geoff Quilley, *Art and the British Empire*, Manchester University Press, 2007.

27 Geeta Kapur, 'When was Modernism in Indian Art?', in *When Was Modernism*, p. 295.

28 On the implicit tensions in 'globalist' art histories, see Blake Gopnik, 'The Oxymoron of Global Art', in eds. Elkins, Valiavicharska and Kim, *Art and Globalization*; and Alain Quemin, 'The Illusion of the Elimination of Borders in the Contemporary Art World: The Role of the Different Countries in the "Era of Globalization and Métissage"', in ed. Ján Bakoš, *Artwork Through the Market: The Past and the Present*, Centre for Contemporary Arts, Bratislava, 2004, pp. 275–301.

29 We could equally well imagine an 'UnAustralian' history of Australian literature, beginning perhaps with our second Nobel Prize winner, JM Coetzee, who besides now living in Australia and writing books set here can perhaps be understood as having always written Australian books, insofar as his subject matter is the lives of a white population in a land that was once black. Such a suggestion takes its inspiration from Robert Dixon and Brigid Rooney's edited collection *Scenes of Reading: Is Australian Literature a World Literature?*, Australian Scholarly Publishing, Melbourne, 2013.

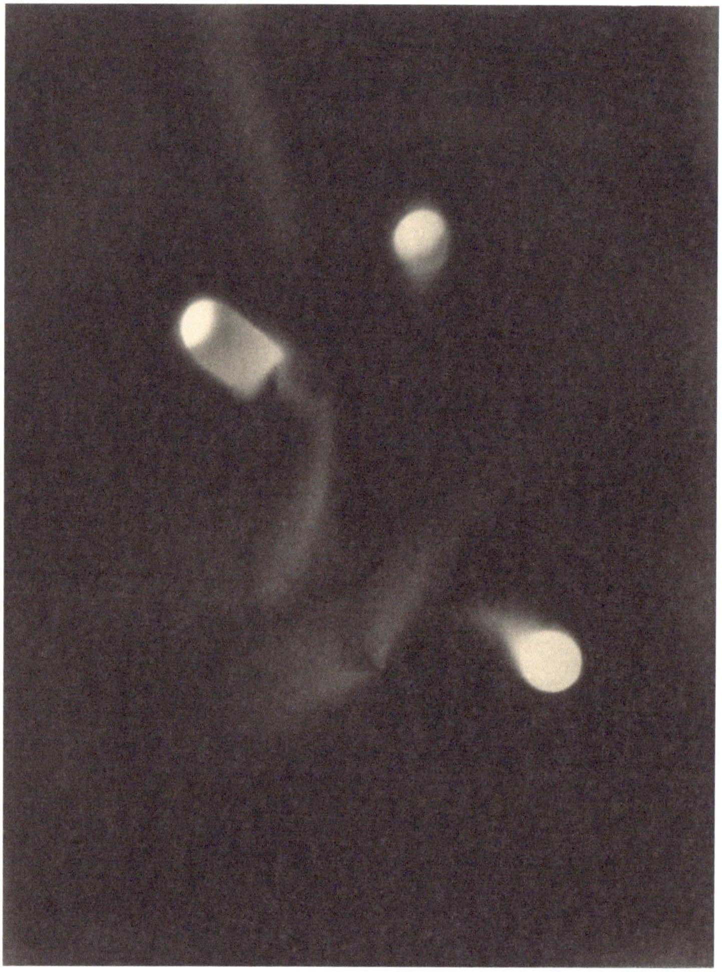

1.1 Sidney Nolan
Illustration for Ulysses, 1936

Outside In
Against a History of Reception

We might begin here with a reflection upon naming. *Art in Australia*, the magazine founded by Sydney Ure Smith, published its first issue in 1916 and its last in 1942. The title spoke very well of Ure Smith's nationalist concerns. For him, only an art of the country and from the country counted. Upon leaving Australia, expatriate artists such as John Russell simply disappeared from the record. Likewise, upon arriving in the country, immigrant artists had to work in an 'Australian' manner or they too would not be part of the story. Thus, long-term Art Gallery of New South Wales trustee Bertrand J Waterhouse featured in the pages of the magazine, but not Bessie Davidson, who lived in Paris from 1914. The revered gumtree painter Hans Heysen featured (and even had a special issue in his honour), but not Anne Dangar, who lived in Sablons on the River Rhône from 1930.

When the magazine re-appeared in 1963 as *Art & Australia*, something else was perhaps implied. Australia is no longer the encompassing category for the art of this country. The art made here or by Australians overseas is not to be explained by its 'Australianness'—as the expression of some spirit of place. Rather, the category 'Australia' sits on the same level as the art, displacing it, shifting it sideways, allowing us to see it differently—posing first of all the problem of how it is Australian, what the connection is between the art and its Australianness.

These are the issues we seek to reinvigorate with the concept of the *UnAustralian*: to open up again the question of what it means to make art here or as an Australian. It is first of all not to place a limit on the artistic activities of this country, to exclude or overlook some art because it does not conform to a specified narrative or does not come out of any *genius loci* or national essence (the latest incarnation of which would be a certain reading of Aboriginal art as Australian). To write a history of UnAustralian art is in some ways simply to open the aperture wider, to include more in the story. It is to look at our history in finer detail, not immediately to generalise it in wanting the art made here always to be an art of nation.

This other history is a possibility that is lost when Bernard Smith publishes his *Australian Painting* in 1962, around the same time that *Art & Australia* appears. Smith's book has gone on to become our canonical history, defining the next forty years of thinking about Australian art. The book is famous for its argument that European artistic sources are transformed by their contact with local conditions (geographical, social, historical). Imported pictorial formulae are consciously adopted and adapted by the inhabitants to satisfy their particular needs. This produces a series of what might be called artistic hybrids or mixtures, as though even in saying this we could identify the works' constituent parts.

What is thereby set forth by and after Smith is a history of *reception*. It is not, needless to say, a history of passive reception. Australians are active in selecting from the art arriving from overseas those features that are most suitable for them; but exactly in this there is an implied distance from these sources, both in time and space. Art appears to happen somewhere else, without us playing a part. It is as though in any account of Australian art there is always a missing cause. This attitude can be seen in the way that narratives of Australian art always begin at some far distant starting point, whether in 1788 with the founding of the colony or earlier with the art of Indigenous peoples. The origins of our national culture would always be lost, unrecoverable, yet arising out of some miraculous first event—to use Smith's biblical imagery, a 'genesis'.

As can be imagined, Smith's history, with its argument for a kind of defining belatedness, had many critics. Undoubtedly, the best of these was the artist and writer Ian Burn, who in a series of publications sought to challenge many of Smith's assumptions. We might think here of Burn's early work on the provincialism problem, which sets out the condition to which we seem to be condemned; his collaborative text with Ann Stephen, Nigel Lendon and Charles Merewether, *The Necessity of Australian Art: An Essay about Interpretation* (1988), which points to the historical alternatives to Smith's account; and his book *National Life & Landscapes: Australian Painting, 1900–1940* (1992), which presents evidence for a new, 'localised', art history in which landscape would contain the possibility of a regional—not national—art (the pairing of 'National Life' and 'Landscapes' in the title of the book is meant to be contradictory, a point not often noticed by its commentators).

It is undeniably Burn who inaugurated the whole postmodern and postcolonial critique of Smith: taking what Smith saw as negative and turning it into a positive; making of our supposed distance and isolation the basis of a new Australian art. Burn's 1988 essay 'The Re-appropriation of Influence' outlines what he sees as Smith's fundamental argument (a still passive history of reception) and seeks to overturn it:

> Style is accepted as a function of the various conceptual strategies involved in representations. In other words, style today is a function of the critical or conceptual mediation of style in its former sense. But, arguably, even in this formulation, there still remains the same instability of stylistic categories at the periphery. The significant difference is that what was formerly perceived negatively [by Smith] as not of the centre has now been transformed into a much sought-after quality by the centre.[1]

This is the basis of Burn's reading of Sidney Nolan's painting *Railway guard, Dimboola* (1943), which he sees not as a second-hand imitation of cubism, or even an unconscious variation of it, but rather as an active and dialogical engagement with aspects of cubism considered as a style. In other words, Burn sees it as an *appropriation* of cubism: a distanced, self-conscious quotation of its formal vocabulary that yet remains outside it (although he nevertheless argues that we cannot now understand cubism outside the ways it has been taken up in countries such as Australia).[2] As Burn points out, it is a quotation of cubism that at once repeats European art while 'mocking' that dependence, and that adopts a dialectical relationship not to tradition but to the 'idea' of a tradition in Australia.

Earlier in 'The Re-appropriation of Influence', Burn speaks of the way that in conceptual art there is a separation of style from content. Style is no longer, as in previous art movements, something that is organically or expressively attached to the object, but can be detached, played with, even falsely applied. All this was part of the breaking of the nexus between the artist and the artwork that was the express aim of conceptual art. But Burn's point is that Australian art—for example, that of Nolan—is *already* conceptual in this sense. Style in Australian art is not something that is natural, unconscious, belonging instinctively to the artist, but is ironic, conscious, attributed to the work by the viewer and not the artist.

As we say, Burn's argument in this is directed against Smith: those hybrids that Smith sees as negative Burn sees as positive; that distance that in Smith condemns us always to being second is what in Burn allows us to come first. But, for all of Burn's claim to break with Smith, he nevertheless shares with him his deepest assumptions. Not only is it true that from *Place, Taste and Tradition* (1945) onwards Smith *does* evaluate positively the same cultural crossovers that Burn says he speaks of negatively, but Smith's *European Vision and the South Pacific* (1960) is already proposing that we cannot understand such European artistic categories as neoclassicism outside of the way they were taken up in Australia. That is to say, both Smith and Burn share the assumption that Australian artistic styles (if not their content) always come from elsewhere. In Smith, it is gumtrees done in the style of Claude Lorrain; in Burn, it is railway guards done in the style of Fernand Léger. In both, we have the same mediated, conceptual, self-distancing relationship to artistic sources. We have the same fundamental history of reception—whether judged positively or negatively, it makes no difference.

For us, by contrast, to think another history of Australian art is to think a history in which Australia is not separate, is not *apart from* but *a part of* the art of the rest of the world. It would be a history written not from the *inside out* but from the *outside in*. It would be a history of what has been excluded from the existing nationalist accounts. It would be a history of what in the art of this country is not defined by distance, of those Australian artists who have worked overseas or those artists arriving from overseas who have continued to work in their own styles. Thus we would tell the story of the Bauhaus-trained light and kinetic artist Ludwig Hirschfeld-Mack living in Geelong in the same way as we would write of Piet Mondrian living in Paris, or indeed in the same way as we would speak of the Australians Alistair Morrison and Dahl and Geoffrey Collings working with the Bauhaus master László Moholy-Nagy in London.

Seen from this perspective, the old nationalist history looks different as well. Take, for example, Sidney Nolan. The retrospective of his work organised by the Art Gallery of New South Wales in 2007 was controversial because it did not include as many of the classic landscapes or Ned Kelly series as people expected.[3] Instead, the show documented Nolan's relentless travel in search of inspiration: Africa, Antarctica, the Australian outback. And there was the almost inadvertent attempt to rehabilitate the later abstract paintings—particularly his spray paintings, which were produced in almost industrial quantities in response to such things as sailing's America's Cup being held in Fremantle in 1987. It can appear as though the elderly Nolan had turned to New York graffiti art in the 1980s, in a belated, if open-minded, search for new artistic sources.

But Nolan had *always* been a spray painter. Predating any of the works in the show, in fact, is his remarkable use of spray paint in a series of works done in 1936 inspired by James Joyce's *Ulysses* (1922). This hitherto unseen emergence of spray painting in Melbourne in the 1930s (and also in Sydney in the 1930s and 1940s by such artists as Frank Hinder and Grace Crowley) appears a true innovation in the history of modernist painting—or at least a local occurrence that does not owe anything to overseas sources. It belongs to a history of innovation not in an all-too-well known Greenbergian modernism, but takes place in what we might call the expanded field of painting: the almost unimaginably varied history of all the things that have been done to and with the notion of painting from the late nineteenth century on. It would be the history of a delta and not a river, a history in which the distinction between major and minor artists no longer holds. *Illustration for Ulysses* (1936) would be a perfect instance of painting always being in an expanded field, because Nolan had worked in a commercial art studio (as did Hinder). Here there would be no external, mediated or distanced relationship to artistic sources in terms of style, but rather a manual, pragmatic and immediate relationship in terms of materials and techniques.

Indeed, Nolan, famous as a painter of images, always insisted that he was 'first of all an abstract painter'. As late as 1982, he emphasised this fact in response to an interviewer asking him about his ultimate place in Australian art.[4] It is thus possible that Nolan's Australianness is merely an interregnum—a long-running artistic impasse or crisis—between two periods of abstraction. Put otherwise, there is an UnAustralian as well as an Australian Nolan. We can write a history of Nolan from the outside in—how he might fit into a world history of spray painting—as well as from the inside out—as a wandering, Ulysses-like Australian always distant from both his proper place and style (an argument that runs all the way from his reception in a series of influential shows of Australian art in London in the 1960s through to Burn and the postmodernists).

So what kind of history would allow us to consider Nolan's (and Hinder's and Crowley's) spray painting? Here perhaps Burn *can* help us. In a 1985 essay, 'Is Art History Any Use to Artists?', Burn proposes taking art history back from art historians.[5] He puts forward a different model from that of historical explanation, individual genius and singular innovation. It would be a story based on illuminating anecdote, unexpected coincidence, artistic collaboration and social exchange. He even gives an example of this other kind of history: William Moore's *The Story of Australian Art* (1934), which is made up of chance meetings and unelected affinities, of stories that seem to have no wider point or that seem to be their own point. It would be an UnAustralian history, a narrative of the numerous connections between Australia and elsewhere: the Dutch-New Zealand artist Petrus van der Velden working in Sydney in the early twentieth century; Thea Proctor being taught by George Lambert in London; Agnes Goodsir belonging to the large cosmopolitan community of lesbian artists in inter-war Paris; Robert Klippel and James Gleeson connecting with André Breton in Paris through the Belgian surrealist ELT Mesens; Wallace Harrison teaching Helen Frankenthaler at his studio school on 14th Street in New York; the postwar School of Paris Sydney artist Mary Webb advocating on behalf of Grace Crowley, Frank Hinder and Ralph Balson for their inclusion in the Belgian Michel Seuphor's 1957 *Dictionary of Abstract Painting* …

There would be no overall world-picture here—no telos, no universal—but also no isolation, no provincialism. Only the endless story of Australia in the world and the world in Australia.

—

1 Ian Burn, 'The Re-appropriation of Influence', in *Dialogue: Writings in Art History*, Allen & Unwin, Sydney, 1991, p. 213.
2 This is a point also made by Lesley Harding and Sue Cramer in their 2009 exhibition *Cubism and Australian Art* at Heide Museum of Modern Art, Melbourne.
3 *Sidney Nolan: A New Retrospective*, ed. Barry Pierce, exhibition catalogue, Art Gallery of New South Wales, Sydney, 2007.
4 Traudi Allen, 'Sidney Nolan', *Art & Text*, vol. 8, 1982, p. 61.
5 Ian Burn, 'Is Art History Any Use to Artists?', in *Dialogue*, pp. 1–14.

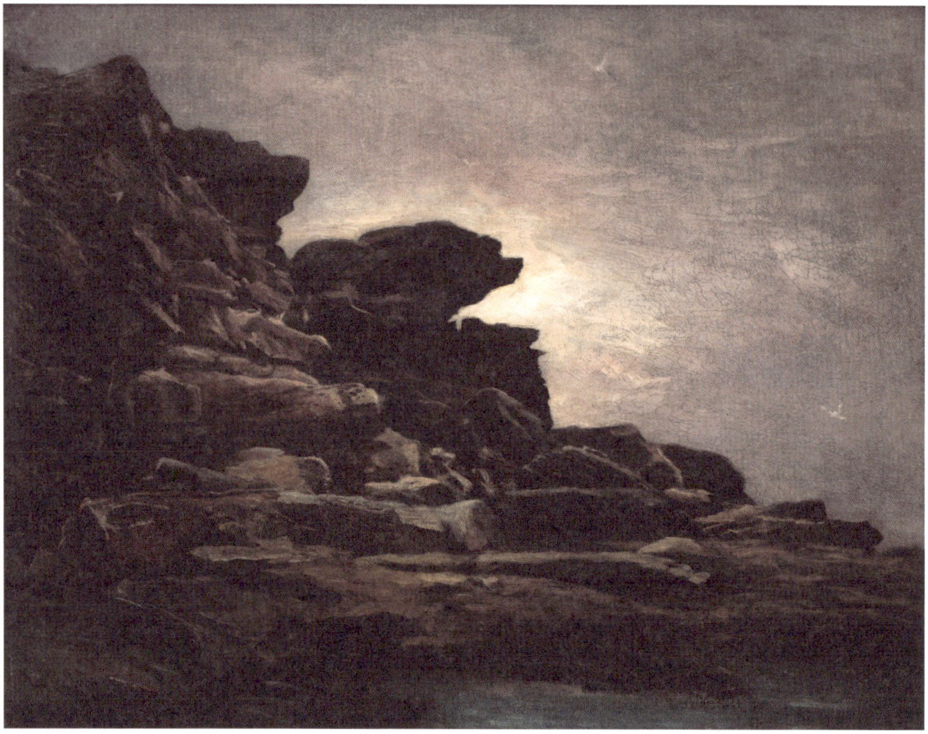

2.1 Petrus van der Velden
Rocks at Bondi, 1903

Cities within Cities
Australian and New Zealand Art in the Twentieth Century

The Christchurch-born painter Raymond McIntyre had been living in England for some sixteen years when in 1925 he reviewed Australian expatriate artist and art critic Edith Fry's second London exhibition of the group Australian Artists in Europe. Arriving in London in 1909, McIntyre had studied first with George Lambert privately and then with William Nicholson and Walter Sickert at the Westminster Technical Institute. He had exhibited regularly at the Goupil Gallery from 1911, with the London Group from 1916 to 1918, and eventually at the Royal Academy in 1924. These experiences, occurring before, during and after World War I, would undoubtedly have attuned him to the questions of expatriatism and national identity at stake in Fry's show. Writing of Fry's exhibition in *Architectural Review*—an international architecture magazine published in London since 1896, for which he had been a reviewer for more than ten years—McIntyre began by asking: 'When is an Australian not an Australian?' He continued:

> The most interesting works in the show have obviously been done under the influence and stimulus of European art. Certainly the most up-to-date and enterprising of the artists show this influence … We might even say that, in proportion as they cease to be Australians, their work becomes more interesting, viewed from the standpoint of modern artistic developments in Europe.

For McIntyre, the Australians who have 'stayed away a long time … have, from any artistic meaning of the word, ceased to be Australians', and thus he confessed himself 'surprised to discover that Mr Horace Brodzky is an Australian'.[1] It is even possible that McIntyre and Brodzky knew each other (without McIntyre knowing Brodzky's nationality), insofar as both had shown at various times with the London

Group. Certainly, McIntyre was familiar with Brodzky's work, and shared with him a concern for a clean and uncluttered line in the portraits he painted.

Other artists in Fry's shows, some of whom were mentioned by McIntyre in his review, included Rupert Bunny, Charles Conder, Agnes Goodsir, Bessie Davidson, Roy de Maistre, Bessie Gibson and Janet Cumbrae Stewart—all of whom were well-established expatriates, thus prompting McIntyre's question of when is an Australian artist not Australian. But the true irony of McIntyre asking this question—a double irony, given that McIntyre was himself a New Zealander—is that some of these 'Australians' were in many regards New Zealanders: JF Scott and Dora Meeson had studied in New Zealand, and Elioth Gruner and Septimus Power were born there. (Scott, for example, was born in Dunedin in 1877 and studied at the Dunedin School of Art. He left for Paris in 1898, where he trained with Benjamin Constant and Jean-Paul Laurens at the Académie Julian. He was at Gallipoli in World War I with the Australian and New Zealand Army Corps, and later worked while enlisted as an artist for the Australian army. Meeson was born in Melbourne in 1869, but moved to New Zealand with her family as a child. She studied art at the Christchurch School of Art, and exhibited with the Canterbury Palette Club and the Canterbury Society of Arts between 1889 and 1895. After returning briefly to Australia to study at the National Gallery School in Melbourne, she left for London to enrol at the Slade School in 1896. In Paris she trained at the Académie Julian, at the same time as Scott, in 1898.)

We might say that the history and conditions of Antipodean expatriatism—even perhaps the forgetting or blurring of that tradition—would also not have been lost on Fry. She, after all, had been the curator of two exhibitions in London: *Australian Artists in Europe*, in 1924 at the Faculty of Arts Gallery; and *Australian Art Exhibition*, the show McIntyre reviewed, at the Springs Gardens Gallery in 1925. She was the author of a series of important newspaper articles on the 'Australian' expatriates in Europe, published in the London and Sydney presses: 'Australian Artists in Paris' (1914 and 1922), 'Australians in Paris' (1917), 'Art and Artists: The Paris Salon' (1919), 'Exiles: The Australian Artists Abroad' (1924) and 'Retrospect: Twelve Years from Home' (1924). For *The British-Australasian* she wrote 'Australasian Artists in Europe' (1921), and for *The British and Australian and New Zealander* she wrote 'Some New Arrivals in Art' (1925).[2] She helped found the Panton Arts Club (whose aim was the 'encouragement of great art and of co-operation between the arts') in 1924, the same year she founded the group Australian Artists in Europe. Fry moved equally between expatriate artistic and literary circles, painting for example *C.R. Allen, novelist and playwright* in 1927, and penning an appreciation of the blind New Zealand writer for the *British Annual of Literature* in 1939.

This question of just who was an Australian—or, more precisely, which New Zealanders were Australian—was also the question asked in the lead article of the inaugural issue of *Art New Zealand* in 1976. More than fifty years after McIntyre's review, the same matters of national identity were still being debated in a magazine notable for having abandoned its original title of *Art in New Zealand*.[3] In 'Memories of Three New Zealand Expatriate Painters', the director of the Auckland City Gallery, Ernest Smith, returned Godfrey Miller, James Cook and Roland Wakelin to New Zealand art history, all of whom up until then had largely been regarded as Australian.[4] (Miller, who served with the New Zealand Expeditionary Force at Gallipoli, had come to Australia in 1919; Cook in 1935; and Wakelin in 1912.) In his essay, Smith was consciously seeking to provide a pre-history to the experiences of a then-contemporary generation of New Zealand artists, such as Billy Apple, John Panting and Eric Macky (husband of Melbourne painter Constance Jenkins, both of whom would go on to contribute to the story of Australasian art in America). And Smith in 1976 was writing in a period when art history was concerned to recover and recuperate hitherto lost or repressed traditions, as seen for instance in the feminist art histories of the 1970s. Smith's anecdotal article is written in testimony to his own personal memories of the three artists and to remind readers of the new journal that these artists were New Zealanders and not Australians, after their disappearance from the New Zealand art histories that were then beginning to be written.

But Smith was only scratching the surface of the phenomenon he identified. From our point of view, there is a whole as yet unrecognised history of New Zealand art in Australia. We have been wanting for some time to write a non-national or what we have called an 'UnAustralian' history of Australian art.[5] It is a history that begins by raising the very same question as McIntyre did: what defines an Australian artist? And our answer, as with Smith, is that we should not confine ourselves merely to artists working in the country. This has been to date the default position of all Australian art histories, from Bernard Smith's canonical *Australian Painting* (1962) on. We have argued, however, that we cannot understand Australian art without taking into account those Australians who did not make art here, and who thereby risked, like Miller, Cook and Wakelin, being excluded from the history of art of the country in which they were born and trained. In this alternative history we find Australian art taking place not just in the usual London and Paris, ultimately cities of Australia's colonisation and cultural marginality. We find it as well taking place in the great metropolis of New York, in Étaples on the coast of France, in Seattle in the north-west of America and in Papunya in the Central Desert, all in their way capitals of art that instead speak of Australia's belonging to the rest of the world.

In this essay, as the necessary complement to the *expatriate* story, we want to write a brief history of New Zealand art taking place in Australia, the *immigrant* story. This would be part of our more general argument—but one that is specific, rooted in historical circumstance, unable to be generalised—that art is translocal, cosmopolitan, caught up in a movement between places. Art is never a matter of countries but always of cities, whether that city be Paris or Wellington; and, more than that, it is ultimately a matter of cities within cities. In Latin, we might say that it is a matter of *partes extra partes* rather than of *genius loci*. And in our UnAustralian history we reverse the perspective of the usual national histories, which are always written from the inside out, and write instead from the outside in. We ask not how other places seem from Australia but how we might appear from other places.[6] Thus, to write a history of New Zealand art from the point of view of Australia is also to write an UnNew Zealand history of art from the point of view of New Zealand. For if from the perspective of Australian art history New Zealand immigrants to Australia are excluded, then from conventional New Zealand art history those New Zealand emigrants to Australia are also rendered invisible. We only have to recall the concluding words to the most recent attempt to write a synoptic history of New Zealand art—Hamish Keith's *The Big Picture: A History of New Zealand Art from 1642* (2007)—to realise that nationalist New Zealand art history is constructed in exactly the same way as the Australian. Keith writes in the concluding chapter, titled 'The Braided River':

> There is no escaping the one simple fact that runs through all of this story. The art made here or influenced by this place is the only art that speaks to us directly about our experience.[7]

In the space that remains, then, we wish to outline some of the global interconnections between Australian and New Zealand art in the twentieth century. In the nineteenth century, the art of the two countries was largely the same thing. It is only in the twentieth century with the rise of national histories that the art of the two countries was divided. We have in common a pre-history, with artists moving between the two countries before their respective art histories were written. Nearly all artists were in effect 'travel' artists, having come from somewhere else and most often moving on again soon after.[8] It is a condition best described by Bernard Smith, who shows the two countries' common roots in his *European Vision and the South Pacific* (1960). As Smith commentator Peter Beilharz writes: 'Australia and New Zealand—Australasia—were one circuit earlier, even if they now pride themselves as culturally distinct'. And, against this more recent sense of cultural distinctiveness, Beilharz goes on to call for a 'renewed sense of the significance of lateral comparison'.[9] Ironically, it would be as much *against* Smith's own Australianist histories that Beilharz's appeal would have to be made. Almost as though describing a mythical time before separation, the classic national histories invariably begin with the same artists. But this commonality then needs to be repressed; the fact that the same artist worked in both countries is rarely, if ever, mentioned. We point here to four such cases of early artistic cross-over, listing one work painted in Australia and the other in New Zealand: the English-born Augustus Earle paints both *Wentworth Falls* (c. 1830) and *Distant view of the Bay of Islands* (c. 1827); the English-born Conrad Martens paints both *View of the crags above Neutral Bay* (1857–59) and *Kororareka in the Bay of Islands* (1841); the Viennese-born Eugene von Guérard paints both *Mount Kosciusko seen from the Victorian border* (1866) and *Milford Sound, New Zealand* (1877–79); and the Amsterdam-born Belgian Jacques Carabain paints both *Queen Street, Auckland*, and *King Street, Sydney* (both 1889).

New Zealand art history proper begins (much like Australia's) with the so-called generation of 1890. We see this generation understood almost as a kind of 'genesis', to use Bernard Smith's phrase from *Australian Painting*,[10] in Michael Dunn's *A Concise History of New Zealand Painting* (1991); in the survey show *Aspects of New Zealand Art 1890–1940* at the National Art Gallery in Wellington (1984); and in—probably the first history to use this date—Gordon Brown and Hamish Keith's *An Introduction to New Zealand Painting 1839–1967* (1969). The argument can take the form either of Brown and Keith's straightforward declaration that the 1890s marked 'the beginning of an era in New Zealand painting',[11] or Dunn speaking of von Guérard's *Milford Sound* as the first 'major masterpiece from the New Zealand landscape',[12] but then, because it was completed in Melbourne from prior studies, reserving this accolade for Petrus van der Velden's *A waterfall in the Otira Gorge* (1891), which was painted entirely *en plein air*.

Petrus van der Velden. Edward Friström. James Nairn. Girolamo Nerli. What is it, ultimately, that distinguishes this generation of 1890—one Dutch, one Swedish, one Scottish and one Italian—from previous New Zealand artists? It is the fact that they *stay* in New Zealand. They teach and exhibit in the emerging arts societies. In short, they introduce the figure of the professional artist. They are *expatriates*, not travel artists (an expatriatism that is possible only when there is the national). They do not simply make art for consumption back in Europe or, like von Guérard, complete a picture of New Zealand back in Australia. They work on the basis that they are creating a tradition in the country of their residence, and indeed their work will significantly inflect that of subsequent generations of artists in New Zealand.

But what is notable about each of these artists, with the exception of Nairn, is that they also work in Australia. The case of Nerli having worked in

Melbourne and Sydney is well known, at least in Australian art history, but van der Velden also worked in Sydney and Friström in Brisbane. Here begins the problem of Australia's and New Zealand's invisibility to each other. Friström, who lived and worked for some seventeen years in Brisbane (where he married an Australian woman), and showed with the Queensland Art Society, on whose council he served, is entirely absent from Australian art history. Van der Velden too is absent from Smith's *Australian Painting*, despite his earlier South Pacific insight. Of course, van der Velden cannot be absent from Brown and Keith; but his Australian years more or less are—and this despite the fact that he returned to Wellington in 1900 after some five-and-a-half years in Sydney, bringing with him, like Friström, his Australian wife-to-be, called indeed Australia. (The van der Veldens would even call their daughter Melba, after the famous soprano, who bought his *Self portrait* of 1909.) Nerli, who arrived in Melbourne with his fellow Italian Ugo Catani in 1885, is in Smith; but, 'after a four year sojourn in Australia, he moved on to Dunedin and became one of the first teachers of Frances Hodgkins'.[13] At that point, he sails out of our narrative, seemingly an Australian artist no longer—this after having been a major influence on Charles Conder, and through him on the entire Heidelberg School, said by Smith to be the first authentically Australian art movement.

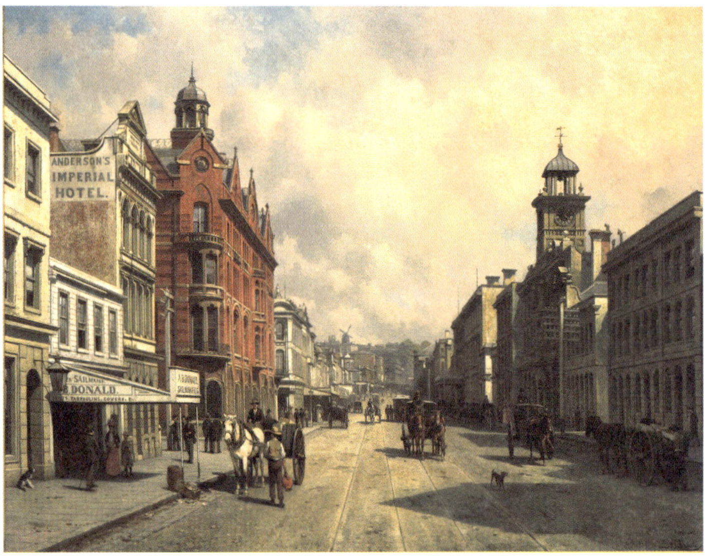

2.2 Jacques Carabain
Queen Street, Auckland, 1889

The presence in Australian art of Nerli's student Frances Hodgkins is also largely unacknowledged. Besides the reference to her with regard to Nerli, Smith remembers her only one other time, in relation to her supposedly two solo exhibitions in this country, in Melbourne in 1912 and Sydney in 1913.[14] In fact, Hodgkins showed also in Adelaide in 1913 and with the Society of Women Painters in Sydney that year too, and had indeed already sent work in 1907 to the *Australian Exhibition of Women's Work* in Melbourne. Brown and Keith conversely do not mention her time in Australia. The two nationalist blindnesses are reciprocal: if Smith is not interested in Hodgkins insofar as she makes *New Zealand* art in Australia, Brown and Keith are not interested in her insofar as she makes New Zealand art *in Australia.*

But let us examine a little more closely the facts of Hodgkins's life and career (most of these are barely represented even in Brown and Keith). In 1910, Hodgkins becomes the first woman teacher of any nationality at the famed Parisian atelier school Académie Colarossi. In 1911, she works and teaches at the French seaside town of Concarneau. That same year, she opens the Frances Hodgkins School of Watercolour Painting at 21 avenue du Maine in Paris. In 1914, she moves to St Ives on the south-west coast of England. From 1915 to 1920, she holds

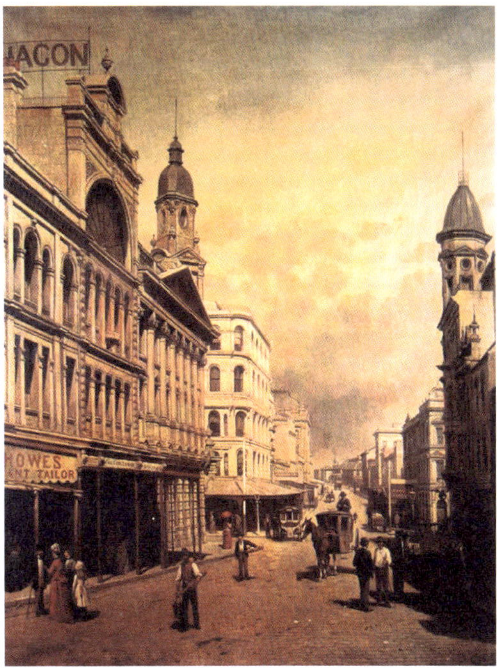

2.3 Jacques Carabain
King Street, Sydney, 1889

summer classes there. From 1921 to 1927, she teaches in both France and England. And whom does she teach during this time? Among many others, the Australasians Ambrose Hallen and Bessie Gibson around 1910 in Paris; Kathleen O'Connor and Owen Merton in 1911 at Concarneau; Maud Sherwood that same year in Paris; and Vida Lahey in 1919 at St Ives.

Thus, Frances Hodgkins is a minor but significant figure in Australian art history because of whom she teaches, and because of her Australian exhibitions, which embodied, as their advertising suggested, 'Modern French Art'.[15] And it is interesting that when Hodgkins fell on hard times in the mid-1920s, she thought of emigrating from England to Australia, 'doubtless remembering', in the words of her biographer Eric McCormick, 'her 1913 tour'.[16] Indeed, in 1925 she even went so far as to book her ticket. She is important to New Zealand art history also because of whom she taught (Sherwood, O'Connor and Merton); but, even more importantly, both New Zealand and Australian artists came to study with her in France and England because she was a New Zealander (just as New Zealanders such as McIntyre and Mina Arndt studied with the Australian George Lambert in London, or New Zealander Edith Collier studied with the Australian Margaret Preston in Ireland and England). That is, Australian and New Zealand artists abroad did not

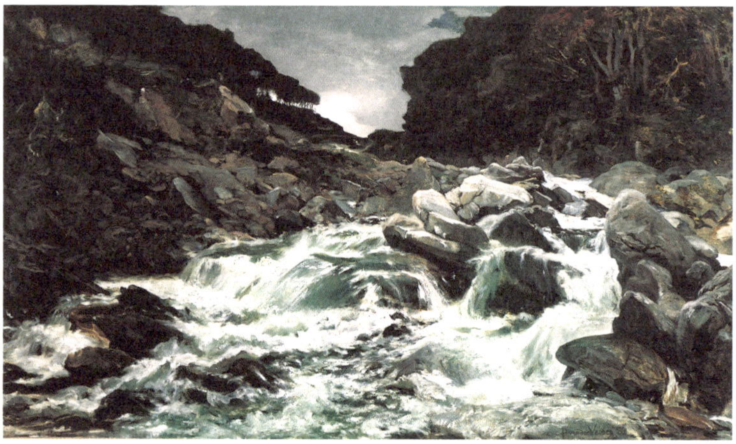

2.4 Petrus van der Velden
A waterfall in the Otira Gorge, 1891

think of themselves as essentially different from each other, as opposed to the way they were thought of by art historians in Australia or New Zealand.

None of the Australians Hodgkins taught are mentioned in McCormick's book on her. This is to leave out one extremely significant aspect of Hodgkins's life and work, which is the knowledge of her shared by artists living in Australia and New Zealand, and more precisely her status as an Australasian expatriate, serving for artists living both in Australasia and Europe as a practical example of an artist living and working in another country.

We could never do more than gesture here towards the rich history of overlap and interaction between Australian and New Zealand artists throughout the twentieth century. But as some way of suggesting the work to be done, we outline ten exemplary instances. Most of them involve New Zealand artists coming to Australia as the larger country, but not all of them. There are important instances of Australian artists and curators going to live and work in New Zealand. And, more revealingly still, there are a number of instances of Australian and New Zealand artists meeting and working together overseas. Again, this is telling us that the artists thought of themselves as similar to each other, even if the histories that were being written about them did not. Certainly, very few of the stories below have made it into the art histories of either Australia or New Zealand. They seem to have fallen between the cracks, to involve either an irrelevant New Zealand aspect in an otherwise Australian story or an irrelevant Australian aspect in an otherwise New Zealand story. But, in truth, it is these kinds of cross-over incidents, involving artists from the two countries, that constitute the real art histories of both, as McIntyre and Ernest Smith saw so long ago. We call here, in other words, for an Australasian art history. This new UnAustralian or UnNew Zealand art history would have to take into account:

- The New Zealander Grace Joel, who was born in Dunedin in 1865, and probably trained with Nerli there. Certainly, she knew him in her home town, but 'possibly also in Melbourne where she went to study in 1888–89 and also later in London, where both painters lived for a time after 1906'.[17] Joel studied at the National Gallery School in Melbourne until 1894, before returning home and eventually leaving for Europe around 1899. She studied in Paris at the Académie Julian with Marcel Baschet and François Schommer, then worked between 1903 and 1906 beside numerous Australasian artists at Étaples. Indeed, the French seaside towns of Étaples and Concarneau in particular were a work- and meeting-place for Australians and New Zealanders from the late nineteenth century on, and Étaples would become an important military base for the ANZACs in

World War I. Following Joel's death in London in 1924, she endowed her old school in Melbourne with a scholarship for painting from the nude.

- The New Zealander Kathleen O'Connor, who left her new home town of Perth in 1906 to go first to London and then to Paris, where she would work with Hodgkins at her School of Watercolour Painting in 1911. She also spent considerable periods at Concarneau. In other words, Australian and New Zealand artists were fully aware of a continuing expatriate tradition, to which they could attach themselves while overseas. Indeed, O'Connor would probably have been aware of the example of another colonial expatriate, the Canadian Emily Carr, who also studied with Hodgkins at Concarneau. However—and this is the important other side of that phenomenon of expatriate recognition we otherwise speak of—both O'Connor and Carr had difficult relations with Hodgkins, perhaps because each had internalised a sense of inferiority as 'colonial' artists (and even women in a still male-dominated world) and projected it onto their teacher.[18]

- The New Zealander Roland Wakelin, who, having already exhibited with the New Zealand Academy of Fine Arts, came to Sydney in 1912 and studied in one of the cradles of Australian modernism with 'the Signor', the Italian-born art teacher Antonio Dattilo-Rubbo. In a milieu that included Grace Cossington Smith and Norah Simpson, Wakelin later teamed up with fellow Dattilo-Rubbo student Roy de Maistre, and together they put on *Colour in Art* at Gayfield Shaw's Art Salon in 1919. The stories of this exhibition and of Simpson's return from Europe with a suitcase of reproductions of the work of French modernism are foundational in the construction of Australian art. That a New Zealander was so central to them has been forgotten, and in many ways Wakelin's esteem rose as his nationality receded, thus reproducing the fate of so many New Zealand artists in Australia.

- The New Zealander Rex Nan Kivell and his well-known Redfern Gallery in Cork Street, London, where in the early 1930s Australian curator Alleyne Zander was encouraged to recover the lost Australian modernist Derwent Lees—a clear case of both Nan Kivell and Zander (like Edith Fry before them) recognising a shared expatriate tradition, and the importance of returning that tradition to its source. After World War II, Nan Kivell employed the Australian Harry Tatlock Miller as his assistant, and showed the Australians Sidney Nolan and Louis James. Nan Kivell generously sold his important collection of Australian and New Zealand colonial art for a fraction of its market value to the National Library of Australia and was knighted on the recommendation of the Australian government.

- The New Zealander Helen Stewart, who came to Sydney in 1928, having studied at Wellington Technical College, the London School of Art, and at Académie Colarossi and La Grande-Chaumière in Paris. In 1931 she returned to London, and like many Australian women worked with Iain MacNab at the Grosvenor School. Again, as so many Australian women did, she went on to study with André Lhote in Paris, thus joining a line that included Grace Crowley, Anne Dangar, Dorrit Black and Eveline Syme, as well as her compatriot John Weeks. Stewart moved among these artists in Sydney, following her return from Europe in 1933. She exhibited at Treania Smith's Macquarie Galleries (where Wakelin had held the inaugural exhibition in 1925), was a withering critic of art criticism in Australia and was at the centre of the so-called colony of New Zealand women painters in Sydney, a loose group that also included Violet Bowring, Maud Sherwood and Adele Younghusband.[19] She returned finally to Wellington in 1946, and from there regularly sent work to Sydney for exhibition throughout the 1950s. She subsequently co-founded 'The Thursday Group' and exhibited with the 'Group of Nine' in Wellington, where she died in 1983.

- The New Zealander Sydney Thompson, who was a student of van der Velden before leaving Christchurch in 1900, thereafter to spend much of the rest of his life in Concarneau. Indeed, we must ask: was it van der Velden who opened Thompson's eyes to the expatriate possibility? In 1925, however, Thompson showed at Macquarie Galleries in Sydney and the New Gallery in Melbourne, and had his work acquired by both the Art Gallery of New South Wales and the National Gallery of Victoria. The following year, he held solo exhibitions in both cities again; and would return to Australia, as also did Frances Hodgkins, as a British artist in *The Murray Fuller Exhibition of Contemporary British Art*, which toured Australia in 1934 and then New Zealand. (This mistaken designation was repeated regularly throughout the 1930s. Derwent Lees, for instance, appeared as a British artist in Alleyne Zander's *Exhibition of British Contemporary Art* in 1933, and Hodgkins and JW Power were likewise identified as British in Basil Burdett's *Exhibition of French and British Modern Art* in 1939.) Thompson was able to work and reside between New Zealand and France for decades, exhibiting regularly in both countries as well as in Australia. He was the very model of a contemporary artist today.

- The New Zealander Owen Merton (father of the well-known and popular American Roman Catholic writer, trappist monk, social critic and spiritualist Thomas Merton), who, after studying at the Christchurch School of Art, left for London in 1909, before joining Hodgkins at her summer school at Concarneau in 1911. Later he studied at Académie Colarossi and was a student of the Canadian Percyval Tudor-Hart at the same time as the Dunedin-born painter Maud Sherwood. Merton had met the Adelaide painter Richard Hayley Lever while painting at St Ives in 1910, and like Hayley Lever before him moved in 1916 with his family from France (where his son was born in 1915) to America, where he remained until 1923. From then until his death in 1931, Merton moved between America, France, England, North Africa and Bermuda. Like his friend from Adelaide, he found the road to America that went through Paris.

- The New Zealander John Weeks, who studied at the Elam School of Arts in Auckland under, among others, Edward Friström, then spent two years at the Sydney Technical School between 1913 and 1915. In 1923 he left Christchurch for the Royal Scottish Academy, but in 1925 left Edinburgh for Paris, where he began to work with André Lhote, something he would do periodically between visits to the south of France, North Africa and Italy (Weeks was also an Orientalist) until 1929. In that year he headed back to Auckland where, in 1930, he began a twenty-four-year teaching career at the Elam School of Art, and in his work became increasingly concerned with abstraction. This trajectory is, to Australian eyes, reminiscent of the careers of, for example, Grace Crowley, Anne Dangar and Dorrit Black, each of whom as a teacher back in Australia was concerned with passing on their understanding of art gained in Europe. Weeks became, as did these women in Australia, a decisive figure in New Zealand art, even if, as Peter Shand has pointed out:

  > the observation in his obituary that he was 'particularly interested in interpreting the New Zealand landscape' sums up the popular perception of John Weeks' place in New Zealand art history, but emphasises the wrong reason for his importance.[20]

- The New Zealander Colin McCahon, who during a trip to Melbourne in 1951 met the Australian returned-expatriate Mary Cockburn Mercer, who was said to have worked for Lhote and to have attended the famous dinner put on by Picasso and friends for Henri Rousseau in Paris in 1908.

McCahon hired the now 'small, elderly woman with a walking stick and crutch' to give him painting lessons and, more importantly, to talk to him about art. It is upon his return to New Zealand that McCahon embarked on a new cubist phase in his work, which can be seen as leading to his artistic maturity. Unlike many examples of Australian–New Zealand relations, McCahon's biographer Gordon Brown fully acknowledges the influence of Cockburn Mercer upon McCahon: 'Although unimportant as a painter, McCahon felt something of the spirit of Cubism flowed through Cockburn-Mercer into his own understanding of what Cubism was about'.[21]

- Finally, we would have to consider among many others the careers of the New Zealand avant-garde sculptor and film-maker Len Lye, who lived in Sydney from 1921 to 1926, where his shift to hand-painted animated films featuring 'primitive' imagery from the region was inspired in part by his viewing of the collection of Aboriginal and South Pacific art and objects at the Australian Museum and his reading at the Mitchell Library in Sydney; and the prematurely deceased Wellington artist Frank Weitzel, who was an important contributor to the de Maistre–driven Burdekin

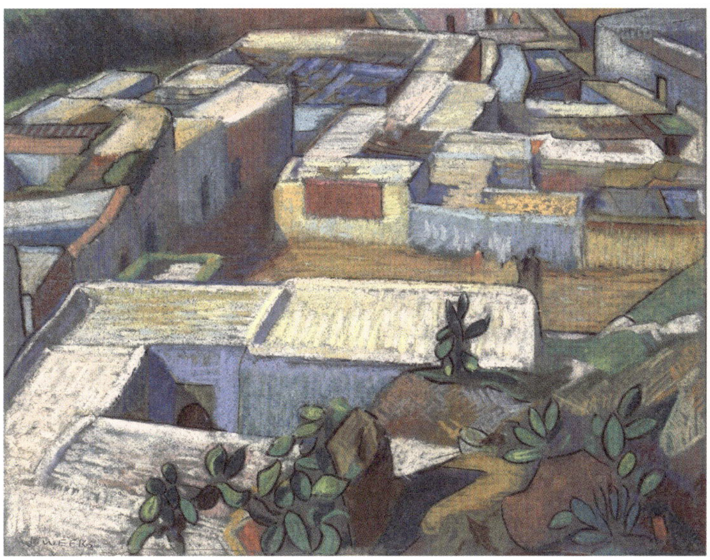

2.5 John Weeks
Moroccan rooftops, 1927–8

House exhibition in Sydney in 1929, which stood at the intersection of modern art and design in Australia. Weitzel, whose family was politically active, anti-conscription (his father was interned as an enemy alien) and subject to local hostility, originally headed to America, where he studied at the California School of Fine Arts. On scholarship, Weitzel enrolled next at the Art Students League of New York in 1926, and then at the Kunstakademie in Munich in 1927. It was only in 1928 that he joined his sister in Sydney, and having established himself there within a few years set off again, this time for London where he exhibited with, and knew, Jacob Epstein, Duncan Grant and Paul and John Nash.[22] While preparing for his first solo exhibition, Weitzel contracted tetanus while digging clay for his sculpture and died in 1932. The following year his work was the subject of a retrospective exhibition organised by Dorrit Black at the Modern Art Centre in Sydney. Indeed, it was through Black that Weitzel had come to work with Claude Flight at the Grosvenor School, which led to his embrace of the linocut. Weitzel, so briefly in Sydney, nonetheless later came to be thought of as important by Australian artists and yet is completely absent from New Zealand art histories.

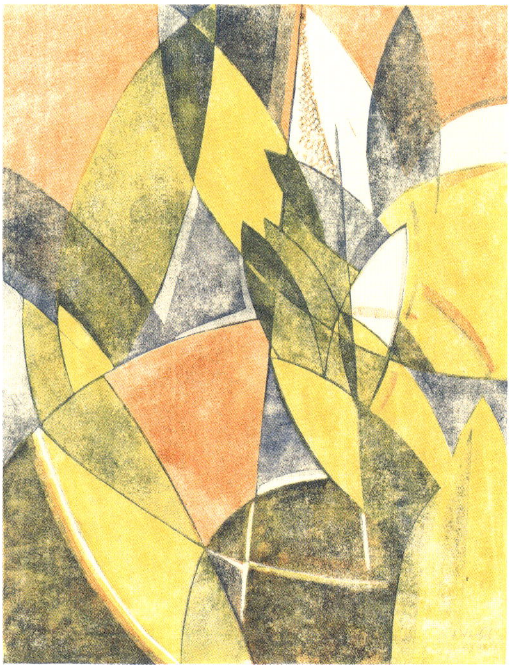

2.6 Frank Weitzel
Abstract design 2, c. 1932

All of this would be to leave out such telling New Zealand figures in Australian art as James R Jackson, Maud Sherwood, Dora Meeson, Harold Cazneaux, Frank Lynch, Dorothy Richmond, Edwin and Mary Murray Fuller, Dorothy Thornhill, Frances D Ellis, Nancy Borlase, Helen Crabb (also known as 'Barc'), Gordon McAuslan, Eileen Mayo and even Sydney's so-called Witch of Kings Cross, Rosaleen Norton, who was born in New Zealand. It would also be to leave out those fewer—and for us this is significant—Australian figures who feature in New Zealand art. This brief list would include the natural history painter and Pacific adventurer Ellis Rowan, the Slade-trained watercolourist and painter Eana Blyth Jeans, the East Sydney Technical College (now National Art School)–trained painter, printmaker and teacher Kate Coolahan, and the National Gallery School–trained landscape painter Shay Docking and her husband, the gallery director and author of *Two Hundred Years of New Zealand Painting* (1971), Gil Docking.

To conclude here, however, let us take up one case study in Australia–New Zealand artistic relationships in a little more detail. *The Invention of New Zealand Art: Art and National Identity, 1930–1970* (2009) by Francis Pound is clearly an attempt to reverse previous histories of New Zealand art. The book is an analysis of the nationalist rhetoric that accompanied New Zealand art throughout the forty years under review, in effect arguing that the distinctiveness of New Zealand art is not real but the creation or invention of a discourse. Moreover, for Pound, this nationalist discourse—as for Ernest Smith some thirty years before—is no longer relevant to the situation of such contemporary New Zealand artists as Michael Parekowhai or Jenny Fraser or the gallerist Peter Vuletic (his examples), who make and show work with galleries and artists around the world. Pound's book ends in the year 1970, and his concluding chapter is entitled 'A Post-Nationalist Art'. But what is notable about Pound's book is that, for all of his criticism of the rhetorics of nationalism, he is unable to present a positive alternative. If he ends with a 'post-national' situation for New Zealand art, he is precisely unable to write the history of this post-nationalism. Indeed, the reader ultimately gets the sense that the book, which was written over a twenty-year period, was originally a nationalist history, and for all of its change of heart along the way cannot get beyond this nationalist horizon.

We might get a sense of the limits of Pound's book and of the possibilities that another, UnNew Zealand, art history might open up if we consider the career of one of the artists Pound takes up in his 'post-national' chapter, Gordon Walters. Pound—as Michael Dunn in *A Concise History of New Zealand Painting* before him—wants to understand Walters's turn towards abstraction as a consequence of his encounter with the art of Paris in 1950. This contact was no doubt crucial, but it arose in the wider context of his life and work in Sydney and Melbourne during the six years between 1946 and 1953. However, Pound, as Dunn, makes no mention of Walters's Australian years (as Australian art historians also do not when writing histories of art in that country), but it was during these years that Walters did his first abstract paintings.

To offer the briefest summary of events: after studying with the Indonesian-born Theo Schoon at Wellington Technical College, Walters went to Sydney for the first time in January 1946, and in that month acquired a copy of the catalogue for the Museum of Modern Art's 1941–42 Joan Miró exhibition. He visited Melbourne and then returned to Wellington in April. He spent July and August with the Dutch-Indonesian-New Zealander Schoon in the South Canterbury caves examining Maori rock art, and over the Christmas period he continued to make drawings and take photographs in the caves alongside him. In June 1947 Walters held his second exhibition at the French Maid coffee shop in Wellington, and left again for Sydney in December, where he would live until February 1949. During this period he recalled 'studying rock engravings in the Sydney area and bark paintings in the museums of Melbourne and Sydney'.[23] Walters' *Untitled* (1956) is even said by him to be 'partly inspired by Australian Aboriginal rock painting'.[24] Walters's imaginative exploration of the Indigenous art of Australia and the Pacific and his use of the Mitchell Library is an almost exact replay of Len Lye's evolution in the same city in the 1920s.

However, 1948 was an important year in the history of abstract art in Sydney. In that year Grace Crowley was appointed to teach the subject at East Sydney Technical College (now the National Art School) but handed over her class to Ralph Balson, who began the first of his twelve years teaching there. Tony Tuckson considered them his most influential teachers, and they in turn remembered him as their most 'sincere' student.[25] Both Balson and Crowley contributed work that year to *Contemporary Australian Art*, which opened in June at Auckland Art Gallery, and both artists were central figures in the seminal group exhibition *Abstract*, which opened in October at David Jones Art Gallery in Sydney. And, between catching up with copies of *Cahiers d'art* at the Mitchell Library, Walters did indeed meet Balson and Crowley.[26] In February the following year he headed back to Wellington, where in November he held his fourth exhibition, this time at the Wellington Public Library. This exhibition, consisting of work mostly done during and after his time in Sydney, would be his last for sixteen years. For Michael Dunn, it either gets a 'hostile reception'[27] or is 'received with indifference'.[28]

In March 1950, Walters sailed to London, which he used as a base for his forays onto the Continent, in particular to Paris, over the following ten months. Already familiar with the work of Auguste Herbin from the November 1949 issue of *Art d'aujourd'hui*, he arrived in Paris at a time when geometric painting was in the ascendant.[29] In April 1950, Galerie Denise René held the group exhibition

Espaces nouveaux, which included the work of Victor Vasarely, and in June put on *Arp-Sophie Taeuber-Arp*, the show at which Walters must have 'warmed to [the work of] Sophie Taeuber-Arp, on the whole preferring it to the work of her husband, Hans Arp'.[30] In the same month, the fifth Salon des Réalités Nouvelles opened at the Palais des Beaux-Arts. This was the expansive and inclusive iteration of the Salon that included artists from around the world, in particular from Switzerland, the Netherlands and America, besides the usual French, Germans, Scandinavians, Italians, Belgians and Hungarians. In this single exhibition, Walters could have seen the work of Herbin, Josef Albers, Etienne Beöthy, Max Bill, Marcelle Cahn, Jo Delahaut, Piero Dorazio, Félix Del Marle, Natalia Dumitresco, Jean Gorin, Paul Gadegaard, Camille Graeser, Janin, František Kupka, Gyula Kosice, Richard Paul Lohse, George Morris, Eric Olson, Antoine Pevsner, Manlio Rho, Hilla Rebay, Mimmo Rotella, Nicolas Schöffer as well as the Australian Mary Webb.[31] The year 1950 was also when Jean Dewasne and Edgar Pillet founded their Atelier d'Art Abstrait in the rue de la Grande-Chaumière.

Then, in January 1951, Walters returned. Not to Wellington but to Melbourne, and it was there that he painted his first abstract painting. In October, he was joined by his friend the expatriate New Zealander George Johnson, and through

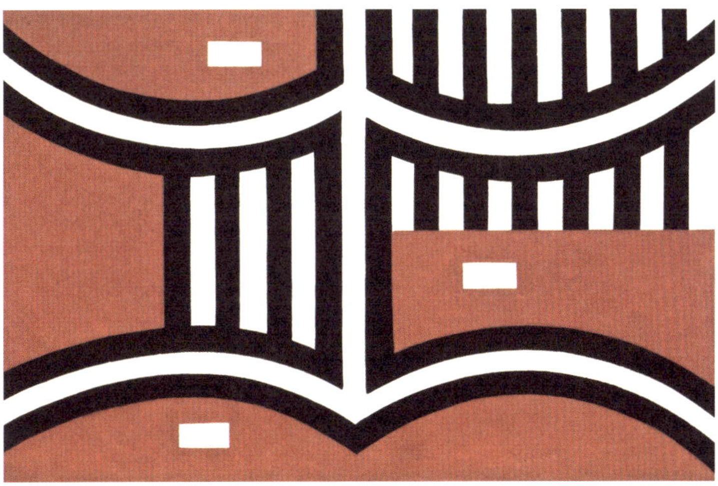

2.7 Gordon Walters
Untitled, 1956

most of 1952 the two artists shared a studio in Nicholson Street, Footscray.[32] Walters spent more than two-and-a-half years in Melbourne, and, although little is known of his time there, it was clearly a productive period for him:[33]

> The influences I was digesting at the time were those of the artists whose work I had studied in Europe, and who were to have a decisive and lasting effect on my work. They were Arp, in his early reliefs and collages, Mondrian, the early Vasarely, Herbin and Capogrossi in particular. On the other hand there was the art of the Pacific, New Zealand, New Guinea (all of it), the Marquesas, the Austral Islands, etc., which I had also studied closely in museums while overseas.[34]

In all, Walters was in Australia for more than six years before he left in August 1953 for Auckland, where he caught up again with Schoon, the first time they had seen each other in more than eight years. In Australia he had done his first abstract works and, when 'he departed from Melbourne in August 1953, Walters left much of his work behind with the intention of soon returning. Instead, he was to remain in New Zealand from that time onwards, based in Wellington'.[35] Walters's lost Melbourne works remain a tantalising prospect. In 1979 Walters returned to Sydney, where he met Bridget Riley as she escorted her touring Australian exhibition, and he made his final trip to that city in 1982 to view the Sydney Biennale.

Let us be very clear here: our point in all of this is not merely a matter of asserting that Walters spent time in Australia, as though this is significant in and of itself. Rather, our point is the much stronger one that we cannot properly understand even the *New Zealand* part of Walters's career—his breakthrough into abstraction—without taking account of the time he spent in Australia. And in all kinds of ways, as we have tried to show here, whether it is the experiences of New Zealand artists overseas before they return or, indeed, the influence of New Zealand artists who remain overseas on the art made in New Zealand, we simply cannot restrict New Zealand art to that made there or influenced by the country, as Keith would have it. New Zealand art also takes place *elsewhere*; its cities always contain *other cities*.

Now, Pound is undoubtedly right when he says that New Zealand art today is 'post-national'. It is to admit that the special relationship that Australia and New Zealand had in the nineteenth and twentieth centuries is over. Today, Australia is no longer a privileged destination for New Zealand artists, as the closest larger culture. Whereas once it was the Sydney film industry that held Len Lye in Sydney, today New Zealand film-makers work all around the world, and make the world and, indeed, other worlds, in New Zealand. But if we were going to write the history of this situation, of how New Zealand got to be like this, we would start with Australia. It was perhaps in Australia more than in any other place that New Zealand art began to move beyond itself. It is only by considering New Zealand's continuing artistic relationship with a country like Australia in the twentieth century that we might understand New Zealand's artistic relationship with the rest of the world in the twenty-first century. And this is true too for Australia.

We might finish our account by reflecting on the famous story of Colin McCahon in Sydney in 1984. He had not been out of New Zealand for twenty-six years and, at the height of his artistic fame and doubtless stressed by the events surrounding his exhibition at the Sydney Biennale, he disappeared and likely went on a drinking spree. For a day he was lost in a place that New Zealand art history does not see and that does not see New Zealand art. By the time of McCahon's alcohol-fuelled wanderings and memory lapses, so incorporated were New Zealand artists in the history of Australian art and so unknown were those New Zealand artists living in Australia by New Zealanders, it had been forgotten that both Walters's and McCahon's old friend Theo Schoon had been in Sydney for years, equally lost. And McCahon himself, walking through the streets of Sydney, was the very embodiment of New Zealand art in Australia: incognito and unrecognised, thought to be just another Australian until he was found and rescued.[36]

An earlier version of this text was published in the *Journal of Art Historiography*, no. 4, 2011.

—

1 Raymond McIntyre, 'Exhibitions', *Architectural Review*, vol. 57, January/June 1925, p. 214.

2 These articles were part of a series written by Edith Fry between 1914 and 1927. They included 'Australian Artists in Paris', *Sydney Morning Herald*, 1 July 1914, p. 5, and 'Australian Artists in Paris', *Sydney Morning Herald*, 18 March 1922, p. 7; 'Australians in Paris', *Sydney Morning Herald*, 2 May 1917, p. 5; 'Art and Artists: The Paris Salon', *Daily Telegraph*, 26 July 1919; 'Australian Art Exhibition in London', *Daily Telegraph*, 17 June 1920; 'Exiles: The Australian Artists Abroad', *Sydney Morning Herald*, 16 February 1924, p. 20; 'Retrospect: Twelve Years from Home', *Sydney Morning Herald*, 12 July 1924, p. 11; 'Australasian Artists in Europe', *British-Australasian*, September 1921, pp. 46–8; and 'Some New Arrivals in Art', *British Australian and New Zealander*, July 1925, pp. 32–4.

3 The same logic would apply in Australia, where the once-titled *Art in Australia* would become *Art & Australia*, in what would appear to be a move against the limiting of Australian art to that made here.

4 Ernest Smith, 'Memories of Three New Zealand Expatriate Painters', *Art New Zealand*, no. 1, August/September 1976, pp. 11–15.

5 For an overview of this history, see Rex Butler and ADS Donaldson, 'A Short History of UnAustralian Art', in ed. Ian North, *Visual Animals: Crossovers, Evolution and New Aesthetics*, Contemporary Art Centre of South Australia, Adelaide, 2007, pp. 107–22. For an attempt to write one of the chapters of this history, see Rex Butler and ADS Donaldson, 'Stay, Go, or Come: A History of Australian Art, 1920–40', *Australian and New Zealand Journal of Art*, vol. 9, nos 1–2, 2009, pp. 118–43.

6 Perhaps the best example of this history so far is Frenchman Jean-Claude Lesage's *Peintres australiens à Étaples* (*Australian painters in Étaples*), Amis du Musée de la Marine d'Étaples, Étaples-sur-mer, 2000, a history of Australian and New Zealand artists at the artist colony of Étaples on the northern coast of France. It is in this book that we have another history of Australasian art as seen through the eyes of an outsider. We draw on *Peintres australiens* throughout what follows.

7 Hamish Keith, *The Big Picture: A History of New Zealand Art from 1642*, Godwit, Auckland, 2007, p. 269.

8 We take the expression 'travel artist' from *Augustus Earle, Travel Artist: Paintings and Drawings in the Rex Nan Kivell Collection, National Library of Australia*, ed. Jocelyn Hackforth-Jones, exhibition catalogue, National Library of Australia, Canberra, 1980.

9 Peter Beilharz, 'Two New Britannias: Modernism and Modernity across the Antipodes', *ACH: The Journal of the History of Culture in Australia*, nos 24–25, 2006, pp. 146, 155. In this, Beilharz would be echoing the words of Australian literary critic Nettie Palmer, who once wrote: 'At the beginning of this century, and before that, Australia and New Zealand knew a good deal more about each other than in the decades that followed', Nettie Palmer, 'New Zealand and Australia', *Meanjin*, vol. 3, no. 3, Summer 1944, p. 165.

10 Bernard Smith, 'Genesis 1885–1914', in *Australian Painting, 1788–1970*, Oxford University Press, Melbourne, 1971, pp. 71–124.

11 Gordon H Brown and Hamish Keith, *An Introduction to New Zealand Painting, 1839–1967*, Collins, Auckland, 1969, p. 49.

12 Michael Dunn, *A Concise History of New Zealand Painting*, David Bateman, Auckland, 1991, p. 40. Dunn is another fascinating example of Australia–New Zealand interrelations, and indeed the tension between the national and the international in the art historiography of the region. Graduating from the Canterbury School of Art with a degree in painting, Dunn then studied at the University of Melbourne in the late 1960s under European émigré Franz Philipp, eventually completing an MA on the topic of New Zealand sculpture, with the title 'Dependent Taste'. Although in *A Concise History* we see the connection made between the landscape and national identity, in Dunn's later *Nerli: An Italian Painter in the South Pacific*, (Auckland University Press, 2005) we have the attempt to think of Nerli—undoubtedly aided by Dunn's trans-Tasman perspective—as belonging exclusively neither to Australian nor New Zealand art history. It is in the acknowledgements to this book that Dunn thanks Philipp for suggesting the topic to him. Is it too much to see the influence of the cosmopolitan Italianist Philipp on Dunn's work on Nerli and that of Smith's *Australian Painting*—for Dunn must have encountered the work of Smith in Melbourne in the late 1960s—on Dunn's own national histories?

13 Smith, *Australian Painting*, p. 74.

14 Ibid., p. 191. At footnote 21 Smith makes clear his reliance on Eric McCormick, Hodgkins's future biographer, for his understanding of Hodgkins.

15 The advertisement for Hodgkins's exhibition in Sydney is reproduced in Eric H McCormick, *Portrait of Frances Hodgkins*, Auckland University Press, 1981, p. 76.

16 Ibid., p. 101.

17 Dunn, *A Concise History*, p. 44

18 See on the similarities between O'Connor and Carr Maria Tippett, *Emily Carr: A Biography*, House of Anansi Press, Toronto, 2007, p. 93. Janda Gooding in her 'Putting Distance Between Us: Katherine O'Connor and the Luxembourg Garden Paintings' points to a certain antagonism between O'Connor and Carr and their teacher and, indeed, implies one between O'Connor and Carr themselves: 'What is fascinating is that each woman either erased their recollections of the other two artists or deliberately belittled their involvement. Carr identified Hodgkins as "an Australian woman whose name I forget"; Hodgkins deliberately omitted from her letters any reference to O'Connor; and O'Connor dismissed Hodgkins as "an opportunist with astigmatism"', in *Painted Women: Australian Artists in Europe at the Turn of the Century*, ed. Anne Gray and Helen Carroll, exhibition catalogue, Lawrence Wilson Art Gallery, Perth, 1998, p. 27. This account is complicated, however, by the fact that it seems likely that O'Connor and Carr did not actually study at Concarneau simultaneously: O'Connor, it appears, had left by April 1911, while Carr for her part did not arrive until the end of October. (We're grateful to Elena Taylor for this information.) Perhaps, then, the antagonism between O'Connor and Carr is as much the result of a 'provincialising' art history as any truth of the respective artists' feelings.

19 HS [Helen Stewart], 'Art Criticism in Australia', *Bulletin*, 4 April 1934. From Art Gallery of New South Wales press clippings folder, Art Gallery of New South Wales Research Library, Sydney. See also Margaret Pearson, 'Colony of New Zealand Women Painters in Sydney', *Sydney Morning Herald*, 2 December 1937, p. 26.

20 Peter Shand, 'John Weeks (1886–1965)', *Dictionary of New Zealand Biography*, updated 22 June 2007, http//www.dnzb.govt.nz/.

21 Gordon H Brown, *Colin McCahon: Artist*, Reed, Wellington, 1984, p. 79. See on this, however, Martin Edmond's 'The Village', delivered as the 2012 Barry Andrews Address at the National Library of Australia, which makes the point that it was actually the Australian artist Lina Bryans who arranged for McCahon and Coburn Mercer to meet. See 'The Village', *The Journal for the Association of the Society of Australian Literature*, vol. 13, no. 2, 2013, pp. 1–14.

22 Coincidentally, Weitzel's sister Hedwig (Hettie) Ross, having been found guilty in 1921 of spreading seditious literature in Wellington—the Australian newspaper *The Communist*—had moved to Sydney, where she rose through the central committee of the Communist Party of Australia to become the leader of the Militant Women's Group, while at the same time completing her training to become a teacher. Working all over New South Wales from the late 1920s, she eventually rose to spend more than ten years on the executive of the Teachers Federation. From Ross's time at Victoria University College in Wellington around 1920, the future New Zealand Prime Minister Peter Fraser remembered her as 'a wonderfully brilliant student'.

23 Gordon Walters, 'Notes', in ed. Michael Dunn, *Gordon Walters*, exhibition catalogue, Auckland City Art Gallery, 1983, p. 34.

24 Ibid., p. 34.

25 *Tony Tuckson, 1921–1973: A Memorial Exhibition*, ed. Daniel Thomas, exhibition catalogue, Art Gallery of New South Wales, Sydney, 1976, p. 9.

26 In fact, after this essay was originally published, Laurence Simmons alerted us to Walters's 'A Difficult Time for Artists', *Landfall*, no. 185, April 1983, in which he writes: 'But I did see good work, and there were a few isolated abstract painters, such as Ralph Balson and Grace Crowley, whom I met briefly at the time' (p. 21).

27 Michael Dunn, 'The Enigma of Gordon Walters' Art', *Art New Zealand*, no. 9, February–March–April 1978, p. 59.

28 'Chronology', *Gordon Walters*, p. 25.

29 Iain Buchanan, 'Walters and Auguste Herbin', in eds. James Ross and Laurence Simmons, *Gordon Walters: Order and Intuition; A Festschrift of Essays Presented to Gordon Walters on the Occasion of his Seventieth Birthday*, Walters Publications, Auckland, 1989, p. 33.

30 Jenny Harper, 'Black, White and "Op": Links Between Gordon Walters, Bridget Riley and Victor Vasarely', in eds. Ross and Simmons, *Gordon Walters: Order and Intuition*, p. 27.

31 Michael Dunn, 'The Art of Gordon Walters', in *Gordon Walters*, p. 12. Dunn writes: 'In Paris, he

saw exhibitions by French non-figurative painters such as Auguste Herbin and Victor Vasarely at the Galerie Denise René'. Neither artist, however, held a solo exhibition in 1950 in Paris, let alone at Galerie Denise René. Both did, however, have work in the group exhibition *Aspects de l'art d'aujourd'hui* at René's gallery in that year, but this was in January, before Walters arrived.

32 George Johnson, interview with Charles Nodrum, November 2008. Curiously, Johnson remembers Walters coming to Melbourne from Hobart, and that he, Johnson, had preceded Walters to Melbourne.

33 In July, Walters made a brief trip to New Zealand to see his parents.

34 Gordon Walters, 'Statements', 15 September 1982, in *Gordon Walters*, p. 24.

35 Michael Dunn, 'The Art of Gordon Walters', in *Gordon Walters*, p. 13. For a more extended account of Walters' time in Australia, see Rex Butler and ADS Donaldson, 'Gordon Walters: *Les années décisives*, 1946–1953', in ed. Zara Stanhope et al., *Gordon Walters: New Vision*, exhibition catalogue, Auckland City Art Gallery, 2017.

36 For an extraordinary reimagining of this episode, see Martin Edmond, *Dark Night: Walking with McCahon*, Auckland University Press, 2011.

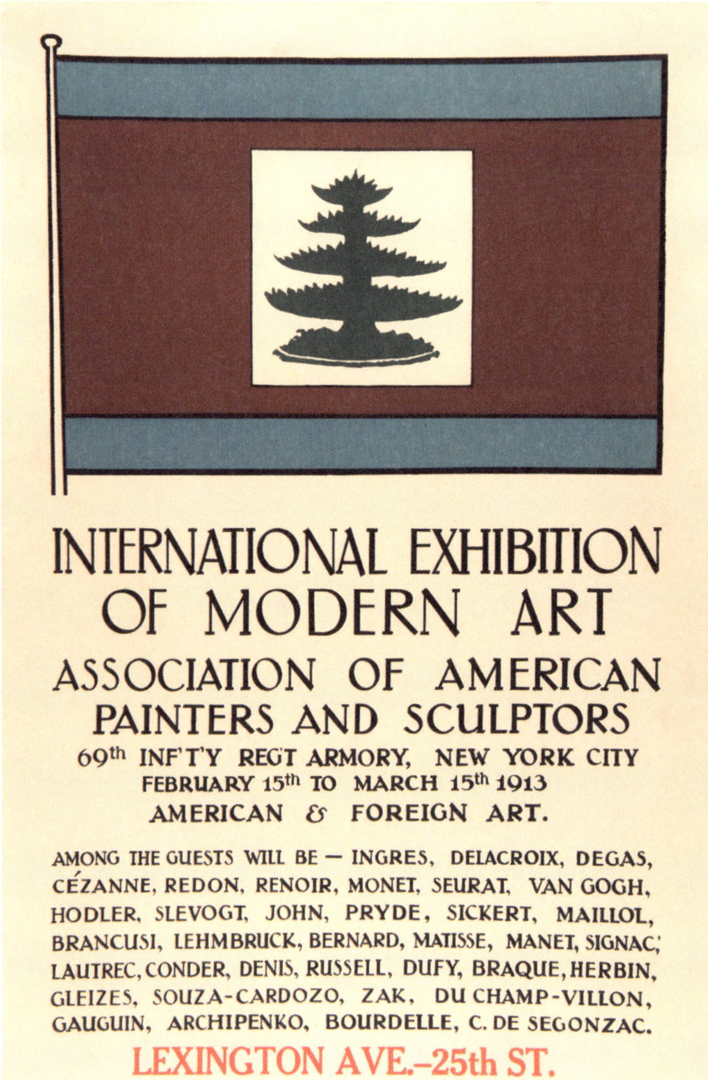

3.1 Armory Show poster, 1913

Against Provincialism
Australian–American Connections 1900–2000

That great America on the other side of the sphere, Australia
—Herman Melville, *Moby-Dick,* 1851

Undoubtedly, one of the most intellectually inventive arguments ever made about Australian art is Terry Smith's 'The Provincialism Problem'. Originally published in 1974 in the New York–based magazine *Artforum*, it is a compelling analysis of peripheral artworlds' positions of dependency on apparently more central and powerful artistic cultures. It takes as its case study Australia's relationship to America, arguing that because of its geographical isolation and temporal delay, Australian art can only ever be 'derivative' and 'second-rate'.[1] To the extent that Australian artists are never in on the 'early struggles', but have access only to the 'mature forms of the style',[2] they are unable to innovate in the terms that count and make works relevant to those beyond the region. Written at the height of Australia's involvement in the Vietnam War and in the wake of anti-colonial movements of liberation, the essay has had a profound and still ongoing effect on Australian art and art criticism. It is probably no exaggeration to say that all thinking today about national identity and Australia's place in the world in the visual arts takes place in its shadow.

More specifically, we might say that the entire subsequent history of Australian art has been nothing less than the attempt to *contest* the terms of Smith's analysis. Art historians such as Heather Barker and Charles Green and, more recently, Anne Sanders have sought to situate Smith's essay in its historical context, pointing out both his intellectual debts (the fact that others had said similar things before) and the specific circumstances in which he made his argument (he had recently studied on a Harkness Fellowship with Robert Goldwater at the Institute of Fine Arts in New York and with Meyer Schapiro at Columbia University).[3] In doing so, they seek to uncover the forces acting upon Smith (America's contest with the Soviet Union during the Cold War) and the assumptions he made when constructing his argument (his adoption of the ideology of artistic modernism), and thus attempt to show that his argument is very much the product of a particular time and place.

Australian art too—both that made after Smith's article and even that made before it—can be seen as an attempt to undermine or otherwise escape the consequences of Smith's argument. From the late 1970s on, the artist Imants Tillers made works whose explicit target was the idea of Australia's provincialism. Through his copying or appropriating of better-known works from overseas, Tillers's paintings could be seen almost as a parody of Australian cultural subservience. In his literal remaking of international art, we have exactly the same work, except that Tillers now claims it as his own. But what Tillers thereby seeks to expose is a kind of *internal* limit to the logic of provincialism: the fact that the dominance of a metropolitan culture is able to operate only insofar as it speaks to provincial cultures in their own language, and these cultures in turn are able to imagine it as their own.[4] And this postmodern appropriation had an influence on Australian art historians too, who applied it to a previous generation of Australian artists. Thus Ian Burn is able to argue that a work like Sidney Nolan's *Railway guard, Dimboola* (1943) is not the unconscious imitation of a cubism that arrives intact from overseas, but is rather engaged in a conscious 'dialogue' with cubism that forces us to re-read cubism itself.[5] Or further back in Australian history, Ross Gibson can say of convict forger Thomas Watling's *Letters* (1794) that they are not the playing out of the familiar tropes of colonial isolation but, on the contrary, express a distinctively Australian experience through their 'mongrel' and 'vernacular' mixing of different rhetorical registers.[6] Even Bernard Smith's great *European Vision and the South Pacific* (1960) has been read within this logic as a form of 'reverse perspective', according to which the neoclassicism of the European explorers is rewritten and sent back as romanticism after contact with the distinctive fauna and flora of the South Pacific.[7]

In fact, Terry Smith himself has subsequently revised or qualified his own original claims. In a series of essays written after 'The Provincialism Problem', he acknowledges that his initial diagnosis may no longer apply to today's art world, in which artistic centres of interest are more widely dispersed and American cultural power is no longer so dominant. In the essay 'Provincialism Refigured', written after the *Australian Biennale 1988: From the Southern Cross: A View of World Art 1940–1988*, held in the Bicentennial year of 1988 in Sydney, Smith responds to the rise of postcolonialism by suggesting that it is not just Europe and America that are of cultural significance: '"The centre" is no longer one place, it is a network of nodal points, dispersing inequalities of power at many levels'.[8] And this logic is extended in a more recent series of essays, in which Smith begins to think of a new global or world art as part of what he calls the 'contemporary'. In this new contemporary art, there are no longer centres of art at all, insofar as no art can be considered more 'advanced' historically than any other. Rather, art from all over the world exists in a kind of 'simultaneity' or belonging to 'the same moment of time'.[9] As Smith writes in 'The State of Art History: Contemporary Art': 'It is no coincidence that a *worldly* art criticism and art-historical scholarship is coming into existence, one that surpasses its modern precedents in European and American art history and criticism'.[10] And it is on the basis of this idea of the contemporary that Smith can imagine the writing of the 'alternative modernities'[11] that become newly visible in the absence of any single modernism.

However, throughout all of this—the historical contextualisation of Smith's original article, the artistic parodies of it, the art-historical revisions of it, and even Smith's own updating of it—one thing remains unquestioned: *the fact that there was provincialism*. Indeed, the arguments concerning appropriation and its subsequent art-historical revisionism precisely rely upon its continued existence. The ironic gestures of appropriation artists or the re-reading of historical works of art would have no meaning outside it. They do not so much attempt to get rid of provincialism as merely reverse its poles, with the provinces becoming the new metropolis. And Smith, in his subsequent writings on provincialism, at no point suggests that it did not once exist, only that the prevailing circumstances have now changed. Indeed, we might even say that this is how provincialism lives on: not directly, but through its negation, reversal, the argument that it no longer applies. As Smith himself writes in 'The Provincialism Problem', it is exactly through its exceptions that provincialism is all the more proved: 'Those who have broken the bind have done so largely because the system is structured so that several artists each year break the bind'.[12] To argue against provincialism or to argue that it no longer applies, therefore, is finally to change nothing, and certainly with regard to the art and art history of the past.

How, then, to do away with provincialism? Everything in Australian art history presupposes it. Indeed, we would even say that the very category of Australian art as such is provincial. All that has been deemed worthy of being written down and recorded in our history has been done so on the basis of our isolation, distance and difference from other countries. Each of the existing histories of Australian art—William Moore's, Bernard Smith's, Robert Hughes's, Andrew Sayers's, Christopher Allen's and John McDonald's—has been based on this assumption.[13] They are histories constructed on the basis of our separation from, and belatedness with regard to, other cultures. They are the history of *here* as opposed to *elsewhere*. Australian artists who leave are not followed once they go. Artists who arrive are not seen as bringing somewhere else with them. It is true: we no longer see ourselves as provincial, but every time we write a history of Australian art, even to contest or update what has previously been written, we renew that provincialism we thought we had left behind.

We offer, then, a brief history of the relationship between Australia and America throughout the twentieth century to try to demonstrate that Australian art was never provincial, was never separate from that of other countries. In some ways, it is to follow Smith's suggestion for the writing of 'alternative modernities'; moreover, it is also to show—to use the terms of his own argument—that art has always been contemporary, that there has never been that non-reciprocal, dominant, one-way relationship between the two countries that he imagines.[14] Australian artists from the beginning were always part of the story of American art, not just as the overcoming of a prior provincialism but as the demonstration that it never existed. This is also to say that there was never just one centre of American art, which is another assumption of the provincialist argument. Seen through the lens of the present, there is a whole variety of places in America where 'modern' art occurred, and any number of Australians were working in—indeed, were sometimes central to—those places.

So to conclude our introductory remarks, our history of Australian artists working in America also opens up a new history of art in that country. It is what we might call a certain history of UnAmerican art. For the story of Australians in America throughout the twentieth century is similar to that of all those artists from other countries—from Japan to Canada, from Scandinavia to South America—who have also been part of American art. And, equally, this new emphasis on the worldwide movement of artists and ideas about art tells us that American art was never provincial, as it is often characterised as being in relation to France in the early twentieth century. We briefly suggest in this essay, for example, that the famous Armory Show of 1913 did not introduce modernism late into America, as it is usually understood to have done. Instead, if we define American art, like that of Australia, as not taking place exclusively within its shores, we might think of the establishment of Gertrude Stein's great collection of modern art in Paris before World War I, or of Stanton MacDonald-Wright and Morgan Russell's formation of the pioneering movement of synchromism in Munich in 1913.[15] And these apparently offshore developments always travelled back to America. When the Australian Ambrose Patterson arrived to teach in Seattle, it was his artistic training in France that was important to his appointment. The same could be said of his fellow Australian Richard Hayley Lever, who likewise arrived in America with European credentials. And, of course, American modernism had from the beginning seen the presence of such well-known French figures as Albert Gleizes, Francis Picabia and Marcel

Duchamp, as well as artists from many other countries, all of them bringing with them the lessons and understandings of 'French' modernism.

All of this could be understood as the importing of 'French' culture (the provincialist conception). It could equally be understood as a particular 'American' response to French culture, making it over and nationalising it (the postcolonial reaction to provincialism). But it was neither of these. As opposed to these abstract and over-general categories, what we see making up the true story of modernism in America is an almost uncountable number of local interactions and scenes, involving hundreds if not thousands of artists. We write here a certain history of American art from the perspective of Australia, just as we write a certain history of Australian art from the perspective of America. Besides making evident the patterns of trans-location, the point of our lists and detailed biographies of artists is that this inclusiveness and inability to generalise not only characterises contemporary art but is also the defining quality of the art of the past. Many of the artists we speak about, both Australian and American, are currently unknown, but this is not because of any inherent lack of art-historical interest. Rather, it is because they have fallen between the respective nationalisms that have so far characterised the art histories of the two countries. Our point, however, is that these artists, more than any others,

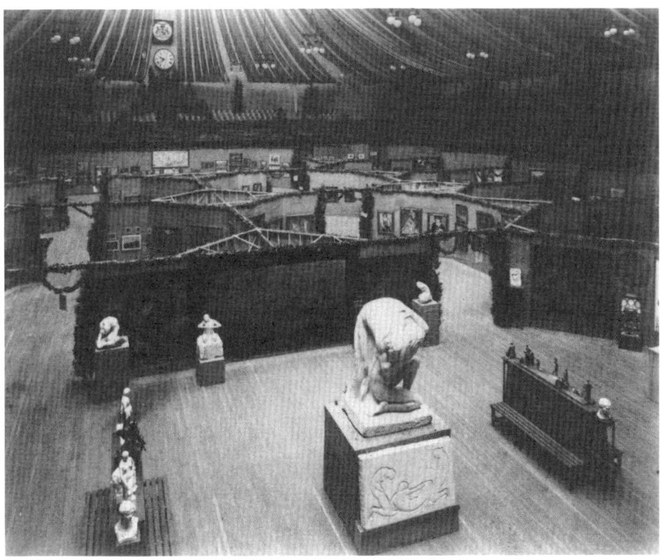

3.2 Installation view of the Armory Show, New York, 1913

are the real precursors to artists today. This international history is the authentic history of the present—that is to say, the generative and productive explanation of how we got to where we are at this moment.

* * *

It is undoubtedly true that, immediately before Smith wrote his essay in 1974, there had been a number of important shows by Australian artists in America. The abstractionist Robert Jacks was part of *Survey '69* at the Montreal Museum of Fine Arts in 1969, had participated in *Group Show* at the Paula Cooper Gallery in 1970 and had been given a solo exhibition at the New York Cultural Center in 1971. The Cultural Center too was the venue for the night 'conceptual art went spectacularly public',[16] when the Ian Burn–curated *Conceptual Art and Conceptual Aspects* opened in April 1970. The sculptor Clement Meadmore had his third and final show with Max Hutchinson Gallery in 1972, and in 1973 was again curated into the Whitney Biennial (having been in two previous Whitney Annuals). The minimal painter Robert Hunter was one of *Eight Contemporary Artists* at the Museum of Modern Art in 1974, a show that was reviewed in glowing terms by the critic Max Kozloff in *Artforum* (and by the Australian critic Robert Hughes in *Time*), just three issues after Smith's article was published there, as though in implicit rebuke.

But in all of this it is perhaps even more astonishing to realise that every Australian who came to New York and wrote about the provincialism problem—for, it is true, Smith was not the first[17]—walked under the Perth artist Charles Basing's celestial mural of 1913, painted on the ceiling of Grand Central Station. Part of a larger project undertaken with the French artist Paul Helleu, it was overseen by the Hewlett Basing Studio of Brooklyn, which he ran together with the architect and muralist J Monroe Hewlett. Basing, in fact, completed a large number of such public murals around New York City, for everyone from the members of the Columbia University Club on Forty-Third Street to the students of public schools numbers 29 and 38 in the Bronx, and even worked on the interiors of Longfellow, Alden & Harlow's Carnegie Institute in Pittsburgh. A member of the prestigious Salmagundi Club, Basing, who had studied at the Académie Julian in Paris with William-Adolphe Bouguereau, was also a successful scenic designer for the New York stage. An Orientalist too, he died in Morocco in 1933 following complications after a camel stepped on his foot, and his work was subsequently the subject of a memorial exhibition at the Fifteen Gallery in New York in 1934. How can we say here, in Smith's terms, that Basing was not 'central' to New York art?[18]

Or—to pick another major American art landmark before beginning our history proper—we might briefly offer an 'Australian' perspective on the famous

1913 Armory Show, which toured New York, Chicago and Boston and is said (erroneously, like all stories of the late import of metropolitan culture into so-called provincial cultures) to have introduced French modernism into America. It is an exhibition that, as is well known, was dominated by the scandal surrounding Duchamp's *Nude descending a staircase* (1912). Duchamp's work was lent to the show by one of its patrons, prominent New York lawyer and collector John Quinn; but, in fact, there were two Australian artists in Quinn's collection whose works were also in the exhibition. The first was the Heidelberg School artist Charles Conder, who had been dead for some four years, and who was represented by five works, including oil paintings, pastels and watercolours on silk. The second was Derwent Lees, the Tasmanian-born then-teacher of drawing at the Slade School, London, where he influenced a generation of English modernists such as Vanessa Bell, Duncan Grant, David Bomberg, Edward Wadsworth and Stanley Spencer. (The story of Lees's 'Australianness' is a familiar one: because he left Australia in his early twenties, he is still remembered today, if he is at all, as a member of the Camden Town Group, as he is in the current hang of his work at the Queensland Art Gallery. But the prominent expatriate curator Alleyne Zander had already attempted several times to reclaim Lees as Australian, both in her *Exhibition of*

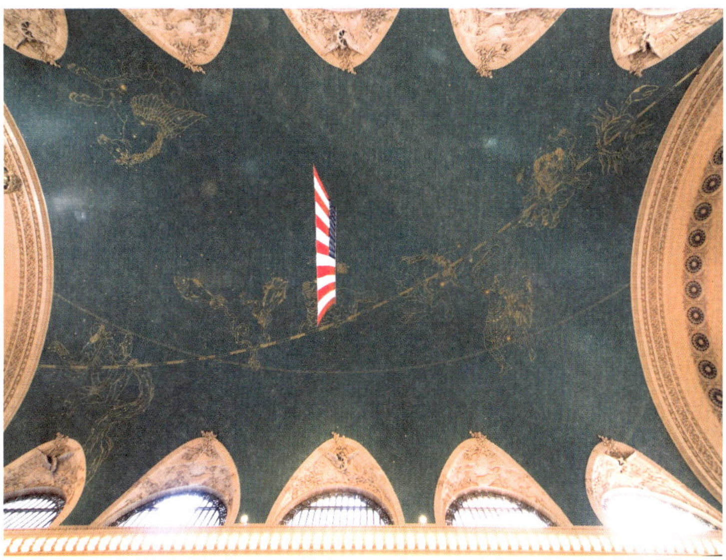

3.3 Charles Basing
View of the ceiling of Grand Central
Station, New York, 1913

British Contemporary Art, which toured Australia in 1933, and in the retrospective of his work she mounted at New Zealander Rex Nan Kivell's Redfern Gallery in London in 1934 after Lees's premature death from tuberculosis, following more than a decade of mental illness.)

And there were two further Australians hanging in the Armory. The first was Francis McComas, who, unlike Conder and Lees, had already had a life and career in America. McComas, born in 1875, left his native Tasmania as a young man to study at the Sydney Technical College and was included in the *Exhibition of Australian Art* at the Grafton Galleries in London in 1898.[19] That same year, he sailed with fellow artist Miles Evergood to San Francisco, where he studied with the French-trained Arthur Mathews, then director of the California School of Design. After further study in Paris, he returned to the West Coast and joined the Monterey Peninsula art colony, where he made a reputation for his landscapes, in particular those of Hopi country and the American South-West. A tonalist and watercolourist, McComas was selected for the Armory Show as one of three representatives of Californian art, and was later honoured at the 1915 *Panama Pacific International Exhibition* with a joint exhibition with his old teacher Mathews. Today he is recognised as California's first modernist.[20] The other was Frank Nankivell, the Victorian artist who had left Australia in 1890 headed for Paris, but was waylaid in Japan for several years before settling in America. In Tokyo he was a crucial influence on Rakuten Kitazawa, the inventor of modern Japanese 'manga', whom Nankivell employed in the office of the English-language illustrated magazine *Box of Curios*. In New York by 1896, he went on to become a founding member of the Association of American Painters and Sculptors (1911–14), the artist's group behind the Armory Show, on whose selection committee Nankivell served. His membership of this crucial driver of American modernism, which never numbered more than twenty-eight members, places him alongside the leading New York artists of the time, including George Bellows, Arthur B Davies (whose prints Nankivell worked on), William Glackens, Robert Henri, Walt Kuhn, Ernest Lawson, George Luks and John Sloan.[21]

Luks, Henri and Sloan were also friends of Miles Evergood, or Myer Blashki as he was known when he studied at the National Gallery School in Melbourne, the other artist on board that boat with McComas bound for America in 1898. After stopovers in Hawai'i and San Francisco, Evergood was in New York the following year, and in the following decade he made his reputation in that city. In 1904 his work was shown in the *First Independent Exhibition of American Impressionists* alongside, for instance, Glackens, Henri, Luks and Bellows, and he held well-received exhibitions at the Lotos Club in 1902, 1903 and 1908.[22] In 1907 his work was hung in the National Academy, and in 1909 he mounted a retrospective at the Salmagundi Club. In 1910, alongside Nankivell, he participated in the landmark first exhibition of the Society of Independent Artists. By 1911, however, Evergood had moved to London, and before World War I he had shown with the New English Art Club and in the New Salon in Paris, and had joined the Chelsea Arts Club, thus reconnecting him with numerous Australian artists. Indeed, at the outbreak of war, alongside John Longstaff, Tom Roberts, Arthur Streeton and George Bell among others, he enlisted in the Royal Army Medical Corps and served at Wandsworth Hospital in London. After the war, the family moved between New York and London, and in 1931 he returned to Australia, where he found 'virtually nothing had changed since his departure in 1898'.[23] Living first in Brisbane and then in Sydney, by 1935 he was back in Melbourne, and in 1937 he organised a remarkable two-person exhibition at the Athenaeum Gallery with his son Philip Evergood, by then a highly respected and well-known social realist in America and considered by his father's old friend John Sloan as 'the heir to the Ash Can School's philosophy'.[24] Subsequently, Philip's painting *Art on the beach* (1934), an image of the artist colony at Provincetown, Massachusetts, first exhibited in the 1934 Whitney Biennial in New York, was acquired by the National Gallery of Victoria. Miles Evergood died suddenly in 1939 with a memorial exhibition held in Melbourne that year and another in 1941.

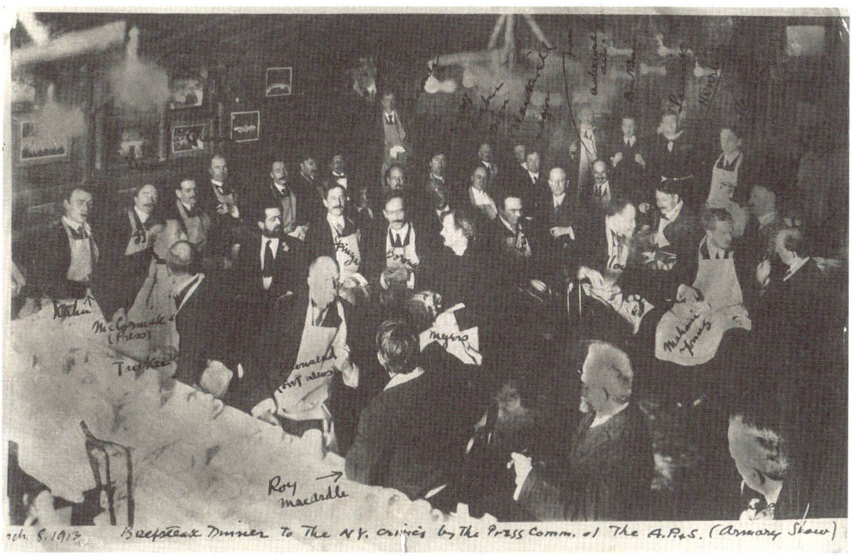

3.4 Armory Show artists and members of the press at the beefsteak dinner given by the Association of American Painters and Sculptors, New York, 8 March 1913. Back, centre: Frank Nankivell.

Another Jewish Melbourne artist, Horace Brodzky, also found the road between America and England.[25] Brodzky first trained at the National Gallery School from 1901 to 1904. Almost immediately upon finishing, he left for America—first for San Francisco in 1904, and then for New York, where in 1906 he studied at the National Academy of Design. But then in 1908 Brodzky packed up again, this time for London, where it could be said that his story truly begins. In 1911, he enrolled briefly at the City and Guilds Art School and held his first solo show in his own studio in Chelsea. From this exhibition PG Konody, later to be the London buyer for the National Gallery of Victoria's Felton Bequest, selected his painting *Girgenti—the pine tree* (1911) for the 1912 Venice Biennale. In that exhibition he was joined by Hayley Lever and identified, of course, as British, although from an UnAustralian point of view he was in fact continuing a line of Australian artists who had already shown at what was then called the *Esposizione d'Arte della Città di Venezia*. It is a line that includes Charles Conder, George Lambert, Arthur Streeton and Tom Roberts, as well as the little-known Australian Scottish impressionist Grosvenor Thomas, who showed at least three times in Venice.[26]

Brodzky, who was close to Henri Gaudier-Brzeska who sculpted his bust in 1913, joined the fledgling London Group in 1914 but nonetheless moved to New York in 1915 with letters of introduction in his pocket to the poet Ezra Pound (remarkable given he was Jewish and Pound an anti-Semite) as well as the collector John Quinn, who subsequently introduced him to Jules Pascin, with whom he became firm friends and about whom, as with Gaudier-Brzeska, he was later to write a book.[27] In 1917 he acted as the clerk of works in the little-known second and final *Vorticist Exhibition*, arranged by Quinn (the first was in London in 1915). It was the inaugural show at the Penguin Club, which was founded by Kuhn and backed by Quinn. That same year Brodzky participated in two group shows with the Penguins and held his solo exhibition there the following year.[28] In 1919 he designed endpapers for the long-running 'Modern Library' series of books, then in 1920 Egmont Arens published *A Portfolio of Linoleum-cuts by Horace Brodzky*, and by 1922 he had designed dust jackets for books such as Upton Sinclair's *Jimmie Higgins* (1919), Ezra Pound's *Instigations* (1920) and Eugene O'Neill's *The Hairy Ape* (1922). Brodzky also edited two so-called little magazines while in New York, *Art Review* and *Rainbow*, in which he introduced the work of the war poet and painter Isaac Rosenberg to the American public. By the time of his departure after eight years in New York, he had been included in the first exhibition of the Modern Artists of America, Inc. (1922) and his work had been compared in *The New York Times* to that of Toulouse-Lautrec and Goya.[29] He was farewelled at a stag dinner at the Penguin Club on 22 March 1923 'to celebrate the departure permanently to England of the honourable and talented Horace Brodzky (alias "Prince Igor" alias "Happy Horace")'.[30]

But Basing, McComas, Nankivell, Evergood and Brodzky were by no means the first Australians to work professionally in America. Australian artists had been in America throughout the nineteenth century. They sometimes went there directly across the Pacific, and sometimes through London and Paris. Perhaps the first figure in our history of Australia–America connections is the Melbourne, London and Paris–trained Eleanor Harrison (née Ritchie). Harrison—who died at the age of forty-one and was, more tellingly, an expatriate—is, in the words of art historian Jane Clark, that 'classic example of the "forgotten" Australian woman artist'.[31]

Harrison met her husband, the noted American plein-airist Lowell Birge Harrison, while working outside Paris in the early 1880s. In 1883 the newlyweds set out to make a home in Santa Fe, New Mexico, and travelled the Wild West, but in 1885 they returned to Philadelphia, from where they left again for Paris the same year. There Harrison continued her studies (with Benjamin Constant, as well as Jules Lefebvre), probably the first woman in a long line of Australian artists to study at the Académie Julian. In 1886 her work was hung in the Paris Salon, where she exhibited regularly thereafter. From 1887 for eighteen months Harrison and her husband lived at Étaples, where she had a studio—the first Australasian artist to live and work on the Picardy Coast. Later she would be followed by such artists as Rupert Bunny, Arthur

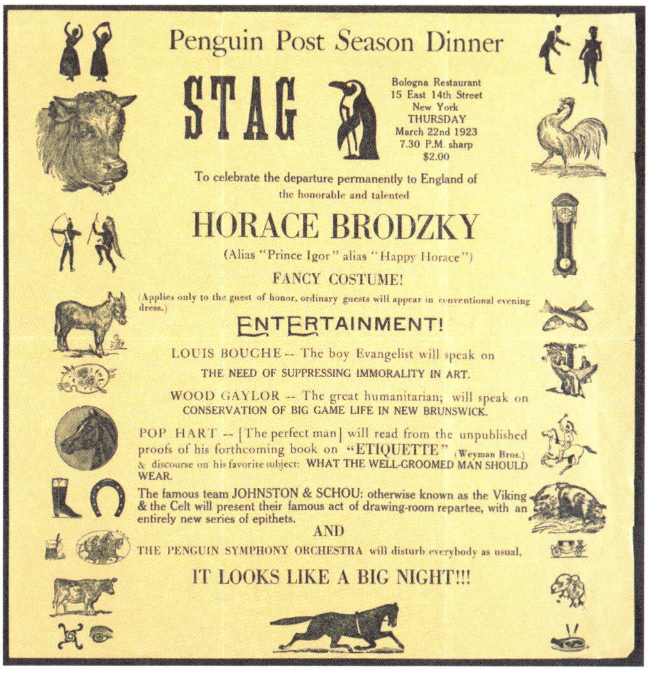

3.5 Flyer for a stag party given by the Penguin Club honouring Horace Brodzky, March 1923

Baker-Clack, Iso Rae and Frances Hodgkins. Harrison and her husband returned to Melbourne in 1889 (proving, of course, that she had never lost her 'Australian' identity, despite all of her years overseas, as the usual nationalist histories would have it), and they had a joint exhibition that year in Tom Roberts's Collins Street studio, where Charles Conder expressed an admiration for Eleanor's work. They then both held an exhibition at Gemmell, Tuckett & Co.'s rooms in 1891, before departing for San Francisco later that year. Eleanor Harrison died in Santa Barbara in May 1895, probably due to complications following the birth of her son.

By the time of her death, however, there was already a regular back-and-forth between Australia and America. This is particularly to be seen in the black-and-white tradition, with an early generation of American cartoonists coming here to be part of a growing market for Australian newspapers, and conversely an uninterrupted line of Australian cartoonists working in the already established newspaper industry in America. There is first of all Luther Bradley, a graduate of Yale, who arrived in 1882 to work for *Melbourne Punch* and *The Bulletin*. He soon departed to become the art director and chief cartoonist for the *Chicago Daily News*. But there is also the much longer-staying Livingston Hopkins, or 'Hop' as he was known, who after contributing work to *Scribner's Monthly*, *Wild Oats*, *Judge* and various Harper's magazines was induced by the Queensland draughtsman WH Traill to join *The Bulletin*. Hopkins arrived in Australia in 1882, the same year as Bradley, bringing with him 'Australia's first photo-engraving equipment, which allowed drawings to be photographed and transferred onto metal plates for printing, thus making topical daily cartoons a possibility'.[32] From 1887, Hopkins was the chief *Bulletin* cartoonist until his retirement in 1913, ending up doing more than 19,000 drawings for the magazine. He made trips to the country with Banjo Patterson, started an artists' camp on his land at Balmoral in Sydney with Julian Ashton, and taught etching to Ashton, Tom Roberts and Arthur Streeton.

Equally, our own cartoonists travelled across the Pacific to work in America. In 2005 the State Library of New South Wales staged an exhibition, *Reclaiming Felix the Cat*, which sought to remind us of the Australian provenance behind the worldwide syndicated comic and animated film favourite *Felix the Cat*. The exhibition, curated by Judy Nelson, argued for the authorship of Sydney-born animator Pat Sullivan, against that of his American assistant Otto Messmer, and made the point that Sullivan's creation of Felix in 1917 preceded Walt Disney's Mickey Mouse by more than a decade.[33] Sullivan's cat was 'the indisputable animated screen cartoon star of the 1920s',[34] and no less a figure than Charlie Chaplin once declared: 'I have only one rival. Felix!'[35]

Along with Sullivan two other well-known Australian black-and-white artists were working in New York: Bert Levy and Reg Russom. Levy, who had done

Jewish jokes for *The Bulletin* in the 1890s, published his celebrated panorama *As an Australian artist saw New York's Christmas streets*, which manages to combine wry humour with cutting social comment, while working for the *New York Times* in 1904. (Later, in 1916, while working in New York, he broke his contract to get out of his well-known series 'Samuels and Sylenz' because he increasingly found the direction he was being asked to take offensive to Jews.) At the same time in New York we have Russom, who for many years was a staff artist on the *New York Times* and 'made his first hit with a series of drawings in *Life*, in which [in a satirical way] he pictured the transit problems of the future'.[36] He had studied at Ashton's and left for San Francisco at age nineteen around 1906, but not before his work was acquired by the Art Gallery of New South Wales when he was seventeen. He eventually returned to Australia and died in Newcastle in 1952.

Basing, McComas, Sullivan, Levy and Russom were all men, but the larger story of Australian expatriatism—as traced by a generation of feminist art historians including Caroline Ambrus, Rachel Biven, Joan Kerr and Helen Topliss—is that of women artists. We have only to think in the first half of the twentieth century of Dora Ohlfsen in Rome, Stella Bowen in London and Paris, Bessie Gibson, Bessie Davidson and Agnes Goodsir in Paris, Anne Dangar at Moly-Sabata on the Rhône,

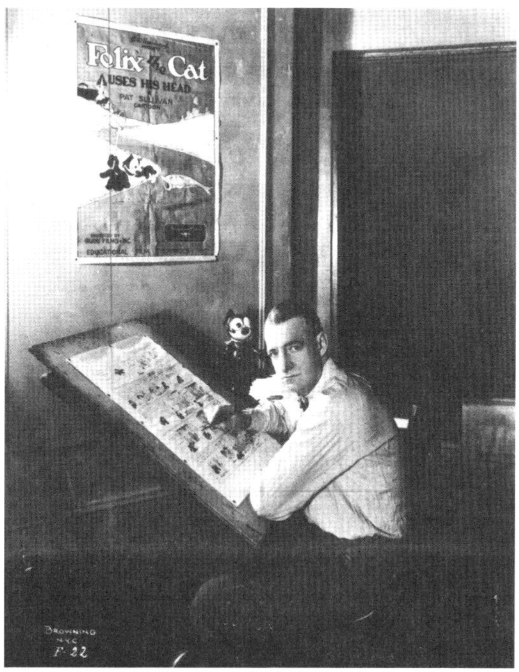

3.6 Pat Sullivan in his studio, New York, 1922

and the Rae sisters, Iso and Alison, in Étaples. In the majority of cases, it was the *women* who wanted to escape the increasingly nationalist and masculinist Australia of the first decades of the twentieth century. And it was no different, as we will see, for those artists who went to America. Indeed, a number of women artists or artists assisted by women found that the path to New York went first through Paris. We have the printmaker Emily Letitia Paul, who was born in Bathurst in 1866 and trained at Ashton's at the same time as Thea Proctor. After studying art in London from 1902 to 1903 and in Paris at the Académie Julian, she went to America in about 1904 before returning to Sydney in 1913. Influenced by American socialism, she abandoned the decorative panels and floral oils she had been doing until then and became a leading public speaker for the Socialist Party in Sydney. In 1914 she unsuccessfully contested the state seat of Cook for that party, before dying suddenly in 1917. We also have the renowned miniaturist Stella Marks, who after studying at the National Gallery School in Melbourne and then in London left for New York in 1914, where she remained for more than twenty years. In 1935 Marks was offered the position of president of the American Society of Miniature Painters, but was unable to accept because her husband, Montagu Marks, was due to go back to London to start a partnership with the well-known British film producer Alexander Korda. The couple returned to Australia in 1937, and in 1938 two of Marks's works were included in the *Sesquicentennial Celebration Exhibition* at the Art Gallery of New South Wales.

Most notable among the early female expatriates, however, is Constance Jenkins. At seventeen she entered the National Gallery School, where she studied from 1900 until 1908. In 1909 she won the prestigious National Gallery of Victoria Travelling Scholarship, the first woman to do so, and went to study at the Académie Julian in Paris and eventually exhibited at the Old Salon. She returned to Australia in 1912, but left soon after for San Francisco via New Zealand. (She had become engaged in the meantime to the New Zealand–born and National Gallery School–trained artist Eric Macky.) The couple opened an art school in San Francisco in 1915, which soon gained the reputation of having 'the most progressive group of art students in the Bay region'.[37] In 1917, the art school was amalgamated with the California School of Fine Arts, a union sponsored by the San Francisco Art Association and that affiliated it with the University of California. Constance (now) Macky remained professor of painting there for some twenty years. She was included in numerous shows of Bay area art that toured America, and according to one account her 'figurative paintings and portraits dominated many group shows in San Francisco museums and galleries'.[38]

The Mackys, however, were not the first Australasian artists to exert an influence over West Coast American painting in the first half of the twentieth century. The son of a boxer, Gordon Coutts moved from Scotland initially to Adelaide and then to Melbourne in his late teens. He returned briefly to Glasgow in 1888 where he married his teenage sweetheart and was back in Australia the following year and almost immediately began studying at the NGV Gallery School in Melbourne. Taught by Frederick McCubbin, following the completion of his studies Coutts quickly began exhibiting and became associated with the Heidelberg artists. Already highly thought of, in 1896 he was appointed instructor in painting at the (Royal) Art Society of New South Wales and taught there until 1899 when it was reported that he was leaving for London. Two years later, however, in Adelaide, where he had family, an article in the paper appears regarding difficulties he is facing in Melbourne. It is headed, 'An Artist's Troubles – Mr Gordon Coutts Sued by His Wife – Conjugal Infelicities'.[39] Although he was directed by the court to pay maintenance to his wife and child, Coutts nonetheless 'carefully neglected compliance with the order of the court, escaped from this country and led [the authorities] in a dance for eight months'.[40] In 1902 he was arrested in Wellington, New Zealand, for failing to comply with the Melbourne court's order, having been found in a hotel in the company of the young artist Alice Hobbs, formerly a student at the NGV Gallery School, and with a ticket to England in the name of another person. Coutts was subsequently extradited to Melbourne, but at his trial the charges were dropped after he agreed to pay the arrears. In 1907 he and his first wife are officially divorced in Melbourne, but by this time Coutts had been in San Francisco for more than four years, during which time he had married Hobbs. Indeed, the first Mrs Coutts only found out about her husband's bigamy when the new Mr and Mrs Coutts were listed in the Melbourne press amongst the Australian survivors of the San Francisco earthquake in 1906. In 1910 Coutts and his new wife moved to Paris where he studied at the Académie Julian and showed in the Old Salon (SAF) in 1912 and 1914. That same year, with the outbreak of war, they returned to the Bay area. In 1916, however, he decided to return to Paris and Tangiers, but Hobbs declined to follow. Instead, she moved to Reno and divorced him in 1918. He is reported as saying at the time, 'She said I love my art more than I did her. Is that an offence? I consider it a fine compliment'.[41] Coutts married for the final time after the war, to Gertrude Russell, a musician and artist, and lived in Spain and maintained a studio in Tangiers, from where he made frequent and regular trips to London to present his academic Orientalist landscapes and portraits at the Royal Academy and other exhibiting societies. In 1924, the couple moved to Mexico for a year, before finally settling in Palm Springs the following year. There he built his fantasy Moorish villa 'Dar Marroc' in the Californian desert. In the interwar years, the Couttses' house was the centre of the fledgling Palm Springs artist's colony. His near neighbour, the transcendentalist abstract painter Agnes Pelton, frequently visited, Rudolph Valentino and Winston Churchill came to stay, and his Los Angeles dealer, Earl Stendahl of the legendary

Stendahl Gallery, where Coutts showed in 1925, had a place just around the corner. In this way, Coutts became a well-known painter of the South-West, like McComas, and a practitioner of what we might call an American-style Orientalism. He even made a brief return to Australia, although not to Melbourne, when he held an exhibition in Adelaide in 1927. His return to Palm Springs from Australia, however, more or less coincided with the Depression, and his work's market, once buoyant, dissipated. When Coutts was confined to bed with tuberculosis, in 1936 his lifelong friend and former Tangiers neighbour, the famed Irish Orientalist Sir John Lavery RA, visited him at 'Dar Marroc', not long before his eventual death in early 1937. Later prevailed upon to return to Palm Springs, Lavery was involved in the car accident that resulted in the death of Gertrude just before Christmas 1937. Lavery then stayed in California and oversaw Coutts's memorial exhibition, held at the Dee Bradford Gallery on Sunset Boulevarde in Los Angeles in early 1938. In 1950, Coutts's daughter Jeanne, an artist and teacher herself, was instrumental in establishing the still-running Desert Art Center in Palm Springs.

Equally, when it came time to disentangle the history of painting in the north-west of America, it was felt to be important to point out that when the later-to-be-major American abstractionist Mark Tobey moved to Seattle in 1922, he did not so much found the Northwest School of painting, as is often claimed, as join an already existing conversation—one gathered around the table of the Melbourne-born painter Ambrose Patterson. In the words of Seattle-based historian Matthew Kangas, Patterson was 'the first modern artist to arrive in Seattle'.[42] Patterson left Australia for the last time in 1916, after his fin-de-siècle French and Belgian years between 1898 and 1909, and lived first in Hawai'i (where he dined with Jack London and Somerset Maugham, and was visited by his old benefactor Nellie Melba), before moving to Seattle in 1918. In 1919 he was invited to establish the University of Washington School of Painting and Design, where he would remain until 1947, and where—again to quote Kangas—he 'set in motion a teaching system which still flourishes today'.[43] Patterson held solo shows all over America, including solo exhibitions at the Seattle Art Museum in 1934, 1947 and 1956, and a retrospective in 1961. He died in 1966, but the true irony is that when the show *American Artists of the North West* toured Australia in 1958, featuring the work of Seattle's so-called Big Four (Tobey, Morris Graves, Kenneth Callahan and Guy Anderson), and already provoking in more enlightened cultural circles here criticisms of American cultural dominance,[44] it was at least in part the influence of an *Australian* on advanced American art that they were seeing.

Australian artists were also influential on the East Coast. Again, if we are looking for an Australian who is 'central' to American culture, achieving recognition at the highest level, why not consider Adelaide-born Richard Hayley

Lever, who in 1925 presented his painting of the presidential yacht to Calvin Coolidge on the Rose Lawn of the White House. Hayley Lever, while living earlier at the artist colony in St Ives, Cornwall, was selected to show his work in the 1910 *Carnegie International Art Exhibition*, and the Carnegie Institute subsequently commissioned work from him. His work had been hung since 1902 at the New Salon in Paris, and he had regularly contributed to the Royal Academy Summer Exhibition and the New English Art Club in London during the Edwardian years. In 1912 Lever moved to America, where he befriended the Canadian-American painter Ernest Lawson, in whose circle he moved following his arrival in New York. Through Lawson he became an associate of The Eight, the so-called rebels of American art. A post-impressionist with symbolist undertones, Lever is 'in the collections of almost all the major American museums',[45] and was grouped with Lawson and William Glackens in a series of influential articles written in the 1920s on 'The Modern Tendency in Art' by the critic Catherine Beach Ely. Writing in *Art in America*, she observed of Lever's painting that 'his colour and atmosphere are handled from the American viewpoint, yet in a way peculiar to himself'.[46] After the war too, Lever's work was reviewed alongside that of Basing and McComas, insofar as they were often

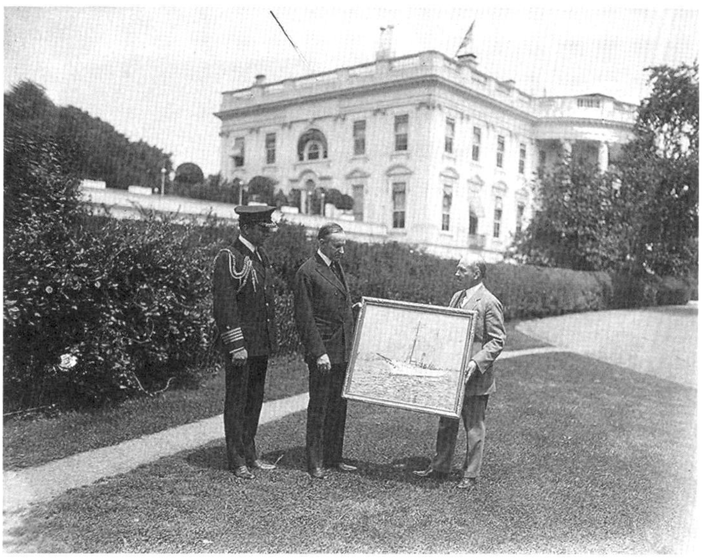

3.7 Richard Hayley Lever presenting *Mayflower* to President Calvin Coolidge, Washington DC, 1925

in the same shows and even won prizes at the same time.[47] Lever taught painting from 1919 to 1931 at the Art Students League of New York, in what art historian Sam Hunter called 'the stronghold of a revived American realism'.[48] He won the 1928 Amsterdam Olympic medal for painting, was elected a full member of the National Academy of the Arts in 1937, and was eventually honoured with a lifetime membership of the National Arts Club. Lever was forced to give up his house during the Great Depression, and died in New York State in 1958, a famous painter, etcher and teacher, but thoroughly impoverished.

Or, again, if we wanted another example of the influence of an Australian on a major American artist, we would only have to look at the relationship between Martin Lewis and the American realist Edward Hopper. (In many ways, we could say that Lewis plays the same role for Hopper as John Russell plays for Matisse.) Lewis, having briefly studied at Julian Ashton's in Sydney in the late 1890s, left for America at the turn of the century. Although largely self-taught, he was able to make a living as a commercial artist, and from 1915 began making etchings, taking as his subject the streets and people of Manhattan. In that year he passed on his knowledge to his fellow art student and friend Edward Hopper, who was also working in illustration. In the 1920s, Lewis moved to Japan for five years, where he painted in oils and studied traditional Japanese printmaking in the style of the *ukiyo-e* masters. Back in New York, Lewis won the first Logan Prize of the Chicago Society of Etchers and in 1929 the Purchase Prize of the Boston Art Club; and it was from this time, as the Depression unfolded, that he began to make the prints for which he is famous. From the late 1930s, like Lever before him, Lewis became a teacher at the Art Students League, where he would remain until 1951, and he died aged eighty-two in 1962. Today his work is highly sought after and of considerable interest to historians of early American realism, being included, for instance, in the British Museum's *The American Scene: Prints from Hopper to Pollock* (2008). Reviewing the show, critic Andrew Graham-Dixon observed that 'Martin Lewis is one of several previously underrated American printmakers who have been collected in particular depth and strength by the British Museum'.[49] As is usual, though admiring the work, he gets Lewis's nationality wrong. However, as art critic Malcolm C Salaman recognised as early as 1931:

> Among the etchers of America the position of Martin Lewis is something of a paradox, for though an Australian by birth, he is perhaps the most essentially American of them all, that is to say, he is pictorially the most psychological interpreter of American life as it is lived in characteristic aspects of New York City.[50]

For their part, scholars of Hopper attribute Hopper's temporary movement into etching when not progressing with his painting—in particular, the work *Evening wind*, made in 1921—as allowing his final, mature mode. Hopper himself, who was notoriously defensive and loath to give credit to others, always denied the influence, even deliberately post-dating his encounter with Lewis. But we prefer to trust the testimony of the first director of MoMA, Alfred Barr, who, in the catalogue of the 1931 retrospective he gave Hopper, spoke of the influence of Lewis on his work. Later, Hopper himself acknowledged, 'After I took up etching, my painting seemed to crystallize'.[51]

The last in our line of artist pedagogues is the best known, and certainly the Australian art critic with the widest reputation in America in the first half of the century: Mary Cecil Allen. Born in Melbourne in 1893 to a prominent family, Cecil Allen first studied at the National Gallery School, then at the Slade in London and then back in Australia with the tonalist Max Meldrum. An American visitor to Melbourne who heard Cecil Allen lecture was so impressed that she employed her as a guide to European galleries, and together they left Australia in 1926. After some eight months on the Continent, mainly in Paris, Cecil Allen was invited to lecture in New York, and thereafter moved to America. Within a few years, she

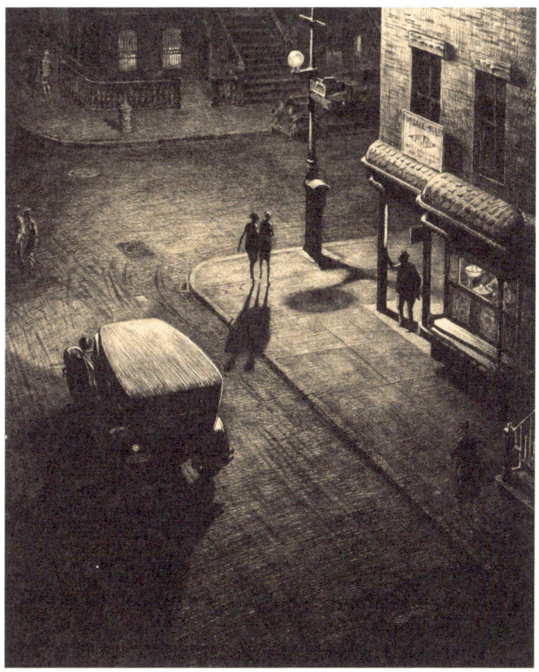

3.8 Martin Lewis
Relics (speakeasy corner), 1928

had authored two influential books on modern art, *Mirror of the Passing World* (1928) and *Painters of the Modern Mind* (1929), the latter important, for instance, for the Canadian painter Emily Carr.[52] In 1930 she organised the first exhibition of Australian art in America, *First Contemporary All-Australian Art Exhibition*, initially at the Roerich Museum in New York and then touring fourteen American cities. Cecil Allen lectured to acclaim throughout the 1930s at the Metropolitan Museum, the Brooklyn Museum, Columbia University and the Center for British Art at Yale University. In 1935 she returned to Melbourne, where she held her first exhibition in Australia. Its 'modern' style provoked considerable reaction, and Cecil Allen arranged a number of discussion groups, studio visits and painting classes in order to introduce her audience to her understanding of art. During World War II, Cecil Allen ran her own art school in New York, but came back to Australia in 1950 to paint, holding another exhibition in Melbourne, which this time met with commercial success. (She was to have another sell-out show at Australian Galleries there in 1959.) Upon her return to America in 1950, she lived at the artists' colony in Provincetown, Massachusetts, where she died in 1962. Often mistaken for an American, despite her evident and long-running identification as an Australian—in 1953, for example, she applied unsuccessfully for the position of head of the National Gallery School in Melbourne—Cecil Allen's work was exhibited, both during her lifetime and after her death, throughout America.

The 1920s and 1930s, of course, saw the rise of Hollywood movies, now accompanied by sound. Again, it is seen to be a moment of American cultural imperialism, leading to the closing of the Australian film industry, swamped by competing films in the same language. But then, as today, many Australians worked in Hollywood, and movement between the two countries was always two-way. Indeed, it was the movies that attracted many Australian artists to America during this time. We might think, for example, of the Brisbane-born Robert Emerson Curtis, who left for America in 1922, sharing his cabin with his good friend the film director Charles Chauvel, himself on his first trip to Hollywood. Curtis studied at the Art Institutes of San Francisco and Chicago, and ended up meeting his American wife in Hollywood. In America, 'he developed his lifelong interest in industrial modernism, and on returning to Sydney in 1928 he set about documenting the construction of the Sydney Harbour Bridge',[53] using the graphic medium of lithography. These images would eventually be published as *Building the Bridge: Fourteen Lithographs Celebrating the Construction of the Sydney Harbour Bridge* (1931).

And speaking of civic construction, 1913 had seen the arrival in Australia of Chicago-trained architects Walter Burley Griffin and Marion Mahony Griffin to oversee the design and building of Canberra. They would be followed more than thirty years later by a different kind of American-trained architect, Harry Seidler, who had studied with Walter Gropius and Marcel Breuer at Harvard, worked with Alvar Aalto in Boston and then with Josef Albers at Black Mountain College, before emigrating to Australia in 1948. But perhaps a more important 'American' arrival was Frank Hinder, back from Taos, New Mexico, with his New York–born wife, the sculptor Margel Harris. Hinder had studied with Antonio Dattilo-Rubbo and at the East Sydney Technical College, before leaving for America in 1927. He studied initially at the Art Institute of Chicago, and then under the important teachers Emil Bisttram and Howard Giles, first at the New York School of Fine and Applied Arts in 1929 and then at the Master Institute at Roerich Museum in 1930. Bisttram and Giles were both friends of Jay Hambidge, whose instructional text *Elements of Dynamic Symmetry* (1926) greatly influenced the Hinders and others in Sydney. In 1930 the Hinders married just outside Boston, where Harris had trained at the School of the Boston Museum of Fine Arts, and where in 1933 Hinder held his first solo exhibition, *Drawings Based on Dynamic Symmetry*. (Hinder was, incidentally, not the only Australian to be showing in America at this time: we have already noted Charles Basing's memorial exhibition of 1934, but in the same year JW Power and Roy de Maistre also showed together in an exhibition of English and European paintings at the Arundell Clarke Gallery in the Rockefeller

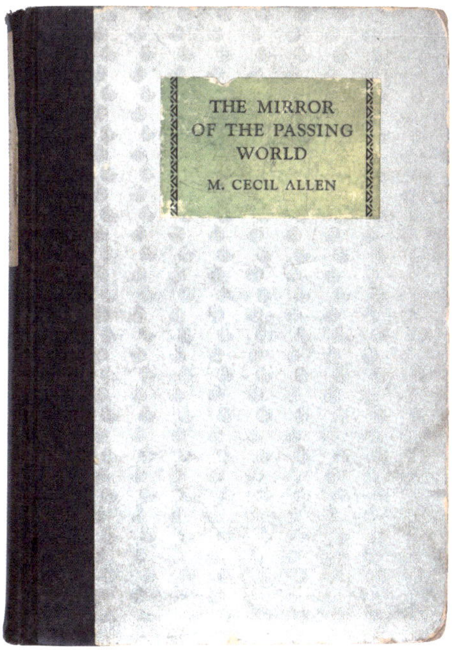

3.9 Mary Cecil Allen,
The Mirror of the Passing World, 1928

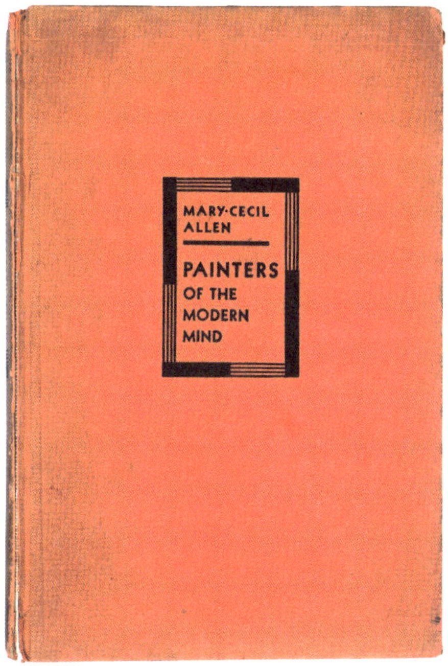

3.10 Mary Cecil Allen,
Painters of the Modern Mind, 1929

Center.) Heading westward in 1933, the Hinders moved to Taos and attended Bisttram's summer school in the New Mexico town, which had already been a crucial generator of American modernism for more than three decades.[54] Bisttram would go on to become one of the decisive advocates of Kandinsky in America, and in his own work brought the Russian's spiritualist abstraction into contact with the art and culture of the indigenous Tiwa people, who had established their Pueblo communities and developed their adobe dwellings centuries before the arrival of European settlers. In 1934 the Hinders made their way to Sydney, never to see Bisttram again, although he continued to send them books and catalogues for a number of years. The similarities between Bisttram's and Hinder's works in the late 1930s and 1940s are remarkable, and in many ways we can understand Hinder as a displaced Taos modernist. Certainly, his *Tribute to Kandinsky* (1938) is the product of his encounter with the American art world. In the year of his return, Hinder co-founded the George Street Group with Ralph Balson, Grace Crowley, Rah Fizelle and Eleonore Lange. It was Australia's first self-consciously avant-garde artist collective. In fact, as much as anything, Hinder is an important transitional figure in Australian art, allowing—against Terry Smith's model for such things—such collaborators as Balson and Crowley to extend the ideas he had introduced, enabling them (unlike him) to become entirely abstract.

We have almost the reverse trajectory with the painter John Vickery, who left Melbourne for the American East Coast in the mid-1930s. Trained at the National Gallery School in the 1920s, Vickery exhibited with the Victorian Artists' Society, painted murals and worked on the interior of the Milky Way Café in Melbourne for the architects Roy Grounds and Geoffrey Mewton. On New Year's Day 1936 Vickery left Australia, heading first to London and then to New York. Again, able to support his practice by working in commercial illustration, he served as a war artist with the US Army during World War II, and today his posters are collected by numerous public institutions. Indeed, the war, if anything, brought Australia and America closer together. We not only had the massive presence of American troops in Australia, producing responses ranging from Melbourne artist Albert Tucker's apocalyptic *Images of modern evil* (1943–47) to Brisbane artist Gwendolyn Grant's ambiguous and almost wistful *Fantasy* (1943), we also had the stepping up of the official cultural interaction between the two countries, both to keep up morale during the war and afterwards as part of the Cold War, in which America contended with the Soviet Union. Before World War II, the Carnegie Corporation had helped build up libraries on, among other things, modern art, as seen, for instance, in the collection of the State Library of Queensland. The exhibition *Art of Australia 1788–1941* toured widely across America and Canada during the war, and *U.S. War Painting from MacArthur's New Guinea Campaign* toured Australia in 1944. In the aftermath, as

Australia turned towards America politically, Sidney Nolan, Russell Drysdale and William Dobell participated in the 1952 *Carnegie International*, where their officially sanctioned nationalist vision was judged by the director of MoMA to be 'many years behind Europe and the United States'.[55]

In fact, any number of Australians were making contemporary art in America after the war. For his part, Vickery returned to his own practice just as the New York School was being announced in the bars of Greenwich Village. During these years, he became friends with Philip Guston (they had studios in the same building), and through him met Willem de Kooning, Jackson Pollock, Joan Mitchell and Franz Kline, with all of whom he rubbed shoulders in the old Cedar Street Tavern, which was to become the semi-official meeting place of the abstract expressionists. In the 1950s Vickery painted his *Cruciforms*, with their crossed beams of massed paint; and in the 1960s and into the 1970s he worked on his hard-edge and Op paintings, the so-called *Linear* and *Split spectrum* works. These latter two series were shown at the Allan Stone Gallery in New York in 1970, by which time Vickery had moved to New Jersey. As the gallerist and art historian Charles Nodrum has observed:

> Many (Australian) hard-edge artists in the '60s used optical effects, but few, if any, settled down to complete a series of specifically Op paintings. It is ironical it fell to a sixty year old expatriate to produce such a group.[56]

Vickery died in America in 1983, aged seventy-seven, his work largely overlooked by those wishing to write a history of Australian art.

Equally, it should not be forgotten that a crucial figure at the origins of the New York School was the expatriate New Zealand-Australian painter Wallace Harrison. When the artist and teacher Paul Feeley advised his students at Bennington College, Vermont, on where they might study during their non-residential work terms, he customarily suggested either Hans Hoffman at his school on Eighth Street or Harrison at his school on Fourteenth Street. In 1949 Helen Frankenthaler chose Harrison, whom she remembered as 'a mad Francophile and crazy about Picasso and Lipchitz', a decision that art historian Barbara Rose describes as being for those 'who were committed to an intense study of art rather than a lifestyle'. Together with James Brooks and his wife Charlotte Park, both of whom also studied with Harrison, Frankenthaler continually visited all the New York galleries during her formative period.[57] Harrison, then—who had studied in Auckland and Sydney; who had lived in Paris in the early 1930s; who had taught at the Cooper Union from 1933 and been part of that institution's modernisation; who had run his own school from 1938 to 1950; and who was the teacher of Frankenthaler, Brooks, Park as well as Robert

Blackburn—is thus one of the hidden sources of the New York School. Indeed, it is interesting to note that Harrison was one of three Australian artists to run their own art school in New York in the 1940s—the others were Cecil Allen and the Meldrumite expatriate painter, illustrator and leading light of the Staten Island artists' colony, Percy Leason, who had moved to America in 1938.

It was a new generation of artists—and women artists in particular—who established the postwar line of Australian émigrés on the East Coast. When critics speak of America becoming the new centre of the art world after World War II—of New York, in the resonant phrase of art critic Serge Guilbaut, 'stealing the idea of modern art'—what is often forgotten is, first, that the artists involved in this were often immigrants to America themselves (for example, Max Ernst, Hans Hoffman and Josef Albers). And, second, that it was largely *women* who were the moving force behind then-advanced American art: Peggy Guggenheim and her gallery The Art of This Century; Betty Parsons and her eponymously named gallery, where she showed Barnett Newman, Mark Rothko and Jackson Pollock; and Hilla Rebay, who was instrumental both in establishing the collection of Solomon Guggenheim and in the building of the Frank Lloyd Wright–designed museum to show it.

The first of our postwar women expatriates is the National Art School–trained Anne Wienholt, who won the New South Wales Travelling Art Scholarship, and, reflecting the mid-century re-orientation away from Europe, headed to New York in 1945, studying first at the Art Students League, then with Rufino Tamayo, and finally with SW Hayter at his Atelier 17, which had relocated from Paris in 1940. In touch with former fellow student Margaret Cilento, she called on her friend to join her. Cilento—a member of a famous artistic family, which included her sister Diane—was in New York by 1946; and she likewise studied with Tamayo and at Hayter's, where she worked beside Roberto Matta, Yves Tanguy, William Baziotes and Robert Motherwell. Cilento once somewhat disingenuously observed of her encounters with another of the artists working there that '[Salvador] Dalí was a lovely man, but always wanted to borrow my paints'.[58] She also went on to study at the important but short-lived The Subjects of the Artist School, named by its co-founder Barnett Newman, and whose studios were to become the centre of abstract expressionist activity well into the 1950s. Returning to Australia in 1951, Cilento 'introduced Abstract Expressionism to Brisbane',[59] and thus to Australia; but, following negative critical reaction to her show at Macquarie Galleries in 1951, she abandoned abstraction, leaving us only with the extraordinary legacy of the prints she made in New York between 1947 and 1952.

From this moment on, the interaction between the two countries increases exponentially. If what we have been sketching so far is a certain 'pre-history' of our present moment, involving artists who are all too little known, then the artists we are now about to discuss are, by and large, recognised in Australian art history. At this point we are of the same historical moment of which we write. But it is now the *character* of the relationship between the two countries that we wish to challenge. In the short series of names we are now about to present, is it a really a 'provincial' relationship between Australia and America that we see? Or is it rather a mutual flow—unequal, but certainly not one-way or non-reciprocal—between the two countries, precisely indicative of a newly contemporary and rapidly globalising art world?

We might provide here just a partial listing of the Australians who by the late 1950s were living and working in New York. (And, again, the point is that many of these would have been known to Smith when he wrote his article. The question must be asked of each and every one of them: do they really seem 'provincial' from where we stand today?) Beginning with the women, we have: Yvonne Audette, who studied at the Art Students League from 1952 to 1954 and then on a Fogg Scholarship at the New York National Academy of Design School of Fine Arts; Janet Alderson, who likewise studied at the Arts Students League in 1962 before heading to Europe to make her career; Ralph Balson's former student Alison McMaugh, who settled in Michigan in 1963 having studied in London, and who

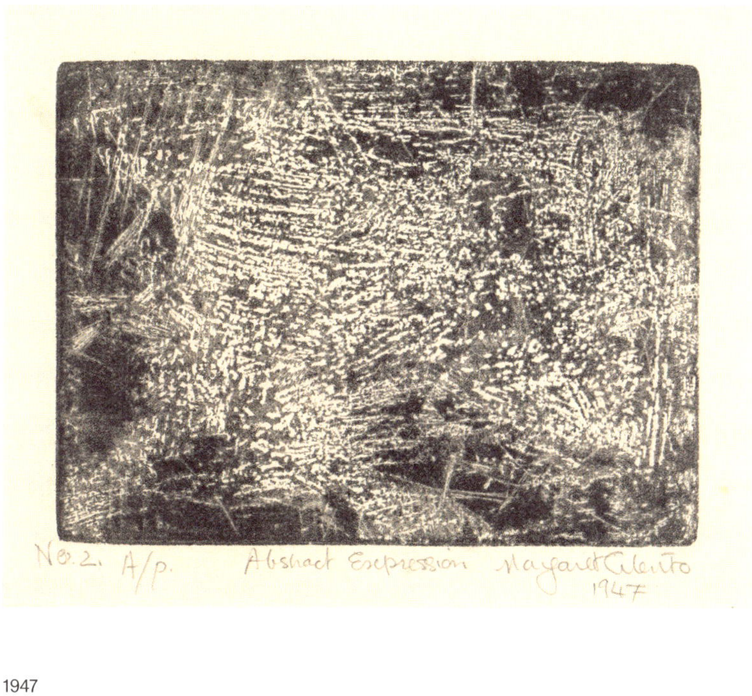

3.11 Margaret Cilento
Abstract expression, 1947

taught at art schools throughout America, maintaining a successful career into the 1990s; Virginia Cuppaidge, who moved to New York in 1969, as Judy Cotton did in 1971, where they are both still exhibiting; Margaret Worth, who moved to New York in 1969; Margery Edwards, who first lived in New York in 1959, but moved there permanently in 1974; Denise Green, who, after studying in Paris, moved to New York in 1969 and trained at Hunter College under Motherwell and Rothko (in his final months); and Ruth Peyser, who arrived in New York in 1978 and subsequently became well known for her animation. We also have, more recently, Toba and Rachel Khedoori, identical twins of Iraqi descent, who were born in Sydney in 1964, moved to Los Angeles in 1990 and have since established important careers. Toba's paintings on large fields of paper were shown in the 1995 Whitney Biennial, the 2004 São Paulo Biennial and the 2009 Venice Biennale, and she has held solo exhibitions at, for instance, the Museum of Contemporary Art, Los Angeles, the Whitechapel Art Gallery, London, and the Hirshhorn Museum, Washington. Rachel, who also exhibited at the 2009 Venice Biennale, has shown her sculptures, photographs and installations in solo exhibitions at, for instance, the Kunsthalle Basel, Nice's Villa Arson, and the Kunstverein Braunschweig.

Then we might mention the men. There is the sculptor Robert Klippel, who, having spent time in London and Paris, headed to New York in 1957, from where he was appointed to the staff of the Minnesota School of Arts. He taught there until 1962, when he returned to Sydney to continue his long and successful career. There is Clement Meadmore, who, having travelled to Europe and Japan, left Sydney for New York in 1963, where he remained until his death (writing a series of reports on the mid-1960s New York scene for *Art & Australia*). There is the painter Sydney Ball, who began studying at the Art Students League of New York and returned home via Japan in 1965. There is the Op and technology artist Frank Eidlitz, who studied with György Kepes from 1966 at the Massachusetts Institute of Technology. And, to bring us back almost to where we began, there is Ian Burn, who moved to New York from London in 1967, where he joined the foundational conceptual art group Art & Language in 1970, thus becoming, in the admittedly mistaken words of French artist Bernar Venet, the '"first Australian in the history of art" to be at the centre of an international movement'.[60]

* * *

The history we have just sketched might be said to end with the important and much-discussed exhibition *The Field*, co-curated by the soon to leave for MoMA John Stringer, and held to open the new building designed by Roy Grounds for the National Gallery of Victoria in 1968. Today the show is understood as the most important event in Australian art history that occurs immediately before Smith's essay, and is often returned to as a forerunner to more contemporary concerns.[61] In most readings, the exhibition is understood as marking the height of the American influence on Australian art, with opposing sets of critics alternately approving or disapproving of this. But there is perhaps another interpretation of the show that opens up before us and that casts both it and Smith's essay in a different light. For, in some ways, *The Field* can be seen to signal the last moment of modernism in Australian art. In the end it is *modernism* that lies at the heart of Smith's analysis, with its distinctions between metropolitan and provincial cultures, advanced and academic art. In other words, after 1968, art history, not only in America but also in Australia, is no longer able to be written according to the linear, teleological progression of modernism. It is an insight shared by Bernard Smith, who in the second edition of *Australian Painting* (1971) concluded that by 1970 provincialism no longer applied to Australian art.[62] That is, at the very moment it was written, 'The provincialism problem' had been historically surpassed and was historically out of date. The conditions of modernism that made it possible no longer applied. But we ultimately want to say more than this. As our brief survey of Australian–American artistic interactions throughout the twentieth century shows, it *never* applied; it was *always* out of date. Instead we see that the art we have looked at was from the beginning *contemporary*. In retrospect what we realise is that it was always decentred, pluralistic, non-teleological, non-critical, and often expressed social concerns through effectively relational or participatory forms of aesthetics. Against the modernism that was thought to define the century, we are now able to observe a whole range of matters that had previously been overlooked: the interaction between high and commercial art, the importance of pedagogy and teaching, the exploration of internal psychology, the questions of femininity and queerness, the continuing investigation of realist modes and colour, unconventional techniques in printmaking and poster-production. To think outside the elitism and exclusions of modernism—which reached its height in America in the 1950s and 1960s, and whose assumptions Smith inherited—and to think outside the elitism and exclusions of nationalism—which reached its height in Australia between 1920 and 1960, and whose assumptions Smith equally inherited—is to enable the presence of Australian art in America to be seen. It is the contemporary that allows us to see this new history of Australian art, but it is this history that allows us to realise that the art produced by Australians has always been contemporary.

An earlier version of this text was published in the *Journal of Australian Studies*, vol. 36, no. 3, 2012.

—

1 Terry Smith, 'The Provincialism Problem', *Artforum*, vol. 13, no. 4, September 1974, p. 57.

2 Ibid., p. 55.

3 See Heather Barker and Charles Green, 'The Provincialism Problem: Terry Smith and Centre-Periphery Art History', *Journal of Art Historiography*, vol. 3, December 2010, pp. 1–17; and Anne Sanders, 'Minefield: Revisiting the Historical Document that is "The Provincialism Problem"', *Broadsheet*, vol. 40, no. 2, 2011, pp. 111–13.

4 See on this Imants Tillers, 'Locality Fails', *Art & Text*, vol. 6, 1982, pp. 51–60.

5 Ian Burn, 'Sidney Nolan: Landscape and Modern Life', in *Dialogue: Writings in Art History*, Allen & Unwin, Sydney, 1991, p. 69.

6 Ross Gibson, 'This Prison This Language: Thomas Watling's *Letters From an Exile at Botany Bay*', in ed. Paul Foss, *Islands in the Stream: Myths of Place in Australian Culture*, Pluto Press, Sydney, 1988, p. 4.

7 Ian McLean, 'Reverse Perspective: Bernard Smith's Worldview and the Cosmopolitan Imagination', *Journal of Art Historiography*, vol. 4, June 2011, pp. 1–18.

8 Terry Smith, 'Provincialism Refigured', *Art Monthly Australia*, vol. 13, August 1988, p. 6.

9 Terry Smith, 'The State of Art History: Contemporary Art', *Art Bulletin*, vol. 92, no. 4, December 2010, p. 369.

10 Ibid., p. 380.

11 Ibid.

12 Smith, 'The Provincialism Problem', p. 59.

13 See William Moore, *The Story of Australian Art: From the Earliest Known Art of the Continent to the Art of To-day*, Angus & Robertson, Sydney, 1934; Bernard Smith, *Australian Painting, 1788–1970*, Oxford University Press, Melbourne, 1971; Robert Hughes, *The Art of Australia*, Penguin, UK, 1970; Andrew Sayers, *Australian Art*, Oxford University Press, 2001; Christopher Allen, *Art in Australia: From Colonization to Postmodernism*, Thames & Hudson, London, 1997; and John McDonald, *The Art of Australia: Vol. 1: Exploration to Federation*, Pan Macmillan, Sydney, 2008.

14 Indeed, Smith writes in 'The State of Art History': 'Contemporaneous qualities may also have been present in art always and everywhere. The art historical quest unleashed by this idea, I venture to suggest, goes all the way back. It pushes us to ask some unexpected questions' (p. 379). It is these questions we seek to ask here, and especially of Smith's own earlier work.

15 Such offshore American events as Wright and Russell's synchromist exhibitions in Europe before the war were important here. Their ideas were particularly influential on, for example, Roy de Maistre and Roland Wakelin's landmark 1919 exhibition *Colour in Art*.

16 Ann Stephen, *On Looking at Looking: The Art and Politics of Ian Burn*, Miegunyah Press, Melbourne, 2006, p. 133.

17 See Ian Burn, 'Art Is What We Do, Culture is What We Do to Other Artists', *Art Dialogue*, vol. 1, no. 1, Melbourne, 1973; reprinted in *Dialogue*, pp. 131–9.

18 On the general fame or cultural capital of Basing's mural, we might give two instances, one from 'high' culture and one from 'low' culture: in Sloan Wilson's classic novel of 1950s America, *The Man in the Gray Flannel Suit*, the central character is described in a moment of crisis: 'As he walked through Grand Central Station, he looked up for the first time, noticed the stars painted on the blue ceiling there. They seemed to be shining brightly, and feeling slightly theatrical, he wondered if it were legitimate to wish on a painted star', Penguin, UK, 2005, p. 69; and in the DreamWorks animated feature *Madagascar* (2005), Alex the lion, when knocked out at Grand Central Station while attempting to escape from the zoo, looks up and confuses the stars in his head with the stars on the ceiling.

19 The American painter and illustrator William Smedley, who had come to Australia in 1886 to draw for *The Picturesque Atlas of Australasia* (1886–88), was also included in the *Exhibition of Australian Art* at the Grafton Galleries.

20 Robert J Pierce, *Francis McComas: Rediscovering California's First Modernist*, Monterey Museum of Art, California, 2021. Today it is even possible to stay at the 'McComas House', his purpose-built studio and residence just moments away from the famed Pebble Beach Golf Links on the Monterey Penninsula, of which he was a member.

21 According to the catalogue from the New York exhibition, Nankivell showed nine works, Conder eight and Lees and McComas three each. McComas and Nankivell showed in Gallery F: 'American Paintings', beside, for example, Bellows, Patrick Henry Bruce, Katherine Dreier and Morgan Russell; Conder and Lees showed in Gallery G: 'English, Irish and German Paintings and Drawings', beside, for example,

JD Innes, Augustus John, Wassily Kandinsky, Ernst Kirchner, Walter Sickert, Max Slevogt and Jack B Yeats; Nankivell showed in Gallery K: 'French and American Watercolours, Drawings, etc.', beside, for example, Henri, Stuart Davis, Dodge MacKnight, John Marin, Marie Laurencin, Wilhelm Lehmbruck, Aristide Maillol, Henri Matisse and Edvard Munch; and also in Gallery L: 'American Watercolours, Drawings, etc.', beside, for example, Bellows, Davies, Kuhn, Luks, Sloan, Marsden Hartley and Walter Pach; and McComas in Gallery N: 'American Paintings and Sculpture', beside, for example, Glackens, Henri, Kuhn and Morton Schamberg; and in Gallery P: 'French, English, Dutch and American Paintings', beside, for example, Camille Corot, Gustave Courbet, Eugène Delacroix, Jacob Epstein, Gwen John, Édouard Manet, Pierre-Auguste Renoir and James McNeill Whistler.

22 The dates of Evergood's Lotos Club exhibitions have been put together with reference to *Philip Evergood: Never Separate from the Heart*, ed. Kendall Taylor, exhibition catalogue, Center Gallery, Bucknell University Press, Lewisburg, Pa, 1987, p. 46; and Gael Hammer, *Miles Evergood: No End of Passion*, Phillip Mathews, Sydney, 2013, p. 103.

23 Hammer, *Miles Evergood*, p. 49.

24 Taylor, *Philip Evergood*, p. 81.

25 See on Brodzky, Henry R Lew, *Horace Brodzky*, Henry Squire, Melbourne, 1987.

26 It is often said of Thea Proctor that she exhibited in 1912 at the 'Venice International Exhibition', but the authors have been unable to confirm this.

27 Horace Brodzky, *Pascin*, Nicholas and Watson, London, 1946; and on Henri Gaudier-Brzeska, *Henri Gaudier-Brzeska 1891–1915*, Faber and Faber, London, 1933. We might also in this context think of the Polish-born realist painter and photographer Joseph Biel, who established the first Jewish library in Melbourne, at the Working Men's College (now RMIT), where he studied before his departure to America, going on to train with George Grosz at the Art Students League. In 1931 he married the artist Lina Gurr and lived in Brooklyn and Cape Cod, where he befriended again Mary Cecil Allen, whom he had known in Melbourne.

28 See on this Christine I Oaklander, 'Walt Kuhn and The Penguin', *Archives of American Art Journal*, vol. 49, no. 3–4, 2010, pp. 51–59.

29 'The World of Art', *New York Times*, 9 April 1922, p. 22.

30 See on this 'Flyer for a stag party given by the Penguin Club honoring Horace Brodzky', March 1923, Louis Bouché papers, 1880–2007, Archives of American Art, https://www.aaa.si.edu/collections/items/detail/flyer-stag-party-given-penguin-club-honoring-horace-brodzky-12165.

31 Jane Clark, 'Eleanor Henderson Harrison', *Design & Art Australia Online*, 1995, updated 2011, https://www.daao.org.au/bio/eleanor-henderson-harrison/biography/.

32 Joan Kerr, 'Livingston Hopkins', 1996, updated 2007, *Design & Art Australia Online*, https://www.daao.org.au/bio/livingston-hopkins/biography/.

33 Sullivan returned to Australia briefly in 1925, and at a civic reception hosted by the Lord Mayor declared: 'I made the cat and the cat made me', Anonymous, 'Pat Sullivan', *Sydney Morning Herald*, 7 December 1925, p. 5.

34 Lindsay Foyle, 'Felix the Animated Cat: The Story of Pat Sullivan', *Vixen Magazine*, 2008, www.vixenmagazine.com/patsullivanandfelix.html.

35 Cited in Courtenay Kidd, 'Artnotes', *Art Monthly* (Australia), vol. 179, May 2005, p. 47.

36 Joan Kerr, 'Reg Russom', *Design & Art Australia Online*, 1996, updated 2007, https://www.daao.org.au/bio/reg-russom/biography/.

37 'Constance Macky', in ed. Gene Hailey, *California Art Research*, vol. 15, no. 1, San Francisco, 1937, p. 103.

38 Ibid., p. 105.

39 Unattributed, 'An Artist's Troubles – Mr Gordon Coutts Sued by His Wife – Conjugal Infelicities', *The Advertiser*, Adelaide, 1 May 1901, p. 5.

40 Unattributed, 'Maintenance Matter – Artist Charged', *The Herald*, Melbourne, 8 July 1902, p. 2.

41 Unattributed, 'Gordon Coutts – World Famous Artist – Divorced, Wife Former Art Student in Melbourne', *Leader*, Melbourne, 2 February 1918, p. 43.

42 Matthew Kangas, 'When "Mystic" Became Modern: Henry Gallery Show Rewrites NW Art History', *Artguide Northwest*, 1999, www.artguidenw.com/NWArt.htm.

43 Ibid.

44 See Bernard Smith mistakenly speaking about 'San Francisco' abstraction a year later in 'The Antipodean Manifesto' (1960), in *The Antipodean Manifesto: Essays in Art and History*, Oxford University Press, Melbourne, 1976, p. 65. Indeed, Callahan himself worked for years until 1928 on a freighter plying its trade between San Francisco

and Sydney, and therefore had already had some contact with Australia.

45 LC, 'Hayley Lever', *Art News*, vol. 60, no. 5, September 1961, p. 52.

46 Catherine Beach Ely, 'The Modern Tendency in Lawson, Lever and Glackens', *Art in America*, vol. 10, December 1921, p. 32.

47 For instance, Nankivell and Lever both showed in *The 'Fifty'* at Montross Gallery, New York, in 1916; McComas was awarded the Dana Watercolor Medal, and Lever the Philadelphia Watercolor Prize, both at the 1918 Philadelphia Water Color Club exhibition; and before the war Nankivell and Evergood appear in the same review of the first *Independent Artists* exhibition in *American Art News*, vol. 8, no. 26, April 1910, p. 2.

48 Sam Hunter and John M Jacobus, *American Art of the Twentieth Century: Painting, Sculpture, Architecture*, Thames & Hudson, London, 1973, p. 137.

49 Andrew Graham-Dixon, 'The American Scene: Prints from Hopper to Pollock', *Sunday Telegraph* (London), 27 April 2008, p. 33.

50 Malcolm C Salaman, *Martin Lewis*, Modern Masters of Etching series, The Studio, London and New York, 1931, np.

51 Cited in Gail Levin, *Edward Hopper: An Intimate Biography*, Knopf, New York, 1995, p. 139.

52 On the influence of Allen on Carr, see Maria Tippett, *Emily Carr: A Biography*, Oxford University Press, Toronto, 1979, pp. 179–86.

53 Jo Holder and Joan Kerr, 'Robert Emerson Curtis', *Design & Art Australia Online*, 1996, updated 2007, https://www.daao.org.au/bio/robert-emerson-curtis/biography/.

54 Indeed, Taos—and the American South-West more generally—was a crucial place for the development of art in Australia too. Following the success in 1927 in Melbourne of Fred Leist's paintings done there, the model of painting in the desert and selling in the city led directly to Rex Battarbee's decision to work in Central Australia, where he would develop his relationship with Albert Namatjira. On this, see Martin Edmond, *Battarbee and Namatjira*, Giramondo Press, Sydney, 2014. Similarly, Patrick White's novel *The Aunt's Story*, written in England, as well as featuring a cover by his lover Roy de Maistre, features a concluding dream sequence that takes place in Taos. In the footsteps of DH Lawrence, White had visited the small New Mexico town on his transcontinental American journey in 1939. He stayed there for more than three weeks during which time he met Lawrence's widow Frieda as well as the famed Mabel Dodge Luhan and the eccentric former Bloomsbury painter Dorothy Brett. In Taos, too, White enjoyed a relationship with the poet, writer and publisher Walter Willard 'Spud' Johnson. On de Maistre's influence in general on White's novel, see Leela Gosfield, 'The Textures of Music, the Sensuousness of Paint: Cubist Influences in Patrick White's *The Aunt's Story*', MA thesis, Curtin University, 2014.

55 See Staff Correspondent, 'Our Art Is "Years Behind"', *Sunday Herald* (Sydney), 19 October 1952, p. 3. To be clear, although this remark reveals a certain understanding of Australia as provincial, our argument is that this provincialism was not the true nature of the relationship between Australia and America and always existed in a wider context of non-provincialism. We might express this also by saying that Nolan, Drysdale and Dobell are not the real story of Australian art in the twentieth century.

56 Charles Nodrum, 'John Vickery (1906–1983)', www.charlesnodrumgallery.com.au/index.html.

57 All quotations from Barbara Rose, *Helen Frankenthaler*, Harry N. Abrams, New York, 1970, p. 21. On Harrison, see also Henriette Harrison, *Wallace Harrison: A Painter*, Ekdotike Hellados, Athens, 1983. See also *James Brooks: The Early 1950s*, ed. Stanley Kunitz, exhibition catalogue, Berry Hill Galleries, New York, 1989.

58 *Margaret Cilento*, ed. Nancy Underhill, exhibition catalogue, University of Queensland Art Gallery, Brisbane, 1982, p. 8.

59 Ibid., p. 11.

60 Ann Stephen quoting Venet in a letter by Burn in *On Looking at Looking*, p. 6. Stephen also repeats John Stringer saying of Burn, equally mistakenly, that he had the 'unique distinction of being the only Australian ever to be central to an internationally significant art movement' (p. 222).

61 See, for example, Ian Burn and Nigel Lendon, 'Purity, Style, Amnesia', in *Dialogue*, pp. 94–100; and *FieldWork: Australian Art 1968–2002*, eds. Jason Smith and Charles Green, exhibition catalogue, National Gallery of Victoria, Melbourne, 2002.

62 Smith, *Australian Painting*, p. 334.

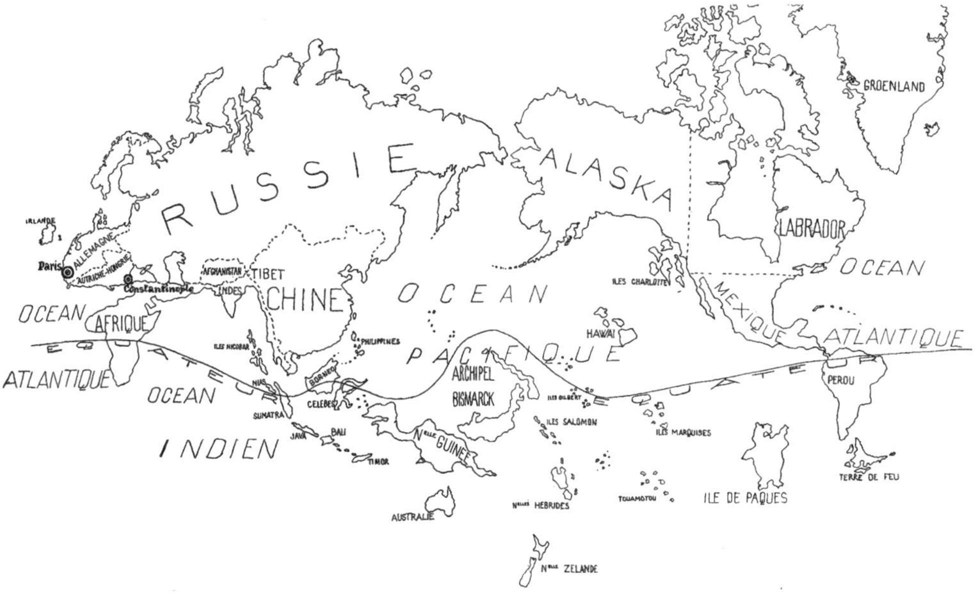

4.1 *Le monde au temps des surrealistes* (*The world at the time of the surrealists*), published in *Variétés*, Brussels, 1929

Surrealism and Australia
Towards a World History of Surrealism

There have been, over the past few decades, several retrospective exhibitions dedicated to global aspects of well-known art movements. World impressionism, feminism and conceptualism have all had their turn at being anthologised.[1] But there has not been, to our knowledge, a similar exhibition on surrealism. We attempt to write here the Australian entry for such an exhibition. However, before doing so, we might speak for a moment about the special place such a project would have, because, if surrealism can now be seen from a global perspective, it also—like those other art movements—casts a particular light upon this globalism. In some ways, we must consider the fact that, if surrealism can be seen today from a global perspective, the very notion of globalism is 'surrealist', that is, not only an aspiration of the original movement (as globalism was also implied in impressionism and feminism), but itself a 'surrealist' idea.

Surrealism is famously—at least at the beginning—a movement strongly identified with a single figure, a single place and a single time: André Breton in Paris in 1924. Breton's particular genius, we might say, was to take the postwar energies of Dada, which emerged variously in Zurich, Hanover, Berlin and New York, and involved artists from many different countries (Belgium, Romania and the Netherlands), and out of this dispersal constitute a coherent, centrally organised art movement. And he was able to keep its fire alight—for surrealism was a particularly long-lived art movement—for some thirty years.

But at the same time, surrealism—we might say due to both Breton's own personal inclinations and the very nature of the movement—was also expansionist. With an internationalism already built into his communism, Breton's expatriatism in New York during the 1940s became crucial to that city's artists.[2] Equally important at the time was Breton's involvement in surrealism in Mexico, which found its ultimate expression in the *International Surrealist Exhibition*, held in Mexico City in 1940. Similarly, Breton's famed collection of so-called *art primitif*, held in his apartment bureau at 42 rue Fontaine in Paris, was an attempt to take surrealism around the world, in something like an extension of Picasso's and others' 'primitivism' some thirty years previously.[3]

However, beyond Breton's own actions, the logic of surrealism is already effectively globalist—and perhaps even more so than those other art movements. It is not about an outer landscape (like impressionism), but about an inner landscape. It is not about a particular social subject (like feminism), but about a universal unconscious subject. It attempts to put forward an argument not about art (like conceptualism), but about life. And, more than this, once surrealism is proposed, it is seen to be everywhere. That is, for all of Breton's efforts to take surrealism to Mexico, he found once there that Mexico was already surrealist. Japan too, which Breton never visited, not only had its own identified surrealist movement, but this movement subsequently discovered that Japan was surrealist before surrealism.[4] More particularly, from the perspective we take here, following on from (but in a way reversing) the 'primitivist' logic of his interest in the art of Oceania, Breton discovers that Indigenous art from Australia is already surreal, as he acknowledges in his preface to Czech artist Karel Kupka's *Un art à l'état brut: Peintures et sculptures des aborigènes d'Australie* (1962, published in English in 1965 as *Dawn*

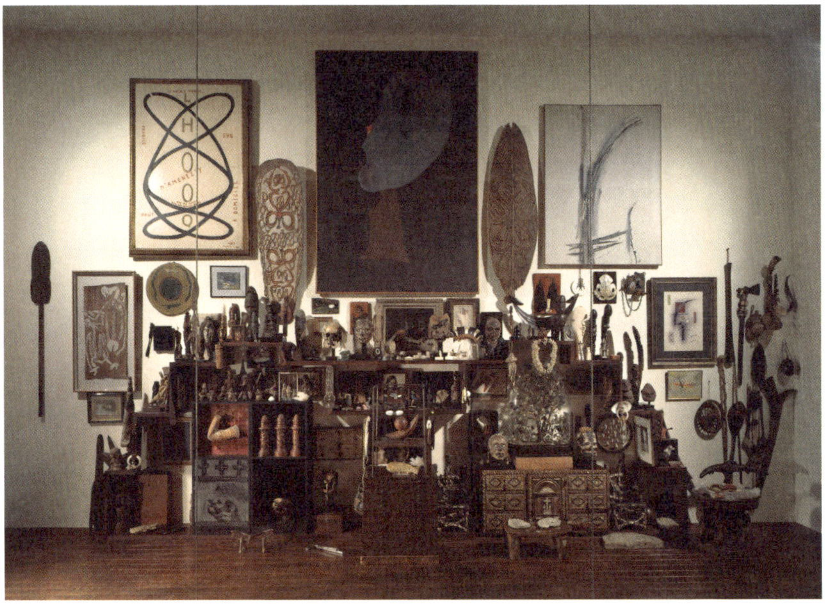

4.2 The second room of André Breton's apartment, reconstructed at the Centre Pompidou, Paris.

of Art: Painting and Sculpture of Australian Aborigines, a forerunner to Kupka's later doctoral thesis at the Sorbonne).[5] Thus it was that Paddy Compass Namatbara's bark painting depicting two Maam figures ended up on the wall of Breton's studio on the Left Bank after the war. It is also something like this that can be seen in Adelaide-born Stella Bowen's *Le masque* (*The mask*) (1930), painted in Paris deep into the failure of her relationship with Ford Madox Ford, with its extraordinary split image of the hands of a white woman (in fact, those of the poet Edith Sitwell) holding up an African mask, her right hand with white bracelet and ring and her left hand with black bracelet and ring. Here too, if there is a similar 'regressive' impulse as in Breton, there is also something like the inevitable search by all avant-garde movements—even Bowen's relatively mild version of surrealism—for historical antecedents, the desire to attach themselves to something in the past.

And all of this was recognised even by those outside the immediate surrealist circle at the time. When the exhibition *Art of Australia 1788–1941* toured America in the midst of the war (we wonder if Breton did not see the exhibition), its American critics inevitably likened Australian art to American art, finding many similarities between them, with one exception. The *New York Sun* review of the show declared that 'Aborigines were surrealists'. 'The exhibition', its critic reported:

> does not differ greatly from those we are accustomed to. Australian art has developed along similar lines to American. But Aboriginal drawings are really surprising, giving evidence that surrealism, of the physiological, if not psychological, order, was an early invention.[6]

* * *

However, we do not immediately in this essay leap to the conclusion that surrealism is already everywhere, but rather begin by tracing its first historical passage out of Paris. For as much as surrealism looked inwards and backwards, it also looked outwards and forwards. Despite its leader's attempts to contain it institutionally (its internal struggles were legendary, its expulsions innumerable), the movement ultimately went beyond Breton. Its popular heroes, Dalí, Magritte, Bataille and Artaud, all worked beyond his official patronage and in one way or another rejected his published manifestos. This is seen no more clearly—involving also surrealism's shift into another language—than in the 1936 *International Surrealist Exhibition*, held at the New Burlington Galleries in London, and involving some 400 works by sixty-nine artists from fourteen countries. For Breton himself, the show 'marked the highest point in the graph of the influence of our movement'.[7] A high-water mark, we might say, but also a shift in the tide, for if the show was the moment of surrealism's first outpouring beyond Europe, it also signalled the ebbing of Breton's own personal control over the movement. Although he, along with his close colleagues Paul Éluard and Man Ray, was on the French organising committee and gave a lecture at it, the show was driven by Englishmen Roland Penrose and Herbert Read. Earlier that year, Read had edited *Surrealism*, the first authoritative account of the movement (which included a reproduction of Christchurch-born Len Lye's *Marks and Spencer in a Japanese garden* of 1930). Indeed, three years before, in 1933, he had written his *Art Now*, which already discussed surrealism (and which included, at least in its first edition, a reproduction of Sydney-born Roy de Maistre's *Composition* of c. 1933).

It is true that no Australians were involved in the original formulation of surrealism.[8] However, by the time of the *International Surrealist Exhibition*, Read through his English-language popularisations, had not only created the conditions for the reception of surrealism in England but also opened more widely English modernism to the outside. As the art historian and aesthetician Harold Osborne was later to write in his 1981 *Oxford Companion to Twentieth-Century Art*: 'The show came upon the backwater of England's 1930s like a bombshell'.[9] For many British artists, the *International Surrealist Exhibition* offered them their first direct access to surrealist works. Nonetheless, the show also included the work of the

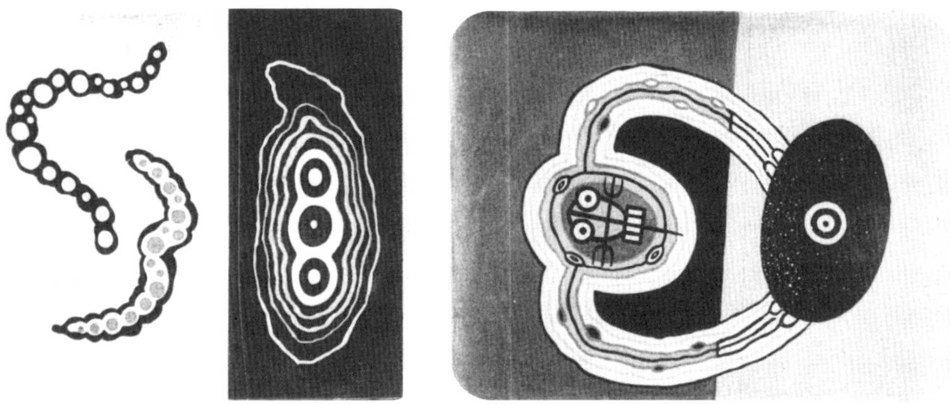

4.3 Len Lye
Film stills from *Tusalava*, 1929

young English surrealists Graham Sutherland, Cecil Collins, John Minton and the Birmingham group, which included Conroy Maddox and John Melville, alongside the more established Alberto Giacometti, Hans Arp, Paul Klee, Joan Miró, Giorgio de Chirico, Salvadore Dalí, Pierre Roy, René Magritte, Max Ernst and André Masson, who came from all over Europe. This selection demonstrates both that by this time surrealism could not be said to come from only one place and that it was also outside any single person's prerogative to adjudicate upon it.[10]

Remarkably, as well as having a crucial impact on Australian artists living in England, the show was extensively reviewed and discussed in Australia under such headlines as 'Painting the Subconscious' (*West Australian*) and 'Surrealism—Exploitation of the Dream World' (*Adelaide Advertiser*). And, after this, the follow-up 1938 surrealist show back in Paris produced such headlines as 'Surrealism—Art or Nonsense' (the *Advertiser* again), 'Freak Art on Exhibition' (*Hobart Mercury*) and, inspired by its signature work, Duchamp's 1200 bags of coal suspended from the ceiling of the gallery, 'Art Show in a Cellar' (*The Argus* in Melbourne).

It could, however, be said that even before Breton repackaged a number of existing cultural tendencies as surrealism, artists from Australia and New Zealand were working through many of the same sources as he was. By late 1922, Lye was copying by hand Sigmund Freud's *Totem and Taboo* and drawing in its margins images of 'primitive' art at the Mitchell Library in Sydney, the same year he had moved to Australia. He had earlier come across Freud through his studies of a number of ethnographic and anthropological texts held in the same library.[11] Their accounts of the Indigenous art of Australia and the Pacific, as well as his own travels through the Pacific Islands, would eventually lead Lye to the cel animation of his first movie, *Tusalava*, which premiered in 1929 at the recently formed London Film Society, with a now-lost live score composed by his Sydney friend the musician and composer Jack Ellitt. Lye would later participate in the 1936 *International Surrealist Exhibition*, for which Penrose and Read selected a painting and two photograms. Indeed, Lye's influences caught up with him there, because the show also included work by African and Oceanic artists.[12] This primitivism, whose prestige by the 1930s was inseparable from that of surrealism, was to influence another Australasian artist with international connections, the New Zealander Frank Weitzel, who had studied in Los Angeles, New York and Munich before his arrival in Sydney. There he collaborated with de Maistre on the 1929 Burdekin House exhibition before leaving for London, where, through Dorrit Black, he came to know the British linocut artist Claude Flight and began to make boldly edged images of 'tribal' masks and figures, showing them in the 1931 and 1932 *Exhibitions of British Linocuts* at the Redfern Gallery.

De Maistre himself left Sydney for London in 1930, and almost immediately held an exhibition with his young friend Francis Bacon at 7 Queensberry

Mews. He had painted works at Bacon's studio and bought two canvases by him from the show. De Maistre's influence on Bacon is clear, despite Bacon's own subsequent attempts to distance himself from his sources.[13] In 1934 de Maistre held an exhibition at the leading Mayor Gallery, with the support of the emerging art historian and collector Douglas Cooper, whose family was Australian and had sold its businesses and considerable holdings of land in Sydney and moved to London. That same year, de Maistre opened his School of Contemporary Painting and Drawing with the German artist Martin Bloch, and the year before had had his work reproduced in Read's *Art Now*. Later in the 1930s, de Maistre would become the first love of Sydney author Patrick White, whom he had met in inter-war queer London, another Australian working at the time in a surrealist idiom. The nexus between de Maistre, Bacon, White and Cooper is a little-recognised but nonetheless crucial encounter in Australian modernism, bringing together two Australian expatriates (de Maistre and White) and two diasporic Australians (Bacon and Cooper, who both had Australian parents).[14]

Another Australian present in London at the explosion of the *International Surrealist Exhibition* was Sydney-born James Cant. De Maistre had introduced Cant to the Mayor Gallery, where he first showed in 1935 in a group exhibition, and he was subsequently invited to become a member of the English Surrealist

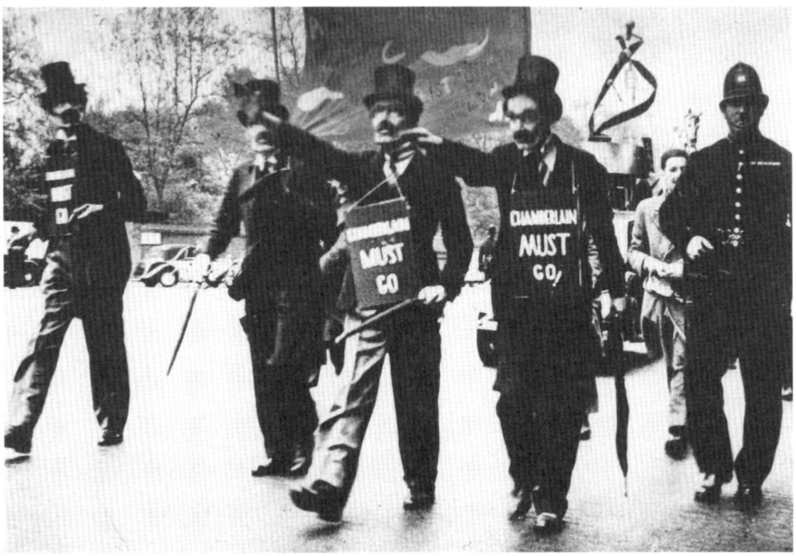

4.4 English Surrealist Group members Roland Penrose, Julian Trevelyan, Geoffrey Graham and James Cant protest Spanish Civil War neutrality in Chamberlain masks, London, 1938

Group. The following year, de Maistre helped organise *An Exhibition of Paintings* at Thomas Agnew & Sons on Bond Street, which was in art historian Heather Johnson's view his 'last tilt at becoming part of the avant-garde', and Cant was included alongside Bacon, Sutherland, Ivon Hitchens, Victor Pasmore, John Piper and Julian Trevelyan.[15] In 1938, Cant along with Trevelyan, Penrose and his compatriot the Australian Geoffrey Graham were all photographed in costume as part of a surrealist action at the May Day march in London, wearing masks of Prime Minister Neville Chamberlain made by the sculptor FE McWilliam, in protest at the British government's appeasement of fascist Spain.[16] That same year, Cant and Graham responded to an advertisement calling for volunteers for medical research, and the two Australians experimented with mescaline. It was after these psychedelic experiences that both Cant and Graham (as well as Trevelyan and Penrose) made works. Cant's *Merchants of death* (1938) is the first artwork produced by an Australian artist having used a drug other than caffeine, nicotine, opium or alcohol. In 1937 he participated in *Surrealist Objects and Poems*, which was opened at midnight by Trevelyan in the guise of a blind explorer at the London Gallery, Penrose's and ELT Mesens's important Anglophone centre for surrealism. In 1938 he was part of the large group exhibition *Realism and Surrealism* at the

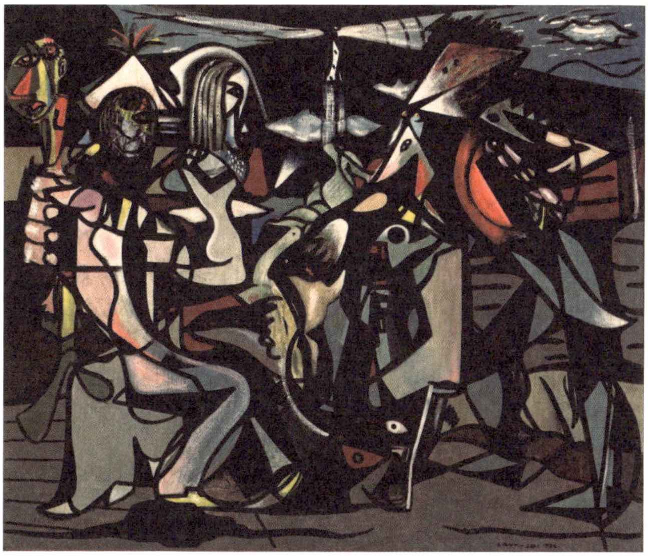

4.5 James Cant
Merchants of death, 1938

Guildhall, Gloucester, and *Collage, Papier-Collés, Photo-Montages* at Peggy Guggenheim's shortlived London gallery, the Guggenheim Jeune.

Cant, however, was not the only Australian artist doing collage at this time. In her monumental *Collage*, German art historian Herta Wescher writes in a margin note that the Australians Graham and Eric Smith, beside Lye and Cant, were doing collage in London in the 1930s—she probably knew the work of Graham and Smith from *Surrealist Objects*, in which they had shown alongside Mesens, Penrose, Trevelyan, John Nash, Henry Moore and the American Lee Miller.[17] Back in Australia, Sidney Nolan was also making his first Max Ernst–indebted collages in Melbourne from 1938. And there is a whole history of surrealist photography—photography that is said to be *the* surrealist medium by such critics as Rosalind Krauss[18]—as exemplified by Max Dupain, which runs through the 1930s in Australia. Indeed, before it was art, surrealism was encountered by the Australian public daily, whenever people were exposed to the mass culture of advertising, driven as it was by photography. In 1939, the year of his departure for Australia and with war approaching, Cant participated in the touring exhibition *British Surrealist and Abstract Paintings*—Graham was also in this exhibition—and was the subject of a spread in the Mesens-edited *London Bulletin*, the chief mouthpiece for surrealism in England.

Much less visible than Cant, the Melbourne artist Clifford Bayliss stayed in London during the war, in charge of a rescue squad. He had arrived in 1936 having won the National Gallery of Victoria Travelling Scholarship the previous year, the first man in more than thirty years to have done so.[19] An intensely personal artist, his drawings are full of images of bound figures, with the winding sheets in his work like 'the unwrapping of his fantasies'.[20] It is not clear how he came to his surrealism—perhaps he saw Breton and Penrose's *International Surrealist Exhibition* when he arrived, perhaps he encountered it in Paris when he soon after studied there with André Lhote, or perhaps it was a result of his wartime experiences. A friend of Nolan's before he left, he was well aware of surrealism before he arrived in England. The reclusive Bayliss never returned to Australia, he barely exhibited, and his works were only rediscovered in the 1990s, at which point Bernard Smith described him as 'a real Ern Malley'.[21]

Bayliss, needless to say, was not the only Australian artist nearly lost to the war. The Melbourne-born Peter Purves Smith was in New York to visit the World Fair when hostilities were declared on 3 September 1939. Returning to London on board the same ship as Patrick White and intending to go on to Australia, he suddenly decided to join the British Army, in which he spent most of the next six years. Among the best known of his paintings of the period is his ghostly and desolate *New York* (1936), notable both for its 'wasteland' theme—a common surrealist trope regarding the city—and its upright cleft sticks, undoubtedly drawing on Dalí's paranoiac-critical method (we might recall such imagery from the end of Dalí and Luis Buñuel's 1929 film *Un chien Andalou*, for instance).

Following his war service, Purves Smith returned to Australia in 1946 and began once again to paint. As reviews of the *International Surrealist Exhibition* already suggest, the Australia he came back to was not as isolated or entirely anti-modernist as conventional accounts of the period would have it.[22] By 1940 and the end of the tour of the Basil Burdett–curated *Exhibition of French and British Modern Art*, both the Australian public and artists had had their first direct experience of surrealist painting from overseas. They had seen the work of Edward Wadsworth, Nash, Sutherland, Dalí, de Chirico and Ernst—Ernst had earlier painted the Australian expatriate musicologist Louise Hanson Dyer in his *Surrealist portrait of Louise Hanson Dyer* (1933)—and the success of the exhibition, which also included a few more-or-less abstract paintings such as Ernst's *Le paysage au germe de blé* (*Landscape with germinating corn*) (1934) and Ben Nicholson's *Composition in black and white* (1933), had inspired the critic Lionel Lindsay to write to publisher Sydney Ure Smith that 'The intrusion of mathematics is the greatest insult ever made to art. Abstract art! You might as well talk of an abstract fuck or an abstract glass of whiskey.'[23]

But it was through the exhibitions of the Contemporary Art Society (CAS) that the Australian public received its first prolonged exposure to surrealism. Formed in Melbourne and then Sydney in reaction to the founding of the Robert Menzies–backed Australian Academy of Art, the CAS at first staged exhibitions dominated by surrealism. Its inaugural (1939) show at the National Gallery of Victoria featured the work of Eric Thake, Sidney Nolan, Albert Tucker and James Gleeson. The second exhibition, in 1940 in both Melbourne and Sydney, featured Thake, Nolan, Gleeson, Max Ebert (pseudonym of the artist Herbert McClintock) and Joseph Tierney (pseudonym of the artist and critic Bernard Smith). The third show, in 1941, continued the surrealist pre-eminence. Many of the same artists exhibited (Cant, Nolan, Graham, McClintock, Oswald Hall), but now also Geoffrey and Dahl Collings, Loudon Sainthill and the near-unknown Dutch-Jewish immigrant artists Robert and Lyalla Benezra. The third show could still earn the headline 'Pictures that Startled Sydney' in the *Sunday Telegraph*[24]—but the CAS had then been doing this for years. The important thing here is that, in the absence of any other exhibition possibilities for advanced art in Australia, this repetition of names makes it clear that these CAS annual exhibitions, held in Sydney and Melbourne and soon to be bi-annual, were making possible the establishment of long-term artistic careers.

In this series of exhibitions, modern and contemporary art effectively meant surrealism, at least from the public's point of view. So when it was time for the old guard to flex its muscles, Howard Ashton, art critic for Sydney's

Sunday Sun, under the title 'Should Artists Paint Spinach on a Moon of Purple Cheese?', predictably found fault with the second CAS show.[25] On the other hand, Perth-born CAS regular Herbert McClintock, in his guise as Max Ebert, defended it strongly. Indeed, Gleeson, now writing as an art critic, sought to explain the movement to the public in the November 1940 edition of the journal *Art in Australia* in an essay entitled 'What is Surrealism?' (The same issue featured a reproduction of Tucker's *Futile city* (1940), another example of the genre of 'wasteland cities', following Purves Smith.) In his essay, Gleeson speaks of the work of Ebert and Tucker, and writes that in his own work *Principles of the rituals of homicide* (1939)—it seems that he too had been reading Freud's *Totem and Taboo*—he attempted to 'express the universal struggle for the liberation of the individual will … to achieve the freedom of his will man must metaphorically murder the father'.[26]

The second CAS exhibition brought Tucker up from Melbourne to Sydney for a roundtable on surrealism with Gleeson and Smith (as Tierney), both of whom were members of the Teachers' Federation Art Society. At this meeting surrealism went national; but the moment was short-lived, as the divisions between the various protagonists quickly became apparent. For his part, Smith was

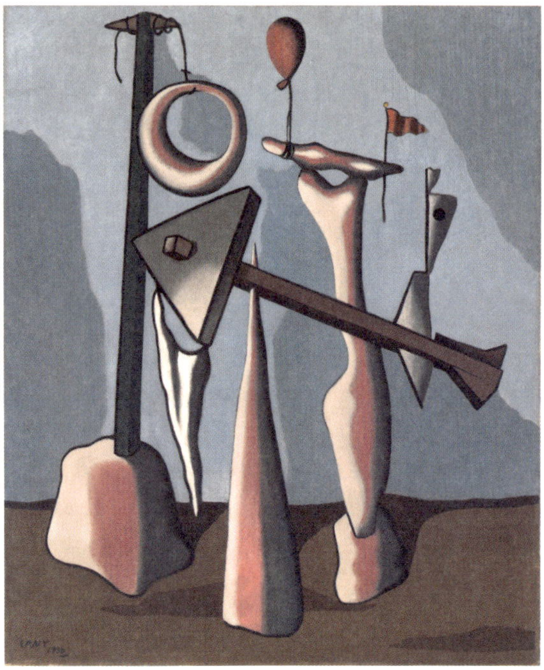

4.6 James Cant
Objects in a landscape, 1936

committed to a political surrealism—and, indeed, he would soon abandon painting to pursue a career as an art historian. In his autobiography *The Boy Adeodatus*, written in a strange third person, Smith remembered that:

> Gleeson was the only person in Sydney that Bernard had been able to find who was seriously interested in surrealism. But not at all in politics. It was the intuitive unpolitical side of the movement that attracted him, Freud and Dalí.[27]

In 1940 Smith joined the teachers' branch of the Australian Communist Party and began to dream of killing *his* 'father': the first historian of Australian art, William Moore. Haunted by the author's fantasies of patricide, *The Boy Adeodatus* ends ominously with Smith recounting that:

> he had seen the old man [Moore] as a harmless old man ploughing a field. He then saw two knives on the table. He threw one at the back of the old man as everything went dark.[28]

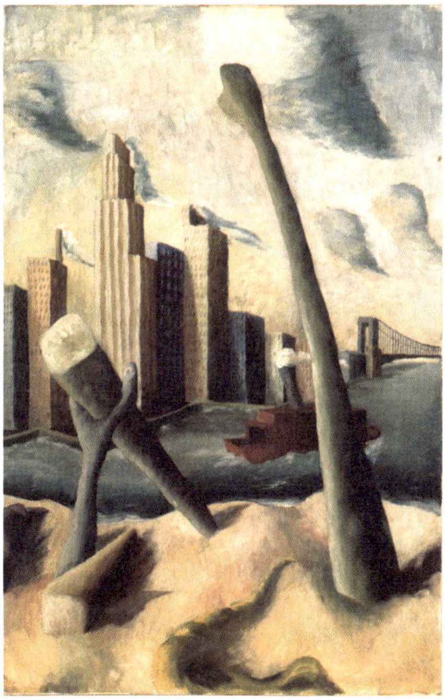

4.7 Peter Purves Smith
New York, c. 1936

Around the same time in 1939 Max Ebert was holding his first solo show in Perth, which included works such as *Dawnbreakers* (1939), with its glowering and confrontational faces. This show was then reprised at Macquarie Galleries in Sydney, where Ebert moved permanently the following year. In Sydney he lived in an apartment in a big city building, using the roof as an open-air studio, and was photographed there in *Pix* magazine not long after his arrival, painting on a ceiling, sitting on the rooftop chimney and creating in a cupboard.[29] Like Smith, he would later abandon his surrealism (and his pseudonym) in favour of a socially committed practice and became a founding member of the Studio of Realist Art, the left-wing exhibition and educational vehicle that saw itself as the 'conscience of a nation'.[30] Russell Drysdale, a kind of barometer of surrealism, moved from Melbourne to Sydney in 1940, and there, and in Albury, he produced such works as the Henry Moore–inspired *Crucifixion* (1946), the Dalí-indebted *The rabbiters* (1947), the Graham Sutherland–inclined *Golden gully* (1949) and the de Chirico–invested *Boy running, Cooktown* (1950).

But the dispersion of surrealism went wider than Sydney and Melbourne, and had other effects. In Brisbane, Vincent Brown, having discovered surrealism while at the Grosvenor School and the Slade from 1936 until 1939—he would

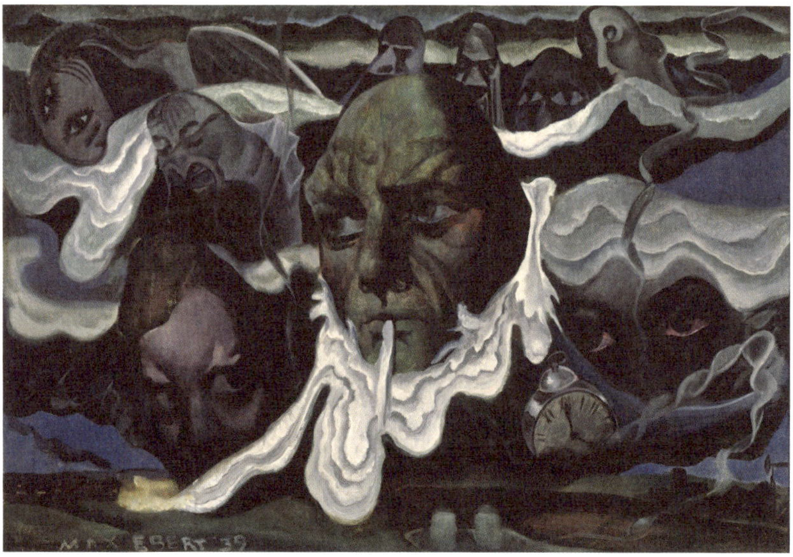

4.8 Herbert McClintock
Dawnbreakers, 1939

undoubtedly have seen the *International Surrealism* show—undertook the opposite journey to McClintock, from realism to surrealism. In 1945 he held his second solo exhibition, at the Canberra Hotel in Brisbane, in what has been described as 'the first insistently modernist experience visited on [that city's] public'.[31] The surrealism of his war years revealed Balinese influences, beside the more conventional Chagall-like dreamscapes. In 1948 he returned to England, where he would stay for twenty-nine years before returning finally to Brisbane, eventually settling into a softer and more decorative version of his original style.

In Adelaide, perhaps the most prominent exponent of surrealism and an important figure in the establishment of the CAS in South Australia was Ivor Francis. In 1939 Francis had met the precocious eighteen-year-old Max Harris, soon to found the cultural journal *Angry Penguins*, its title indicative of its surrealist leanings. During the war Adelaide had become an important centre for modernism in Australia, and with surrealism, in Harris's words, it managed to turn 'nice Adelaides into angry Adelaides'.[32] Francis painted his Dalí-esque *Schizophrenia* in 1943 after a period of dramatic change in his life. Recently returned from several years of teaching on South Australia's isolated Eyre Peninsula, he first exhibited the work at the Royal South Australian Society of Artists' Gallery (a true surrealist mouthful) in Adelaide, alongside that of fellow Adelaide surrealist Douglas Roberts. Francis wrote at the time of its purchase by the Art Gallery of South Australia: '*Schizophrenia* is a work symbolic of frustration … To the artist this [schizophrenia] was the malady of the world itself in 1943'.[33]

In Melbourne, there was Eric Thake, who not only painted, but was also a graphic artist and photographer. From 1932 he belonged to the Melbourne Contemporary Group, and in 1939 became a founding member of the CAS. An early exponent of surrealism in Australia, Thake shared the CAS prize in 1940 with James Gleeson for his *Salvation from the evils of earthly existence* (1940), the painting drawing on typical surreal imagery from aircraft and shipping, with its turning propellers driving machines of paper through the air. Thake's aerial imagery and precise line here remind us of the Auckland-born surrealist Felix Kelly, in particular Kelly's *Christmas card* from 1939 (and, by coincidence, Thake printed his own long-running series of surrealist Christmas cards between 1941 and 1975). A surrealist all his life, Thake worked in advertising from 1926 to 1956, designing stamps, murals, newspaper advertisements and billboards. His photograph *Torn posters* of 1963 both reflects on his own professional work and looks at once back to the French Affichistes and forward to Pop.

In Melbourne also, the painter, art writer and activist Bernard Boles began his own excursions into surrealism. Like Gleeson in Sydney and the lesser-known Percy Watson in Melbourne, Boles drew on the biomorphic marine imagery typical of surrealism all around the world, as seen, for example, in the work of painters from Edward Wadsworth to Yves Tanguy. (Indeed, the Sydney-born artist JW Power was working in this idiom in Paris and, in an exhibition of the artists' group Abstraction-Création devoted to its members who used organic imagery, he showed alongside Barbara Hepworth, Enrico Prampolini and Sophie Taeuber-Arp, among others. See p. 242.) In 1948, Boles, having been rejected from the Victorian Artists' Society, would hang his pair of refused paintings from a fence outside the show and spend the ensuing two weeks sharing his views on art with passers-by. Later that year, he held a solo exhibition on the launch *Fairyland*, which was moored near the Princes Bridge on the Yarra River in Melbourne. An early critic of our art schools, he advocated a system of art education exemplified by the experimental approach of the Chicago Institute of Design:

> Let him explore the sensory collage of Schwitters, the shapes and experience of volumes from Arp and Hepworth, the divided flat rectilinears and colour-values of Mondrian, the constructions of Tatlin and Gabo, the mobiles of Calder and the virtual volumes of Moholy-Nagy …[34]

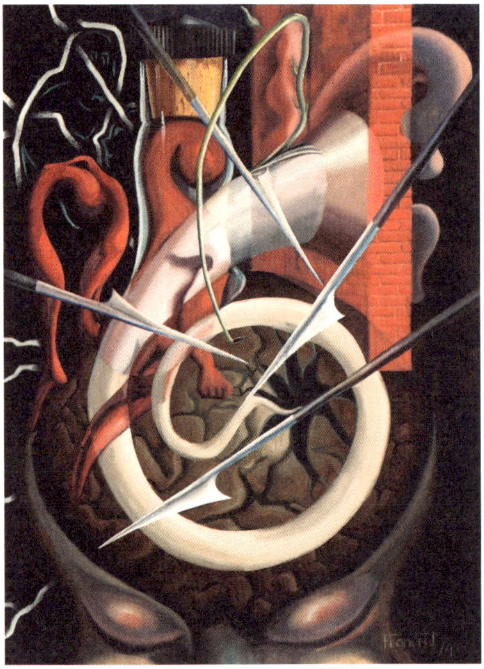

4.9 Ivor Francis
Schizophrenia, 1943

If all of this dispersal is dizzying, it is nothing compared to the forced movement of our wartime immigrants, some of whom were artists. The infamous HMT *Dunera*, the brutal transport ship that brought from Britain some 2500 so-called enemy aliens, the majority of whom were, of course, Jewish, arrived in Sydney on 6 September 1940, after a terrible fifty-seven-day journey that saw detainees confined below deck and some beaten. Among the ship's passengers were the artists Klaus Friedeberger, Erwin Fabian, Ludwig Hirschfeld-Mack and Hein Heckroth. It is hard not to see Friedeberger's and Fabian's subsequent work as a response to their ordeal, and from their experience a particular subcategory of surrealism in Australia developed. Hirschfeld-Mack's *Desolation* (1941, see p. 160) is well known. Less well known but its equal is Berlin-born Friedeberger's *Camp dream* (1943) and Berlin-born Fabian's *Coffin* (1941). These internment camp works are remarkable early examples of the depiction of the *homo sacer*, that extra-judicial figure stripped of all legal rights. The same sense of isolation and aloneness is evident in Hein Heckroth's *Australia* (1941), completed at the internment camp in Hay; and later his surrealism would be expressed through, for example, his 1948 Oscar-winning design for Michael Powell and Emeric Pressburger's ballet film *The Red Shoes* (1948). Also arriving in Australia in 1940 was the Austrian Vera Rudner, a little-known painter who worked from

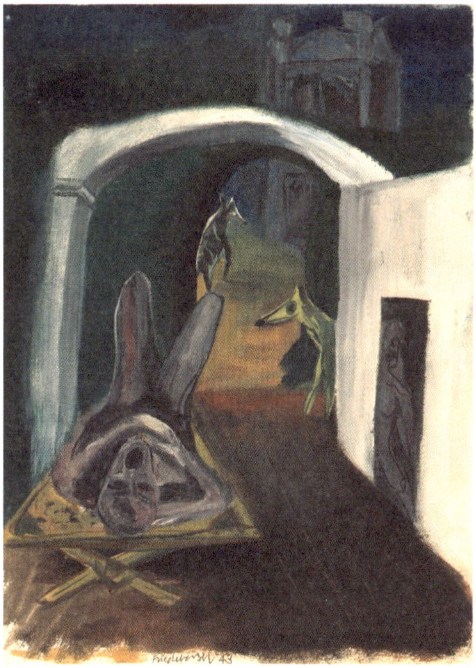

4.10 Klaus Friedeberger
Camp dream, 1943

the early 1940s until 1948, in which year she painted her scarifying *Sacrilege*, just months before she abandoned her practice, haunted by her experiences in Europe.

But, against this surrealism with its internationalism, Freudianism, internal landscapes, and emigrants and immigrants, there was the use of surrealism to express something said to be particularly Australian. Sidney Nolan, Russell Drysdale, Albert Tucker, Donald Friend, Jeffrey Smart and Arthur Boyd all secreted surrealism in their Australian landscapes. Eventually each of these artists would distance himself from surrealism and become central to the creation of a new nationalist iconography. It is these artists who will become emblematic of Bernard Smith's Australian art, and in their insistence on a simultaneously mythic and vernacular figuration stood beside him in his so-called defence of the image against what he saw as the overwhelming tide of international abstraction. This 'defence' motivated Smith's *Antipodeans* exhibition in 1959, as much as it did his *Australian Painting*, published three years later.[35] Just as Smith disavowed his original surrealism in favour of a local realism, so the artists he supported increasingly saw themselves as uniquely Australian, even if they actually lived elsewhere.

We can see all of this in the celebrated and by now over-analysed Ern Malley 'affair'. The mock poems concocted by anti-modernists Harold Stewart

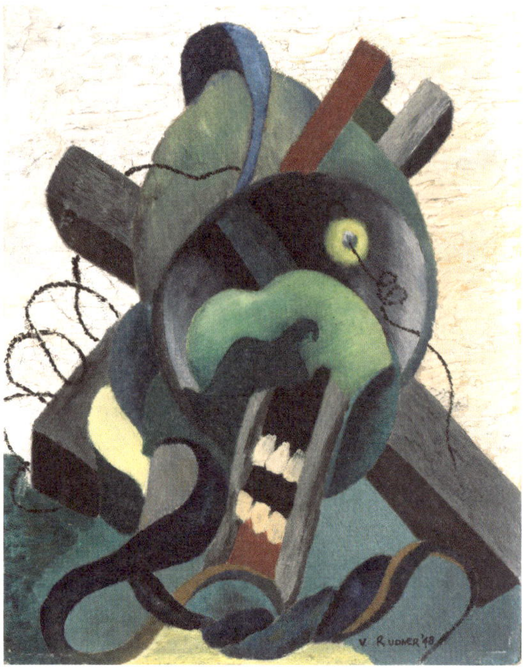

4.11 Vera Rudner
Sacrilege, 1948

and James McAuley were imitative surrealist collages, directed against Max Harris and his by then Heide-based magazine *Angry Penguins*. This episode is as well known as it is because it has been used by art historians to argue for the inevitability of the Antipodeans, that is, surrealism seen as a mere precursor to the 'rebellion' of realism.[36] The tale is also used in a cautionary manner by such polemicists as Smith, who treat it as an example of what not to do—an instance of a wrong turning in the development of Australian art.[37] However, the artistic success and long-running influence of the actual poems—for all of the bad faith of their original composition—inadvertently reveals just what the Australianists were never able to do. They were, ironically, the best-known things that Stewart and McAuley would ever write; and indeed they have been shown, against their creators' own claims, to be carefully and deliberately constructed works of art.

Against this Australianism, the immediate postwar years saw an influx and rise of immigrant artists. As usual, New Zealanders were coming to the country and rising to prominence. It was in the late 1930s in Sydney that the Te Awamutu–born Adele Younghusband began her exploration of surrealism. In 1947 Gordon Walters moved to Sydney and started his own studies into the Indigenous cultures of the Pacific and Australia in the Mitchell Library, repeating the earlier trajectory of Len Lye. The same year, Riverton-born Gordon McAuslan moved to Sydney, where he continued to develop the biomorphic surrealism he had begun in New Zealand, and like Lye and Walters carried on his studies of Pacific cultures. Walters's informal teacher, the Indonesian-born Theo Schoon, his whole life a kind of surrealism, was vitally concerned with Maori rock art, and in 1947 and 1948 the two friends spent the months between Walters's trips to Australia drawing and photographing the South Canterbury caves. Interested in the living cultures around them, these New Zealand artists became involved with Indigenous art and society before 1950 in a way no European-Australian artist, with the exception of Margaret Preston, and perhaps James Cant, had ever been.[38] When the Timaru-born born Colin McCahon came to Australia in 1951, however, it was not an encounter with Indigenous art that he had but with the now elderly Mary Cockburn Mercer, who gave him lessons that were to be decisive to his future work. Familiar with cubism from her time in Paris—she was said to have been at the famous dinner hosted by Picasso for Henri Rousseau in 1908 and to have worked with André Lhote in the 1920s—her later work both betrays these roots and indicates her own continuing involvement with surrealism. Her *Birth of Venus* (1941) is a perverse reimagining of Boucher's equally perverse *Triumph of Venus* (1740), painted some 200 years before and undoubtedly a form of surrealism *avant la lettre* (and the penguins in Cockburn Mercer's picture do not exactly appear to be angry!). Finally, in London, Auckland-born Felix Kelly first made his reputation with a three-person show alongside Lucian Freud and Julian

Trevelyan at the Lefevre Gallery in 1943, and this reputation was confirmed when Herbert Read, who had bought a painting from the show, wrote the introduction to the book *Felix Kelly*, published in 1946. After the war, Kelly's benign but sinister landscapes were popular on both sides of the Atlantic, his career as a surrealist reaching its zenith in 1980 when the future king, Prince Charles, consulted him about his 'somewhat grim' Highgrove House, and Kelly subsequently painted an alternative, which became the basis for the prince's remodelling of his residence.[39]

The striking Dunedin-born Rosaleen Norton had been in Sydney since 1925. At high school she was expelled for producing 'depraved' drawings of vampires, ghouls and werewolves, and she subsequently enrolled at the East Sydney Technical College (now National Art School) under sculptor Rayner Hoff, who encouraged her 'pagan' creativity.[40] She first attracted controversy when she exhibited a series of sexually explicit drawings at the Rowden White Library at the University of Melbourne in 1949. It led to a raid by the police and Norton being charged with obscenity. Many of her works were based on supposed trance encounters, induced by self-hypnosis, with archetypal beings, whom she considered had their own independent existence (although they are all, in fact, disguised self-portraits). *The Art of Rosaleen Norton* was published in 1952 and

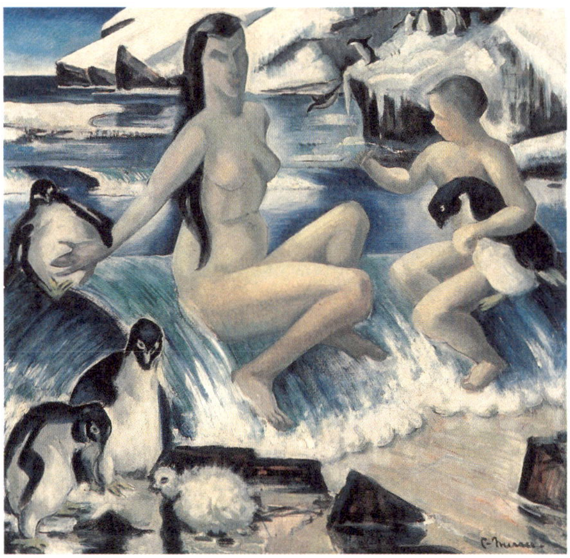

4.12 Mary Cockburn Mercer
Birth of Venus, 1941

led to the publisher being charged with producing an obscene publication, and the book was subsequently only released with its sexually explicit images blacked out. From the 1950s on, Norton became known as the 'witch of Kings Cross'. She was falsely accused of holding black masses and engaging in 'unnatural sexual acts'. Perhaps she is most famous, however, for her association with Sir Eugene Goossens, the first permanent conductor of the Sydney Symphony Orchestra and a member of her occult group, who was charged in 1956 with importing ritual pornographic objects, charges that led to his deportation from Australia and in part to his death six years later.

But by far the greater proportion of Australia's postwar immigrants came from Europe. Ready-formed surrealists Dušan and Voitre Marek arrived from Prague in 1948, bringing with them a particularly Central European surrealism steeped in cosmic fairytale and folklore. They moved initially to Adelaide but Dušan in particular was restless and moved from there to Hobart, Sydney, and then to Papua New Guinea. It is perhaps the brothers' presence in Adelaide, as the first of a series of Central European immigrants who were to make that city their home, that allows us to see their work as a forerunner to what curator Daniel Thomas would later dub 'Slavic space-age Adelaide'.[41] Indeed, not long after his arrival in Port Moresby,

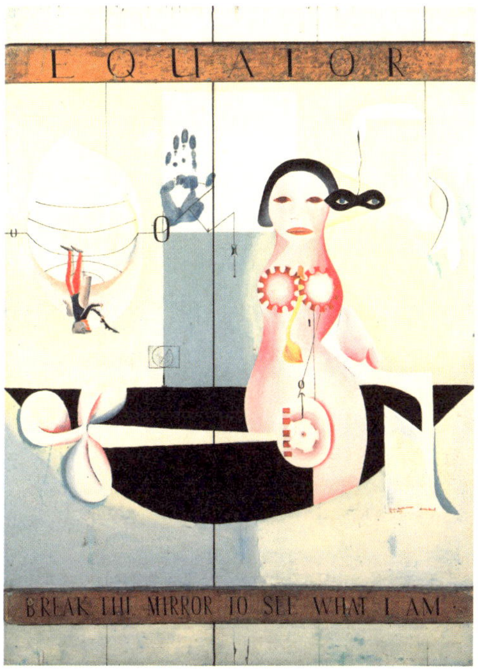

4.13 Dušan Marek
Equator, 1948

Dušan Marek held his *Surrealist Exhibition* there, another important milestone in the worldwide dispersion of surrealism (although, of course, by this time New Guinea was already hanging above the hearth of surrealism in Breton's apartment and was twice as big as Australia, at least in French-speaking surrealists' eyes).

We might finish our entry here by returning to Europe. While the years after the war saw an influx of migrants, it also saw an outflow as Australian artists began once again to reconnect with Europe. In London, Gleeson met Sydney sculptor Robert Klippel at the studio complex known as the Abbey, and together at the invitation of Mesens they held a joint exhibition at the London Gallery in 1948.[42] This collaboration was important for them both. The painted wood figure *No. 35 Madame Sophie Sesostoris (a Pre-Raphaelite satire)*, its title derived from a character in TS Eliot's *The Waste Land*, which was the centrepiece of the show, brought together Gleeson's painting and Klippel's sculpture in one work. For his part, not long after their London show, Gleeson returned to Australia and became an art critic and our best-known surrealist. His work from the 1970s on, a more erotic reprise of his earlier painting, reminds us of a queer version of the American painter of soft-core female nudes Mel Ramos. For his part, Klippel moved to Paris after the show, where he warmed himself by the embers of Breton's

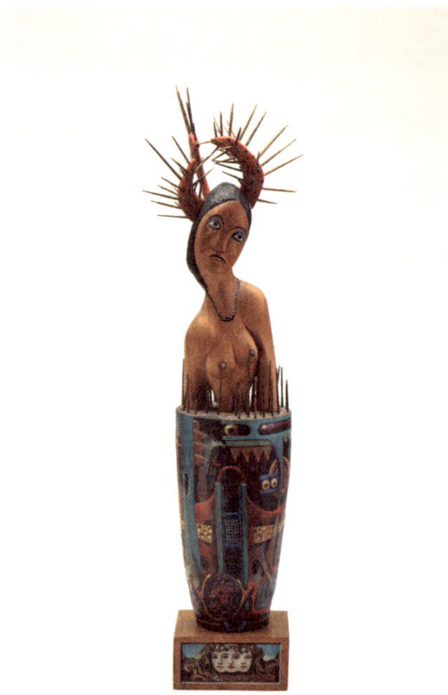

4.14 Robert Klippel and James Gleeson
No. 35 Madame Sophie Sesostoris (a Pre-Raphaelite satire), 1947–8

official surrealism and held his first solo exhibition at Nina Dausette's gallery, La Dragonne. Slowly fading in *la ville de lumière*, the surrealist movement would not last much longer in Australia. Its final resting place, at least in the official histories of art in this country, would be among the Antipodeans.

* * *

These few pages point to a possible Australian (or even Australasian) contribution to a show of world surrealism. But they would not constitute any kind of *Australian* surrealism, as Smith and those who followed him have desired. Nor would they constitute a surrealism *in* Australia, as curator Christopher Chapman once proposed in an exhibition of that title.[43] Rather, we might speak of what we have done as an essay on surrealism *and* Australia, the two terms lying next to each other, to use Lautréamont's well-worn phrase, like an umbrella and a sewing machine on an operating table. Or we might even say that what we have pointed to is an *UnAustralian* surrealism: the fact that to consider the relationship between surrealism and Australia is to make clear that we never had an identifiable Australian art; that Australian art was always global, never simply existing within national boundaries but, rather, always part of the world.

And this is what the surrealists always understood. It was clear as early as 1929 when *The world at the time of the Surrealists* was published in an issue of the Belgian periodical *Variétés* devoted to surrealism. It was probably drawn by the surrealist poet Paul Éluard, who had travelled through the Pacific and into Southeast Asia following his overnight disappearance from Paris in April 1924. Éluard had fled his gambling debts, having absconded with some family money, chiefly because of the pressure he felt under as a result of the *ménage-à-trois* he was maintaining with his wife Gala, later to marry Dalí, and Max Ernst.[44] Departing from Marseille on the SS *Antinous*, Éluard headed first across the Atlantic and then through the Panama Canal, bound for Noumea. Travelling under his real name, Eugène Grindel, by early June Éluard had left Papeete destined for New Zealand, where he eventually disembarked in Wellington. (And Éluard reminds us so much of Lye, who was moving around Tonga, Fiji and Samoa at the very same time.) From there it is thought that he travelled by a Dutch steamer, first to Sydney, then to Brisbane, to New Guinea, through the Torres Strait, and on to Indonesia and eventually to Singapore, where the threesome was reunited (Gala and Ernst having travelled eastwards from Europe to meet him there).[45]

Remarkably, Éluard is only the first of a number of surrealists who visit the South Pacific in the inter-war years. He was, however, preceded by the poet and writer Victor Segelan before World War I (Segalen wrote an account of

Gauguin's last days in *Gauguin dans son dernier décor* in 1909). And after him came the writer, poet and art dealer Jacques Viot in 1925–26, then the Saigon-born painter, and later photographer, Émile Savitry and the painter Georges Malkine, who travelled there together in 1929 until they fell out over a woman. In 1930 Savitry worked in Tahiti as a stills photographer on the set of FW Murnau's *Tabu*. As well, in 1933 the photographers Jacques-André Boiffard and Eli Lotar worked in the Pacific on their way around the world (reminiscent of German photographer EA Hoppé's world travels at the same time), and in 1934 Roger Parry published *Tahiti*, his book of photographs of the island. 'Yet', as art historian Robert McNab has pointed out, 'this Pacific diaspora of surrealism is little known, and the story of the decade during which seven surrealists trailed around Oceania remains untold'.[46] On the map, along with the disappearance of America and its replacement by Mexico, is the recognition that Australia is just another island in the Pacific, part of a wider Oceanic flow that has always existed. On the surrealist map, boundaries waver, the equator is not a straight line separating North and South, and the Pacific Ocean is the centre of the world. It was a point already made by Matisse, who travelled to Tahiti in 1930, in his *Oceania* of 1946.

But Matisse was only following Gauguin's voyage to the same island, and to Sydney, Melbourne and Auckland, a journey that led to the incorporation of Javanese and Polynesian art directly into Gauguin's Parisian studio at 6 rue Vercingétorix in the mid-1890s.[47] And Gauguin's installation reminds us of Adelaide artist Mortimer Menpes' own 'surrealistic' insertion of original Japanese interiors into his London house at 25 Cadogan Gardens in the late 1890s. All of this is merely to point out how the Pacific has always opened up alternative histories, never more obviously than in the encyclopaedic study *Art in Oceania* (2012),[48] which must be understood as directed against the *October* School's *Art Since 1900* (2004), which for all of its apparent 'revision' of received art history still remains deeply Euro-American-centric in its emphases. It is what Gauguin, Breton, Kupka and Namatbara knew all along. We would write a history of surrealism and Australia, then, only to make evident this fact, and to reveal that, if these global anthologising exercises are a phenomenon of the early twenty-first century, the global itself has been with us since at least the beginning of the last century.

An earlier version of this text was published in *Journal of Art Historiography*, no. 9, 2013.

1 See *World Impressionism: The International Movement, 1860–1920*, ed. Norma Broude, Harry Abrams, New York, 1994; *WACK! Art and the Feminist Revolution*, eds. Lisa Mark and Cornelia Butler, exhibition catalogue, MIT Press, Cambridge, Mass., 2007; and *Global Conceptualism: Points of Origin, 1950s–1980s*, ed. Jane Farver, exhibition catalogue, Queens Museum of Art, New York, 1999.

2 It was from New York in 1941 that Breton sent his article 'Originality and Liberty' to be published in *Art in Australia* (vol. 4, no. 1, December 1941, pp. 11–12). Writing at the beginning of World War II, Breton in this call from the New World again re-imagines the points on the globe, declaring: 'Each one of us, from Paris to Sydney, from New York to the depths of Asia, has an actual physical part in this world convulsion'.

3 Near the end of his life, Breton was still in his apartment thinking about 'far-off Arnhem Land' when he wrote the preface to Karel Kupka's *Dawn of Art: Painting and Sculpture of Australian Aborigines*, Angus & Robertson, Sydney, 1962; reprinted in eds. Ann Stephen, Andrew McNamara and Phillip Goad, *Modernism and Australia: Documents of Art, Design and Architecture*, Miegunyah Press, Melbourne, 2006, pp. 722–4.

4 On this, see Majella Munroe, *Communicating Vessels: The Surrealist Movement in Japan, 1925–70*, Enzon Press, Cambridge, 2012.

5 Karel Kupka, *Un art à l'état brut: Peintures et sculptures des aborigènes d'Australie*, La Guilde du Livre, Lausanne, 1962. Kupka completed his doctorate at the Sorbonne in 1968 and later wrote his better-known *Peintres Aborigènes d'Australie*, Publications de la Société des Océaniste 24, Musée de l'Homme, Paris, 1972. For an excellent account of Kupka and his relationship to Aboriginal art, see Nicholas Rothwell, 'The Collector', *The Monthly* (Melbourne), October 2007, pp. 28–37.

6 Cited in Anonymous, 'Aborigines Were Surrealists', *Daily News* (Perth), 22 November 1941, p. 27.

7 Breton, cited in Roger Horrocks, *Len Lye: A Biography*, Auckland University Press, 2001, p. 159, fn. 3.

8 Oceania, however, was central to surrealism. Its 'primitive' objects and imagery were essential to its art; and, indeed, the *International Surrealist Exhibition* included sculptures from Australia and New Guinea lent by the Museum of Archaeology and Anthropology at Cambridge. This museum houses material drawn from James Cook's voyages to the South Pacific in the 1770s, as well as material from Alfred Haddon's expedition to the Torres Strait in 1898. See Our correspondent, 'Surrealism in Europe', *The Age*, 4 July 1936, p. 20. For images of the exhibition installation, see Lee Miller's photographs, reproduced in ed. Phillip van den Bossche et al., *The Star Alphabet of E.L.T. Mesens: Dada and Surrealism in Brussels, Paris and London*, exhibition catalogue, Mu.ZEE, Ostend, 2013, pp. 163–4.

9 Harold Osborne, *The Oxford Companion to Twentieth-Century Art*, Oxford University Press, 1981, p. 530.

10 A temptation to which not even the Birmingham surrealists were immune, accusing other British artists of being 'overnight surrealists'. On this, see Michel Remy, 'Towards the Magnetic North: Surrealism in Birmingham', in ed. Silvano Levy, *Surrealism in Birmingham: 1935–1954*, exhibition catalogue, Birmingham Museum and Art Gallery, Birmingham, UK, 2000, pp. 7–14.

11 Horrocks, *Len Lye*, p. 48.

12 From Lee Miller's photographs of the exhibition it is apparent that this work by unnamed artists was hung equally beside the surrealists.

13 Patrick Schaefer, 'Francis Bacon Tate Britain jusqu'au 4 Janvier 2009', *L'art en jeu*, no. 7, February 2009, http://www.art-en-jeu.ch/home_wp/francis-bacon.

14 See on this John Richardson, *The Sorcerer's Apprentice: Picasso, Provence and Douglas Cooper*, Knopf, New York, 1999; and John Richardson, 'Bacon Agonistes', *New York Review of Books*, 17 December 2009, pp. 38–44. For a more extended discussion of Cooper's place in Australian art, see Rex Butler and ADS Donaldson, 'Douglas Cooper and Australian Art History', *Broadsheet*, vol. 39, no. 2, 2010, pp. 131–3.

15 Heather Johnson, *Roy de Maistre: The English Years, 1930–1968*, Craftsman House, Sydney, 1995, p. 97.

16 See 'We ask your attention! The British Surrealist Group Takes Arms', https://kv53139.blogspot.com/2014/12/we-ask-your-attention-british.html.

17 Herta Wescher, *Collage*, Harry N. Abrams, New York, 1968, p. 246.

18 On this, see *L'Amour Fou: Photography and Surrealism*, eds. Rosalind Krauss, Jane Livingston

and Dawn Ades, exhibition catalogue, Hayward Gallery, Abbeville Press, New York, 1985.

19 Juliet Peers, 'Clifford Bayliss: A Secret History', in *Clifford Bayliss, 1912–1989: Surrealist Drawings from the 1940s*, exhibition catalogue, Bridget McDonnell Gallery, Melbourne, 1995, p. 5.

20 Elena Taylor, 'Surrealism and Australian Artists in France and Britain: 1930s', in eds. Simon Maidment and Elena Taylor, *Lurid Beauty: Australian Surrealism and Its Echoes*, exhibition catalogue, National Gallery of Victoria, Melbourne, 2015, p. 21.

21 Bernard Smith, cited in Peers, 'Clifford Bayliss: A Secret History', p. 3.

22 On this, see Geoffrey Blainey, *The Tyranny of Distance: How Distance Shaped Australia's History*, Sun Books, Melbourne, 1996. JF Williams's *The Quarantined Culture: Australian Reactions to Modernism, 1913–1939* (Cambridge University Press, 1996), is more ambivalent on this, pointing to instances of Australia's connection to overseas (for example, the reproduction of Marinetti's *Futurist Manifesto* in Australian newspapers at the time) while maintaining the thesis that Australia remained 'quarantined' from international cultural influences.

23 Cited in Joanna Mendelssohn, *Lionel Lindsay: An Artist and His Family*, Chatto & Windus, London, 1998, p. 198.

24 Anonymous, 'Pictures That Startled Sydney', *Sunday Telegraph*, 21 September 1941, p. 2.

25 Howard Ashton, 'Should Artists Paint Spinach on a Moon of Purple Cheese?', *Sunday Sun*, 6 October 1940 (Art Gallery of New South Wales press clippings folder).

26 James Gleeson, 'What Is Surrealism?', *Art in Australia*, no. 81, November 1940, p. 30.

27 Bernard Smith, *The Boy Adeodatus: The Portrait of a Lucky Young Bastard*, Oxford University Press, Melbourne, 1990, p. 258.

28 Ibid., pp. 299–300.

29 'Dreams Inspire Australia's Art', *Pix* (Sydney), 28 September 1940, p. 7.

30 Bernard Smith, 'Foreword', in *3rd Annual Exhibition by the Studio of Realist Art*, exhibition catalogue, David Jones Art Gallery, Sydney, 1948, np.

31 Sheryl McDonald, 'Vincent Brown and Modernism in Brisbane 1940–48', in eds. Christopher Saines and Sheryl McDonald, *Vincent Brown: An Early Brisbane Modernist*, exhibition catalogue, Queensland Art Gallery, Brisbane, 1990, p. 9.

32 Max Harris, 'Introduction', in ed. Jane Hilton, *Adelaide Angries: South Australian Painting of the 1940s*, exhibition catalogue, Art Gallery of South Australia, Adelaide, 1990, p. 11.

33 Ivor Francis, cited in Robert M. Caplin, 'The First Australian Painting of Schizophrenia by Ivor Francis', *Australasian Psychiatry*, vol. 22, no. 3, 2014, p. 300.

34 Bernard Boles, 'A Blueprint for Today's Art Education', *The Australian Artist* (Melbourne), July 1947, p. 13.

35 See Bernard Smith, 'The Antipodean Manifesto', *Antipodeans*, exhibition catalogue, Victorian Artists' Society Gallery, Spotlight Press, Melbourne, 1959, np.

36 Richard Haese, *Rebels and Precursors: The Revolutionary Years of Australian Art*, Penguin, Melbourne, 1988, pp. 141–4.

37 Bernard Smith, *Australian Painting, 1788–1970*, Oxford University Press, Melbourne, 1971, p. 233.

38 In 1949, having befriended the anthropologist Charles Mountford and having become interested in Aboriginal art through his job at the Australian Museum in Sydney, Cant would paint and exhibit his 'own' Obiri Cave paintings, first in Sydney and then in London. These have been exhibited at Charles Nodrum Gallery, Melbourne, 8–26 May 2015, with an essay by Sheridan Palmer, 'James Cant's Aboriginal Paintings', www.charlesnodrumgallery.com.au/exhibitions/james-cant-five-paintings-from-the-william-ohly-collection/essay-by-sheridan-palmer.

39 See on this 'Obituaries: Peter Falconer', *The Telegraph* (London), 5 February 2003, www.telegraph.co.uk/news/obituaries/1421095/Peter-Falconer.

40 Nevill Drury, 'Rosaleen Norton', 1995, updated 2011, *Design & Art Australia Online*, www.daao.org.au/bio/rosaleen-norton/biography.

41 Daniel Thomas, 'Five Ages of Contemporary', *Advertiser* (Adelaide), 13 February 1993, Arts, p. 12.

42 In 1949 the German-Australian sculptor Inge King also held an exhibition at the London Gallery. It included the surrealist *Flower dancer* (1948), remarkably similar to Klippel's *No. 40 (red sandstone carving)* (1948), with both works brought together in Maidment and Taylor's *Lurid beauty*.

43 *Surrealism in Australia*, ed. Christopher Chapman, exhibition catalogue, National Gallery of Australia, Canberra, 1993.

44 Both Éluard and Ernst were collectors of Oceanic art. In 1985 the National Gallery of Australia acquired ninety-six works from Ernst's collection of 'tribal' art through his widow, the painter Dorothea Tanning. Now called the Max Ernst Collection, it includes one work from Australia, one from New Zealand and more than twenty-four from Papua, as well as work from other Pacific nations.

45 Robert MacNab points out that, while 'we cannot tell how long he spent in the ports he marked, nor how he travelled', we do know that Éluard was in Wellington, Sydney and Brisbane, because he traced his route in black ink on a map he kept with him, further suggesting that the surrealist map published in *Variétés* was his. See Robert McNab, *Ghost Ships: A Surrealist Love Triangle*, Yale University Press, New Haven, 2006, p. 68.

46 McNab, *Ghost Ships*, p. 68.

47 See Bronwen Nicholson and Roger Neich, *Gauguin and Maori Art*, University of Washington Press, Seattle, 1996; and John Milner, *The Studios of Paris: The Capital of Art in the Late Nineteenth Century*, Yale University Press, New Haven, 1988, pp. 227ff.

48 Peter Brunt and Nicholas Thomas, *Art in Oceania: A History*, Thames & Hudson, London, 2012.

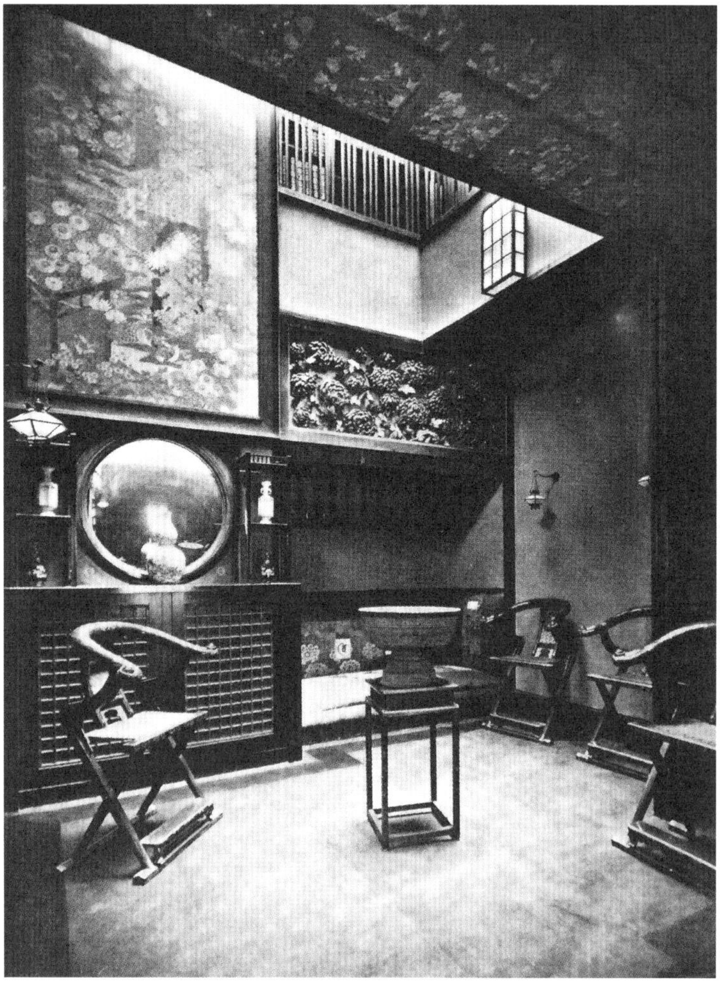

5.1 Installation view of the inner hall and drawing room of Mortimer Menpes's house at Cadogan Gardens, London, c. 1899

Ten Rooms
The Real Spaces of Asian–Australian Artistic Interaction

On 28 October 2012, on the occasion of a government white paper on the topic, Australia's Prime Minister Julia Gillard stood up in front of an assembled crowd of business leaders, academics and community representatives at Sydney's Lowy Institute and announced the next 100 years as Australia's 'Asian century'.[1] The sentiment was commendable, overturning as it did long political indifference to the region and even actual racist and exclusionist practices. The only problem was that it was about a century, perhaps even centuries, too late. It has always been an 'Asian' century in Australia. Before the country was colonised by Europeans, Australia was part of Asia, and Indigenous and Asian peoples traded with each other along the northern reaches of the continent. Even after colonisation, but before there was an 'Australia', much of the world mixed and dealt with Asia through Australia. Yet none of this economic, political and cultural exchange has ever featured in our art histories, which have always emphasised the art of white Europeans above any expression of 'regional' aesthetics.

It has always been tempting from this perspective to think of Australia as a remote, underpopulated and only recently settled nation, hanging precariously off the bottom of Asia. The country would be a cultural and geographical exception, separated by its English colonialist past from its neighbours to the north. It would be the same old provincialist story of isolation and belatedness, only this time in relation to a different centre (and we can see this narrative gaining currency in the twenty-first century with the rise of the new Asian superpowers). But, for us, nowhere is marginal to anywhere else. Everywhere is connected to everywhere. The world is a sphere and there are no edges. To paraphrase one of our favourite authors, the centre is everywhere and the circumference nowhere. It is this conception that the Asia-Pacific Triennial in Brisbane, founded more than twenty years ago, has attempted to grapple with since its inception. But, in truth, the Asia-Pacific has been with us since at least the celebrated *9 by 5 Impression Exhibition*, held at Buxton's Rooms in Melbourne in 1889, which was undoubtedly one of the most important art exhibitions ever held in Australia, but not for the reasons usually given.

In this essay, therefore, as a way of exploring the true Asian century, the one that has just ended, we will take up a number of the real artistic spaces in which Asia and Australia have found themselves alongside each other, echoing their actual geographical proximity. We will select ten exemplary 'rooms', **indicated in bold**, each telling us something different about Asian–Australian artistic exchange. In doing so, we want to point to a certain history of what we might call 'UnAustralian' art, which is not merely a particular set of artists or even works of art, but a different way of thinking about space, looking at Australia from the outside in and not the inside out, turning the world upside down, so that Asia, Africa and South America are on top, and not Europe and America. In doing so, we also offer an alternative way of writing the history of Australian art: as a story not of private patronage and large state-sponsored exhibitions and institutions, but of incessant, small, 'local' interactions between artists, exchanging ideas, techniques and ways of life.

1. So let us begin with that foundational Australian exhibition—said to mark the very 'genesis' of Australian art[2]—held in the **small gallery** above an art supply shop on Swanston Street, Melbourne. The show, of so-called impressions, many painted on cigar box lids, proved controversial, and Tom Roberts, Charles Conder and Arthur Streeton published a defence of their aims in *The Argus* of 3 September 1889, which finishes with the shared hope that their work would lead 'towards the development of what we believe will be a great school of painting in Australia'.[3] Now, Bernard Smith in his *Australian Painting* reads this as a proposal for a nationalist art that would see culture here as something distinct. But for Alison Broinowski in her *Yellow Lady*, who sets the artists' work in a wider geographical context, this apparently 'Australian' moment was in fact 'Asian'.[4] Conder's cover of the catalogue for the show featured a Japanese cherry blossom. Roberts for his part had in all likelihood seen James McNeill Whistler's 1884 exhibition at Dowdeswell's Gallery in London, featuring quickly painted pictures on small panels; and it was Whistler's broadly brushed tonalism with minimal highlights, which he had got from his study of Japanese woodblock prints, that largely defined the style of the Australian 'impressionists', as critics of the time recognised.[5] Indeed, borrowing from the *mise-en-scène* of Whistler's 1884 show, the artists hung the room of the *9 by 5 Impression Exhibition* in 'draperies of soft Liberty silks of many colours … Japanese umbrellas, screens and handsome Bretby Jardinières completed a most harmonious arrangement of colour'.[6] Roberts's own studio was decorated with Oriental rugs and Japanese vases, and Conder's with Madras muslin, Liberty silks and Japanese fans, all of which were readily available in Australia.

2. But if Japanese art was in Australia, Australian art was also in Japan. In a **small office** in Tokyo in 1891, the National Gallery School–trained Frank Nankivell, having run out of money on his way to Paris, found himself working as a cartoonist for the English-language satirical magazine *Box of Curios*. There he employed Rakuten Kitazawa, the only Japanese-born member of staff, and crucially taught him Western-style cartooning. Today, Kitazawa is widely considered the 'father' of that late-twentieth-century globe-spanning phenomenon of Japanese *manga* and *anime*. For, after leaving *Box of Curios*, he went on to found *Tokyo Puck*, based on the American magazine *Puck*, and there trained Ippei Okamoto, the first newspaper *manga* artist, and Hekoten Shimokawa, the inventor of *anime*. These two in turn were decisive for Osamu Tezuka, the creator of the *Astroboy* and *Kimba the White Lion* cartoon series and rightfully called Japan's Walt Disney; and Tezuka was extremely important for Hayao Miyazaki and Takashi Murakami, two of the world's leading post-Pop artists. Thus it is perhaps not too much to say that, for all of the distance of the connection, Japanese *manga* and *anime* are ultimately an Australian thing. For his part, Nankivell, after four years in Japan, headed off to America, where he became instrumental in the establishment of the Association of American Painters and Sculptors and their organising of the Armory Show in

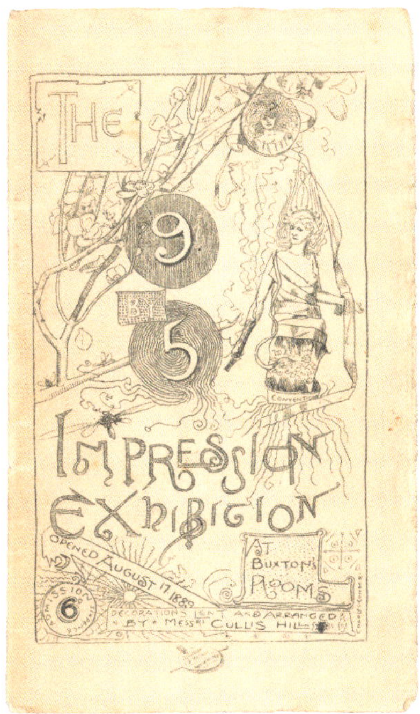

5.2 Charles Conder
9 by 5 Impression Exhibition catalogue cover, 1889

New York, Boston and Chicago in 1913—said to be (although it was not) America's introduction to the international avant-garde. Indeed, if it was true that an Australian was at the root of something uniquely Japanese, it is also true that the first person to photograph Korea was Australian. In 1903 the Clunes-born photographer George Rose travelled to what was then known as the 'hermit kingdom', where he photographed the people and the place, including the Japanese invasion of 1904, a remarkable foundational document that today allows Koreans to see themselves at the turn of the last century.[7]

3. And Japan was in Europe, and therefore in the Australia that was also in Europe. At 25 Cadogan Gardens in Chelsea in 1899, the Adelaide-born artist Mortimer Menpes installed an entire **Japanese interior** at the centre of his house. Menpes, already renowned for his technically brilliant etchings, had first gone to Japan in 1887 and worked with Hokusai's pupil Kawanabe Kyōsai, one of the so-called interface Japanese working with Europeans.[8] It was, indeed, Menpes's 1888 show of paintings, drawings and etchings based on his time in Japan at Dowdeswell's Gallery in London that led to Oscar Wilde's immortal observation in his essay 'The Decay of Lying' (whether positive or negative of Menpes, it is hard to decide) that 'There is no such country. There is no such people. In fact, the whole

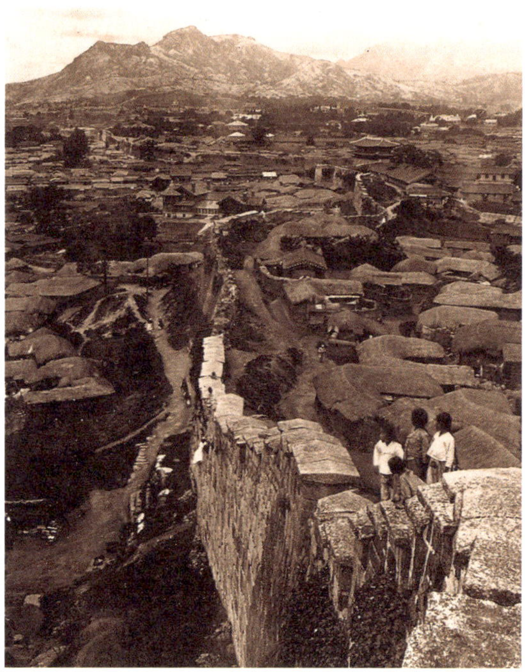

5.3 George Rose
Seoul, 1904

of Japan is a pure invention'.[9] In 1890, Menpes travelled throughout India, Burma and Kashmir with his daughter Dorothy, who had previously been the subject of paintings by Menpes's friend Whistler (and her middle name was Whistler in honour of her godfather). In 1896, Menpes returned to Japan and in 1901 produced with his daughter the best-selling *Japan: A Record in Colour*, two years later setting up the Menpes Press to put out a long-running series of books recording his travels (*China*, *India*, *Venice*, *Paris*). It was while he was in Kyoto during his second visit that he had built the fittings that he would later install in his otherwise Arthur Mackmurdo–designed Arts and Crafts house in Chelsea. Generally understood as a follower of Whistler, Menpes in his interactions with Asia went further than Whistler, who never actually visited there and, indeed, resented Menpes for having done so, which was part of the reason for their acrimonious falling-out. He performed what Broinowski calls the 'expatriate shift'.[10] For Menpes, it was a question not merely of the distant mimicry of a supposed Japanese aesthetic, but of the direct incorporation of a real Japanese space. In the entrance hall of Cadogan Gardens, every plane supported a Japanese fitting or piece of furniture, not as a style but as a physical object (on the floor were lacquer chairs, on the walls silks, and towards the ceiling wood-and-paper light-shades).

4. We see a similar paper lantern in the **background** of Rupert Bunny's 1900 portrait of the world-renowned Japanese actress Sada Yacco on stage in Paris in the role of 'Kesa'. Yacco was there at the time enacting the role at the Paris Exposition, as part of the Japanese Court Company, the first Japanese theatre company ever to tour the West. Bunny was later to make another portrait of Yacco in 1907, this time performing the mad scene in the role of 'Le shogun'. In the first painting, Bunny shows her with her face and body turned away from the audience, and in the second she faces towards them wearing full theatrical make-up. In the former, her nationality is not part of the meaning or narrative of the picture, while in the latter we have the traditional mask of Japan staged for the world. In the first, as opposed to the second, that is, it is her femininity that Bunny seeks to capture, her quality as an 'everywoman'. After all, Yacco was a celebrity with whom Western women identified (and even something of a feminist, for she insisted on performing with her husband's company, despite his traditional disapproval of women performing on stage with men).[11] And, indeed, aren't we struck by the similarity between Bunny's portrait of Yacco and his images of Frenchwomen emulating Eastern odalisques in his series of bathing paintings? That is to say, against either a simple Western view of Japan or an Orientalism, perhaps what Bunny is most interested in is a form of universal *Belle Époque* femininity—dreamy, theatrical, other-worldly—with little regard to any kind of cultural 'truth'?

5. But it was not only in Paris that Yacco performed. Like the Australian operatic soprano Dame Nellie Melba, also the subject of a famous Bunny portrait, she was a global superstar. On the same world tour that had gone through Paris and other European capitals, the Kawakami Theatre Company also toured America, staging seasons in New York and San Francisco. America was an option for Australian artists too. For example, in 1900 the nineteen-year-old Castlemaine-born printmaker Martin Lewis, who had briefly trained at Julian Ashton's in Sydney and already been published in *The Bulletin*, left for America. After stopping over in San Francisco and Chicago, he eventually ended up in New York, where he found work as a commercial artist and illustrator. It was there that he taught his friend Edward Hopper how to etch, which is the technique that led Hopper on to his mature work.[12] Already something of an 'Orientalist' before leaving Australia—besides his knowledge of the *ukiyo-e* masters, he was also inspired by the etchings of Dutchman Marius Bauer—in the 1920s Lewis moved to Japan for five years, where he painted in oil and studied traditional methods of Japanese printmaking. Particularly of interest to him was what might be called Japanese art's de-dramatised and anti-picturesque quality, in which the 'firmament twinkles with lofty indifference to the little human scene'.[13] It was a directness that he would bring to his depictions of

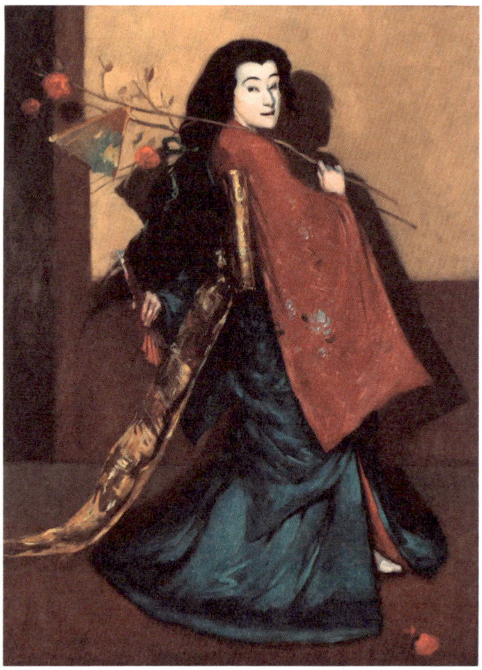

5.4 Rupert Bunny
Mme Sada Yacco, Le Shogun (scène de la folie), c. 1907

inter-war New York, which can appear so much like the work of Edward Hopper, although in truth the influence flows the other way. Indeed, Lewis has been described as 'pictorially the most psychological interpreter of American life as it is lived in its characteristic aspects'[14]—but, of course, the great irony here is that this archetypal American artist was both Australian and saw America through Japanese eyes. The author of a book on Lewis as an etcher, Malcolm C Salaman, for example, writes of the atmospheric effect of Lewis's ***Street booth**, Tokyo, New Year's Eve* (1927) that Lewis shows 'artificial light glaringly contrasted with the comparative darkness of a starlit night',[15] a description that would apply equally to his later New York–based *Glow of the city* (1929), or indeed Hopper's *Summer evening* (1947).

6. We wonder whether, when Lewis was in Tokyo, he might have seen the 1924 show by the Sydney Camera Circle, held at the still-running **Shiseido Gallery** in Ginza, which was a kind of alternative national exhibition to *The Exhibition of Australian Art* held the year before in London at the Royal Academy. The Sydney Camera Circle show included work by Harold Cazneaux, Cecil Bostock, Henri Mallard and the recently-returned-to-Japan Kiichiro Ishida. Ishida had been introduced to photography by a Japanese photographer living in Sydney, Ichiro Kagiyama, who had already exhibited in Japan and who, unlike Ichida, would go

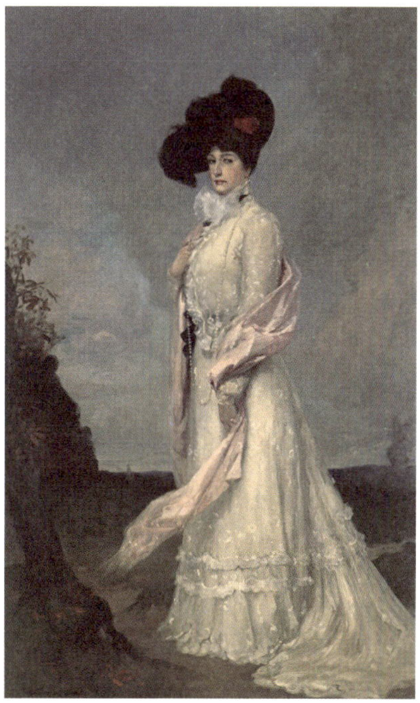

5.5 Rupert Bunny
Madame Melba, 1901–2

on to have a considerable career, with many of his photographs being published by *The Home* in the 1930s. Indeed, it was only in 1941 with Japan's entry into the war that Kagiyama returned to Japan, after some thirty-five years in Australia. But the real point here is that the 'pictorialism' of the Camera Circle—and it is undoubtedly ironic that Kagiyama was never admitted into the group—was nevertheless influenced by Japanese aesthetics.[16] We can see it in its misty atmospherics, its dispersion of the viewer's attention, its lack of focus and its frequently decentred compositions. Again, the vaunted 'Australianness' of the Camera Circle—the fact that it is said to have founded a national school of photography—reveals its debt not only to a general Japanese aesthetic but also to particular Japanese photographers: Kagiyama, who was one of its first practitioners; and Ishida, who enabled the group's first overseas showing.

7. Also arriving from Japan in the 1920s was the Oxford University–educated professor of Oriental studies at the University of Sydney, Arthur Lindsay Sadler, author of *The Art of Flower Arrangement in Japan: A Sketch of Its History and Development* (1933) and part of a circle of intellectuals in Sydney interested in China and Japan that included architect Hardy Wilson, Professor Alexander Mackie and Professor EJ Waterhouse. Sadler is today best known for his so-called

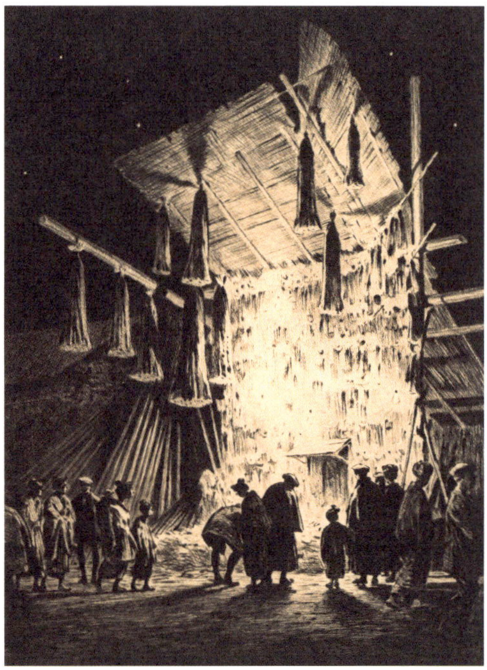

5.6 Martin Lewis
Street booth, Tokyo, New Year's Eve, 1927

Japanese Room in the Roy de Maistre–curated 1929 Burdekin House exhibition in Sydney, which consisted of much of his own furniture collection and was an early attempt to fuse both art and design and European modernism and Japanese aesthetics—and in this, of course, it might remind us of Menpes's Cadogan Gardens. But the connection with Menpes goes deeper than this: the Burdekin House exhibition was sponsored by the wife of the governor of New South Wales, Lady de Chair; and de Maistre when he left for England the following year painted for de Chair's dining room at Carrington House in London an Orientalist fantasia in gold and silver, based on Ernest Fenollosa's influential *Epochs of Chinese and Japanese Art*, originally published in 1912.[17] Along the same lines, back in Australia there was the Melbourne modernist Isabel Tweddle's now forgotten 'Pink House' in Toorak in the 1930s, designed to store her extensive collection of Japanese paintings and prints, many of which were collected on her travels there, and, like Menpes and de Chair, a permanent built environment, as opposed to any merely temporary installation.

8. Hardy Wilson, as already mentioned, was part of Sydney's Orientalist circle. A visit to China as a young man in 1922 had decisively changed his ideas about architecture, leading him to try to produce a fusion of Greek and Chinese

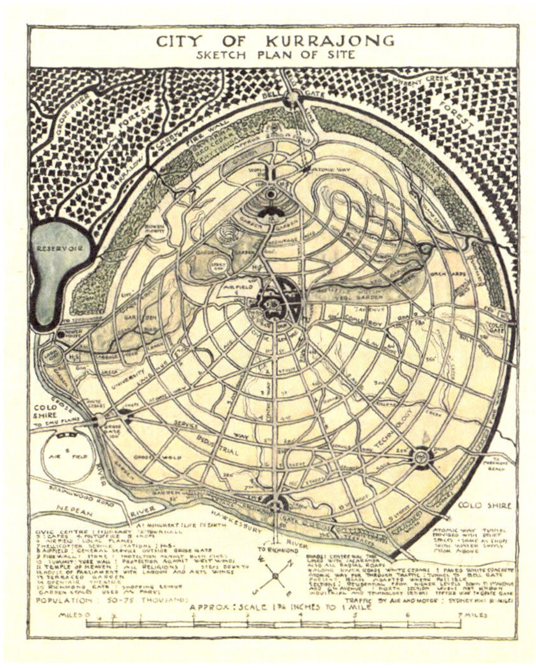

5.7 William Hardy Wilson
City of Kurrajong, 1951

styles. In the 1950s he planned an ideal Australian city, named—of all things—Kurrajong, which was dismissed as eccentric and never finished. But, in fact, our national capital is itself a kind of ideal city built by an architect influenced by Asian culture and religion. The University of Illinois–trained Walter Burley Griffin was a practising Theosophist at the time he designed **Canberra**, which incorporates a number of 'Asian' design elements, such as *feng shui*. Indeed, the drawings done by his architect wife, Marion Mahony Griffin, which are said to have been what won the commission, were extremely *japoniste* in inspiration.[18] Certainly, the Chicago office of Frank Lloyd Wright, where Mahony worked before coming to Australia, was said to be 'filled with the spirit of *Japonisme*'.[19] Walter Griffin would eventually move to the Indian city of Lucknow in the 1930s to build another ideal city, bringing to his designs much of his experience of Canberra. Griffin was by that time merely the latest in a long line of Australian artists, particularly Theosophists, who had made the pilgrimage to India: Aby Altson, who had worked for an Indian prince in 1904; Ethel Carrick, who travelled through Asia after the death of her husband in 1915; and later Flora Beresford, who would leave for India in 1950 and return only in the late 1970s.

9. If in each of these examples Asia is a single place or country, it is also a region, a network, a passage between places. And no one better embodies this than the Scottish-born Ian Fairweather, who was raised by his aunt until the age of six, before his father returned from India where he had been the surgeon-general of the Twenty-Second Punjabi Rifles. While studying later at the Slade School of Art in the 1920s, Fairweather also attended classes in Japanese and Chinese languages at the **School of Oriental and African Studies at the University of London**. In 1929 he left for Shanghai for the first time. He was in Bali by 1933; before arriving in Melbourne in 1934, he is said to have visited Sri Lanka. Less than a year later, he was in the Philippines, before he returned to China. In 1936, he left China for Japan, Taiwan, Hong Kong and Borneo, before going back to the Philippines. In 1938 he was living near Brisbane, and then in Cairns in 1939, before moving to Singapore in 1940 to work at a desk job as part of the war effort, before being transferred to Calcutta and then Bombay, where he was temporarily in charge of an Italian prisoner-of-war camp. Upon discharge, he returned to Melbourne in June 1943, before moving to Cooktown in north Queensland; in 1945 he launched his celebrated raft from Darwin to Timor, and the rest is national mythology. From one perspective, Fairweather can be seen as a Scottish Gauguin, but from another perspective he was a kind of 'constellation', connecting distant places and embodying an already globalised art world, in which no culture is marginal and there is cubism in Aboriginal art, Western perspective in Asian art, and both Aboriginal and Asian art in Western art. He might be considered Australasia's first truly 'Asian' artist, as opposed to an artist from a particular culture. For was

Fairweather's art not as much Japanese as Chinese, as Balinese as Aboriginal? Can the distinction between East and West truly hold any more with regard to his work? Put simply, there could be no Tim Johnson or Simryn Gill without Fairweather. Fairweather himself was preceded less famously by Ambrose Patterson in Hawai'i, Theo Schoon and Guelda Pyke in Bali, Len Lye in Samoa and all of them by Ellis Rowan, the celebrated botanical artist, naturalist, explorer and self-proclaimed 'flower hunter', who travelled throughout the Pacific.

10. To conclude our brief survey here, we come back to the famous *9 by 5* exhibition. If Australian art began with 'impressions' painted on wood whose *japonisme* was later repressed for fear of an anti-Asian sentiment,[20] this same repression was not possible in the face of what appeared to be the 'impression' of bodies on the panels depicting the effects of the dropping of the atomic bomb in Iri and Toshi Maruki's **installation** of their *Hiroshima panels*, which toured Australia throughout 1958. The postwar period was a time of official occupation followed by repatriation and diplomatic reparation (peace parks, Japanese gardens, Japan's joining of the Western Bloc). We could indeed draw up a list of Allied soldiers who spent time in Japan after the war as part of the occupying forces and became heavily influenced by Japanese culture and aesthetics, such as the Californian

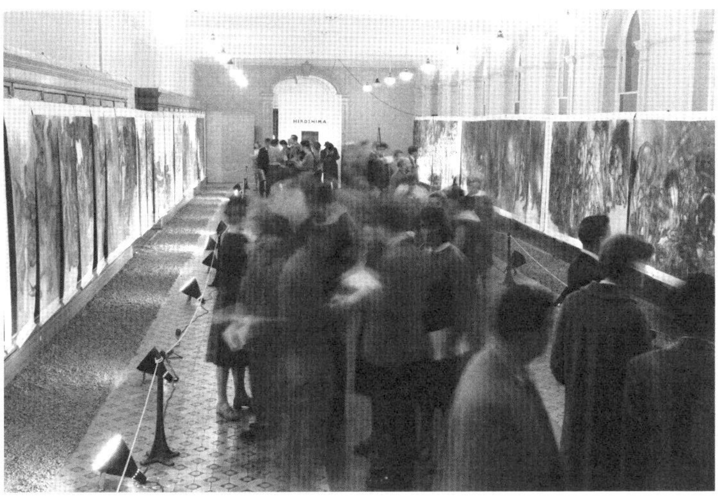

5.8 Iri and Toshi Maruki
The Hiroshima panels, 1950–52. Photo by Mark Strizic, National Gallery of Victoria, Melbourne, 1958

hard-edged painter John McLaughlin. But McLaughlin can also be seen as part of a tradition of Asian-Pacific artists, which included the earlier abstract expressionist Mark Tobey, who was himself part of a Northwest School centred in Seattle and founded by the Australian Ambrose Patterson, which itself included many Asian-American artists. This new Asia-Pacific connection is only one aspect of a century of increasingly globalised art-making. If it has only recently been noticed and turned into an ongoing exhibition, it has been experienced by artists for a lot longer than that.[21] Asia has always been part of the Pacific, like a series of islands in a wider interconnecting ocean, or like rooms in a house. And it is in this ocean or house that Australian art must first of all be located: outside itself, among others, not just a *here*, but also a *there*.

An earlier version of this text was published in *Broadsheet*, vol. 42, no. 3, 2013.

—

1 See Rowan Callick, 'Back to the Big Picture: Asian Century White Paper', *The Australian*, 29 October 2012, p. 13.

2 Bernard Smith, *Australian Painting, 1788–1970*, Oxford University Press, Melbourne, 1971, p. 78.

3 Tom Roberts, Charles Conder and Arthur Streeton, 'Concerning "Impressions" in Painting', *Argus*, 3 September 1889, p. 7.

4 Alison Broinowski, *The Yellow Lady: Australian Impressions of Asia*, Oxford University Press, Melbourne, 1996, pp. 27–8. As will be obvious in what follows, like all scholars of Asian-Australian relations, we are indebted to Broinowski's ground-breaking book.

5 The reviewer for *Table Talk*, 16 August 1889, for example, writes: 'Messrs Tom Roberts, Conder and Streeton are not at all free from the charge of "Whistlerism"'. Cited in Virginia Spate, *Tom Roberts*, Landsdowne Press, Melbourne, 1972, p. 65.

6 *Table Talk*, 16 and 23 August 1889. Cited in Spate, *Tom Roberts*, p. 65.

7 See Catherine Croll, *In The Spirit of George Rose*, Clunes, Victoria, 2015.

8 Broinowski, *Yellow Lady*, p. 40. For further details of Menpes's life and work, see Gary Morgan's foundational three-volume *The Etched Works of Mortimer Menpes (1855–1938)*, Stuart Galleries, Adelaide, 2012. In 2014, Menpes was the subject of a retrospective by the Art Gallery of South Australia, *Mortimer Menpes: Painter, Etcher, Raconteur*.

9 Oscar Wilde, *The Major Works*, Oxford University Press, 2008, p. 235. Paul Foss will later use Wilde's essay to argue that 'Australia' does not exist, in 'Theatrum nondum cognitorum', in eds. Peter Botsman, Chris Burns and Peter Hutchings, *The Foreign Bodies Papers*, Local Consumption Publications, Sydney, 1981, pp. 15–38.

10 Broinowski, *Yellow Lady*, p. 45.

11 For a detailed account of Yacco and her widespread cultural meaning, see Shelley C Berg, 'Sada Yacco: The American Tour, 1899–1900', *Dance Chronicles*, vol. 16, no. 2, 1993, pp. 147–96, especially p. 155.

12 See the chapter 'The Detour Through Etching', in Gail Levin, *Edward Hopper: An Intimate Biography*, Alfred A. Knopf, New York, 1995.

13 Malcolm C Salaman, *Martin Lewis*, Modern Masters of Etching series, The Studio, London and New York, 1931, p. 5.

14 Ibid., p. 1.

15 Ibid., p. 5.

16 See *Kiichiro Ishida and the Sydney Camera Circle 1920s–1940s*, ed. Yuri Mitsuda, exhibition catalogue, Museum of Sydney, 2003.

17 See ed. Deborah Edwards, *The Roy de Maistre Mural Room*, Art Gallery of New South Wales, Sydney, 1993; see also Heather Johnson, *Roy de Maistre: The English Years, 1930–1968*, Craftsman House, Sydney, 1995, p. 59.

18 On the Griffins, see Broinowski, *Yellow Lady*, pp. 38–9.

19 Ibid., p. 39.

20 Ibid., pp. 52–3.

21 On this, see *Art in Oceania: A New History*, eds. Peter Brunt and Nicholas Thomas, Thames & Hudson, London, 2012.

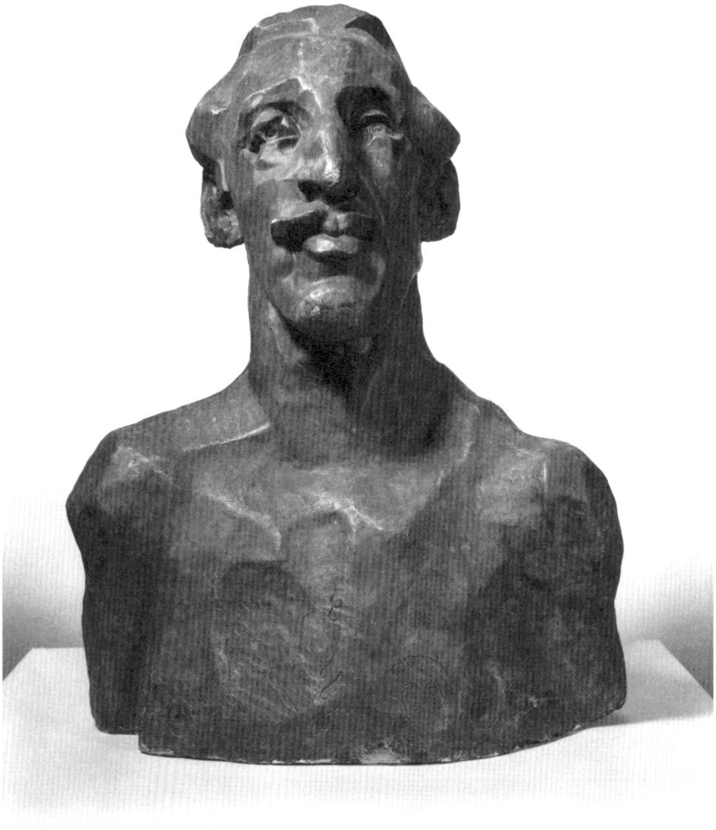

6.1 Henri Gaudier-Brzeska
Horace Brodzky, c. 1913

Another Australia
British-Australian Art 1880–1970

What follows is a proposal for a show, an alternative or complement to the *Australia* exhibition held at the Royal Academy in London in 2013. It was an exhibition that took the supposedly unique landscape of Australia as its guiding curatorial principle. It was a landscape exhibition disguised as a national one, or perhaps a national exhibition disguised as a landscape one.[1] As the catalogue for the exhibition makes clear, *Australia* stands at the end of a line that began in 1898 with the first 'Australian' exhibition at the Grafton Galleries in London. This *Exhibition of Australian Art* in London was followed by a long series of similar exhibitions—similar in that they involved many of the same artists, as indeed this most recent version does—a series that arguably reached its climax with *Recent Australian Painting* at the Whitechapel in 1961 and *Australian Painting* at the Tate Gallery in 1963. All of these exhibitions were an attempt to represent, or rather create, a national Australian art for an overseas audience. And they have succeeded in implanting 'Australian' imagery as firmly in British consciousness—their stated intention and justification—as they have in our own. Indeed, it would be a significant study to trace the invention of Australian art as a response to the felt necessity to present ourselves to others. Have we not written our art history as though it were to be read by someone outside Australia? Have we not in effect looked at ourselves as though through the eyes of another: wanting to attract their attention, seeking to be more distinctive, more identifiable, more idiosyncratic, than we actually are? For truly, we are tempted to ask, does the category of Australian art exist anywhere but in these shows destined for overseas with the word 'Australian' inscribed in their titles?

All of this is perhaps why the 2013 exhibition met with such condescension. Because, ultimately, it repeated the same story. Because Australian art history insists on presenting itself in a way already known to the outside. This 'Australia', we would suggest, is not the same Australia that would be presented, for example, in New York. Because Australia and England have always traded expectations, which is also to say blind spots. They have both always preferred stereotypes to self-reflection or to thinking how they represent themselves to their narcissistic partner. We have always arranged ourselves for the eyes of Britain, knowing secretly that this is not the real us. Hence the permanent unease in our relationship, a sort of passive-aggressivity, alternating between a colonial cringe and assertions of independence. But if Shaun Gladwell, channelling both Ned Kelly and Mad Max, turned his back on his British audience in the show, as he did in his video in the exhibition, *Approach to Mundi Mundi* (2007), it was only because he was assured he was being watched by them. This is the whole 'bad faith' of Australian difference or exoticism, all the way from the first images of Indigenous people through to Clive James. It is performed only to gain the approval or recognition of the establishment it would otherwise seek to contest. Is not our dry red desert ultimately the same as their green and pleasant British land? Or, indeed, because it is always a matter of a mutual and mutually reinforcing blindness, is not their green and pleasant land—say, the Midsomer of *Midsomer Murders*—a version of our dusty red desert, say, Boney's Centralia?

The question for us, writing this today, is how to refuse this? It is a question that no Australian art show put on in Britain has yet asked itself. But, for us, it would not be by emphasising our difference or distance. It would, paradoxically, be by emphasising our sameness and proximity. It would be the history not of Australian artists working in an exotic otherness on the other side of the earth, but of Australians already in Britain, indistinguishable from those around them. For whom London is the end of the earth—except that they are already there. And once there making not Australian but British art. Indeed, we would say that British art is ultimately not possible without Australians. Now, clearly, this position is somewhat satirical, along the lines of *Gulliver's Travels*—and we might suggest, as is the case with *Gulliver's Travels*, that satire is a response to colonisation or to the great European empires opening up and claiming the world. For, if parody is the discovery of small differences beneath the same, then satire is the putting together of what appears different, so that we become aware of the hidden affinities between them. A great Australian satire in the Swiftian mode is undoubtedly Bernard Smith's *European Vision and the South Pacific*, which famously looks at Europe through foreign eyes. But so also is the Australasian satirist John Clarke's *The Even More Complete Book of Australian Verse*, which precisely begins from the conceit that all the great British poets were in fact Australian. Thus we have Warren Keats and Walter Burley Yeats, Very Manly Hopkins, Sir Don Betjeman and Sylvia Blath, the conclusion of whose 'Self Defence', obviously a version of the real Sylvia Plath's 'Daddy', we cannot resist quoting: 'Big brute fatso bastard / Still bugger bum fuck poos, / Daddy, Daddy, I'm through, Hello? / Germaine I can hardly hear you, / This is a very bad line'.[2]

Accordingly, what we offer here is not so much a criticism of the *Australia* show, but a *satire* of it. It is a satire that, as always, puts together two terms usually held apart: Australia and Britain. For, on the one hand, the artists we include are part of British art and, on the other, the exhibition we propose is still called *Australia*. And this is done, as also with satire, not to suggest a recognisable difference from the usual Australian shows, but to point to the indiscernible condition for them. To make this lack of differentiation even more apparent, we attempt to replicate the structure of the *Australia* show, with the same thematic rooms, the same chronological account of Australian (or perhaps British-Australian) art. Ultimately our point would be, as with all satire, to demonstrate that our inversion is not necessary, that there is no need to put on such an exhibition of British-Australian art, because this is actually the case for every apparently British and Australian art show. As we will make clear, virtually every British and Australian art exhibition that has attempted to point to the unique and irreconcilable quality of each country's art has included an artist from the other place. As satire always demonstrates, the world—we might say especially the art world—is already its own satire. And, furthermore, we would even admit the historical unnecessariness of our little exercise here by pointing to a series of exhibitions curated in London by the great early twentieth-century Australian art critic Edith Fry, *Australian Artists in Europe*, held at the Faculty of Arts Gallery in 1924, and *Australian Art Exhibition*, held at the Spring Gardens Gallery in 1925, which were both directed against Sydney Ure Smith's earlier and nationalist *Exhibition of Australian Art*, held at the Royal Academy in 1923, and evidenced the true and continuing history of Australian artists working in Britain and Europe from at least the early twentieth century on.

Entrance—Anthony Martin Fernando

So here, without further ado—in all of its unnecessariness—is our version of another exhibition in London, also called *Australia*. Room by room, artist by artist. But how to begin? The *Australia* show began with a room of Aboriginal art, in all of its ultimate otherness and exoticism. After all, despite existing long before the concept of Australia, what could be more uniquely 'Australian' than Aboriginal art? Anything more distant and unknowable? And, therefore, anything more attractive to the Western (British) eye? Except that Aborignal art and culture do not exist entirely outside of Britain. So we refuse this initial gesture of the *Australia* show, including Aboriginal art only at the end. Instead, at the entrance, before we enter the main galleries, a certain figure haunts our exhibition, lingering at its borders: Anthony Martin Fernando, a Dharug man, Sydney-born, who, suggests historian Fiona Paisley, might even have been descended from John Martin, an African-American convict on the First Fleet, who had several children with Dharug women. Where might Fernando have been seen in London in the 1920s? He was a regular speaker, the so-called lone protester, at Hyde Park. And he would stand outside Australia House on the Strand, wearing a coat pinned all over with toy skeletons, where he explained to passers-by: 'This is all Australia has left of my people'.[3] Here we show him in Sikh-Australian Raj Nagi's painting *Portrait of Anthony Martin Fernando* (2007), which does not show his face. We place him where we do in our exhibition because he represents more than simply an 'Australian' problem. Rather, his multicultural background reminds us of the way that Britain has always been part of the definition of 'Aboriginal', just as the skeletons on his coat also remind us of the presence of Indigenous people (and Aboriginal art, artefacts and, more tragically still, bodies) in Britain. As art historian Paul Wood argues, the category of the 'indigenous' is an essential part of British art and culture, without which the British would not be 'British'.[4]

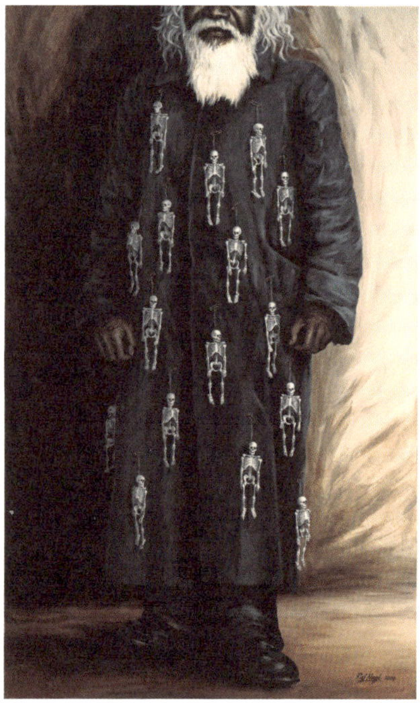

6.2 Raj Nagi
Portrait of Anthony Martin Fernando, 2007

Rooms 1 and 2—The Royal Academy and the Royal Art Societies

The Royal Academy is Englishness invented in an artistic way with its founding through the personal act of George II in 1768 and its first president in Sir Joshua Reynolds. It was started to raise the status of the professional artist and to make a permanent place for the exhibition of art, but inseparably it was intended to foster a 'national' school of art. Consider nevertheless how many Australians contributed to this project of a national art. A partial listing of the Australians who exhibited at the Royal Academy or studied at its schools, including before their arrival in Australia, would include, chronologically arranged: in the nineteenth century, William Dexter, Nicholas Chevalier, Margaret Thomas, Robert Dowling, William Strutt, Julian Ashton, Mortimer Menpes, Tom Roberts, Charles Douglas Richardson, Bertram Mackennal, Rupert Bunny, Arthur Merric Boyd, Emma Minnie Boyd, John Longstaff, Aby Altson, Arthur Streeton and David Davies; by the end of World War I, Emanuel Phillips Fox, George Coates, Harold Parker, BE Minns, Will Ashton, Bessie Gibson, George Lambert, Richard Hayley Lever, Albert Henry Fullwood, Thea Proctor, James Quinn, George Bell, Bess Norriss Tait, Grace Joel, Jessie Traill, Clewin Harcourt, Fred Leist, Charles Bryant, Penleigh Boyd, Fairlie Cunningham, Agnes Goodsir, Sydney Long, Norman Carter, Margaret Preston, Gladys Reynell, Christina Asquith Baker, Charles Web Gilbert, Eva Benson, Dora Meeson and Blamire Young; between the wars, Charles Wheeler, Elioth Gruner, Hans Heysen, Marion Jones, Daniel Meyer Altson, Hilda Rix Nicholas, John Eldershaw, WB McInnes, Winifred Honey, Daryl Lindsay and AME Bale; and, even after World War II, Grace Cossington Smith and Sidney Nolan.

All of the Australians listed above (and we apologise for the listiness of our essay, but we do want to point out the extent to which Australian artists working in a range of styles are ingrained in British art history) exhibited with the RA—a matter of juried selection. Many more also studied at its associated Royal Academy schools, but did not exhibit in the RA. Portia Geach, for instance, the first Australian to win a scholarship to study there in 1896, did not participate in the RA's exhibitions. Certainly, from the 1860s until post–World War II, there was a near-uninterrupted line of Australian artists who trained at the RA. Their presence gained momentum in the 1890s, accelerated in the first decade of the new century and peaked in the decades before and after World War I. And these Australians were not just painters, but made important contributions to sculpture and miniatures, and women were represented almost equally with men. (There is undoubtedly a utopian 'satirical' aspect to this royally decreed kingdom.) In other words, the years after 1889 and the invention of Australian art are characterised by an outpouring of Australians to London, and more generally around the globe. Indeed, it might even be said that the history of Australian art between 1900 and 1915 took place largely on the walls of European art galleries and museums, so little of it was shown here. But the dominant accounts of our art have not recognised this, and the occlusion of this history of Australian art at the RA until this proposed exhibition tells us that this expatriate condition of Australian art has largely been rendered invisible, even in so visible a place as the RA.[5] (And, of course, we would want to put on our exhibition at the RA too.) Let us just look here in a little more detail at four artists from our list, none of whom fit the mould of the 2013 edition of *Australia*, but who each represent a certain kind of British-Australianness.

In rooms one and two of our proposed exhibition, we have the Adelaide painter and etcher Mortimer Menpes, who first exhibited in London in 1880, was a friend to James McNeill Whistler, stood godfather to Oscar Wilde's son, and who through his press helped popularise Orientalism in Britain. We have also the Melbourne artist Bertram Mackennal, who was the first Australian to be knighted for art and was elected an associate of the Royal Academy in 1909 and a full member in 1922. As a sculptor, he was a symbolist, then part of the New Sculpture movement. We have George Lambert, who was elected an associate in 1922, the first Australian painter so chosen, but who had decided to return to Australia permanently the year

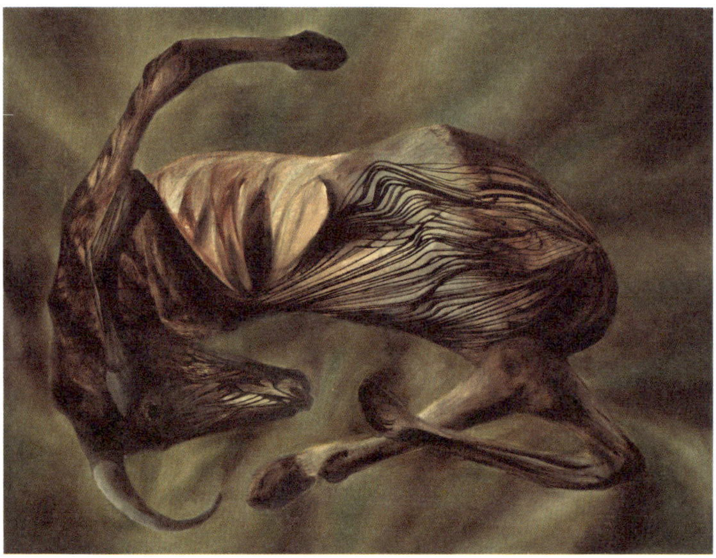

6.3 Sidney Nolan
Carcass, 1953

before to capitalise on his fame and where he lent support to the emergent 'modern' movement. We have as well the Melbourne artist Sidney Nolan, a war deserter who in the 1950s began a series of paintings of Gallipoli, moved permanently to Britain in 1953 and was once filmed watching on at an Anzac Day march, and who, surprisingly for an artist so identified with outlaws and bushrangers, received his Commander of the British Empire in 1963, was knighted in 1981 and two years later towards the end of his life became a member, alongside Henry Moore, Ben Nicholson and Lucian Freud, of the British monarch's Order of Merit, which is limited to twenty-four living people. We include here his *Carcass* from 1953, a few years before his 1957 Whitechapel Gallery show, which was widely regarded as the greatest success of an Australian artist in England up until that time. Indeed, as evidenced by the choice of Nolan's *Ned Kelly in the desert* for its catalogue cover, the real source for the 2013 *Australia* was the alien, desolate Australia that Nolan invented fifty-six years earlier for that exhibition.

To display the work of the aforementioned artists in these rooms would be to show the work of Australians who were not seen as exhibiting an irreconcilable 'Australianness' but rather were sanctioned by their peers as part of an official British art scene. They were included in the Royal Academy, studied at the Royal Academy schools and exhibited with the Royal Institute of Painters in Oils, the Royal Drawing Society, the Royal Society of British Sculptors, the Royal British Colonial Society of Artists, the Royal Society of British Artists, the Royal Society of Portrait Painters, the Royal Watercolour Society, the Royal Miniaturist Society, the Royal Scottish Academy, the Royal Glasgow Institute, the Scottish Society of Artists, the Society of Mural Decorators and Painters in Tempera, the Society of Animal Painters, the International Society of Sculptors and Painters and Gravers and the so-called Modern Society of Portrait Painters (Lambert and Gerald Kelly were foundation members). And insofar as these artists worked across all genres, we would feature portraits by John Longstaff, Emanuel Phillips Fox, George Coates, James Quinn and Agnes Goodsir; sculptures by Harold Parker, Eva Benson and Charles Webb; miniatures by Bess Tait; landscapes by Richard Hayley Lever, Hilda Rix Nicholas, David Davies and Penleigh Boyd; and still lives by Margaret Preston and Gladys Reynell.

Room 3—The New English Art Club

Moving through twentieth-century British art history, we come to the Australian artists who participated in the New English Art Club (NEAC), which was founded in 1886 by artists who had been rejected by the Royal Academy and who were influenced by French impressionism, including George Clausen, Stanhope Forbes, Walter Sickert and Philip Steer. The poet and essayist Alice Meynell outlined its aims as 'following, in England, the methods being practised in France—the vivid and simple study of nature'[6] or, as art historian Simon Watney describes it, the NEAC was 'more or less the Slade's unofficial shop window to the world'.[7] But the NEAC proved to be not that 'modern', and in 1889 Steer and Sickert led a rebel group in the Club that staged the group exhibition *London Impressionists*—and it is undoubtedly interesting in this context that English impressionism went public in exactly the same year as the Australian version did in the *9 by 5 Impression Exhibition* in Melbourne. Nonetheless, the NEAC's annual exhibitions until at least 1910 continued, in the words of its chronicler Kenneth McConkey, to 'argue the case for modern art, in the only significant opposition [to the Royal Academy]'.[8] Artists who showed and were associated with the NEAC include Whistler, Augustus and Gwen John, Henry Tonks, William Rothenstein, Roger Fry, Lucien Pissarro, Bernard Meninsky, Paul Nash and Mark Gertler—in other words, the origins of Australia's British modernism.

To the extent that the NEAC was reformist, it looked to France. Thus it looked outwards to impressionism and post-impressionism, and many of its members had Continental connections. It is in this context that Charles Conder, who was elected to the NEAC in 1891, the same year he was elected associate of

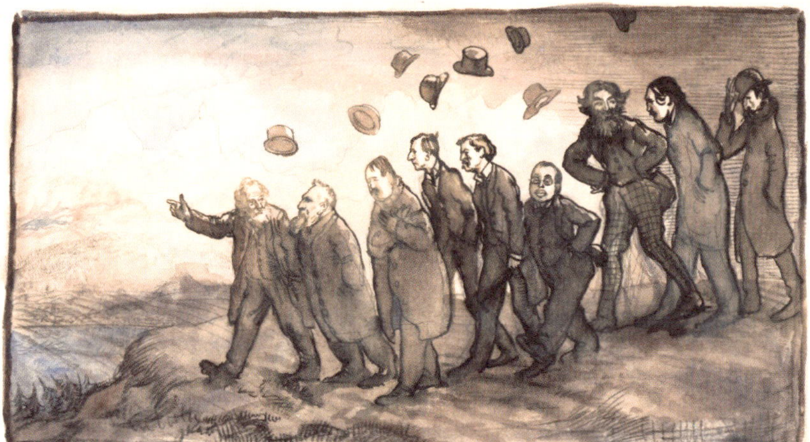

6.4 William Orpen
Group associated with the New English Art Club, c. 1904

the New Salon in Paris, is the central Australian for us in this room (see Conder, second from the right in Orpen's drawing, fig. 6.4). Important later members such as Meninsky and Gertler, who lectured at the Westminster School of Art in London from the 1910s until the 1940s, would become foundational teachers for a generation of Australian artists immediately before and after World War I, as we will see. The NEAC is usually understood as testament to the insufficiency of English art at this point because it was only by looking to France that British modernism was born. However, it was the Tasmanian Derwent Lees—who showed continuously with the NEAC from 1911 until 1919—who taught not only Meninsky and Gertler but also Stanley Spencer and David Bomberg at the Slade School, and who therefore helped transform postwar British painting. Lees was even briefly a member of that very Bloomsbury group, the Friday Club.

In this room we also feature the work of the Australians Bernard Hall, who, before emigrating, showed in the inaugural exhibition of the NEAC; John Russell, who showed in 1891; Miles Evergood, Margaret Preston and George Bell, who showed with the NEAC during the teens; and Max Martin, Miguel Mackinlay and Vida Lahey, who all showed in the 1920s. We would also include—for our British-Australian history precisely wants to see similarities between Australia and the rest of the world—the New Zealanders Frances Hodgkins and Raymond McIntyre, who both showed in 1911. Interestingly, the Heidelberg School stalwart Arthur Streeton always wanted but failed to become a member. As Streeton rather poignantly wrote to Roberts that same year:

> I have been down this summer painting his [Steer's] favourite subject and painting it in my own way and I begin to feel I am alright. They'll have to accept me yet.[9]

Consider his *Corfe Castle* (1907), now held at the National Gallery of Victoria, and compare it to NEAC heavyweight Steer's version of the same subject. Or think of his earlier *Chepstowe Castle, Wye Valley* (1902), now held at the Art Gallery of New South Wales, and compare it again to Steer's version. So much for the Australian impressionists embodying some distinctive idea of Australianness.

Room 4—The Artist Colonies at Newlyn and St Ives

Britain's first art colony, the Newlyn school, was established near Land's End on the tip of the Cornish coast in the early 1880s and was soon to be followed by another just down the road at St Ives in 1885. As the Bendigo Art Gallery's

2012 exhibition *Wild Colonials* pointed out, these were important places in the construction in British modernism, and the secreting of Australian artists in it.[10] Reproducing the logic of the artist colonies at Étaples and Concarneau in France, these small fishing villages provided cheap studios and an abundance, for Britain, of that newly discovered holy grail, natural light.

By 1884 there were as many as twenty-seven artists resident in the small fishing village at Newlyn. In that year Mortimer Menpes worked there, together with Walter Sickert and James McNeill Whistler; and two of its founding artists, Thomas Cooper Gotch (another co-founder of the NEAC) and his wife Caroline Yeats, held a shared exhibition in Melbourne in 1884.[11] Following the success of the Anglo-Australian Society exhibitions that began in 1885, Cornish subjects were as popular with the Australian public as they were with the acquisition committees of our state galleries. Between 1889 and 1892, for example, the AGNSW bought the work of five West Country artists, including the work of its leading lights, Stanhope and Elizabeth Forbes.

The St Ives artist colony was from the beginning, as all coastal artist colonies are, international in character. Its leaders, English artist Henry Harewood Robinson and his Irish wife, Dorethea Robinson (née Webb), were joined by friends

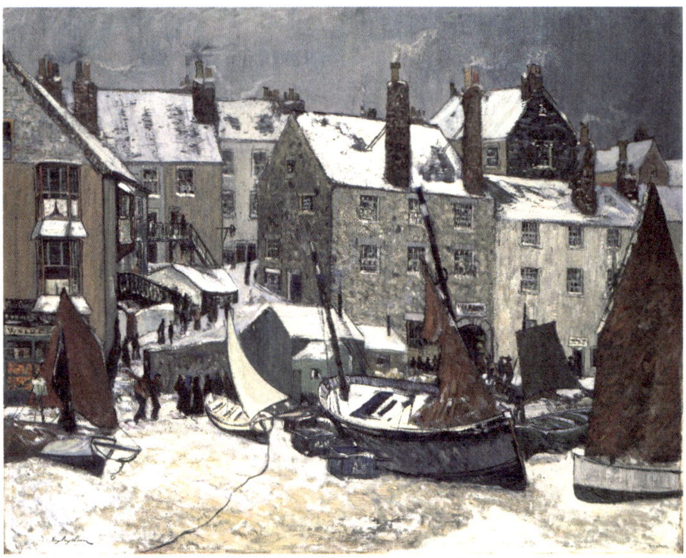

6.5 Richard Hayley Lever
Winter, St Ives, c. 1914

from their Concarneau days, the Americans Edward and Vesta Simmons, Howard Butler and Frank Chadwick and his Swedish wife Emma Lowstadt, as well as their fellow Scandinavian Anders Zorn. And here is just a partial list of the Australian and New Zealand artists who worked or studied at either the Newlyn or St Ives art colonies: Dorothy Richmond, Richard Hayley Lever, Will Ashton, Charles Bryant, Hans Heysen, Arthur Burgess, Charles Conder, David Davies, William Osborne, Emanuel Phillips Fox, George Bell, George Lambert, Mortimer Menpes, Edith Fry, Owen Merton and Frances Hodgkins.

Perhaps the story of Hayley Lever is the most telling among them, as artist colonies tend to be migratory—everyone comes from somewhere, but will almost inevitably then go somewhere else—and it is his work that we present in this room. Leaving Adelaide in 1899, Hayley Lever headed for St Ives, where at James Ashton's suggestion he studied at the Cornish School of Landscape, Figure and Sea Painting with the influential teacher and painter Julius Olsson, and with Algernon Talmage.[12] (It is interesting to remember that in 1888 Olsson and the Melbourne-born English painter Louis Grier opened a painting school in St Ives, and that Grier returned to Australia in 1892 where he held an exhibition of his work at the Athenaeum Gallery in Melbourne.) Hayley Lever, a member of the St Ives Art Club, sent his work from Cornwall to the NEAC, the RA and the Salons of Paris as well as to numerous other associations and exhibitions, and travelled regularly to London and France and made painting trips there with artists including Frank Brangwyn. Before he left finally in 1914 for New York, where his career would blossom and he would become by some margin Australia's most represented artist in American institutions, at St Ives Hayley Lever 'could rightly be called the most innovative artist working in the colony in this period' with his painterly post-impressionism.[13]

But here we might recall the story of the New Zealand artists in Cornwall, in particular Frances Hodgkins, and it is her work we would also present in this room. In 1902, during her first trip to Europe, she rented a studio in Penzance and participated in her first exhibition in Britain when she took part in the annual show of the Newlyn artists. Hodgkins returned permanently to Europe in 1906 and moved between Italy, England, the Netherlands and France, where she became the first female teacher at Académie Colarossi in Paris and opened her School for Watercolour there in 1911. At the end of that year she accompanied an exhibition of her work through Australia and New Zealand and on her return to England settled in St Ives in 1914. After the war she returned to her nomadic ways, but was living in Manchester by 1925, from where she established her reputation. By the early 1930s she was one of Britain's leading modernists, having shown with the Seven and Five Society since 1929 and having been invited to be a founding member of Unit 1, which she declined. She died in 1947, the year after her retrospective at

Lefevre Gallery in London, an acknowledged and celebrated 'English' artist, her fame cemented in the following year by the publication of the monograph *Frances Hodgkins* by Myfanwy Evans, part of the popular Penguin Modern Art series.[14] It would be at least four decades before New Zealand art history—just as parochial as Australia's—realised what it had and claimed her as a New Zealander.

Room 5—The Allied Artists Association, the London Group, and the Seven and Five Society

Founded in 1908 by art critic Frank Rutter, the Allied Artists Association (AAA) held its inaugural exhibition that year at the Royal Albert Hall. It self-consciously drew on the model of the Salon des Indépendents in Paris and the various secessionist movements around Europe, and its members included Sickert, Spencer Gore, Harold Gilman, Lucien Pissarro, Augustus John and the Australians John Russell (1908, 1909) and George Bell (also 1908 and 1909). The paintings in this room show us that Australian artists were able to exploit both the official and unofficial channels of recognition that operated in London before World War I.

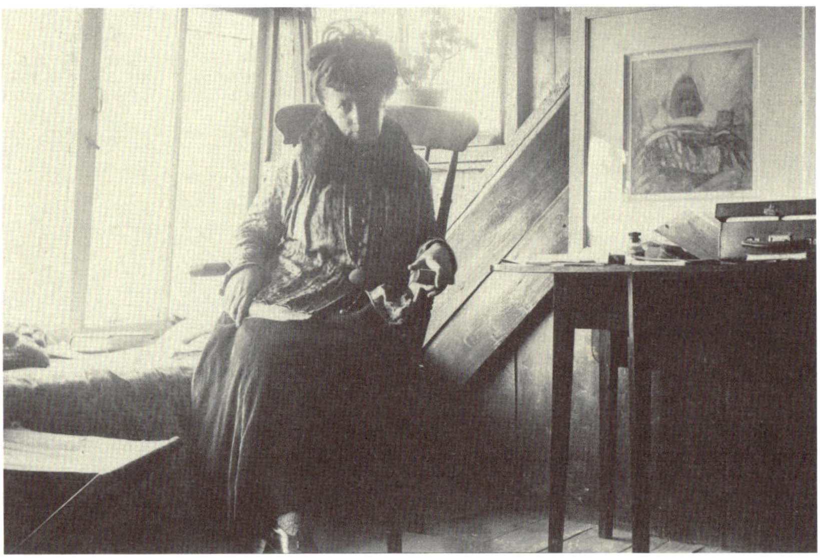

6.6 Frances Hodgkins in the Wharf Studio, St Ives, Cornwall, 1918

Emerging from the AAA in 1911, the Camden Town Group was formed with Spencer Gore as president. Its members included all of the artists above, as well as JD Innes, Wyndham Lewis and Duncan Grant. Sometimes called the 'English post-impressionists', they held two exhibitions, in 1911 and 1912, and included Henry Lamb among their number. Lamb would admittedly be 'Australian' only in a wider definition of what the term could mean, having been born but not having trained here. He was certainly listed until recently exclusively as British in the Queensland Art Gallery's small collection of Camden Town Group paintings, but the aperture is widening and he is now listed as 'British/Australian'.

The Camden Town Group in turn gave way to the London Group in 1913. The London Group came about through the merging of the Camden Town Group with other smaller groups, including some of the Vorticists. It was anti–Royal Academy and pro-France. After World War I, its importance diminished as it became a kind of halfway house, although it regained energy in the 1920s, and undoubtedly this still-running institution's golden years were the decades between the wars. Its founding members included Lamb, Wyndham Lewis, Harold Gilman, Jacob Epstein and Henri Gaudier-Brzeska. By the 1920s, they had been joined, for instance, by Edward Wadsworth, Stanley Spencer, Roger Fry, Bomberg, Gertler and Meninsky. The first Australian to join was Horace Brodzky in 1914, followed by Sydney artist JW Power in 1923. Frances Hodgkins joined in 1940, by which time its members included Eileen Agar, Barbara Hepworth, Henry Moore, Graham Sutherland and Victor Pasmore. The Australian expatriate Roy de Maistre joined after the war in 1945, the soon-to-be Australian immigrant Inge King in 1948, and Hobart-born sculptor Oliffe Richmond in the mid-1950s. Littered with Australians, it is the London Group that might be said to have institutionalised modernism in England between the wars.

The Seven and Five Society, notionally made up of seven painters and five sculptors, was formed in 1919. It positioned itself against Fry and the Bloomsbury Circle in wanting to be more 'forceful' and 'up-to-date', with its members re-elected each year. JW Power was a member in 1922 and 1923, and by the end of the 1920s and beginning of the 1930s its bias was towards abstraction. By 1935 the society was wholly abstract and renamed 'The Seven and Five Abstract Group', and in that year held the first exhibition entirely of abstract art in England.

Christchurch-born Len Lye eventually left Sydney, where he was living, for London in 1926, where he was almost immediately elected to the Seven and Five, and exhibited with them well into the 1930s. Lye's well-known animated film *Tusalava* (1929), which he first showed at the London Film Society, drew heavily on the Indigenous and Pacific art he had studied at the Australian Museum and was accompanied by an original musical score by his Sydney friend the composer Jack Ellitt. In 1935, Lye made *A colour box*, the world's first direct film, which was sound edited by Ellitt and produced by hand-painting the film strip itself, and again employing an Oceanic art–derived vocabulary of lines and stripes.[15] In this room devoted to the London Group among others, it is Lye's films we would feature; and we would also include paintings by Power, de Maistre and the New Zealanders (this other *Australia* is in fact Australasian) Raymond McIntyre and Frances Hodgkins, as well as sculpture by Inge King and Oliffe Richmond.

Rooms 6 and 7—The Grosvenor School, the Westminster Art School and Ozenfant's Academy of Fine Art

Bernard Meninsky, Mark Gertler and Amédée Ozenfant are little-known sources of Australia's modernism, but each was influential and formative on the work of numerous Australian artists. Meninsky and Gertler taught at the Grosvenor and Westminster art schools in London, which became leading generators of British inter-war modernism in large part through their efforts. In a sense, the schools fulfilled the same role as the Slade had in Edwardian England. The Grosvenor School in Pimlico was founded in 1925 by printmakers and linocut artists Claude Flight, Iain MacNab, Cyril Power and Sybil Andrews. It was always international in scope, with numerous Australians studying alongside, for example, the Swiss printmaker Lill Tschudi. The Westminster School in central London came about in its modern form as the result of a merger with the Westminster Technical Institute in 1904. It is where Norah Simpson studied with Harold Gilman and Charles Ginner, from whom it was said she first heard about modern art, leading her to Paris and to collect reproductions of Cézanne et al., and in this way on her return to Sydney in 1913 she famously though erroneously is said to have 'introduced modern art to this country'.[16] But it was in the 1930s that the Westminster School was at its most progressive, incorporating by that time many of England's leading modernist artists, who had studied at the same time as Simpson, even beside her in the same classes.

It is largely in these inter-war years that Australian students sought to study with Flight, MacNab and Cyril Power at the Grosvenor School, with Gertler or Meninsky at the Westminster School, or even with the uprooted Purist Ozenfant at his atelier school in London in the late 1930s. These artist-teachers with roots in Scotland, France, Poland and the Ukraine, as well as in England, are foundational for English art, but they are also important for Australian modernism (both in England and back in Australia). And their teaching should be recognised for its international scope. Like the French ateliers of the turn of the century, English art schools of the 1930s, as today, brought together students from all around the world, including Australia.

The first of our rooms here belongs to the Grosvenor School, and it features the prints of Dorrit Black, Ethel Spowers, Eveline Syme, Frank Weitzel and Horace Brodzky. Black had lived with Grace Crowley and Anne Dangar in Sydney before heading to London, where she studied at the Grosvenor and was taught by Flight. Together with Crowley, she later studied with André Lhote and Albert Gleizes in Paris before returning to Sydney, where in 1932 she set up the Modern Art Centre (MAC), at which Crowley later also taught. Besides functioning as an exhibition space, the MAC also conducted art classes and operated as a retail outlet for ceramics and other *objets d'art*. The opening of the MAC was a significant occasion and its first show, *Exhibition of Progressive Art*, was launched by educator and advocate of modernism Ethel Anderson, and included works by Syme, Roland Wakelin, Eleonore Lange, Ralph Balson and Black herself. Later the MAC put on both Crowley's and Balson's first solo exhibitions, as well as a memorial exhibition dedicated to New Zealand artist and Flight associate Frank Weitzel, who died in England of tetanus in 1932 aged twenty-six. However, financial pressures caused by the Depression and the death of Black's father led to its closure in 1933. Black eventually returned to her home town, Adelaide, where she became a foundational figure in that city's modernism and one of Australia's pre-eminent linocut artists.

Ethel Spowers, a National Gallery School graduate, was first shown the work of Flight by Eveline Syme in 1928, and together a few months later they enrolled in his class at the Grosvenor School. In 1932 the pair returned to Australia, where they propagated Flight's ideas through their teaching, collecting and work, and thus made the Grosvenor School truly international. (Indeed, the second-last exhibition of Grosvenor School linocuts was held in Melbourne in 1937.) Black, Syme and Spowers all participated in the first *Exhibition of British Linocuts* in 1929 at the Redfern Gallery in London, and in the year of their return the threesome held their joint *Linocut Exhibition* at the Everyman Library in Melbourne. And, as we say, Australia itself was an essential centre for the promotion of the Grosvenor School and its ideas. Indeed, it is important to mark the contributions that Australian and New Zealand artists have made to British linocuts and woodcuts more generally, for example, the enthusiastic proto-modernists Sydney-born Gladys Owen and Dunedin-born Maud Sherwood, who both worked in England between and through the wars. In terms of British printmaking, they join a line begun by Mortimer Menpes, who was famous for his etchings and press at the turn of the century, and continued after World War I by Royal Academy–trained Henry Rayner, who is said to have produced the largest body of drypoint etchings by any twentieth-century artist (as well as the first informal portrait of a member of the British royal family), and by Horace Brodzky, whose printmaking also gained him renown before the war. Like Black, Spowers and Syme, Brodzky participated (as British, naturally) in the first *Exhibition of British Linocuts* and was indeed the first artist in Britain to make a linocut, and thus could be seen to be the very origin of the so-called British Linocut School.

For its part, the Westminster School, represented in our second room, also attracted an international cohort of students, including many Australians, in particular to Gertler and Meninsky, who were themselves outsiders of sorts in British art. Both, as we say, had been students of Derwent Lees at the Slade around 1910 and perhaps had a certain affinity with Australians. We begin with Vera Blackburn, who, after studying with Thea Proctor and Adelaide Perry in Australia, travelled to England in 1937 following the death of her mother, where she studied at the Westminster School for two years with Gertler and Meninsky. While there she made friends with Jean Bellette and her husband Paul Haefliger, who were also studying with both artists—Bellette's desolate landscapes of Hill End in western New South Wales are often seen in terms of their Merioola-style neoclassicism (along with Justin O'Brien and Jeffrey Smart), but in fact they come just as much from Gertler's emphatic edge and what has been called Meninsky's 'structuralism' and sense of composition.[17] And we see the same influence also on Nora Heysen, whom we also take away from the assumed influence of her father and find in her work the brightness of Gertler's colour and Meninsky's concern for underlying structure.

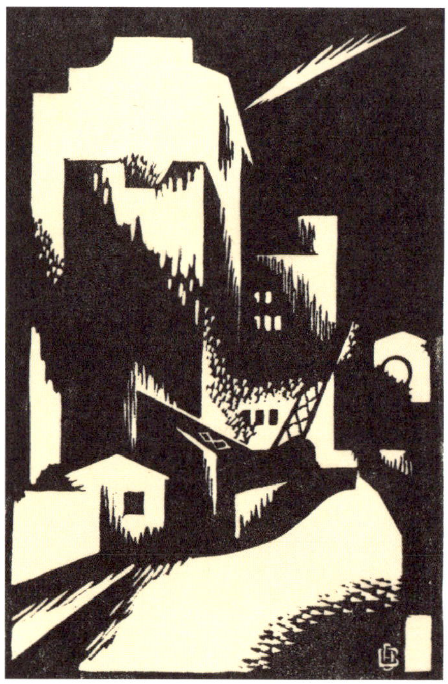

6.7 Dorrit Black
Nocturne, Wynyard Square, 1932

Finally, in this room we look at the French artist Amédée Ozenfant's Academy of Fine Art, which opened in London in 1936 and relocated soon after to New York. The artist couple we present here is Eric Wilson and Jean Appleton, who both attended Ozenfant's atelier school in 1938, as did Crowley for a week in 1929 when it was still in Paris. Wilson had earlier studied at the Westminster School with Gertler and Meninsky, where he met his life-partner Appleton (both were also influenced by Elmslie Owen's abstract composition class). Bernard Smith for his part claimed Wilson as the maker of the first abstract work to be collected by an Australian gallery when it was acquired in 1946 by the Art Gallery of New South Wales, but *Abstract—The kitchen stove* (1943) is plainly nothing more than a late-cubist still life with a cat. Appleton, on the other hand, was never more radical than when she was in London in 1937, where she painted her truly abstract post-Purist *Painting IX*.

And beside the paintings of Blackburn, Bellette, Haefliger, Wilson and Appleton, we would hang the work of those artists who studied at the Grosvenor School with MacNab, including Gladys Owen, Helen Stewart, Alison Rehfisch, George Bell, Peter Purves Smith, Nutter Buzacott, Russell Drysdale and Vincent Brown; as well as others who studied with either Gertler or Meninsky in the 1930s, including Nora Heysen, Amie Kingston, Vera Blackburn, Carl Plate and

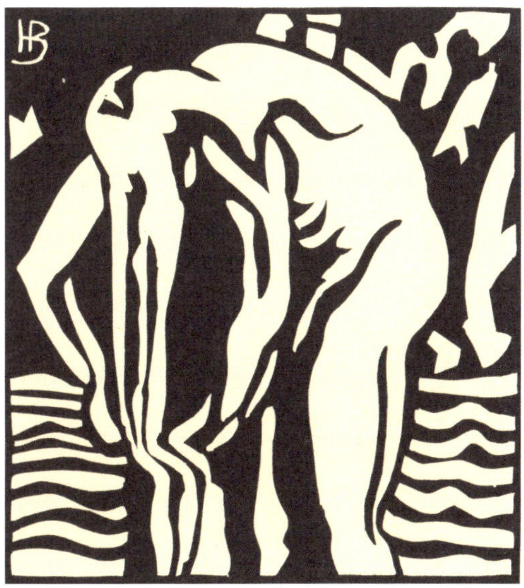

6.8 Horace Brodzky
Expulsion, 1914

John Passmore. None of these artists could have featured in *Australia*, chiefly because they were not first of all landscape painters and because their work has a psychological dimension and tends to look inwards and not outwards.

Room 8—Diasporic and Expatriate Modernism in 1930s London: Roy de Maistre, Francis Bacon, Douglas Cooper and Patrick White

It is not just Australian or even Australasian artists, however, who play a role in English culture. It is also writers (Ngaio Marsh), art historians (Jack Lindsay), collectors (Lady de Chair), gallery directors (Rex Nan Kivell) and critics (Raymond McIntyre). And this room is given over not just to the work of an artist (Roy de Maistre), but also to the circle he moved in and the wider milieu of homosexual Australian men in London in the 1930s. We want to point out here that, if expatriatism has been buried in our history, even more so has been the notion of an Australian diaspora. Yet it can be shown to be the hidden link to so much of the history that we take to be self-explanatory. It is the kind of secret bond that lies behind the visible surface of our national and canonical histories. Let us start here with the obvious: the relationship between the Australian artist Roy de Maistre and perhaps the best-known British artist of the twentieth century, Francis Bacon. This connection has been the subject of increasing scholarly attention, most recently—although as much as anything it was for us a lost opportunity—in the 2013 exhibition *Francis Bacon: Five Decades* at the Art Gallery of New South Wales.[18] The indebtedness of Bacon to de Maistre, not only personally (it was de Maistre who encouraged the then–interior designer Bacon to become a painter) but also artistically, is becoming increasingly evident to art historians. The influence on Bacon's early work of such paintings of de Maistre's as *Francis Bacon's Queensbury Mews* (1930), with its mysterious figure hanging on the stairwell screen, and more particularly on his *Conflict* (1932), is well recognised. But the more profound connection between the two men is the recently discovered fact that Bacon's father (supposedly archetypically and repressively Irish-Catholic) was actually born in Adelaide. What brought these two men together was not just the not-at-all repressed fact that they both were queer, but the truly unspeakable fact that both were Australian.

This room, however, is dominated by the collection of the diasporic Australian Douglas Cooper, whose wealth was based on his family's colonial businesses, which included the distilling of gin and the transporting of gold to the Bank of England in nineteenth-century Australia. It was Cooper who introduced de Maistre to Freddy Mayor of the Mayor Gallery in London, which he part owned, from where de Maistre established his reputation as an English surrealist in the

1930s. (De Maistre was included, for instance, in the first edition of Herbert Read's influential 1932 primer *Art Now.*) Cooper had studied at Cambridge, Freiburg and the Sorbonne, spoke four languages fluently, and upon coming into his inheritance in 1932 decided to dedicate a third of the sum each year to the acquisition of the first generation of cubist work made between 1907 and 1914. In doing so, he stood against not only the market, but also Roger Fry and his post-impressionist taste-making. And he thereby established what his once-lover, the biographer and art critic John Richardson, justifiably called 'the finest collection of modern art in England'.[19] But profoundly anti-English himself—and what could be more Australian than that?—Cooper moved to France in 1938, and during the war served as an *ambulancier* and, because of his language skills and knowledge of art, as the war wound up became one of the 'monuments men', an interrogator of captured German officers with information regarding looted art. Eventually—for the military was not to know of his penchant for sado-masochism—he was relieved of his role because of what was euphemistically called his 'over-zealous' interrogation techniques. In the early 1950s, Cooper moved to Uzès in the south of France, where he commissioned Fernand Léger's *Les trapezistes* (1954), now part of the collection of the National Gallery of Australia, to hang in the stairwell of his château. In 1954

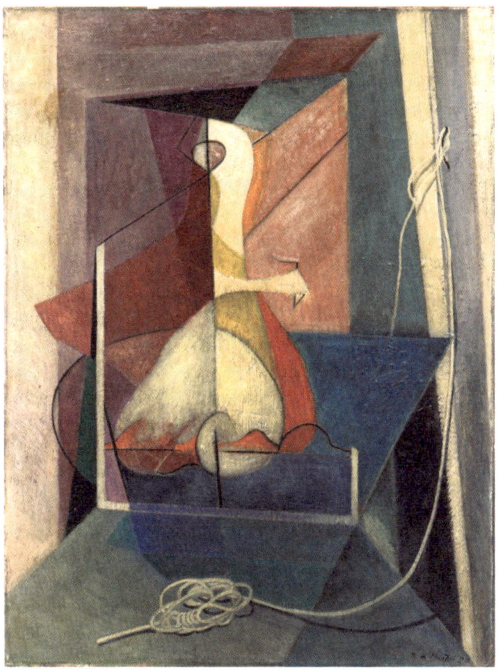

6.9 Roy de Maistre
Conflict, 1932

he also published the catalogue of the Courtauld collection, thus adding to the long list of books he had already published since the war dedicated to early cubist and modern art, including the catalogue raisonné of Gris as well as studies of Braque, Klee, Léger, Rousseau and Degas. (It is arguable that Cooper is the major postwar Anglophone art historian of cubism, introducing several generations of English-speaking students to the work of its artists.) In the mid-1950s, he conducted the so-called Tate Wars, during which he attempted to remove Sir John Rothenstein as the director of that flagship museum because, in his words, 'somebody had to stop those feeble hacks at the Tate Gallery from buying all that genteel British rubbish'.[20] The stand-off is alleged to have come to blows when Rothenstein attacked Cooper at an opening, and it was said by Rothenstein that he was sent a congratulatory telegram by no less than Winston Churchill, who had earlier crossed swords with Cooper following Cooper's attempts to recover works of art from a German dealer after the war. Thwarted at the time by Churchill, it was later revealed that before the war that same dealer had taught the British Prime Minister how to paint.

De Maistre was also the first love of Patrick White, who dedicated his first novel, *Happy Valley* (1939), to him. (Its modernism too was rooted in London, even though its actual setting was the Monaro region in southern New South

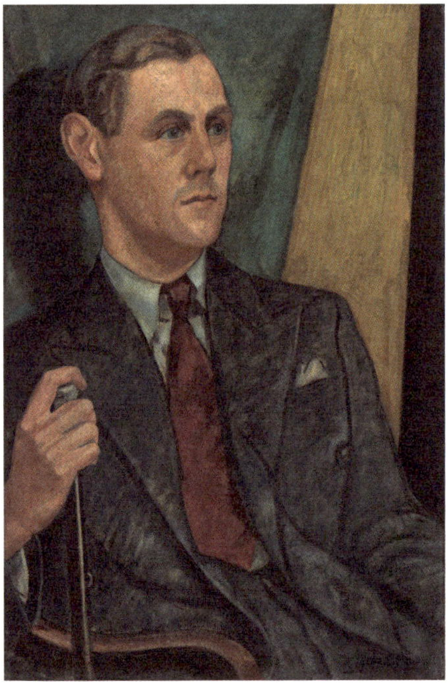

6.10 Roy de Maistre
Patrick White, 1939

Wales.) White too, like Cooper, once commissioned a table from Bacon, when he was a furniture designer. Indeed, White even had it copied when he returned to Australia after the war. The table is now the subject of a work by contemporary British artist Simon Starling, no doubt recognising the importance of White and this connection between Bacon, Cooper and de Maistre for British modernism. We simply cannot consider the history of a certain British modernism—a kind of renegade and anti-establishment modernism—before and after the war without taking into account the contribution of these four queer expatriate or diasporic Australians, a connection repressed not only by their sexuality but by the blindness of Australian art history to Australians in Britain and of British art history to the role played by artists of other nationalities in the creation of their own national art. In the end, Cooper after his death did bequeath much of his collection to the Tate Gallery; and it is not too much to say that the cubism we see on the walls of England's national gallery is the product of the workers of many nations who laboured on the Australian gold fields throughout the late nineteenth century to build up the Cooper family fortune. We are indeed looking at the Australian landscape up on the walls of the Tate Gallery today, alchemically transferred from a distant British colonial outpost to the epicentre of British collecting culture. Or as Cooper put it on the title page of a copy of van Gogh's *Letters to Émile Bernard* he once gave to de Maistre but with whom he had now fallen out: 'For Roi at Xmas time 1938. Tu m'as donné ta boue, j'en ai fait de l'or' or 'You gave me your dirt and I made it gold'.

Our room, then, would include paintings by de Maistre alongside Bacon's, as well as a selection of cubist work drawn from Cooper's gift to the Tate Gallery. We would also display White's copy of Bacon's desk, on which we would place his books besides Cooper's.

Room 9—The London Gallery and the Redfern Gallery

Surrealism also had a home in Britain in these inter-war years, thanks to the efforts of their outward-looking artists and political pressures in Europe; and in 1936, following the success of the *International Surrealist Exhibition*, the London Gallery was set up by the young English critic and artist Roland Penrose and the Belgian artist, writer and gallerist ELT Mesens to become the English headquarters for the movement. It was during these years in London that Sydney's James Cant became our first official surrealist. Cant had studied at East Sydney Technical College (now National Art School), before he left for London in 1934, where he enrolled at the Central School of Arts and Crafts;

and in the following year participated through the agency of de Maistre in a group show at the Mayor Gallery, after which he was invited to join the English Surrealist Group. Again via de Maistre—proving that, queer or not, Australian artists identified as Australian in England, even when everybody else saw them as British—his work was included in *Young British Painters,* which was held in 1937 at Thomas Agnew & Sons in London. In this show Cant hung beside Bacon, Sutherland, Ivon Hitchens, Victor Pasmore, John Piper, Robert Medley, Ceri Richards, Julian Trevelyan and de Maistre himself, and he was thus marked as one of Britain's up-and-comers. In the same year, he participated in the exhibition *Surrealist Objects and Poems* at the London Gallery, as also did his compatriots Geoffrey Graham and Eric Smith. In 1938 Cant participated in *Realism and Surrealism: An Exhibition of Several Phases of Contemporary Art* at the Guildhall in Eastgate, Gloucester, where he showed alongside Geoffrey Graham and Ian Fairweather, as well as Arp, Tanguy, Dalí, Masson, Cocteau and Magritte. In the same year, he contributed to the exhibition *Pintores Ingleses no Segundo* held at the Salão de Maio in São Paulo, and in *Collage, Papier-Collés, Photo-Montages* at Peggy Guggenheim's gallery Guggenheim Jeune in London; and then in 1939, the year he returned to Australia, he was identified as British in *British Surrealist and Abstract Painting*, which toured the United Kingdom, and contributed to ELT Mesen's exhibition *Living Art in England* at the London Gallery. Back in Sydney, Cant showed in the first Contemporary Art Society shows in 1939 and 1940, and in 1948 managed to exhibit in both the Studio of Realist Art show and in *Abstract* at the David Jones Gallery. In England in 1948, on the other hand, through the invitation of Mesens, both Inge King and Robert Klippel and James Gleeson as a pair held exhibitions at the London Gallery. King, Klippel and Gleeson had not long arrived in London and were living and working at the Abbey studio complex when Mesens, a regular visitor there, invited them to exhibit. The offer to Klippel and Gleeson led them to combine their work in the painted wooden figure *Madame Sophie Sesostoris*, its title derived from a character in TS Eliot's *The Waste Land* and, in its constructed juxtapositions, brilliantly capturing the atmosphere of quiet desperation and dead geraniums in planter boxes that pervades that haunting and elegiac poem.

But—and the writing-out of Cant as Australian in Britain reminds us of this—Edith Fry was not the only protagonist in the inter-war years determined to remind the public of the continuing presence of Australian artists in Europe (and thus, in a way, a precursor to what we are trying to do here). The other was the Coleraine-born Alleyne Zander, who, having run the New Gallery in Melbourne in the late 1920s, moved in 1930 with her partner, the great black-and-white artist Will Dyson (perhaps his biggest success was his collection *Kultur Cartoons* from 1915, with a foreword written by HG Wells), to London, where she worked as the manager of the Redfern Gallery. Employed by the New Zealander Rex Nan Kivell, Zander organised the *Exhibition of British Contemporary Art* and accompanied it to Australia in 1933, which was the first introduction of Australian audiences to modern art, and not, as is so often asserted, the later 1939 *Exhibition of French and British Modern Art*. Zander included in her exhibition the work of Charles Conder and Derwent Lees, the latter of whom she called 'perhaps the most notable painter Australia has yet contributed to contemporary art',[21] and also organised a series of exhibitions in the 1930s at the Redfern Gallery to recuperate Lees for English art, therefore not seeing his (and Conder's) Britishness and Australianness as mutually exclusive. But Zander's incipient globalism is soon lost, for when Lees and Power are included in Basil Burdett's 1939 exhibition they are both returned as British.

Therefore, in our room based on the Redfern Gallery and the London Gallery, we would show work by Cant, Graham, Smith and King; by Gleeson and Klippel; and by Lees and Loudon Sainthill.

Rooms 10 and 11—The Abbey

No Australian artists, either before or after, have ever been given such an entrée into the English art world as that received by the generation of expatriates at the Abbey Art Centre in the years following the end of World War II. But English art history does not acknowledge this cosmopolitan centre in its midst. Owned and run by collector and dealer William Ohly, who also owned the Berkeley Galleries, it was his desire that 'a mix of people and disciplines at the Abbey should stimulate artistic activity and a multi-disciplinary approach to art'.[22] Situated in about three acres of gardens and orchards in the outer-London suburb of New Barnet, the Abbey was a small complex of structures set around a large, nineteenth-century, three-storey building, which was said to be one of the first houses in Britain to be built entirely out of concrete. This central house, where meals were served twice a day, was 'cold and sometimes felt damp', and was surrounded by a 'motley array of garden dwellings', which were let as studios.[23] By the end of the 1940s, the Abbey had been home at one time or another to Klippel, Gleeson, Richmond, Noel Counihan, Peter Graham, Leonard French, Grahame King, Douglas Green, Arthur Rose, Stephen Walker and Mary Webb, who introduced Bernard Smith into its midst. Through Ohly's extended circle, these Australians at the Abbey met such critics and artists as Mesens, Penrose, Read, Rothenstein, Henry Moore and Matthew Smith, whose paintings hung in the dining room and which Gleeson remembered well. Numerous British and European artists also made it their base, including Scottish painter Alan Davie, English sculptor Peter King, Austrian ceramicist Lucie Rie and English film-maker Mike Figgis. John Coplans, the English photographer and future founding editor of *Artforum*, was a resident at one time, as was Hungarian Peter Foldes, who subsequently held numerous exhibitions in Australia in the 1950s. Noel Counihan even remembers a visit from the German collage artist John Heartfield.[24]

Bernard Smith's great books on Australian art (most notably *European Vision and the South Pacific*, but also *Australian Painting*) were largely conceived and planned there. What Smith wanted above all, not just for the artists of his 1959 *Antipodeans* show but for himself, was English recognition. This, after all, was the explicit aim of the late 1950s artists' group known as the Antipodeans, for which he was the mouthpiece; and it is fitting that he ended *Australian Painting* with the unattributed manifesto that he in fact wrote for the group's only, as it turned out, exhibition, for it was this desire for acknowledgement that drove his construction of Australian art. In fact, Smith's Antipodeans project was born from a double rejection: the first by him of abstraction, in part following his all-night exchanges with fellow resident, the abstract expressionist Davie, who had recently returned from the 1950 Venice Biennale, where he had seen the work of Jackson Pollock; the second of him by Anthony Blunt, who was dismissive of his work when he arrived to study at the Courtauld in the late 1940s. As Smith acknowledged in the conclusion to his autobiography *The Boy Adeodatus*, his intellectual formation was profoundly Oedipal, contradictorily wanting his father's (or let us say his motherland's) approval at the same time as wanting to kill him, and all the more poignant for his own life experience of having been given up for adoption by his mother at birth and never knowing his biological father.

In these rooms, then, we would feature the work of postwar Australian artists whose work mirrored that of their English colleagues and emerged from the surprisingly international atmosphere extant in the still-recovering London of the late 1940s and early 1950s. On the walls we would hang paintings by Webb, French, Counihan and Foldes. On the floor, we would have the sculpture of Richmond, who after winning a travelling scholarship studied at the Royal College of Art in 1948, before moving into the Abbey the same year. And next to him, we would have Berlin-born Inge King, who trained at the Royal Academy as well as at the Glasgow School of Art, before arriving at the Abbey, where she met Grahame King, with whom she later moved to Melbourne, where she led that city's important postwar modernist school of sculpture, Centre 5.

Room 12—Australian Artists and Henry Moore

A continuing emphasis on sculpture leads into our next room, which is inspired by the extensive *Henry Moore* show that toured Australian capital cities from 1947 to 1948, sponsored by the British Government through the British Council. This exhibition of England's then-pre-eminent sculptor—by then as recognisably 'British' as Big Ben, the bulldog and the pound note—was patently an attempt by Britain to compete with America for ideological influence in rapidly changing postwar circumstances, and as it were impose British culture on its distant ex-colonies. But if the British Council had done its homework, it would have realised that this shipping over of Moore's bronzes to the Antipodes also represented something of a homecoming. For since at least the 1920s, Australians had been studying with or assisting Moore, and it is their work we would display in this room. We would include the work of Ola Cohn, who studied with Moore at the Royal College of Art between 1926 and 1930; Edith Moore, the sister of the art historian William Moore, who studied with him at the Chelsea Polytechnic between 1933 and 1935; Eileen Mayo, who likewise studied with him there in 1936 before coming to Australasia in 1952; Guy Grey-Smith, who studied with him at the Chelsea School of Art between 1945 and 1947, around the same time Arthur Boothroyd did; and Richmond, who was Moore's assistant, and the first to be paid by him, between 1949 and 1951. Later Richmond lectured in sculpture at the Chelsea School of Art from 1956 to 1977, in which capacity he influenced several generations of English sculptors. He exhibited in London and all over Europe and America throughout the 1960s and 1970s, including in *Contemporary British Sculpture* in Norwich in 1961 and *British Sculpture* at the Tate Gallery in 1965. But he also showed in the exhibition *Australian Art* at the South London Gallery in 1966 and the *Commonwealth Festival of Australian Art* in Leicester in 1967, as well as *Recent Australian Sculpture: Form in Action*, which toured New Zealand in 1968. Richmond was part of that generation of British sculptors that included Bernard Meadows, Reg Butler and Keith Armitage, all of whom continued to cast in bronze and work figuratively through the 1950s and into the 1960s. We would also include here the New Zealander Alan Ingham, who followed Richmond as Moore's assistant between 1950 and 1953; Owen Broughton, who assisted between 1950 and 1952; Lenton Parr between 1955 and 1956; Daryl Hill between 1955 and 1958; and, finally, Ron Robertson-Swann between 1963 and 1965. We feel sure this list is not complete. Indeed, it is perhaps not too much to say that Henry Moore was the single most influential artist on the sculpture of Australia in the twentieth century, as he was on the sculpture of Britain during the same period.

Room 13—The Swinging '60s

Our next room is given over to the generation of Australian artists who first went to London in the late 1950s and continued into the 1960s, as travelling by ship gave way to jet. The year 1962 was marked by the opening of the Commonwealth Institute in London as a place to showcase the art and culture of Australia (and other Commonwealth countries), which at once represented a last cultural throw—there is undoubtedly something of a Sir Les Patterson aspect to it—and pointed towards the end of that history we have been narrating here because the presence of artists from all around the world in Britain is now noted and we can no longer have anything like a specifically British or Australian history of art—the Young British Artists and the recent *Australia* show notwithstanding. So we would feature in our room the abstract expressionist Peter Upward, the psychedelic Pop artist Martin Sharp, the sculptor Bill Culbert from New Zealand, who all showed at the Commonwealth Institute, as well as *Field* artists Ian Burn, Vernon Treweeke, Wendy Paramor, Rollin Schlicht, Tony McGillick and New Zealand–born, Royal Academy–trained and then-teacher of sculpture John Panting and New Zealand–born Royal College of Art–trained Pop conceptualist Billy Apple; but not, say, Brett Whiteley, who was already part of our

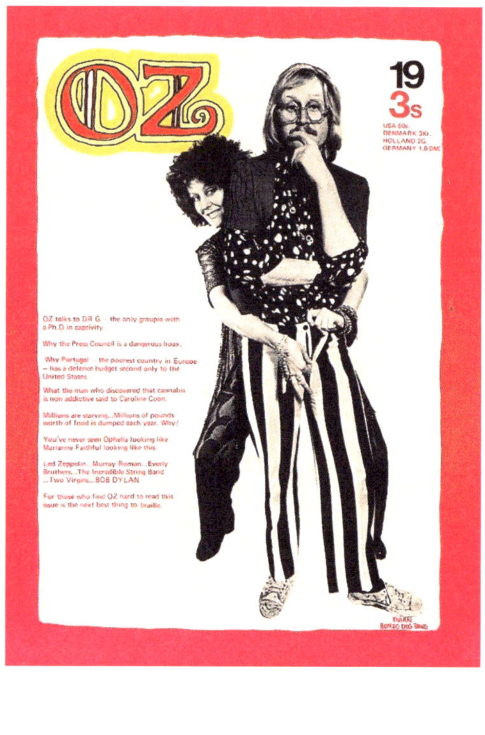

6.11 Germain Greer and Vivian Stanshall of the Bonzo Dog Doo-Dah Band on the cover of *Oz Magazine*, Issue 19, 1969

famous 'expatriate generation' that had earlier included Clive James, Barry Humphries, Germaine Greer, Peter Porter and Robert Hughes. The room would be finished with the addition of the kinetic minimalism of Michael McKinnon, who showed with the experimental artists group Continuum at the Hayward Gallery in 1970.

Room 14—Indigenous Art in Britain

In our final room, to come back to Fernando at the beginning, we include Indigenous Australian art. But as opposed to the exoticising of contemporary Western Desert painting in the *Australia* show, understanding it like everything else there as something coming from far away and from a distant culture, we want to think Aboriginal art as British or rather British art as Aboriginal. We would include in this room the Indigenous art and artefacts shown in Penrose, Read and Breton's 1936 *International Surrealist Exhibition*, held at the New Burlington Galleries in London. In that show they were displayed as part of the avant-garde's enthusiasm for 'primitive' art alongside, for example, the work of de Chirico, Dalí, Duchamp, Magritte, Nash and Moore. Aboriginal art and artefacts were to exert a considerable influence over a generation of British artists, just as they had over the French, and as they had already over another of the other exhibitors in the show, the New Zealander Len Lye. The fact that many of these objects came from British collections reminds us of the enormous and tragic inventories of First Nations peoples and cultures held in British collections. Accordingly, we end our exhibition with Brook Andrew's *Gun-metal grey* (2007) and Christian Thompson's *Down under world* (2012), which draw on the photographic archives of the Royal Anthropological Institute in London, the Museum of Archaelogy and Anthropology at the University of Cambridge and, just as Read and Penrose had for their 1936 show, the Pitt Rivers Museum at Oxford University. Indeed, the collection of the Pitt Rivers Museum was drawn upon again in 1948 by Read and Penrose for their postwar curated *40,000 Years of Modern Art: A Comparison of Primitive and Modern* at the newly founded Institute of Contemporary Art in London, which coincidentally was where Bernard Smith ran into Mary Webb at a lecture the following year by the anthropologist William Fagg, leading to the newly arrived Smith becoming resident at the Abbey. In effect, we would want to suggest, Andrew and Thompson are here making British art. And behind all of this, of course, is Smith's Swiftian claim that British Romanticism itself arises as result of the encounter of the European explorers with the Pacific.

* * *

Our point throughout has been that the art histories of Australia and Great Britain, and the possibility of an identifiable Australian art, have arisen because of a kind of mutual blindness. It is only insofar as we do not see our expatriates in Britain contributing to British art that we can have an identifiable Australian art. Or, to put it otherwise, we can now finally see them as part of Australian art, despite their also contributing to British art. The two are no longer mutually exclusive: there is now a category of British-Australian art, as there is the category of Australian-British art. By 1970, when our account ends, and not coincidentally the bicentenary of Cook's first voyage, we might say that it is a matter not merely of England 'discovering' Australia, but of the discovery of Australia in England.

Now all of this might seem new, or an inversion of common sense, but that could not be further from the truth. The satire of the *Australia* show we have proposed here has already been undertaken.[25] By the time of Edith Fry's second exhibition of *Australian Artists in Europe* in 1925, the New Zealand artist and critic Raymond McIntyre had been writing art criticism for the prestigious *Architecture Review* in London for more than ten years. Arriving in the United Kingdom in 1909, he had studied privately with George Lambert and then with William Nicholson and Walter Sickert at the Westminster Technical Institute. He had exhibited regularly

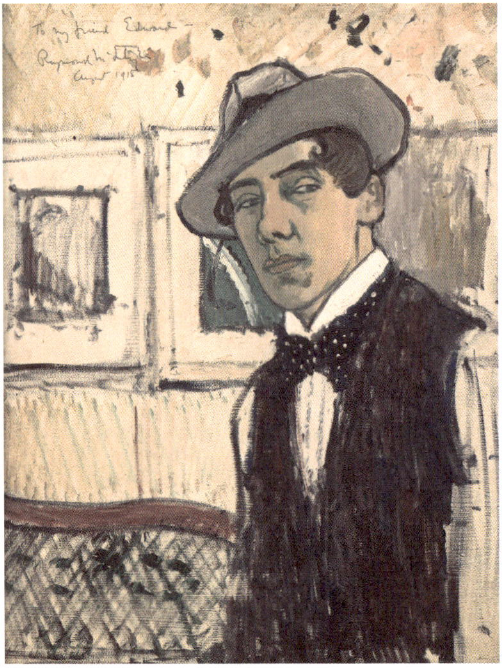

6.12 Raymond McIntyre
Self portrait, 1915

at the Goupil Gallery from 1911, with the London Group from 1916 to 1918, and eventually at the Royal Academy in 1924. These experiences would undoubtedly have attuned him to the questions of expatriatism at stake in Fry's show and her implicit critique of Sydney Ure Smith's *Exhibition of Australian Art*, held two years before. McIntyre begins his review of Fry's show by asking: 'When is an Australian not an Australian?' He then goes on:

> The most interesting works in the show have obviously been done under the influence of and stimulus of European art. Certainly the most up-to-date and enterprising of the artists show this influence … We might even say that, in proportion as they cease to be Australians, their work becomes more interesting, viewed from the standpoint of modern artistic developments in Europe.[26]

It is depressing for us to think that some ninety years later, this insight had been forgotten by the organisers of the *Australia* show at the Royal Academy. But this is what history is for: to remind us of lessons that have been lost, of alternatives that have not been taken, of how things could have been otherwise and perhaps, in the thinking through of this, how they might be already.

An earlier version of this essay was delivered as a lecture to accompany the exhibition *Genius and Ambition: The Royal Academy of Arts 1768–1918*, Bendigo Art Gallery, 2 March – 9 June 2014.

—

1 *Australia* was jointly organised by the Royal Academy, London, and the National Gallery of Australia, Canberra, and ran from 21 September to 8 December 2013. It included, among others, John Glover, Eugene von Guérard, Tom Roberts, Arthur Streeton, Frederick McCubbin, Margaret Preston, Albert Namatjira, Sidney Nolan, Albert Tucker, William Dobell, Russell Drysdale, Fred Williams, Brett Whiteley and John Olsen, before finishing with Shaun Gladwell's *Approach to Mundi Mundi* (2007). The show was widely panned, both in Britain and Australia. Our favourite review of the exhibition is Adrian Searle's 'Australia at the Royal Academy: Ned Kelly to the Rescue': 'This is Australia, the official version—the exhibition as potted history and pop-up continent, the penal colony, the abyss. Nineteenth-century writers, quoted by Thomas Keneally in the catalogue, saw Australia as the afterbirth, the last of lands. Miserably represented and explained, and hung with so few meaningful conversations between them, the artists here might suspect a continuing plot to keep them in a similarly dystopian limbo.' *The Guardian*, 17 September 2013, www.theguardian.com/artanddesign/2013/sep/16/australia-royal-academy-exhibition-review. But for sheer vituperation, it's hard to go past Waldemar Januszczak's description of the work of Fred Williams and John Olsen in his 'A Desert of New Ideas': 'Fred Williams, a particularly mannered member of the less-is-more school, splatters the delicate emptiness of the desert with thick cowpats of minimalism. As the show grows ever browner and yellower, John Olsen's *Sydney Sun*, a giant panel of art installed above your head, successfully evokes the sensation of standing under a cascade of diarrhoea. I think he was actually trying to record the harsh tangibility of the Australian sun.' *The Sunday Times*, 22 September 2013, www.thetimes.co.uk/article/a-desert-of-new-ideas-znd7t2s3j66.

2 John Clarke, *The Even More Complete Book of Australian Verse*, Text Publishing, Melbourne, 2012, p. 102.

3 Alison Holland and Fiona Paisley, 'Fernando, Anthony Martin (1864–1949)', *Australian Dictionary of Biography*, supplementary volume, Melbourne University Press, 2005, http://adb.anu.edu.au/biography/fernando-anthony-martin-12918.

4 Paul Wood, 'The Other Side of the World', in ed. Emma Barker, *Art & Visual Culture, 1600–1850: Academy to Avant-Garde*, Yale University Press in association with the Tate Gallery, London, 2013, pp. 261–97.

5 Of course, in some way this is what the Bendigo Art Gallery was already doing when it complemented its showing of *Genius and Ambition: The Royal Academy of Arts, London, 1768–1918*, with works by Australian artists who had exhibited at the Royal Academy, including Nicholas Chevalier, Tom Roberts, John Longstaff, Rupert Bunny, Margaret Preston and E Phillips Fox.

6 Alice Meynell, 'Newlyn', *The Art Journal*, April 1888, p. 98.

7 Simon Watney, *English Post-Impressionism*, Eastview Editions, New Jersey, 1980, p. 26. We are grateful to Pamela Gerrish Nunn for this reference.

8 Kenneth McConkey, *The New English: A History of the New English Art Club*, Royal Academy Publications, London, 2006, p. 90.

9 Arthur Streeton, letter to Tom Roberts, 27 December 1902, in eds. Ann Galbally and Anne Gray, *Letters from Smike: The Letters of Arthur Streeton, 1890–1943*, Oxford University Press, Melbourne, 1989, p. 94.

10 *Wild Colonials: Australian Artists and the Newlyn and St Ives Art Colonies*, ed. Tracey Cooper-Laverty, exhibition catalogue, Bendigo Art Gallery, Bendigo, Vic., 2009.

11 Gotch once wrote a remarkable letter to the editor entitled 'The Realistic School in Art', (*Argus*, 27 February 1884, p. 6), in which he outlined his artistic credo.

12 For a good account of Hayley Lever, see *Hayley Lever and the Modern Spirit*, ed. Carol Lowrey, exhibition catalogue, Spanierman Gallery, New York, 2010, p. 9.

13 *Pioneers of St. Ives Art at Home and Abroad (1889–1914)*, ed. David Tovey, exhibiton catalogue, Wilson Books, Tewkesbury, England, 2008, p. 238. Cited in *Hayley Lever*, p. 7.

14 Myfanwy Evans, *Frances Hodgkins*, Penguin, England, 1948.

15 See Roger Horrocks, *Len Lye: A Biography*, Auckland University Press, 2001, esp. chapter 'A Colour Box', pp. 133–41.

16 Smith, *Australian Painting*, pp. 171ff.

17 On Meninsky and Bellette, see Christine France, 'Jean Bellette: Early Life and Times', in ed. Christine France, *Jean Bellette Retrospective*, exhibition catalogue, National Trust of Australia and Bathurst Art Gallery, 2005, p. 12.

18 *Francis Bacon: Five Decades*, ed. Anthony Bond et al., exhibition catalogue, Art Gallery of New South Wales, Sydney, 2013.

19 John Richardson, *The Sorcerer's Apprentice: Picasso, Provence, and Douglas Cooper*, Pimlico, London, 2001, p. 11. Earlier on the same page Richardson writes that before he met Cooper he 'knew very little about him except that he was reputed to have the finest collection of modern art in England, to be "mad, bad and dangerous to know", and worse, Australian' (p. 11).

20 Richardson, *The Sorcerer's Apprentice*, p. 24. See on this John Richardson, 'Bacon Agonistes', *New York Review of Books*, 17 December 2009, www.nybooks.com/articles/2009/12/17/bacon-agonistes/.

21 Clarice Alleyne Zander, 'Derwent Lees', in ed. Alleyne Zander, *Exhibition of British Contemporary Art, Melbourne, Sydney, 1933*, exhibition catalogue, Redfern Gallery, London, 1933, np.

22 Steven Miller, 'The Abbey', in *James Gleeson & Robert Klippel: Madame Sophie Sesostoris (A Pre-Raphaelite Satire), 1947–48*, exhibition catalogue, Art Gallery of New South Wales, Sydney, 1998, np.

23 Bernard Smith, *A Pavane for Another Time*, Macmillan, Melbourne, 2002, p. 346.

24 Judith Trimble, *Inge King: Sculptor*, Craftsman House, Sydney, 1996, p. 10.

25 And, indeed, would soon be undertaken again: in 2016 the *Australian Impressionists* exhibition was held at the National Gallery in London, which at least attempted to acknowledge the activities of Australian impressionists in Britain.

26 Raymond McIntyre, 'Exhibitions', *Architectural Review*, vol. 57, January/June 1925, p. 214.

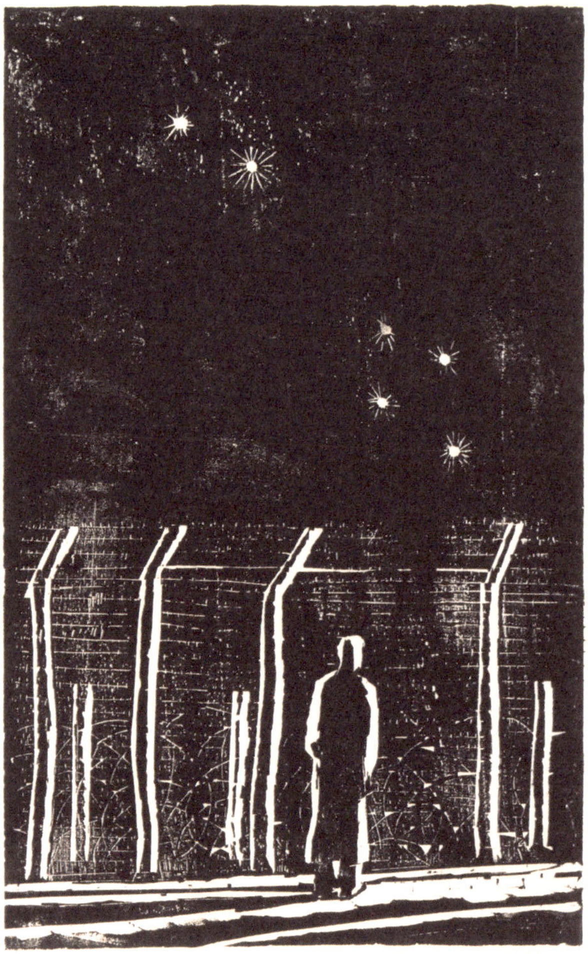

7.1 Ludwig Hirschfeld-Mack
Desolation, Internment Camp, Orange, NSW, 1941

War and Peace
150 Years of Germany and Australia

The guns on the Western Front were barely silent when on 23 November 1918 Belgian-born Henri Verbrugghen took the stage of the recently established New South Wales Conservatorium of Music and softly tapped his baton, bringing the audience to silence. Then into this silence, Verbrugghen called down the immortal opening chords of Beethoven's Ninth Symphony, the 'Choral', with its celebrated final movement 'Ode to Joy', based on Schiller's words. A difficult piece to stage because of the considerable orchestral and vocal forces required, the performance was nevertheless a triumph, all the more so for the occasion it marked: the Allied victory over Germany and the Central Powers. Due to the long lead-time and the necessity for extensive rehearsal, its being played at the signing of peace was a coincidence, but nevertheless a very serendipitous one. The point was not lost on the critic for the *Sydney Morning Herald*:

> The armistice and the blessings of peace were not in sight when the program of the Conservatorium Orchestra on Saturday afternoon was projected, but by an extraordinary coincidence the inclusion of Beethoven's 'Choral Symphony' with the Ode to 'Joy, thou spark from heaven descending', brought the whole body of players and singers into line for the celebration of the glorious Allied victory.[1]

However, the real coincidence here was not the fortuitous programming of Beethoven at the moment of national exultation before the signing of the Treaty of Versailles, but that of Germany and Australia itself. The fact that the very music able to express in Australia the Allied victory was German attests certainly to those values of 'universality' expressed in Schiller's poem; but it attests as well to the reception of those ideals in Australia and the fact that, even at this moment, Australia could express itself through German culture, finding its sounds in German music and words in the German language. And it is true that the relations between Germany and Australia are mostly one-way and there was, indeed, a German influence on Australia before there was even an Australia. We could thus never entirely separate ourselves from Germany, even in this moment of victory over them. We could never truly fight them because in some ways we would also be fighting ourselves. If there have at times been in our shared history anti-German moments—and we will show some of them here—it is undoubtedly true that there has been a much longer running German or pro-German aesthetic in our culture, which is for us part of the real history of where we are today.[2]

All of this, of course, is true not just of music—although music is privileged in its seeming abstraction, spirituality and breaking of boundaries—but also of the visual arts. After all, the first head of our first art school and the first curator of our first state art gallery was Eugene von Guérard, a Viennese-born Kunstakademie Düsseldorf–trained painter, who came to Australia aged forty-two in 1852. He panned and painted on the Ballarat goldfields and then travelled and painted throughout Victoria for some eighteen years (working beside his good friend, the Swiss artist Nicholas Chevalier, on Professor Georg Balthasar von Neumayer's meteorological expedition to Cape Otway in 1862; he also accompanied Neumayer's magnetic survey expedition to north-east Victoria and Mount Kosciuszko that same year), before being appointed Master of the Painting School and Curator of the National Gallery of Victoria in 1870. (The Swiss Louis Buvelot was one of the unsuccessful candidates.) In that year, von Guérard both became a charter member of the Victorian Academy of Arts and was awarded the Cross of the Order of Franz Josef by the Emperor of Austria. Von Guérard was always able to send work to exhibitions in Europe: he sent work to the London International Exhibition in 1862, to the Royal Academy in 1865, to the Exposition Universelle de Paris in 1867 and 1878, to Düsseldorf and Vienna in 1873 and to the Philadelphia Centennial Exhibition in 1876. In that year too, von Guérard travelled to the South Island of New Zealand, where he made his preparatory sketches for that country's first 'national' painting, his *Milford Sound, New Zealand* of 1877–79. (There is a New Zealand–German—or, better put, Australasian–German—art as well.) In 1881 von Guérard resigned from his position in Melbourne, and in 1882 he returned to Düsseldorf, from where he sent work back to Melbourne in 1884 and 1885. In 1891, ten years before his death, he moved to London, from where he travelled to St Ives and the Lake District, which he sketched in his old age. (We might think here of Margaret Preston, who worked for a summer at St Ives during World War I following her own German experience, as we will see.) After losing all of his Australian investments in the crash of 1893, von Guérard spent his final years in poverty, and after his death was buried next to his wife, who had predeceased him by ten years, in Brompton Cemetery in Chelsea, where his grave can still be visited today.

Dating the return of von Guérard to Australian art history to the 1960s, curator Daniel Thomas, writing in 1980 in the appendix to Candice Bruce's *Eugen von Guérard*, begins: 'Australia's neglect of von Guérard's art during the past hundred years requires some explanation', and he points first of all to 'chauvinism', which we would call racism. He suggests furthermore that, unlike Chevalier, von Guérard's English was poor and that he was unpopular among his students for insisting on a 'tight and detailed' rendering and not the more 'broad and loose' handling of the popular, French-inclined Buvelot. 'The most significant reason', however, Thomas explains, 'was the lasting canonisation of a later generation of artists, McCubbin, Roberts and Streeton, who emerged in the later 1880s', and for Thomas their reification—or is it deification?—as *the* Australian artists excludes other possible Australias. As he goes on to write:

> In fact, earlier artists, including von Guérard, were at times equally 'Australian' in their accurate observation of or feeling for Australian life, while the nationalist generation was often 'Un-Australian', for example, in its Japanese or Rococo aestheticism.[3]

Thus we might say that the UnAustralian artist is the more Australian, and the apparently Australian artists are the more UnAustralian. But after his death von Guérard was in no exhibition of Australian art, nor was his work even photographically illustrated until 1962, and his work was first reproduced in colour only in 1969.

Von Guérard, however, was not the first German artist in Melbourne. A fuller account would begin perhaps in the mid-nineteenth century with the explorer Ludwig Leichhardt and the Frankfurt-trained artist Ludwig Becker. Becker worked on Burke and Wills's ill-fated 1860 expedition into the interior, becoming the first German we know of to die in the desert.[4] It would include JW Lindt, the Frankfurt-born painter and photographer, who arrived in Brisbane in 1862, aged seventeen, and who eighteen years later published his world-renowned *Album of Australian Aborigines* (c. 1875), as well as the Vienna-born Carl Pinschof, who moved to Melbourne in 1880 to oversee Austria's participation in the *International Exhibition* of that year and became a much-loved patron of the Heidelberg School painters, and who in 1901 bought the expatriate sculptor Bertram Mackennal's *Circe* (1893), now in the National Gallery of Victoria, paying for its casting. The Pinschof house, Studley Hall in Kew, was a well-known turn-of-the-century salon, its influence ending only with the outbreak of World War I. A wider account of the time would also have to include the Russian-born Swiss Nicholas Chevalier, and the Austrian-born Carl Kahler, who painted the panoramic *Lawn at Flemington on Melbourne cup day* (1887), one of three paintings by him on this theme, as well as all the German work presented in the various international exhibitions held in Australia during the second half of the nineteenth century.

But these fin-de-siècle German–Australian relations in late nineteenth-century Victoria remind us of that Melbourne-born prodigy, composer, pianist, educator and eventual follower of Masoch—we might even call him a painist—Percy Grainger, who moved to Frankfurt in 1895 at age thirteen, where he studied for five years, before beginning his celebrated concert career. His German musical links also remind us that the great Australian soprano Nellie Melba was introduced to Mathilde Marchesi, who as her vocal teacher was crucial to Melba's success, by Elise Wiedermann, the wife of Pinschof, herself a former opera singer. (Later, Joan Sutherland, Australia's other great soprano, would be trained by a pupil of Marchesi.) Indeed, Melbourne altogether was something of a little Germany at the end of the nineteenth century. We might think here, for instance, of von Guérard's successor at the Gallery School in Melbourne, the Irish-born George Folingsby, who had lived for some twenty-five years in Munich, where he had studied

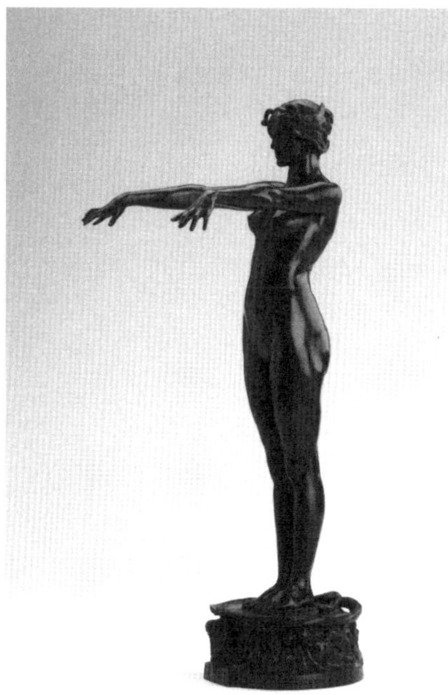

7.2 Bertram Mackennal
Circe, 1893

under Karl von Piloty, before accepting the position. At the Kunstakademie, he had learned the Munich 'method' or 'system', the technique of working from a bituminous base; and from Folingsby and his successor at the Gallery School, the English-born Bernard Hall, who likewise studied in Munich, we get the so-called browning of Melbourne art at the turn of the twentieth century.[5]

But it was during this time that Australia came to be—as the amalgamation of its various states, all of which had significantly different histories and ethnic populations. South Australia, the only free colony, was also the most German, as it still is today. The first state to give women the vote, it was both the home of Hamburg-born Hans Heysen, the founding figure of Australia's 'gum tree' nationalist school, and where Arrernte artist Albert Namatjira first made his reputation. Actually, we might say, Heysen's house, 'The Cedars', and Namatjira's painting *Hermannsburg Gorge* (1945) are at once equally indigenous and a product of the German presence in Australia. The Bibles in Namatjira's Hermannsburg, there because of the Lutheran mission, were in German, so that for many Central Desert Indigenous people German and not English was the first non-Indigenous language they learned.[6] For their part, Adelaide-born artists Bessie Davidson and Margaret Preston both studied in Munich: Davidson at the Künstlerinnen-Verein München in 1904 and Preston at the School for Illustrators the same year. This pedagogical line runs all the way through to Stanislaus Ostoja-Kotkowski, the Polish-born and Kunstakademie Düsseldorf–trained painter and experimental film-maker, who eventually settled in the Adelaide Hills after originally arriving in Australia in 1949, and whose science-fiction themes and engagement with technology can perhaps be understood as a combination of Central European folklore and German industrial modernism. And there is undoubtedly something of Ostoja-Kotkowski in the Czech-born but Kunstakademie Stuttgart–trained Otto Hajek, whose outdoor concrete environment *Adelaide urban iconography*, made for the Adelaide Festival Centre Plaza in 1975, was destroyed in 2016. Indeed, Adelaide's festival has consistently been an outlet for not only German art but also German theatre, music and literature. Is it too much to suggest that the internationalism of the festival, which has been running since 1962 as the first in Australia, is at least in part a result of German cultural cosmopolitanism?

And speaking of Ostoja-Kotkowski's cosmologies, it is little understood just how influential Russian-born but long-term German-resident Wassily Kandinsky's spiritualism was in early twentieth-century Australia, even before he went to work at the Bauhaus. Just a year after its publication in German, reviews of the English translation of his book *Über das Geistige in der Kunst* (*Concerning the Spiritual in Art*) were published in the Australian press.[7] In fact, we might say that the inventor AB Hector's Colour Light Organs, which were demonstrated at the music shop Palings in Sydney in 1912, looked back more to Goethe's experiential, eye-including light than to Newton's mathematical, eye-excluding light, and at the same time across to Kandinsky's contemporaneous theatre piece *Der gelbe Klang* (*The yellow sound*) (1909–12). These events preceded and inspired the landmark *Colour in Art* exhibition of Roland Wakelin and Roy de Maistre in Sydney in 1919, which by coincidence Verbrugghen opened just a year after his performance of Beethoven.[8] And all of this was followed by the Frankfurt-educated Eleonore Lange's sculpture *Seraph of light* of 1932; indeed, Lange in her role as art lecturer introduced colour theories to an interested audience at the Art Gallery of New South Wales (AGNSW) in the 1930s and the Teachers' Federation in Sydney in the 1940s. Others influenced by Kandinsky included the painters Frank Hinder, who painted his *Tribute to Kandinsky* in 1938 (the same year his erstwhile teacher Emil Bisttram co-founded the Transcendental Painting Group in Taos, New Mexico), and the English-born house-painter-turned-artist and pioneer of abstraction Ralph Balson.

But Kandinsky was not the only Bauhaus artist to influence Australian artists. The Swiss-born Bauhaus master Paul Klee also had a considerable impact on Australian art. The Sydney-born and inter-war School of Paris painter

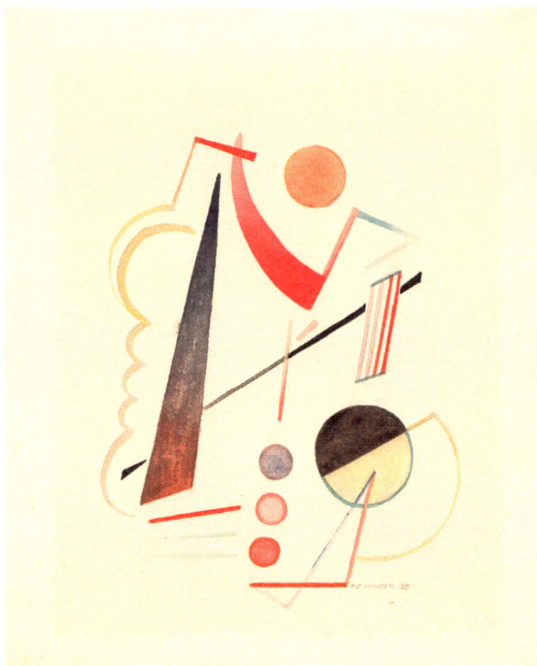

7.3 Frank Hinder
Tribute to Kandinsky, 1938

JW Power translated Leopold Zahn's book *Paul Klee* (1920) for his own use in 1924, and Klee's work certainly helped shape the work of the first generation of Sydney's abstractionists (Frank and Margel Hinder, Ralph Balson) between the wars. The Bauhaus in general had a significant effect on Australian art. No Australian studied there, but a new Australia emerged from there. When the infamous transport ship full of internees, HMT *Dunera*, eventually docked in Melbourne in 1940 after its nightmare journey from London, it included the *Bauhäusler* Ludwig Hirschfeld-Mack. Hirschfeld-Mack, who had won an Iron Cross for his military service in World War I and subsequently became a lifelong Quaker, had been a radical and inventive artist following his period at the Bauhaus (1920–25) but was entirely unknown upon his arrival in Australia. Although he exhibited with the Contemporary Art Society (CAS) in 1947 and held his own small one-person show at the Rowden White Library at the University of Melbourne the following year, his most significant legacy in Australia is in the field of art education, where as both an art teacher and a teacher of art teachers he transformed art education in Victoria. Less directly but no less consequentially, the influence of the Bauhaus can be seen in the founding by Adelaidean Dorrit Black of the Modern Art Centre (MAC) in Sydney in 1931, an institution that sought to combine the manufacturing and selling of commercial art and its applications with the teaching and exhibiting of contemporary art. It is possible that Black was also influenced by her 1928 meeting with Franz Cižek, the Austrian painter, teacher and founder of the Child Art Movement, who gave her a personal tour of his school in Prague (he had already been influential on Johannes Itten before Itten began teaching in 1919 at the Bauhaus) and by her attendance in Prague at the International Congress of Art Applied to Industry on the same journey. In opening the MAC, Black became the first woman to found an art gallery in Australia, and her gallery was the first in this country to use 'modern' in its name.[9] And later our modernist architecture, which is often said to have emerged around the time of the 1956 Melbourne Olympics, was kick-started in the 1940s by the Chinese-born and Swiss-trained German architect Frederick Romberg and by the Vienna-born Harry Seidler.[10] Seidler had trained under Walter Gropius and Marcel Breuer at Harvard University, and with Josef Albers for a summer at Black Mountain College during the late 1940s. It is interesting, however, that when Gropius visited Australia in 1954, the one person he went out of his way to meet with again, and indeed to offer a job in America to, was Hirschfeld-Mack, who was then, as he had been since 1942, teaching at a boys' school in Geelong.

But the first Bauhaus student to visit Australia, so far as we are aware, was Tilli Frankel, who when interviewed on board ship in Sydney en route to Wellington in 1936 spent her time promoting Bauhaus principles. Speaking of Gropius, she said:

> His idea is that in this highly advanced machine age artists should not be employed creating a few beautiful things by hand, but that their time should be spent evolving good ideas which could be carried into factories by machine.[11]

Frankel's husband, geneticist Otto Frankel, was subsequently secretary of a committee chaired by philosopher of science Karl Popper that brought Austrian refugees to New Zealand, the two men having known each other in Vienna before emigrating. Thus through this mechanism New Zealand became home to, for example, the Vienna-born Ernst Plischke, its first modernist architect. And just this kind of architectural exchange happened in reverse in London where the Hungarian-born Bauhaus master László Moholy-Nagy hired the Australians Dahl and Geoffrey Collings and Alistair Morrison in 1935 to help him in his design of Simpsons of Piccadilly. But this German–Australasian connection didn't only happen in Australasia. It also happened in New Guinea, where Australia shared a land border with Germany; put another way, where the Territory of Papua, administered by Australia, was bordered by Kaiser Wilhelmsland, German New Guinea. The German-Danish expressionist Emil Nolde was the official artist on

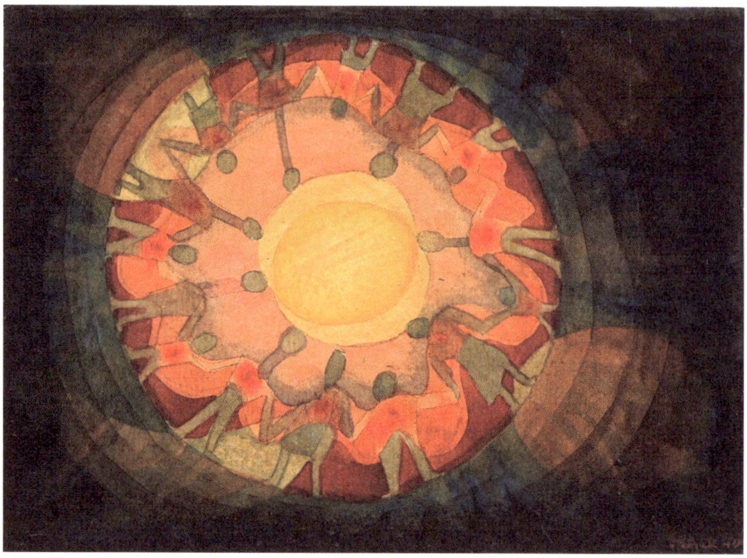

7.4 Ludwig Hirschfeld-Mack
The world to come, 1940

the Külz-Leber medical expedition, sent in 1913 to German New Guinea, as it was called then, to study the causes of its precipitous decline in population. It was in response to the region's 'primitivism' that Nolde's work changed, making watercolours, in his own words, 'so genuine and crude that they could not under any circumstances be hung in perfumed salons'.[12] An example of the work he produced during his time in New Guinea is in the Art Gallery of New South Wales, *Head of a South Sea Islander* (1913–14). This must have been one of the works impounded by the British when the German ship on which Nolde was returning home at the end of his trip attempted to pass through the Suez Canal after war had been declared. Nolde after the war managed to track down his confiscated watercolours to a loft in Plymouth, England, from where he retrieved them. Nolde was a contradictory figure: a Nazi sympathiser and an avowed anti-Semite, he was nonetheless forbidden to paint by the Nazis and his works were removed from museums and included in the infamous *Entartete Kunst* (*Degenerate Art*) exhibition of 1937.[13] And this reminds us of Nolde's fellow Die Brücke artist Max Pechstein, who was likewise included in *Entartete Kunst* and likewise interested in so-called 'primitive' cultures. Pechstein travelled to Palau in the Pacific in 1914, then also administered as part of German New Guinea, and subsequently

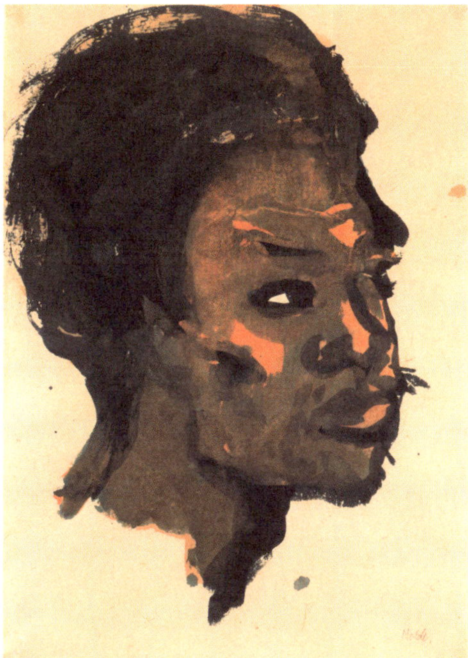

7.5 Emil Nolde
Head of a South Sea Islander, 1913–4

completed numerous paintings and later his own woodcut portrait of a Pacific man, his *Klouruback*, also now part of the collection of the Art Gallery of New South Wales. Interned by the Japanese upon the outbreak of World War I, he eventually made his way back to Germany, where he was conscripted and sent to the Somme.

It would be worth remembering here too that, at the time Nolde and Pechstein were across the border from Australia, Australia's then most successful art dealer was adjusting to the new realities of life during wartime in Sydney. Described by Julian Ashton in 1916 as 'a very slippery German Jew', but in fact a Hanoverian, Adolph Albers had arrived in Sydney as a sixteen-year-old in 1894, was apprenticed to the art framer WL Schmidt and was managing that business by the age of twenty-two. By 1910 he had established his own business buying and selling art, and at that time Ashton wrote: 'He will touch nothing that is not Australian'.[14] By 1917, so successful was he that he had established his home in Gordon and had built his Tudor-style sandstone castle weekender on Bungan Head at Newport. Albers represented artists (he did well with Sydney Long and JJ Hilder in particular), managed exhibitions for the Society of Artists, submitted works for sale to the Art Gallery of New South Wales, took exhibitions to regional New South Wales, broadcast talks on art in Brisbane in the 1930s and 1940s, published booklets on art, was instrumental in getting artists involved in designing stamps in the 1930s, and was director of the gallery in Murdoch's department store after 1945. A globalist, Albers sold Australian pictures to expatriates in London and was importing the work of expatriate artists such as Richard Hayley Lever and Francis McComas to sell in Sydney. He disliked modern art, but his conservative views and his advocacy for the paintings he dealt in allowed him to become the first successful art dealer in Australia. Nevertheless, as art historian Heather Johnson has pointed out, 'his presence in the Sydney art network is scarcely visible in orthodox art history'.[15]

However, if the universal cosmopolitanism of the Bauhaus, whether understood as spiritual or industrial, is one side of our connection to Germany, it is important to acknowledge the other side. Undoubtedly at times, the two countries' relationship has been characterised by conflict and antagonism, and their cultures by mutually excluding nationalisms and chauvinisms. These contradictory impulses can indeed be seen not just in each country but in a single family: the Lindsays. On the one hand, the family produced perhaps Australia's most celebrated and productive émigré art historian (*pace* Robert Hughes), Jack Lindsay, who from 1926 until his death in 1990 lived in England and whose communism was shared by many intellectuals of the time, but who was nevertheless deeply influenced by Nietzsche, about whom he wrote a little-known and under-rated book, *Dionysius: Nietzsche Contra Nietzsche*, in 1928. He also published on Turner, Cézanne and William Blake, and in 1978 a book of poems, illustrated by Noel Counihan, whose title, *War or Peace*, we play on in this essay. We then come to the rest of the family. There is his father Norman, who during World War I became an über-nationalist, creating many menacing anti-German works, none more 'Australian' than his recruiting poster *The arm of the Kaiser reaches around the world* (1918). And then there is his uncle Lionel, who was a vicious anti-Semite and author of the notorious *Addled Art* (1942), in which he railed against the so-called Jewish conspiracy and its threat to Australian art in the form of modernism:

> I have often watched these [Jewish] modernist dealers snaring a gull, and listened to their blandishments. An air of profound conviction surrounds their utterances; never for a moment do they relax an eyelid, as they flatter the taste of snobs and give them to imagine they are the happy few capable of rising to the heights of modern art.[16]

The irony here is that, as with the performance of Beethoven, in the same way that the Allied victory could be expressed only through German music, so Lindsay could defend the integrity of Australian culture only by imitating Nazi racism. And he was not the only one to do so. Perhaps the most surprising was the painter Hilda Rix Nicholas, who on returning from Europe in 1926 decried, like Lindsay, the conspiracy between Jewish art dealers, collectors and artists with regard to modern art, claiming that it was 'immoral, reflecting a state of decadence which began just before the war', and going on to suggest that its success was to be explained because 'the pictures were bought up in most cases by Jewish dealers, who then offered them for sale at greatly enhanced prices and created a small boom'.[17] This was the same 'conspiracy' that was evident to the society painter Ernest Buckmaster upon his return from Europe and that the director of the then-National Gallery of New South Wales, JS MacDonald, also discerned and condemned.

But there was no more committed Nazi-Australian artist than the subject of Violet Teague's well-known *Boy with a palette* (1911), a portrait of the artistically precocious son of German-born musician Eduard Scharf and Bendigo-born pianist Olive de Hugard. (They mixed in the same circles as the Pinschofs.) The young Theo Scharf was hailed by Emanuel Phillips Fox as a prodigy when he held an exhibition at the Athenaeum Gallery in Melbourne as a fifteen-year-old in 1914. Then, on the eve of war, with not a word of German between them, he and his mother decided to go to Munich. From 1916 until 1924, Scharf trained in that city's academy, and in the 1920s he made his reputation with his expressionist etchings of the Bavarian capital's street life, in particular the well-known series 'Night in the city' (1923), a copy of which was acquired at the time by Nellie Melba. (Indeed the last known photograph of her was taken at Scharf's house at Feldafing, just outside

Munich, on what truly turned out to be her final farewell tour of Europe in 1931.) Scharf taught drawing at the State School of Applied Art, later the Academy of Applied Art, from 1934, rising to the position of professor in 1938. An early fascist, he joined the Nazi Party in 1932, the same year he began illustrating for such magazines as *Der SA-Mann* (*The Storm Division Man*), an organisation he joined the following year. In 1941 Scharf is said to have welcomed such School of Paris artists as André Derain, Maurice de Vlaminck and Kees van Dongen to Munich on their infamous tour of Nazi Germany.[18] During World War II he accepted a position as an official war artist, establishing what he called his 'career as a Kriegsmaler' in the Staffel der Bildenden Künstler, part of the Propaganda-Kompanie run out of Berlin and overseen by Joseph Goebbels. He ended his account of his war service by pointing out that, following his time as a prisoner of war, although he had been discharged from the Wehrmacht, 'I have never been discharged from the Staffel der Bildenden Künstler'. In 1950 Scharf returned to Melbourne, where he taught with the Box Hill Art Group and was unknowingly received as a prominent 'professor' by the Australian press, little aware of his Nazi past. In 1956, following the German pension becoming available to him, he returned once more to Munich, where he lived quietly, perhaps just catching up with old friends, until he died in 1987.

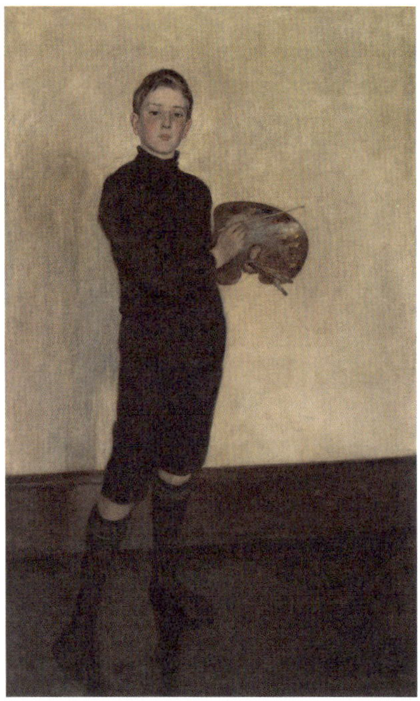

7.6 Violet Teague
Boy with a palette, 1911

But Scharf here again is only one side of the Australian relationship to Germany under Nazism. We should equally not forget JW Power, who served for the Allied Forces as a doctor during World War I, after which he painted his memorial *Ypres* (1918), and who participated in the signal 1936 anti-Fascist exhibition *D.O.O.D.* (*De Olympiade Onder Dictatuur, The Olympics under dictatorship*) in Amsterdam, alongside Max Ernst, Georges Vantongerloo and his friend Otto Freundlich, whose work was to feature on the cover of the catalogue for the *Entartete Kunst* (*Degenerate Art*) exhibition the following year. In 1942 the CAS held its own well-known *Anti-Fascist Exhibition* at the Athenaeum in Melbourne, which featured Albert Tucker, Noel Counihan and Ailsa O'Connor, with a catalogue that quoted from German social realist artist Käthe Kollwitz.

However, World War II came to Australia in other ways. We have already briefly mentioned HMT *Dunera*, which left England in July 1940, overcrowded with mostly Jewish-German and Jewish-Austrian 'enemy aliens', its battened-down transportees robbed and beaten during their two-month trip to Melbourne and Sydney by brutal (and more than likely anti-semitic) British guards. Sigmund Freud's grandson Walter Freud, himself a transportee on the *Dunera*, once calculated that 'each man would have had an average of seven minutes per day to

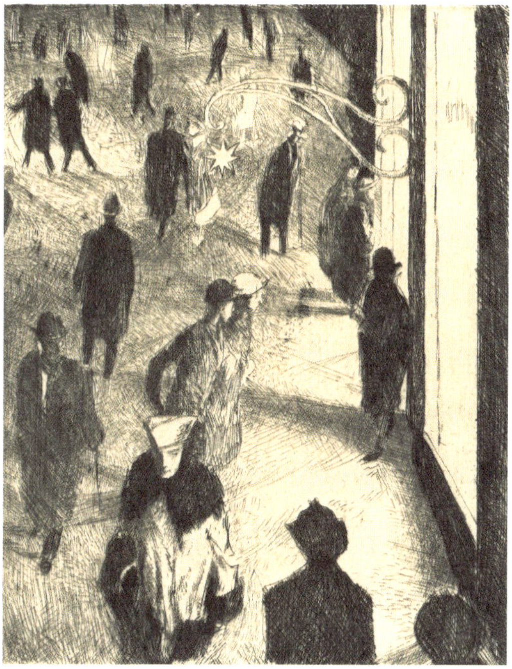

7.7 Theo Scharf
Promenade, from the 'Night in the city', c. 1923

empty his bowels and bladder and to peer through the only portholes not covered by iron plates', before being locked below deck in the dark again.[20]

To tell the story once more, those who disembarked in Melbourne were sent to Tatura in northern Victoria, and those who went on to Sydney were accompanied by armed guards on a nineteen-hour train ride to Hay, where they were interned in two camps, before being transported down to Tatura. Imprisoned, this mostly male community, the so-called Dunera Boys, created a society that replicated Weimar Germany, characterised by the cosmopolitanism of the Austro-Hungarian empire and sustained by an ad hoc and improvised practice of mutual exchange. (Not only was a kind of university set up in the camps, but the many accomplished musicians interned there set up orchestras, which frequently played German music as an implicit rebuke to its appropriation by the Nazis.) Indeed, from late 1941, it became possible to request a return to England or to emigrate elsewhere, but many of those detained decided to stay on in Australia.

We have already mentioned the *Bauhäusler* Ludwig Hirschfeld-Mack, but there were several others younger than he who acquired or extended their artistic skills in the camps. There was Klaus Friedeberger, who was born in Berlin in 1922 and exhibited for the first time at the CAS in 1944, taught by Hirschfeld-Mack. There was Erwin Fabian, who was born in Berlin in 1915 and was similarly taught by Hirschfeld-Mack, although by coincidence a painting by his father Max Fabian had been included in the German section of Penleigh Boyd's 1923 *Exhibition of European Art*, held in Sydney and Melbourne. Finally, out of many others, we might mention Peter Kaiser, who was born in 1918 in Berlin, had trained at the Berlin Academy from 1936 to 1938, and who when he left the camp originally lived and showed with the Merioola Group in Sydney until 1950, when he left for Paris and became part of that city's postwar École de Paris. He continued, however, to exhibit in Australia, with critic James Gleeson writing of the Tachist-inspired works of his 1963 show at Macquarie Galleries that, 'like most modern Spaniards, he makes the most of textures'.[21] But we perhaps cannot refrain here from mentioning artist and set designer Hein Heckroth who, after being freed from Hay following pressure from Herbert Read and returning to London, won an Oscar for his dream-like art direction for Michael Powell and Emeric Pressburger's *The Red Shoes* in 1948, which reminds us that another South Australian, Robert Helpmann (whose second 'n' was a German affectation), choreographed and starred in the movie.

We also draw attention to two other German-speaking figures, who would become Australia's first professional art historians: Franz Philipp and Ursula Hoff. The Viennese Philipp had studied art history there until 1938, when he was expelled as he pursued his study on Mannerist portraiture in northern Italy. Arrested days after *Kristallnacht*, he was sent to Dachau, until his mother was able to secure his release, and then travelled to London, where he was interned by the British as an 'enemy alien', and then at the last moment was squeezed onto the *Dunera*. In 1947 he was appointed tutor in the Italian Renaissance at the University of Melbourne and in 1950 became a lecturer. Ursula Hoff for her part was born to German parents in London in 1909 and moved to Hamburg as a baby. Spreading her university studies between Munich, Cologne and Hamburg, she ended up studying with Erwin Panofsky, Aby Warburg and Fritz Saxl, before arriving in Australia on the eve of the war in 1939. In 1943 she was appointed to the National Gallery of Victoria, the first woman to work there and the first qualified art historian to work in any Australian state gallery, and in 1949 also began to lecture in art history at the University of Melbourne.[22] Just as with von Guérard 'Australian' art could be said to begin with a German, so we might also say that the discipline of art history in Australia, at least as it is practised in universities and museums, effectively began with an Austrian and a German.[23]

But outside of the institutions, there was no greater categorical challenge to the status of art than photography. In the late 1930s, the pioneering modernist photographers Wolfgang Sievers and Margaret Michaelis both came to Australia on German passports; they were joined in 1940 by Henry Talbot (Heinz Tichauer), who arrived on the *Dunera*, and separately and together they began to produce a

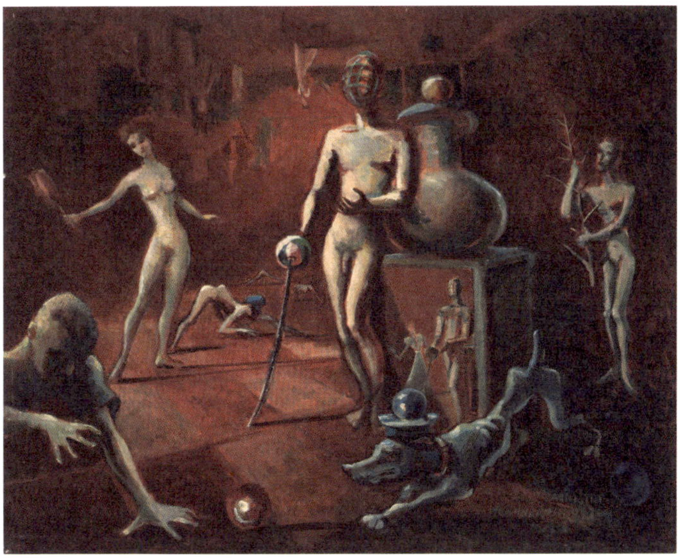

7.8 Hein Heckroth
Australia, 1941

new photography, characterised by its high contrast, Central European studio-training and emphasis on the graphic qualities of architectural space. Inheriting all of these qualities, but with an emphasis more on human than architectural form, was Helmut Newton (Helmut Neustädter), another 'enemy alien' who arrived from war-ravaged Berlin in 1940 and was interned for several years. After the war, he soon started working in advertising, partnered with Talbot; and in 1948 he married his assistant, Melbourne-born photographer June Browne, who subsequently changed her name to Alice Springs (which reminds us of the tendency of our female musicians to adopt a pseudonym relating to their Australian origins to present themselves overseas; for example, Nellie Melba, who came from Melbourne, June Bronhill, who came from Broken Hill, and of course Florence Austral). Newton's work mines his personal history, especially, we might conjecture, his years in Berlin under Nazism as a young boy, expressing itself, for example, in the fascist-themed, goose-stepping perfect Aryan bodies of his female *Nudes* (c. 1970).

But the potential obscenity with which Newton flirts here is laid bare by another kind of body: that of the Jewish victims of the Final Solution's insane logic. In this regard, the remarkable photographs and drawings of official war artist

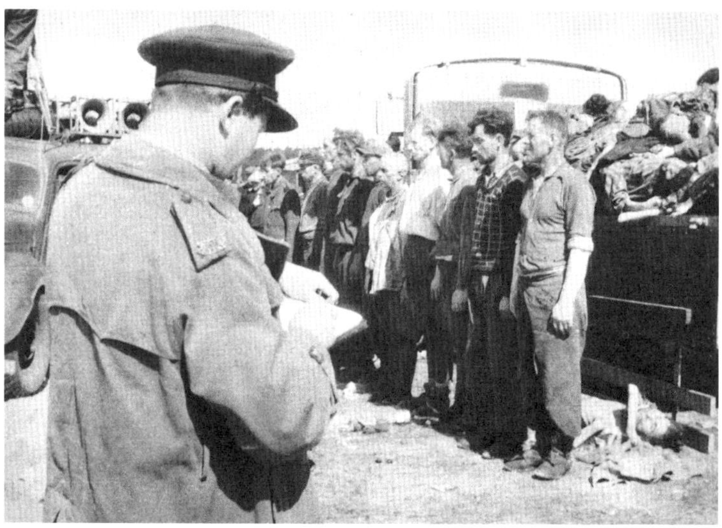

7.9 Alan Moore drawing SS guards in front of a truck loaded with the bodies of concentration camp victims, Bergen-Belsen, 1945

Alan Moore sketching at the scene of the immediate aftermath of the liberation of the concentration camp at Belsen are testament to what in some ways cannot be spoken of. The Australian experience of the Holocaust, if it began with the forced expatriation of Jews from Europe from the mid-1930s and the arrival of the *Dunera*, ended with these appalling images. Another Australian war artist present at the defeat of Nazism was the Meldrumite Colin Colahan, whose paintings depict both the mass movements of populations and the justice wrought upon selected individuals that accompanied Germany's defeat. But we also cannot help compare Moore's images of the prisoners at Belsen with Hirschfeld-Mack's image of an enemy alien at the internment camp at Orange, *Desolation, internment camp, Orange, NSW* (1941). Both are extraordinary premonitions of that new class of human in the twentieth century, the *homo sacer*. And Colahan's images of collaborators imprisoned in a lion's cage in Antwerp and of traitors at an Allied court martial turn the black-and-white of war into shades of grey.

The artists who came to Australia from Germany in the 1950s differed from those who came before and during the war, however, in that they were for the most part already artists before they arrived. We offer only a small selection here. There is, as we have already mentioned, the Kunstakademie Düsseldorf–trained Ostoja-

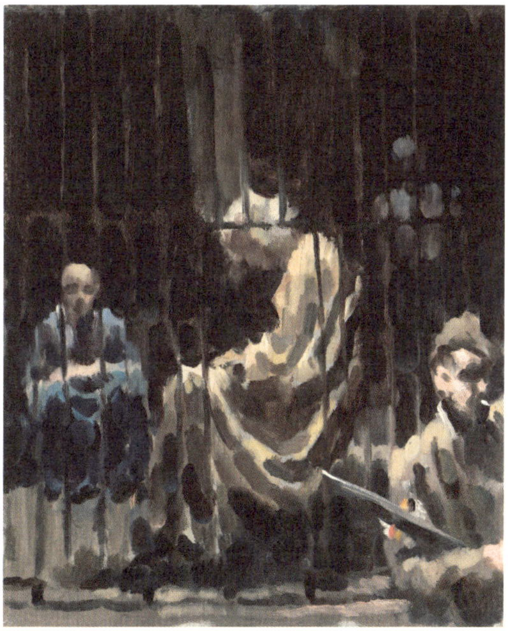

7.10 Colin Colahan
Collaborators in the lion's cage in Antwerp, 1944

Kotkowski. There is also Maximilian Feuerring, who went on to exhibit at the 1961 São Paulo Biennial and who likewise studied at the academy in Düsseldorf. There is the Berlin-born Inge King, who was mentored by Kollwitz, who once advised her about becoming an artist, 'Don't do it if you can help it, it is so difficult'.[24] King, who was Jewish, was able to get to England in 1939, and after studying in Glasgow she was living and working at the artist's studio complex known as the Abbey just outside London when she met her husband, the Melbourne printmaker Grahame King. The couple moved to Melbourne in 1951, where King established her career, and in 2014 at the age of ninety-eight she was the subject of a retrospective at the National Gallery of Victoria. There is the Kölner Werkschulen–trained Udo Sellbach, who in 1966 was a founding member of the Print Council of Australia and in 1977 the founding director of the Canberra School of Art and was represented with one of his graphic abstractions with expressive edges in *The Field*. There is Marcella Hempel, who studied at the Berlin College of Textiles and Fashions and lectured at the Academy of Applied and Fine Art in Dresden from 1946 until 1950, before leaving East Berlin in 1952 because 'I did not want my child to grow up under a totalitarian regime which took the life of my husband, who had been a political prisoner under Hitler'.[25] After arriving in Australia in 1954, she began teaching textile design at the East Sydney Technical College (now National Art School) and later established a long-running course in woven textiles with a number of other women émigrés at Wagga Wagga. There is Jutta Feddersen, who after studying weaving in Bremen arrived in 1957 and taught at the Sturt Weaving workshops at Mittagong, where she was employed by the founder of the workshop, Erika Gretschel, herself a refugee from Germany after the war. And, finally, we have Berlin-born painter Gunter Christmann, who arrived in 1959, was also included in *The Field* in 1968, was an important member of the Central Street group of artists in the 1970s, represented Australia at the São Paulo Biennial and participated in two Biennales of Sydney. All of this is to leave out such pre-war arrivals as Gustav Pillig and Elise Blumann, wartime arrivals as Fred Lowen and Karl Duldig (like Feuerring from the Austro-Hungarian Empire), postwar arrivals as John Krzywokulski and Ernest Fries, and even Cold War arrivals as Karl Wiebke and Alex Spremberg.

But if the generation of German artists coming immediately before and after the war was largely untrained or only recently established in art, after the construction of the Berlin Wall between the two Germanys in 1961, Australia also became a destination for West German artists who had already acquired a worldwide reputation. They include the Swiss-German museum director Harald Szeemann, who came to curate *I Want to Leave a Nice Well-Done Child Here*, an exhibition of Australian artists for Kaldor Public Art Projects in 1971; Klaus Rinke, who came initially for the Mildura Sculpture Triennial in 1976 and then made a number of lengthy return trips into the early 1980s;[26] Niklaus Lang, who came for the third Biennale of Sydney in 1979 (he showed again in the seventh in 1988) and then undertook 'fieldwork' in South Australia from 1986 until 1989, holding the exhibition *Australian Imaginary Figurations 1986–1988* at the Art Gallery of South Australia in 1988; Sigmar Polke, who travelled through Tasmania, Central Australia, the Northern Territory and Papua New Guinea in 1981–82, where he made short films and collected materials for his work; Joseph Beuys, who came to install his *Stripes from the house of the shaman, 1966–76* (1980) for the opening of the National Gallery of Australia in 1982; Werner Herzog, who filmed *Where the green ants dream* in the Northern Territory in 1984; Jörg Immendorff, who performed himself in full-leather-rings-and-piercings mode in 1984 for the fifth Biennale of Sydney, with his three-month residency in Auckland three years later becoming the subject of a series of exhibitions by New Zealand artist Michael Stevenson, who showed *Call me Immendorff* at Galerie Kapinos in Berlin in 2000, *Immendorff in Wellington* at Hamish McKay Gallery in Wellington in 2001 and *An evening with Jörg Immendorff* at The Hyatt in Auckland in 2002; Wolfgang Laib, whose *Milk stone* (1980) was acquired by the National Gallery of Australia before it opened, who came to Australia for the sixth Biennale of Sydney in 1986 and then returned to do one-person exhibitions around Australasia between 2004 and 2006; and Martin Kippenberger, who subsequently exorcised his own participation in the 1994 Biennale of Sydney, but was nonetheless well known to the Sydney art scene and other visiting artists during the week he was there.

From the late 1960s until the 1980s, there was also a more general flow of exhibitions of German art to Australia, beginning with *German Painters of Today* at the Adelaide Festival in 1968. *Paul Klee* and *Graphic Art in Germany Today* toured the country in 1974, the same year *Two Masters of the Weimar Bauhaus: Lyonel Feininger, Ludwig Hirschfeld Mack* was held at the Art Gallery of New South Wales, all of this culminating in *Wild Visionary Spectral: New German Art*, which was staged at the Art Gallery of South Australia, the Art Gallery of Western Australia and the New Zealand National Art Gallery in Wellington in 1986, an exhibition that reflected the so-called return to figurative painting already evident in the work of such Australian artists and artist collectives as Dale Frank, Peter Booth, Mandy Martin, even the previously hard-edge and lyrical abstract painter Sydney Ball, and Roar Studios in Melbourne. The Goethe-Institut as well has been an important conduit for artists' residencies since the 1990s, supporting, for instance, Leni Hoffmann, Manuel Franke and Andreas Exner. German-speaking Austria and Switzerland have been concerned to promote their artists, too, and thus we have seen exhibitions here of the work of such artists as Heimo Zobernig, Anne Schneider and Beat Zoderer. Equally, Australian artists during this time have studied and worked in Germany. The Sydney artists

Tim Maguire, Maria Cruz and ADS Donaldson all trained at the Kunstakademie Düsseldorf in the 1980s and '90s, continuing the line begun some 140 years before by von Guérard, and extended by John Hennings, Pillig, Feuerring and Ostoja-Kotkowski. And likewise, the Melbourne artist Stephen Bram has studied at the Kunstakademie München in the 1990s, continuing the line begun in the nineteenth century by George Folingsby, and continued by Bernard Hall, Frank Weitzel and Erica McGilchrist.

Equally, if it is true that Australasian artists have always studied with German artists in Germany, it is also true that Germans have been taught there by Australasians. It is a line begun at the end of the last century by the new media artist Jeffrey Shaw, who was the founding director of the ZKM Centre for Art and Media Karlsruhe in 1991 and was appointed Professor of Media Art at the Karlsruhe University of Arts and Design (HfG) in 1995, and followed by the video artist Jill Scott, who was a Professor in the Media Department of the Bauhaus Universität in Weimar from 1998 until 2002 and has been a Professor at the Zurich University of the Arts since 2003. It has been continued by the New Zealander Michael Stevenson, who has been a Professor of Sculpture at the Akademie der Bildenden Künste Nürnberg since 2011, by his compatriot Simon Denny, who has been a Professor of Time-based Media at the Kunstakademie Hamburg since 2018, and most recently by the Melbourne artist Gerry Bibby, who replaced Olaf Metzel in 2020 as a Professor of Sculpture at the Kunstakademie in Munich.

In 1985 the influential German curator René Block put on a show called *5/5 Fünf vom Fünften (5/5 Five From the Fifth)*, which featured five contemporary Australian artists, at Berlin's DAAD Gallery. We think the title was deliberately intended to evoke the early twentieth-century German photographer EO Hoppé, who in 1929 came to Australia, initially intending to spend only six months, but eventually staying here an entire year, and in 1931 published *The Fifth Continent*, the first photographic record of Australia by a photographer of any nationality. In the words of photography curator Gael Newton:

> While many hundreds of photographers had made hundreds of thousands of images of different places and had photographed notable journeys, including the rugged transcontinental trips by pioneer motorist Francis Birtles before World War I, no local photographer had published an equivalent, all-encompassing work.[27]

It was an epic transcontinental undertaking by camel, car and train, with Hoppé's son Frank acting as his father's assistant. It was funded largely by Hoppé himself, who had started life as a banker for Deutsche Bank in London in 1900, shooting with amateur photographic societies in his spare time. In 1907 he opened his own photographic studio, and by 1930 he had attained worldwide fame as an ocean-hopping documentary photo-essayist working in a style that combined, in Newton's words, 'tonal impressionism' with a 'sharp-focus realism'.[28]

The Fifth Continent, we might say, owes something to August Sander's great Weimar period photographic taxonomies of German society, except that with Hoppé the logic is cross-sectional not vertical, panoramic and not classificatory. His project might even be seen as a complement to that of the Austrian botanical illustrator Ferdinand Bauer, 'widely acclaimed as one of the greatest botanical artists of all time',[29] who accompanied Matthew Flinders on his circumnavigation of Australia in 1801 and 1802, thus becoming the first artist to see at least all of the *outside* of Australia. Hoppé while here also exhibited his work at the David Jones Art Gallery, where it had a considerable influence on the first Australian modernist photographers, the ultimately more Bauhaus-inclined and even surrealistic Max Dupain and Olive Cotton.

The image of Hoppé at work at an Aboriginal mission reminds us uncannily of Tracey Moffatt's 1999 *Self portrait*, and we wonder here about coincidence and cause and effect. Is Moffatt not reversing the roles from ethnographic subject to ethnographer of her own subjectivity in light of Hoppé? Does she not keep Hoppé's camera and train it on herself? During the writing of this essay, we have sometimes flirted with the seemingly outrageous slogan, in homage to Richard Bell, 'Aboriginal Art Is a German Thing'. And perhaps it applies, if it applies at all, to no one more than Albert Namatjira (whose very name indicates his dual identity—for the forename Albert is ultimately German, popularised in Britain in the mid-nineteenth century following Queen Victoria's marriage to Prince Albert, who anglicised his name from Albrecht). During his own lifetime, there were two predominant attitudes towards Namatjira's work. He was either disdained by the likes of his 'teacher' Rex Battarbee (who ended up preferring the more 'primitive' Edwin Pareroultja) or criticised, as by the eminent French anthropologist Claude Lévi-Strauss, for losing his Aboriginality; or he was positively lauded for being the first Indigenous Australian to show that the 'black man' could paint like the white (this being more or less Margaret Preston's view).[30] But, as has been more recently revealed (take, for instance, his pokerwork boomerangs done in the early 1930s, well before he 'learned' to paint), Namatjira was surrounded by Western artefacts, in a situation neither of primitivism nor of sudden modernism but of what we might call *contemporaneity*.[31] And this contemporaneity, as we say, was largely German. The Hermannsburg mission where Namatjira lived was as much as anything a small German town, from the late 1880s on to an equal degree as in touch with Berlin and Munich as it was with Sydney and Melbourne. More particularly, in terms of an actual artistic lineage, we can say, taking into account whatever internal revisions, Namatjira was also part of a German desert landscape school that started with Becker and ran through Heysen to Battarbee. Indeed, it was the newly appointed Pastor Friedrich Albrecht who originally invited Battarbee and John Gardner to hold a show of their watercolours at the Lutheran mission at Hermannsburg, an exhibition that also included Heysen. Albrecht then encouraged Battarbee to send Namatjira some painting materials; in 1935 Namatjira produced his first watercolour, the oddly prophetic *Fleeing kangaroo*. (Coincidentally, this was the same year the Dresden artist Hans Grundig produced his etching *Warten* (*Waiting*), his own image of the kangaroo, as part of his cycle of prints *Tiere und Menschen* (*Animals and people*), itself a kind of echo of the Soviet artist Vladimir Lebedev's lithograph *Okhota* (*The hunt*) of 1925 with its depiction of kangaroos being hunted by Indigenous men bearing shields and boomerangs.) Later in 1935 Albrecht took ten of Namatjira's works to the Lutheran synodical conference at Nurioopta, where six were sold; and the following year Battarbee included a number of Namatjira's paintings in his own exhibition in Adelaide, where Heysen saw them for the first time and remarked upon their 'freshness'.[32]

This interrelationship between Germany and Indigenous art has always been with us—indeed, is even part of us. On the one hand, in 1994 the Cologne Art Fair famously rejected work by Kuninjku artist John Mawurndjul

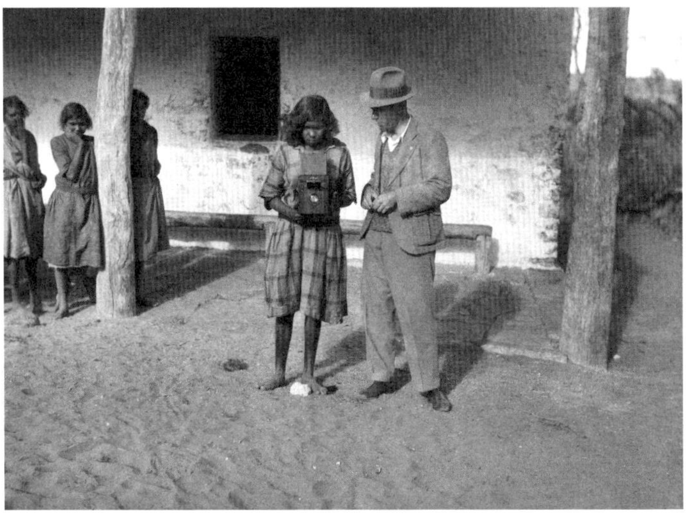

7.11 EO Hoppé and a young woman at the Hermannsburg Lutheran Mission Station, Central Australia, 1930

from Australia's Gallery Gabrielle Pizzi for being 'folk art'.[33] On the other, it is German art historiography from Alois Riegl on that has largely made the case to treat Aboriginal art not as primitive ethnography. Indeed, there is an entire thesis by Friederike Krishnabhakdi-Vasilakis entitled 'On the Reception of Aboriginal Art in German Art Spaces' that investigates this duality, describing an intellectual war between those high-art spaces at the top of the hierarchy that reinforce what she describes as a 'self-reflexive notion of culture' and ethnographic museums that increasingly have 'provided the context against which European, specifically German, identity and culture are pitched'.[34] And Krishnabhakdi-Vasilakis discusses a number of these apparently ethnographic shows that have done so much to make clear that Aboriginal art is in fact contemporary, particularly two held at the Iwalewa House at the University of Bayreuth: *Papunya: Moderne Malerei von australischen Ureinwohnern* (*Papunya: Modern Painting by Australian Aborigines*) in 1982 and *Traumzeit–Maschinenzeit: Neue Kunst der australischen Ureinwohnern* (*Dreamtime–Machine Time: New Australian Aboriginal Art*) in 1987. She then looks at two more recent exhibitions held in more conventional art galleries, after the battle for the status of Aboriginal art had largely been won, one of which was *Aratjara: Art of the First Australians* at the Kunstsammlung

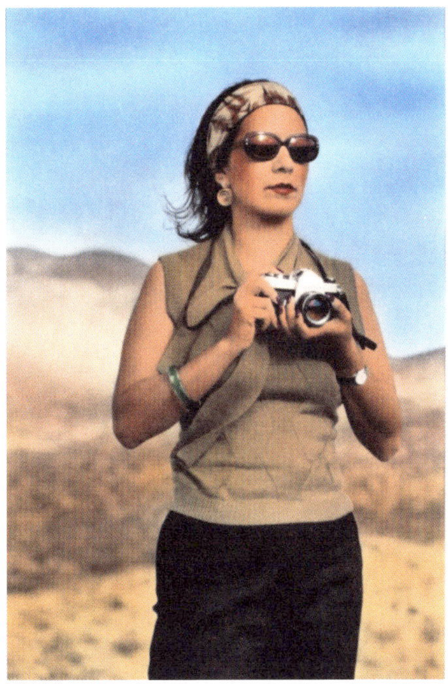

7.12 Tracey Moffatt
Self portrait, 1999

Nordrhein-Westfalen, Düsseldorf, in 1993. This show was jointly curated by Indigenous activist Gary Foley and the German Bernard Lüthi, who had been the curator of the Aboriginal art for the ground-breaking *Magiciens de la Terre* at the Centre Pompidou in Paris in 1989. It included work by Rover Thomas, Clifford Possum Tjapaltjarri and Pansy Napangati, and subsequently toured to London and Humlebaek in Denmark. And since 1995 there have been at least four major surveys of Aboriginal art in Germany, of which we will speak of only one: *Rarrk: John Mawurndjul—Journey Through Time in Northern Australia*, a 2005 retrospective of the Western Arnhem Land painter John Mawurndjul at the Sprengel Museum in Hanover.[35] Again, Lüthi was one of the curators, and the exhibition was the first retrospective of an Indigenous artist in Germany. And when the show travelled to the Jean Tinguely Museum in Basel there was a symposium held in conjunction with it, involving scholars from Australia and Germany, on the topic of world contemporary art and particularly the place of Aboriginal art in the new global context—remember, this was the artist rejected from the Cologne Art Fair just ten years earlier for being 'too folkloric'. (And all of this is in a way to take us back to von Guérard, who collected Aboriginal shields from western Victoria and sent them back to German ethnographic museums while working for the National Gallery of Victoria.[36])

What would it mean for us to imagine such a conference taking place in German—which in all probability it did not, insofar as we presume all the Germans would have spoken English—such that it would have been *in German* that Australia could once again have thought its place in the world? It would be a language, a little like music, that would not only speak of the breaking down of our national boundaries but actually *be* the breaking down of these boundaries. It would be a language that, throughout our history, would remind us, even if it was not understood, even in not being understood, that there were others outside us. And this against all of Australia's periods of xenophobic and self-isolating nationalism (a nationalism that runs parallel to, even if it is not quite as so virulent as, Germany's throughout the twentieth century). We might indeed compare this possible German-Australian art history to something like the staging of music sung in German, which in some ways is even harder to translate, but is nevertheless not just the message but also the very medium of a kind of universalism.

We finish here by jumping forward some twenty-six years from our first mention of Beethoven to the legendary performance of his Ninth Symphony by conductor Eugene Ormandy and the Sydney Symphony Orchestra in Sydney in 1944 at the height of World War II. Again, it is not exactly clear what Ormandy was wanting to say by staging the piece—he refused to spell it out when asked—but the musical language of Beethoven speaks to us in a way that makes us actually enact the words of Schiller across the divide of conflict as we listen:

> Your magic brings together
> What custom has sternly divided.
> All men shall become brothers
> Wherever your gentle wings hover.

In this imaginary pairing of German and Australian art histories, we are reminded that during World War I, a persistent rumour crossed both sides, who were stalled facing each other in deadly trench warfare, that beneath the ground between them was a secret cavern where troops of opposite sides mixed and fraternised. It was obviously a kind of fantasy erected against the horrors of war, intended to make them bearable: utopian, unrealisable, subterranean. But, in some way, art *is* this fantasy. It runs below or against all conflict, all opposition, all partisanship, all exclusionist and nationalist histories, whether Australian or German. And this is not simply utopian or unrealisable, but, as we have hoped to show here, is to be seen in the intersection of our two respective art histories.

An earlier version of this text was delivered as a lecture at the Goethe-Institut, Sydney, for the commemoration of the centenary of World War I, 24 July 2014. Subsequently published in *emaj*, no. 8, 2015.

—

1 'Conservatorium Matinee', *Sydney Morning Herald*, 25 November 1918, p. 4. We are grateful to Samantha Owens of the School of Music at the University of Queensland for her assistance with the musical references in this essay.

2 By 'German' here, we refer not only to Germany as defined by its changing borders throughout the twentieth century, but also to German ethnicity, the German language and German culture (including Austria and Switzerland).

3 Daniel Thomas, 'Appendix: Von Guerard's Reputation', in ed. Candice Bruce, *Eugen von Guérard*, exhibition catalogue, National Gallery of Australia, Canberra, 1980, p. 131. It is important to recognise that among von Guérard's pupils were McCubbin and Roberts.

4 On Becker and Burke and Wills, see Martin Edmond, *The Supply Party: Ludwig Becker on the Burke and Wills Expedition*, East Street Publications, Adelaide, 2009.

5 See Ruth Zubans, 'Folingsby, George Frederick (1828–1891)', in *Australian Dictionary of Biography*, vol. 4, Melbourne University Press, 1972, http://adb.anu.edu.au/biography/folingsby-george-frederick-3545; and Ann E Galbally, 'Hall, Lindsay Bernard (1859–1935)', in *Australian Dictionary of Biography*, vol. 9, Melbourne University Press, 1983, http://adb.anu.edu.au/biography/hall-lindsay-bernard-6528.

6 For a detailed history of Lutheranism at Hermannsburg, see Diane Austin-Broos, *Arrernte Present, Arrernte Past: Invasion, Violence, and Imagination in Indigenous Central Australia*, University of Chicago Press, 2009.

7 See 'New Books: Art for a Purpose', *Argus*, 15 May 1915, p. 4; and classified advertising in *Argus*, 31 July 1915, p. 4.

8 It must be said, however, that Synchromism (as founded by the Americans Stanton MacDonald-Wright and Morgan Russell in 1912 in Munich) and books by MacDonald-Wright's brother Willard Huntington Wright (*Modern Painting: Its Tendency and Meaning*, 1915) and Beatrice Irwin (*The New Science of Colour*, 1915) influenced de Maistre and Wakelin—more than AB Hector did.

9 See Tracey Lock-Weir, 'Chronicle', in ed. Tracey Lock-Weir, *Dorrit Black: Unseen Forces*, exhibition catalogue, Art Gallery of South Australia, Adelaide, 2014, p. 176.

10 Harriet Edquist even dates the introduction of modernist architecture into Australia back to the 1930s with the German-born and Swiss-trained Frederick Romberg. See Harriet Edquist, 'Romberg, Frederick (1913–1992)', *Australian Dictionary of Biography*, National Centre of Biography, Australian National University, 2016, http://adb.anu.edu.au/biography/romberg-frederick-16350.

11 Tilli Frankel, cited in 'How London Is Changing: Visitor's Impressions: Art and Machines', *Sydney Morning Herald*, 26 June 1936, p. 4.

12 Emil Nolde, quoted in Florian Illies, *1913: The Year Before the Storm*, Clerkenwell Press, London, 2013, p. 256. On Nolde in the Pacific, see also Jean-David Jumeau-Lafond, 'Emil Nolde (1867–1956)', *Art Tribune*, 11 November 2008, http://www.thearttribune.com/Emil-Nolde-1867-1956.html; and Christian Ring, *Emil Nolde: The South Seas*, DuMont Buchverlag, Cologne, 2018.

13 Frank Whitford, 'The Nazi Who Painted "Degenerate" Art', *Art Newspaper*, June 2014, vol. 23, no. 258, p. 79.

14 Heather Johnson, 'The Specialist Art Dealer: Adolph Albers', in *The Sydney Art Patronage System 1890–1940*, Bungoona Technologies, Sydney, 1997, p. 86.

15 Ibid., p. 86.

16 Lionel Lindsay, *Addled Art*, Hollis and Carter, London, 1946, p. 12.

17 'Modernism in Art: New Cult Condemned', *Argus*, 26 October 1926, p. 21.

18 Alan McCulloch, 'Theo Scharf', *Encyclopedia of Australian Art*, Hutchinson, Melbourne, 1984, p. 1068.

19 Theo Scharf, 'The First-Hand Account of Theo Scharf', in ed. William Yenne, *German War Art, 1939–1945*, Crescent Books, New York, 1983, p. 148.

20 Walter Freud, cited in Ken Inglis, 'From Berlin to the Bush', *The Monthly* (Melbourne), October 2010, p. 56.

21 James Gleeson, 'Strange But Fascinating Blend', *The Sun*, February 1963. Cited in Charles Nodrum, *Peter Kaiser*, exhibition catalogue, Charles Nodrum Gallery, September 1985, np.

22 For a more detailed account of this, see Sheridan Palmer, *Centre of the Periphery: Three European Art Historians in Melbourne*, Australian Scholarly Publishing, Melbourne, 2008.

23 The Englishman Joseph Burke was given the founding chair of art history at the University of Melbourne, but he was appointed chiefly for his administrative abilities, for being a safe pair of hands. Also on the *Dunera* were the primitivist

Leonhard Adam, the historian George Nadel and the philosophers Kurt Baier and Peter Herbst, among many others. For a general overview of the *Dunera* and its effect upon Australian culture, see Ken Inglis, Seumas Spark and Jay Winter, *Dunera Lives: A Visual History*, Monash University Publishing, Melbourne, 2018.

24 See 'James Gleeson Interviews Inge King', 18 October 1979, p. 22, https://nga.gov.au/research/gleeson/pdf/king_inge.pdf.

25 Marcella Hempell, letter to John McPhee, 11 October 1990; cited in John McPhee, 'Sanctuaries: Three Textile Artists in Australia', in ed. Roger Butler, *The Europeans: Emigré Artists in Australia 1930–1960*, exhibition catalogue, National Gallery of Australia, Canberra, 1997, p. 83.

26 David Galloway, 'The Passionate Pilgrimage of Klaus Rinke', in ed. Suzanne Davies, *Klaus Rinke: Recent Drawings; Rhine-Ruhr-Danube-Loire-Pacific Connection-re-Australia*, exhibition catalogue, RMIT Gallery, Melbourne, 2008, p. 11.

27 Gael Newton, 'Fame, Fortune and the Fifth Continent', *The World of Antiques & Art* (Sydney), no. 72, February–August 2007, p. 14.

28 Ibid., p. 15.

29 Marlene J Norst, *Ferdinand Bauer: The Australian Natural History Drawings*, British Museum of Natural History, London, 1989, p. 9. Norst goes on to say: 'His paintings and drawings of [Flinders'] and other journeys are treasured in museums and libraries around the world: Lichtenstein, Oxford, Gottingen, Vienna and London; and his own contemporaries as well as botanists today compete in extolling the excellence of his work' (p. 9).

30 For a reading that opens up the possibility of a 'deterritorialised' Namatjira along the lines we are suggesting, see Astarte Rowe, 'Of Conceptual Deserts: A Deleuzian Approach to Aboriginal Art', PhD thesis, University of Melbourne, 2013, www.minerva-access.unimelb.edu.au/handle/11343/39775.

31 See on this Ian McLean, 'Aboriginal Modernism in Central Australia', in ed. Kobena Mercer, *Exiles, Diasporas and Strangers*, MIT Press, Cambridge, Mass., 2009, pp. 72–95. Indeed, we might recall in this context that it was from the German missionary and ethnologist Carl Strehlow, working at Hermannsburg, that Tristan Tzara got the ceremonial songs that he turned into his Dadaist 'Song of the serpent' and 'Song of the cockatoo' (1917). We are grateful to the anonymous reviewer of this essay for reminding us of this.

32 On this 'freshness', see Peter W Wilkins, 'Albert Namitjira—Aboriginal Artist', www.wilmap.com.au/people/namatjira.html.

33 See Djon Mundine, 'Aboriginal Art Abroad: Responses to Touring Exhibitions in Europe, the United States and Asia', *Art and Australia*, vol. 35, no. 1, 1997, p. 70.

34 See Friederike Krishnabhakdi-Vasilakis, 'On the Reception of Aboriginal Art in German Arts Spaces: Art Historical and Anthropological Perspectives', PhD thesis, University of Wollongong, 2011, www.ro.uow.edu.au/creartspapers/254/.

35 Another exhibition that certainly deserves mention is *Remembering Forward: Australian Aboriginal Painting Since 1960*, curated by Emily Evans and Claus Volkenandt and held at the Museum Ludwig in Cologne in 2010.

36 These papers have been published in eds. Claus Volkenandt and Christian Kaufmann, *Between Indigenous Australia and Europe: John Mawurndjul; Art Histories in Context*, Aboriginal Studies Press, Canberra, 2009.

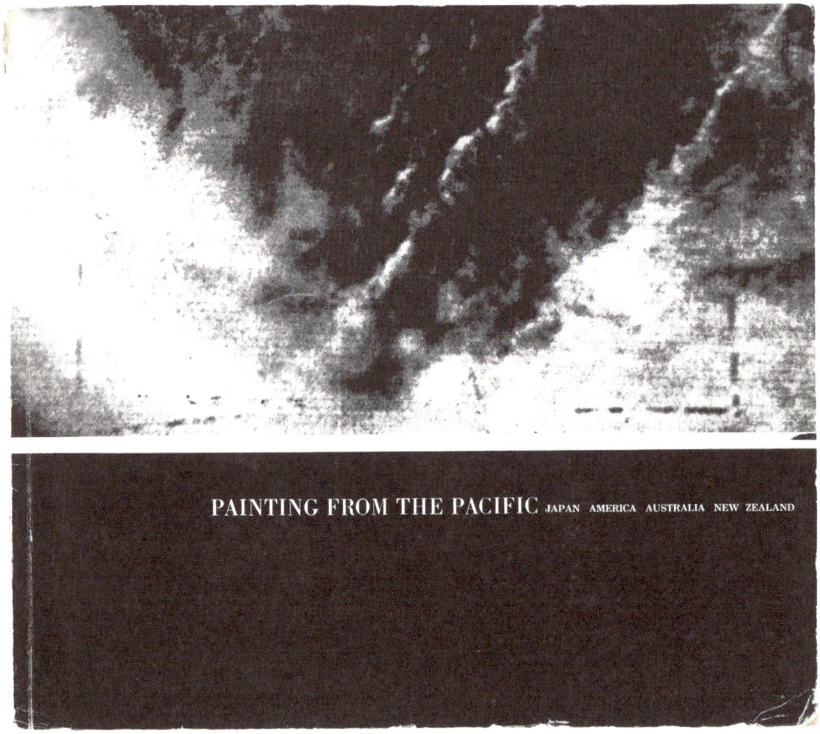

8.1 *Painting from the Pacific: Japan, America, Australia, New Zealand*, exhibition catalogue, 1961

Trans-Pacific
Abstract Painting in Australia, New Zealand and America 1930–1960

Art history begins with coincidence. So let us begin here with a few of our own. The year 2013 was the one hundredth anniversary of Duchamp's readymade, and was celebrated around the world. But besides the appearance of *Bicycle wheel* (1913) in Paris, what else happened in 1913? There was the emergence of abstract painting—be it František Kupka's *The first step* (1909–13), Robert Delaunay's *The first disk* (1912–13) or Fernand Léger's *Contrast of forms* (1913)—and the coincidence, or impossibility of coincidence, between abstraction and the readymade is extremely interesting for us. In America in 2013, the famous 1913 Armory Show also enjoyed its centenary celebrations. But uncelebrated and largely unrecognised was the one hundredth anniversary of contemporary Aboriginal art, which arguably began when anthropologist Baldwin Spencer reproduced in his *Preliminary Report on the Aborigines of the Northern Territory*, presented to the Commonwealth minister for external affairs in 1913, images of Aboriginal shelters on Melville Island. It was from constructions like these from Oenpelli that Spencer extracted the bark paintings that he then took back to Melbourne, later to enter the collection of the National Museum of Victoria.[1] It is precisely in cutting these paintings out of their original context as part of the Indigenous integration of art and architecture, so that they could travel and be shown, that Spencer can be seen to have turned them into art in the Western sense—indeed, into something like readymades. Now the work insofar as it entered the museum no longer had an original context; but from the beginning, these shelters could be seen only as a place for the temporary exhibition of art, a little like the Bazar de l'Hôtel de Ville, the Paris department store from which Duchamp selected his bottle-drying rack. Indeed, we might even say that after Spencer's gesture not only are bark paintings created by artists who knew that their work would eventually be seen by a white audience, but even their first Indigenous audience could now only see them this way. (Spencer after this first series of works commissioned the Arnhem

Land artists to paint directly onto bark supports so that they could be transported.) Their original creators therefore saw themselves differently, as though through the eyes of an other. It is from this moment on that we might properly speak of the formation in Western discourse of the general category of Aboriginal art rather than works being understood according to the ethnographic production of particular peoples and language groups.

But Aboriginal art was not the only Indigenous art to emerge into the mainstream in 1913—and to come about in a way through its coincidence with Duchamp. Navajo art was not included in the 1913 Armory Show in New York, but was made present through a remark made by ex-President Theodore Roosevelt, in which he compared Duchamp's *Nude descending a staircase* (1912), which was the *succès de scandale* of the exhibition, with a Navajo rug on his bathroom floor: 'From the standpoint of decorative simplicity, of sincerity, and of artistic merit, the Navajo rug is infinitely ahead of the picture'.[2] But, again, what is crucial is that this coincidence is not at all stated following the usual modernist model of 'primitivism', in which Indigenous art is merely a precursor to or source material for Western art. Rather, what makes it a coincidence is that the two events occur at the same time, with each allowing the other to be seen. It is indeed something like this coincidence that is often noted in Australian art, from early explorers mistaking Wandjina figures for gods,[3] to Imants Tillers making a work about the shared birthdays of Duchamp and Hans Heysen,[4] to the work of Tillers and Western Desert artist Michael Nelson Jagamara being reproduced on successive pages of a catalogue for the 1986 Biennale of Sydney, thanks to an accident of orthography ('Jagamara' on this occasion being spelled with a 'Tj' instead of the usual 'J'), leading to the two artists working collaboratively.[5] This coincidence between Tillers and Jagamara marks a break, argues art historian Ian McLean, from Aboriginal art being seen in a modernist paradigm, with its linear passage or succession of styles, to being understood as a form of contemporary art, which is characterised by a certain simultaneity of times and places.[6] But, in fact, as is evident from the coincidental appearance of Aboriginal and Navajo art, both unknown to each other, in the same year in Melbourne and New York, Indigenous art has been contemporary since at least 1913.

In this essay, however, we want to concentrate on another 'coincidence': the simultaneous emergence in the 1930s and 1940s of abstract painting in Australia, New Zealand and America, but more particularly in Sydney, Auckland, Taos and Los Angeles. It is what we might speak of as a trans-Pacific abstraction. The causal occasion of our observations—a truth revealed only after the event, as is always the case with coincidence—is a show, *Paintings from the Pacific*, held at the Auckland City Gallery in May 1961, curated by its director, Peter Tomory, and including work from New Zealand, Australia, America and Japan. It was a large show, bringing together recent work by more than eighty artists, including Richard Diebenkorn, Mark Tobey, Billy Al Bengston, Karl Benjamin, Lorser Feitelson, Helen Lundeberg, Gordon Onslow Ford and Stanton MacDonald-Wright from America; Margo Lewers, Carl Plate, William Rose and Stanislaus Rapotec from Australia; Colin McCahon, Jean Horsley and Milan Mrkusich from New Zealand; and Yuichi Inoue, Hisao Domoto, Kaoru Yamaguchi and Eien Iwahashi from Japan. In his foreword to the catalogue, Tomory writes:

> Three years ago, there was an exhibition held here including some of the West Coast American painters. Two years ago, an exhibition came from Japan including a number of Western-style painters. There have also been two Australian exhibitions in the last five years. Amongst these artists and our own here there seemed to lie a certain homogeneity—a sympathetic link, perhaps tangible, and certainly indefinable.
>
> Our thought was, therefore, in arranging this exhibition, to bring all four regions together in order to see whether the Pacific provided some characteristic: perhaps light, or topography, or perhaps, again, some identifiable content. It is with this in mind that these paintings have been selected.[7]

What Tomory is looking for here is some explanation of why the artists he has chosen all emerged at the same time looking so similar. He runs through all of the usual explanations for such a coincidence—climate, landscape, national character—before stopping and admitting that, even if these were true, they would be insufficient. Thwarted in his ambition, he ultimately gestures towards an indefinable 'sympathetic link'—and this is always worrying for the art historian because it comes close to the notorious mistake of pseudomorphism, of thinking that because two works of art look the same they must mean the same thing or come from the same place.

In this essay, we attempt to answer Tomory's question. The answer, however, is not to be found in art history, as either the retrospective reconstitution of an original or the genealogical tracking of a style that is preserved and passed on. Rather, what Tomory observes did happen enigmatically all at once, and was understood and theorised by the artists at the time as such. In some ways, we have a word for this, which is globalism. What Tomory is observing is, in the words of English art historian Sarah Wilson, an instance of 'globalisation before globalisation'.[8] But there is another word for it—or perhaps two—both of which have associations with art: 'spirit' and the 'unconscious' (unconscious not in the corporeal individual or at best social Freudian sense, but in the incorporeal universal, if not cosmic, Jungian sense).

Of course, mention of the spiritual in art cannot but remind us of Wassily Kandinsky. Kandinsky—to start with Tomory's American selections—is not an artist often remembered as being one of the other stars of the 1913 Armory Show. Excerpts of his 1911 book *Über das Geistige in der Kunst* (*Concerning the Spiritual in Art*) had already been translated and published in Alfred Steiglitz's *Camerawork* in 1912. (Even in Melbourne, it was possible to read a review of the book in *The Argus* as early as 1914, following its translation that year into English.[9]) A Russian-born Theosophist who taught at the Weimar, Dessau and Berlin Bauhauses before being forced to flee to Paris by the rise of National Socialism (his work was included in *Entartete Kunst*, the infamous *Degenerate Art* exhibition), Kandinsky was entirely pan-European in outlook, coming out of a long tradition connecting the cosmopolitan to the spiritual—and the European to the global—that went all the way back to Kant. For him, the true task of art was to represent not the external but the internal world. At this early stage of his career in *Über das Geistige* (*Concerning the Spiritual*), however, he is not proposing any literal alphabet or transliteration of soul states, as in his later book *Punkt und Linie zu Fläche* (*Point and Line to Plane*) of 1926 (or as Auguste Herbin was to do in his *Alphabet plastique* of the 1940s). On the contrary, as art historian Matthias Haldemann points out, Kandinsky, through a hyper-reflexive process of searching for what lies behind abstraction, seeks to pass beyond visual symbolisation altogether.[10] In Kandinsky, there is a kind of *coincidentia oppositorum* between on the one hand his quasi-scientific reflection on the principles underlying abstraction and on the other his painterly 'improvisations', in which he breaks with any language-like translation of inner spiritual states (for example, the diagram for 'Obstinacy with forbearance', the analysis of *Little dream in red* (1925) or the visual translation of the opening bars of Beethoven's Fifth Symphony in *Point and Line to Plane*).[11]

When the Sydney painter Frank Hinder joined the American artist and pedagogue Emil Bisttram's first-ever class in Taos in New Mexico in 1933, they already had Jay Hambidge's *Dynamic symmetry* and Howard Giles's magazine *The Diagonal* in common.[12] From 1922 Bisttram had also been acquainted with Russian artist and polymath Nicholas Roerich, whose spiritualism and Theosophy deeply informed the Roerich Museum he founded in 1929. (Indeed, before heading to America's south west, Hinder had studied with both Giles and Bisttram at Parsons School of Fine and Applied Art and at Roerich's Master Institute attached to the Museum.) But what more truly lies behind both Hinder and Bisttram is Kandinsky. Bisttram later recalled that he encountered Kandinsky for the first time only in 1933, when he copied his work and discovered *The Spiritual in Art*, all after his move to Taos the previous year.[13] And immediately before returning to

Sydney, Frank and his wife, the sculptor Margel Hinder (née Harris), whom he had first met at a Bisttram summer school in upstate New York in 1929, travelled to Taos and began working again with Bisttram, with their time there coinciding with Bisttram's 'discovery' of Kandinsky. For his part, Kandinsky had his work promoted in America by the art dealer and collector Galka Scheyer from 1924, was appointed vice-president by Katherine Dreier of her and Duchamp's Societé Anonyme in 1925 (a position he would hold until his death) and participated in the ground-breaking *International Exhibition of Modern Art* at the Brooklyn Museum in 1926. This, then, is Bisttram on the connection he saw between what he was trying to do with his painting and the art of the Native American Pueblos of New Mexico, now visible in the light of his reading and knowledge of Kandinsky:

> They were never permitted to paint anything realistic. They were painting ideas. Something to do with the spirit of man's inner nature … I realized for the first time what the abstract artists were trying to do.[14]

Frank Hinder returned with Margel to Sydney in 1934, where they formed a circle that included Grace Crowley and Ralph Balson, whose artistic roots lay in French post-cubism and its attendant analysis of the picture plane and figure–ground relations. In 1937 these two divergent streams (Crowley and Balson's French post-cubism after Lhote and Gleizes, and the Hinders' Kandinsky-influenced abstraction coming from America) joined together formally to found the George Street Group, the cradle of abstract art in Australia. It was the same year, coincidentally, that the Manhattan-centric American Abstract Artists held their first exhibition in New York. Almost exactly one year later, in 1938, Bisttram co-founded the Transcendental Painting Group in Taos, the organisation that brought together such artists as Raymond Jonson, Florence Miller, Agnes Pelton, Ed Garman and the Canadian Lawren Harris, and that, in the words of their 'Statement of Purpose', 'aimed to stimulate in others, through the deep and spontaneous emotional experiences of form and colour, a more intense participation in the life of the spirit'.[15]

It was in 1938 too that Bisttram sent a copy of Hilla Rebay's third, expanded edition of the *Solomon Guggenheim Collection of Non-Objective Painting*, which featured the work of Delaunay, Léger, Klee, Gleizes and Georges Valmier as well as Rudolf Bauer and Kandinsky, to Frank Hinder, who subsequently shared it with Crowley and Balson. It thus formed a companion volume to their copy of Alfred Barr's *Cubism and Abstract Art* (1936), which also reproduced the work of Kandinsky. While it is true that only Hinder had by this time done truly abstract work—his two *Squares* of 1931 and 1932 are remarkable and almost completely unrecognised—in the time between the George Street Group's *Exhibition I* in

1939 (coincidentally, opening the same week war was declared) and Balson's solo exhibition in 1941, both Balson and Crowley had become abstract artists and would never again paint representationally. In Balson's landmark 1941 exhibition, we see not his oft-professed admiration of Mondrian, or even Klee. Instead, with cosmological space and the overlapping and transparent circles and triangles set within his canvases, it is Kandinsky whose influence is more evident than anyone else—and, indeed, they might be seen to be closer still to the work of Bisttram, whose work Balson could never have seen. Later, in the 1950s, both Balson and Bisttram would relate their work to science, particularly Einsteinian physics, and again separately and at the same time they painted nuclear and atomic cosmologies. For his part, Hinder was more open about the influence of Kandinsky, which was made clear in his watercolour *Tribute to Kandinsky* of 1938.

In the early 1930s, Sydney-born artist JW Power, whose own abstract paintings used biomorphic imagery, influenced perhaps by his earlier medical studies, was—like Kandinsky, following his flight from Germany in 1933—a member of the Paris-based artist collective Abstraction-Création. Power was part of that stream of Abstraction-Création that worked with biomorphic and cosmological imagery, the infinitely far and the infinitely near, which included Sophie Taeuber-Arp, Barbara

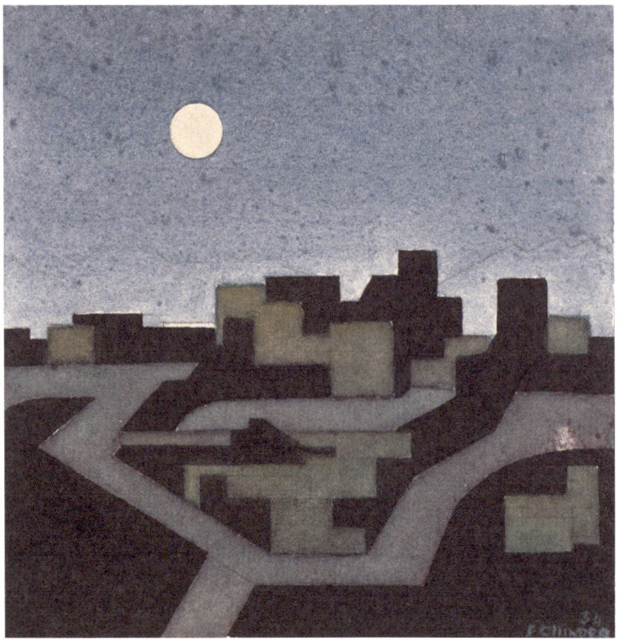

8.2 Frank Hinder
Taos landscape, 1934

Hepworth and Enrico Prampolini.[16] Later that decade back in Sydney, Balson, Crowley and the Hinders were joined in their activities by a small number of other artists, many of whom were likewise interested in Kandinsky. Their work was brought together in the little-known 1948 exhibition *Abstract* at the David Jones Gallery, which included Gordon Andrews and Alistair Morrison, both of whose practices showed the influence of Kandinsky. Indeed, another who had joined the George Street Group earlier in the 1930s was the Frankfurt-born artist and teacher Eleonore Lange, who in 1939 had written the catalogue essay for the group's *Exhibition I*, in which she declared that 'painting today is abandoning the representation of objects in order to establish a new realm of visual existence. This leads step by step to "abstract art"'.[17] Lange, who was a well known and popular public advocate for modern art following her arrival in 1930, also lectured, for instance, in 1943 on such subjects as 'Impressionism and Chinese brushwork', 'Futurism and the rendering of time in earlier periods', 'Cubism and some Pacific arts', 'Surrealism and the magic arts of the past' and 'Constructivism, past and present', in a series of talks arranged by the Contemporary Art Society and the Teachers' Federation Art Society, whose leading light was Bernard Smith. In his otherwise nationalist account, Smith could nonetheless see the globalism of his rival, writing:

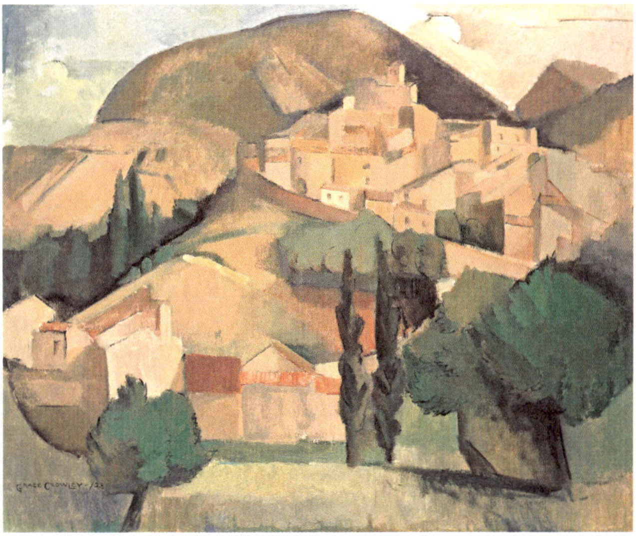

8.3 Grace Crowley
Mirmande, 1928

> She [Lange] did much to raise the level of understanding in art in Sydney by asserting international values and the aesthetic equality of style and played a most significant role in creating an informed audience for contemporary art, especially abstract and non-figurative painting and sculpture.[18]

Years earlier, and anticipating our own work, the title of Lange's final lecture at the Crowley-Fizelle studio in George Street of her 1937 course on 'The modern scientific research on art, and an introduction to its present-day problems', was 'National or international art'.[19]

It is likely that New Zealand artist Gordon Walters, who was living in Sydney in 1948, saw the *Abstract* exhibition.[20] As well as Andrews's and Morrison's work, it included the work of James Cant, who had begun the year before painting a kind of 'Aboriginal' modernism and who the following year would 'repaint' Aboriginal rock art from the Ubirr cave in Arnhem Land, based on photographs and drawings made by his friend the Adelaide anthropologist Charles Mountford. Cant's paintings were subsequently shown in London in 1950, in an exhibition that was acclaimed as 'the first introduction of Australian Aboriginal rock paintings to a European public'.[21] For his part, before leaving Wellington, Walters had worked

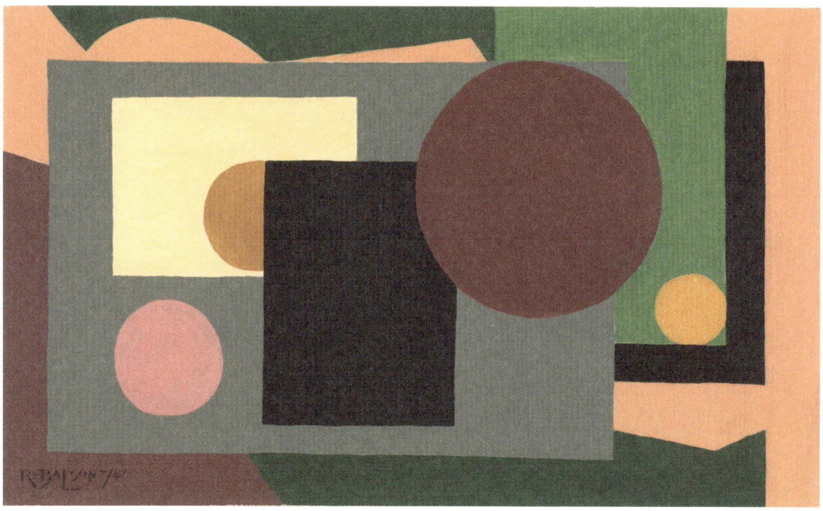

8.4 Ralph Balson
Painting, 1941

with Dutch-Indonesian–New Zealand artist Theo Schoon documenting Maori rock art in South Canterbury, and had produced his own rock art–like painting *The poet* (1947), not so different from such Cant Ubirr paintings as *Symbolic figures ascribed by the modern natives to an earlier people, the 'MIMI'* (1948/49). Then, once in Sydney, repeating the trajectory of fellow New Zealand artist Len Lye some twenty-five years earlier, Walters immediately went to the Australian Museum (where at this time, coincidentally, Cant worked as a preparator), the Mitchell Library and other museums in Australia to study, in particular, Indigenous art. Two years after the *Abstract* show, Walters travelled to Europe for the first time, where he saw the work of Herbin, Sophie Taeuber-Arp and Victor Vasarely, amongst many others. Then, returning to Melbourne in 1951, Walters painted his first abstract canvases. He later became celebrated for his great *Koru* paintings, one of the mainstays of a national New Zealand art, which he began in 1956; but what is perhaps less well known is that, just the year before, he had done a series 'inspired', he says, 'by Australian rock drawings. In Australia I had studied rock engravings in the Sydney area and bark paintings in the museums of Melbourne and Sydney'.[22] In the national histories where his work is almost invariably considered, and particularly in more recent revisionist versions of them, Walters's interest in Maori and Indigenous Australian work is said to show how prevalent ideas of 'primitivism' still were by the middle of the century, but we suggest that it is just as likely that a Kandinsky-like vision of spiritual universality was the real motivation behind the work.[23]

The New Zealand artist Milan Mrkusich—who, unlike Walters, was included in Tomory's show—had preceded Walters to abstraction by some five years. And he did it, unlike Walters, without the formative experience of travel. Rather, it was through his own individual study of such artists as Mondrian and Ben Nicholson, but also importantly through reproductions of Kandinsky's *Improvisations*, an influence local critics identified at the time.[24] Mrkusich has long been a problem for New Zealand art historiography: he didn't travel, he had no 'primitive' roots, he did not appear particularly New Zealandish (think of his name), he had no contact with Walters (there was no school of New Zealand abstraction, no internal New Zealand dialogue). He stayed put in his country and was an autodidact like Balson, whom he never met and whose work he could only have seen, alongside Crowley's, in the little-known exhibition *Contemporary Australian Art*, held at the Auckland City Gallery in 1948. However, despite or even because of this, his work actually resembles Balson's. His *City lights* (1955) is reminiscent of Balson's *Painting* (1954), with its small multicoloured squares on top of a tessellated rectangular ground and its residual transparencies. Mrkusich appears perhaps an inexplicable lone outcrop without comparison in New Zealand art history, but actually this aloneness is found throughout the world. It is a global phenomenon, and we might even say one of contemporaneity. We could compare Mrkusich not only to Balson but also, for example, to the Argentinians Esteban Lisa and Juan Del Prete, the Russian Léopold Survage, the French Félix Del Marle, and the German Henri Nouveau. Again, art history is the history of these repeated singularities, despite any critique we might make of pseudomorphism. Art history starts with these coincidences and its task is to try to explain them.

Across the other side of the Pacific, Los Angeles after the war was also going geometric. The 1961 show *Painting from the Pacific* included the work of Lorser Feitelson, Helen Lundeberg and Karl Benjamin. Of these, Feitelson was the senior figure, by this time in his fifties, who had studied in 1919 at the Académie Colarossi in Paris, made numerous trips back there in the 1920s and exhibited at the Salon d'Automne, before moving to Los Angeles in 1927. After his so-called *Kinetic* series from 1916–23, and following his years in Paris and move to the West Coast, he undertook what might be called his 'neoclassical' paintings, followed by his surrealism of the 1930s into the 1940s, before his final move into abstraction in 1948 with his *Magical space forms*. Like Crowley, that is, Feitelson had studied in France in the 1920s, had passed through various modernist modes and figuration and then, turning away from this, never painted representationally again. And, if we are

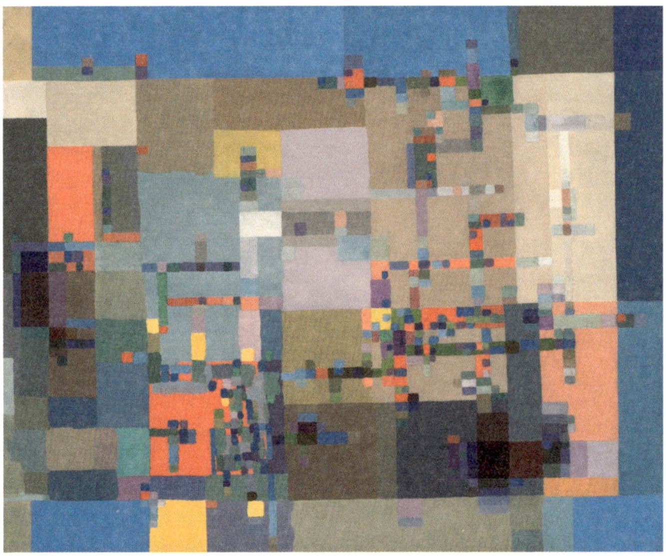

8.5 Milan Mrkusich
City lights, 1955

tempted to attribute the similar trajectories of both artists to their training in Paris, it must be remembered that this training in both cases reflected the 1920s *rappel à l'ordre*, and their move to abstraction necessarily took place against this influence.

Like Crowley in Sydney, Feitelson was at the centre of a circle of artists in Los Angeles working in an abstract style, including most notably his wife, Helen Lundeberg. In many ways Feitelson plays Crowley to Lundeberg's Balson. In 1946 Feitelson organised an exhibition of Stanton MacDonald-Wright at the Art Center School at Pasadena, where he had started teaching in 1944. And, remarkably, MacDonald-Wright was included among the Pacific artists in the Auckland show, represented by his 1955 canvas *Solution*. MacDonald-Wright was the founder, along with his fellow expatriate Morgan Russell, of the art movement Synchromism—the American Kandinskyism, we might say—when they were in Munich in 1912, and they held its inaugural exhibition coincidentally in Paris in 1913. But to return to Feitelson, by 1961 when Tomory included him in his show, he had already organised and held the meetings with Karl Benjamin, Frederick Hammersley and John McLaughlin that would lead to the landmark *Four Abstract Classicists*, organised by Jules Langsner, at the Los Angeles County Museum of Art in 1959. This exhibition established the West Coast line of abstraction dubbed

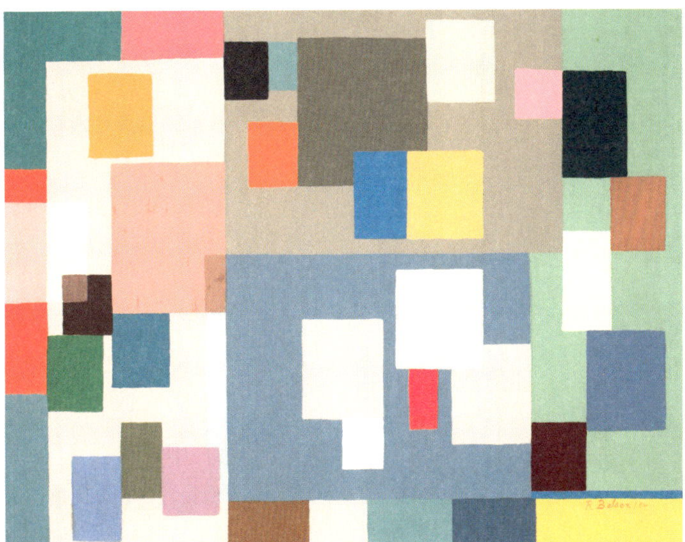

8.6 Ralph Balson
Constructive painting, 1954

'Hard-edge'; and it was in fact from Los Angeles and Laguna Beach that this term arose and not, as it is often assumed, from the East Coast with such artists as Ellsworth Kelly, Frank Stella and the Washington School painters.

However, these younger-generation painters such as McLaughlin, Benjamin and Hammersley emerged independently of Feitelson, just as there was never really a West Coast tradition. Unlike Feitelson, who was the same age, the Massachusetts-born McLaughlin was entirely self-trained, his work informed not just by his experiences in New England, but importantly by his immersion in the culture of Japan, where he moved in 1935. On his return to Boston in 1938, he opened a gallery specialising in Asian art and objects. During World War II, he served as a translator in the Pacific, before settling in 1946 in California, where he began to paint full time at the age of forty-eight (and in this he reminds us of Balson, who held his first solo exhibition at the age of forty-one, but began to show regularly only in his fifties). Twenty-seven years younger than McLaughlin (and Feitelson), the Chicago-born Benjamin likewise served during the war and was likewise self-taught. More formally trained, Utah-born Hammersley had also served in the war, before studying briefly at the École des Beaux-Arts in Paris in 1945 between his extensive studies at various Californian art schools. All of the West Coast artists,

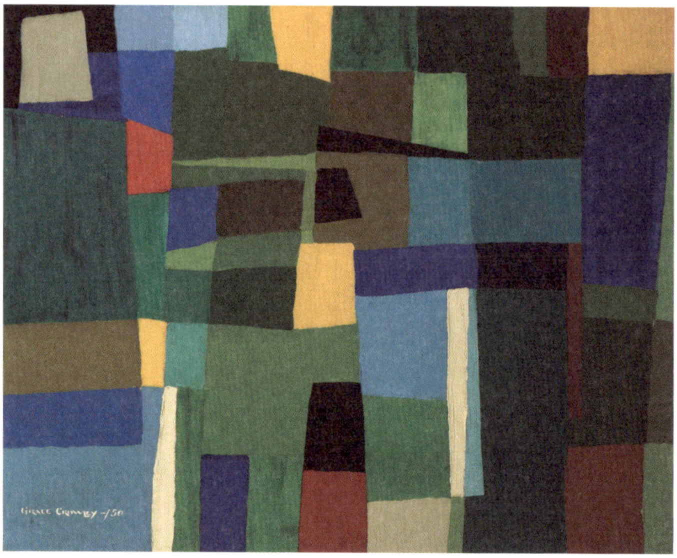

8.7 Grace Crowley
Abstract painting, 1950

Feitelson, McLaughlin, Hammersley and Benjamin, came to abstraction after the war or in the early 1950s, later than their decade-older Australian counterparts Crowley and Balson; but what they had in common—and this would include even Walters and Mrkusich—was that, having come to abstraction, none of them would return to representation. Academically trained artists joined autodidacts, and in the years following the war these trans-Pacific painters, each committed to edge, colour and geometry, pioneered abstraction in their respective realms.

So what, to conclude, is the lesson of Tomory's 1961 show? The disconnected outbreaks we speak of were recognised immediately, at least by the artists, who invariably used to speak of themselves as part of a wider global artistic undertaking, even if they couldn't name their actual contemporaries. But revisiting the show again allows us to see something that is clear only today: that the Pacific *is* the connector. Through art we are trying to understand a Jungian world where relations can be seen between seemingly disparate places and nothing happens by chance. In some ways, the remarkable similarity of the abstraction we have looked at and the simultaneity of its appearance in the 1940s and maturity in the 1950s are a precursor to the world of the internet, where everything is connected to everything else and everything is equally available at once. But this abstraction, as with the

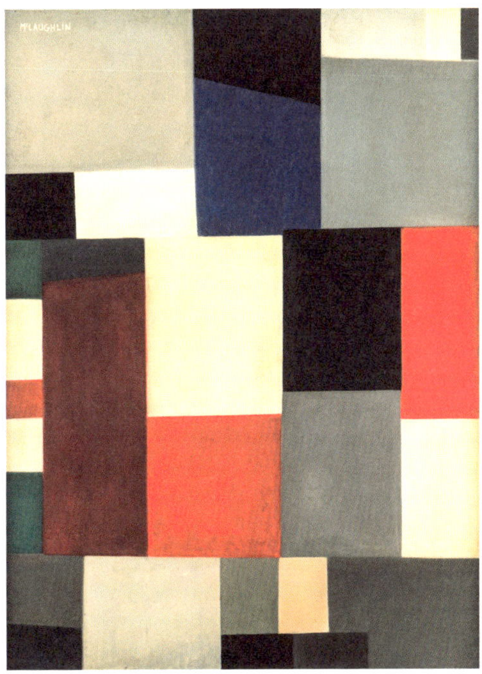

8.8 John McLaughlin
Untitled, 1948

internet, despite all conspiracy theories, is not ultimately the product of a single central influence. Each of these so-called peripheral locations—Auckland, Sydney, Los Angeles, Tokyo—is a city that explains itself, is its own cause and effect, independent of but not unrelated to the others. In speaking of the global, then, this is not to say that there is something like a single world or world spirit causing them (and here we perhaps differ from Kandinsky). It is not some pre-existing underlying condition that produces what we have detailed here. Rather, we might say that these outbreaks allow us to see—or, better, glimpse—a plurality of worlds. (To use a Deleuzian diction, we would say that 'abstraction' here is like the Event of battle that hovers over but is not to be confused with the actual events of the battlefield.[25]) In the end, we cannot produce a history of abstraction only from New York or Paris. Those two cities are as regional and coincidental as everywhere else, and possibly even more so, insofar as they do not see themselves as coincidental, that is, existing only in a relationship with somewhere else. In any attempt to globalise the experience of abstraction at mid-century, we must include the 'sympathetic' perspective that Tomory announced in his foreword. Put simply, it is possible to see the world from where he stands in a way not possible from New York, or Paris.

Art history often forgets this in constituting its linear and centralised histories and genealogies. Contrast, for example, the Eurocentric *Inventing Abstraction 1910–1924* at MoMA in 2012 or *Pacific Standard Time* at the Getty in 2011, which precisely overlooked the word 'Pacific' in its title, seeing the art of the West Coast only in relation to the East, or the more decentralised *Constructive Spirit: Abstract Art in South and North America* at the Newark Museum in 2010, which nevertheless maintained the category 'American', with the eccentric *The Geometric Unconscious: A Century of Abstraction* at the University of Nebraska in 2012 and the truly global *Weltsprache Abstraktion* at the Ethnological Museum Berlin in 2006, the proper equivalent today of Tomory's show.[26] Against the abstraction that most of us have inherited—Greenberg's New York School and its search for origins, in either other cultures or the unconscious—it is not with origins that art begins but with *coincidence*. Not with one but two. Other cultures are not the origins of or sources for our art—Newman's, Rothko's and Pollock's attitude to Native American art, for example—but they are like ours, existing at the same time as ours. To return to what we began by speaking of: when Baldwin Spencer asked Indigenous artists to paint on bark so that their work could be transported, this request would not have been possible unless the artists were ready—and in a way willing—for this to happen. And, similarly, if Kandinsky is posited as a kind of source here, he is ultimately only the name of a coincidence, and we would still have to explain why his work was taken up independently in so many places at once. That is, Kandinsky was not the *origin* of anything. Rather, it is a matter of working *backwards* from Kandinsky.

Perhaps, in the end, Tomory's exhibition showed the logic of world-making as it always was. For when artists produce their work, they necessarily do so with an image of a world in mind. They immerse themselves in an imagined contemporary art, which has today become defined as con-temporary, a being with others at the same time, even though we do not know who they are.[27] The point being that the contemporaneity that we now see (and Tomory saw) was already theirs. Perhaps geometric abstraction especially recognised this in a way that released it from any particular time and place. But the surprising thing, as we say, is that many of the recent accounts of twentieth-century abstraction still fail to realise that the globalism at stake in abstraction is already historical. Indeed, we might speak even more generally of a Pacific *modernism*. Can't we now see Gauguin's *Woman on the beach* (1891) and Matisse's *Oceania* series (1952–53) in relation to Indigenous Australian art? Can't we see Frank Hinder as a displaced Taos modernist as well as a Sydney abstract artist? Isn't Bribie Island's Ian Fairweather also Scotland's Gauguin? As the painter and art historian Herbert Badham once wrote of Ralph Balson:

> Balson believes that the source of true design is to be found in cosmic laws, and that this truth offers a better basis for progress than any other. The speed of books, prints and the victory over space made possible by the radio, Balson believed, will mean that in time the old individualised egos will be submerged in a kind of universal ego.[28]

Or as Kandinsky and his colleague Franz Marc once wrote in their introduction to the *Blaue Reiter Almanac* in 1912, the year before everything we have been speaking of here, and in a way predicting it:

> In our case the principle of internationalism is the only one possible … We must say that an individual nation is only one of the creators of all art; one alone can never be a whole. As with a personality, the national element is automatically reflected in each great work. But in the last resort, this national colouration is merely incidental. The whole work, called art, knows no borders or nations, only humanity.[29]

An earlier version of this text was published in *Discipline*, no. 5, 2015.

—

1 Although the expedition to Arnhem Land during which Spencer obtained the barks occurred in 1912, Spencer did not show them (and then probably only in reproduction) until early 1913 when he gave a lecture at the Australasian Association for the Advancement of Science annual congress in Melbourne. On this, see DJ Mulvaney and JH Calaby, *'So Much That Is New': Baldwin Spencer 1860–1929: A Biography*, Melbourne University Press, 1985, pp. 305–6. It will be our argument that it is the showing of these barks, or more exactly the taking of them out of their 'original' context so that they are able to be shown, that transforms them into an artistic commodity.

2 Theodore Roosevelt, cited in Vivien Johnson, *Once Upon a Time in Papunya*, University of New South Wales Press, Sydney, 2010, p. 279.

3 Paul Carter, 'Gondolas in Gondwanaland', *Art & Text*, nos 23–24, 1987, pp. 114–23. See also Carter's 'Culture of Coincidence: Notes on a Performance Piece Called Mirror States', *Continuum*, vol. 3, no. 1, 1990, pp. 115–26.

4 This is Tillers' *Conversations with the bride* (1975). We might also think of his later *Rendezvous with configuration 8* (1978) (with George Baldessin) and *Three facts* (1981), among many other works.

5 The two works shown in the catalogue were Jagamara's *Five stories* (1984) and Tillers's appropriation of *Five stories, The nine shots* (1985), but appropriation for Tillers is itself to be understood as a form of coincidence. See on this, for example, Graham Coulter-Smith *The Postmodern Art of Imants Tillers: Appropriation en abyme, 1971–2001*, Fine Art Research Centre, Southampton, 2002, especially the chapter '"The Beginner's Guide to Oil Painting" and Creation without a Creator', pp. 97–102.

6 Ian McLean, '9 Shots 5 Stories: Imants Tillers and Indigenous Difference', *Art Monthly Australia*, no. 228, April 2010, p. 15.

7 Peter Tomory, 'Foreword', *Painting From the Pacific,* Auckland Art Gallery, 1961, np.

8 See biography of Sarah Wilson for 2013 AAANZ Conference, aaanz.info/aaanz.home/conferences/2013-conference/

9 For a review of Kandinsky's *Concerning the Spiritual in Art*, see 'New books: art for a purpose', *Argus*, 31 July 1915, p. 4.

10 Matthias Haldemann, 'The Theatre of Pictures: Kandinsky's Abstraction of Abstraction', in ed. Helmut Friedel, *Kandinsky: Absolute, Abstract*, exhibition catalogue, Prestel, Munich, 2008, pp. 242–55.

11 See Wassily Kandinsky, *Point and Line and Plane*, Dover Books, New York, 1979, p. 43 and 'Appendix'.

12 On the influence of Kandinsky in America, see *Theme and Improvisation: Kandinsky and the American Avant-Garde, 1912–1950*, eds. Gail Levin and Marianne Lorenz, exhibition catalogue, Little Brown & Co., Boston, 1992.

13 On Bisttram and Kandinsky, see Marianne Lorenz, 'Kandinsky and Regional America', in *Theme and Improvisation*, pp. 153–4.

14 Bisttram cited in Nathan K. Rees, 'Synthesising Transcendental Painting: Race, Religion and Aesthetics in the Art of Emil Bisttram, Raymond Johnson and Agnes Pelton', PhD thesis, University of Maryland, 2010, p. 143, www.drum.lib.umd.edu/bitstream/handle/1903/11221/Rees_umd_0117E_11785.pdf?sequence=1&isAllowed=y.

15 Transcendental Painting Group, '1938 Statement of Purpose', reprinted in *The Transcendental Painting Group: Major Paintings*, exhibition catalogue, Michael Rosenfeld Gallery, New York, 1999, p. 11.

16 The exhibition *Hepworth, Beothy, Closon, Fernandez, Helion, Power, Prampolini, Seligman, Taeuber-Arp, Valmier* was held in Abstraction-Création's exhibition space at 44 Avenue de Wagram, Paris, 2–14 February 1934.

17 Eleonore Lange, 'Foreword', *Exhibition I*, 1939, in eds. Ann Stephen, Andrew McNamara and Philip Goad, *Modernism & Australia: Documents on Art, Design and Architecture 1917–1967*, Miegunyah Press, Melbourne, 2006, p. 391.

18 Bernard Smith, Australian Painting, 1788–1970, Oxford University Press, Melbourne, 1971, p. 212. On the other hand, Smith will speak of Lange as 'mystical' and recall his distaste for her lecturing style in *Pavane for Another Time*, Macmillan, Melbourne, 2002, p. 47.

19 MS 1990.1, Papers of Eleonore Lange, Research Library and Archive, Art Gallery of New South Wales, Sydney.

20 For more on Walters in Sydney, see Rex Butler and ADS Donaldson, 'Gordon Walters: *Les années décisives*, 1946–1953', in eds. Lucy Hammonds, Julia Waites and Laurence Simmons, *Gordon Walters: New Vision*, exhibition catalogue, Toi o Tāmaki, 2017, pp. 132–45.

21 Elizabeth Young, *James Cant*, Brolga Books, Adelaide, 1970, np.

22 Gordon Walters, 1982, quoted in ed. Michael Dunn, *Gordon Walters*, exhibition catalogue, Auckland City Art Gallery, 1983, p. 34.

23 See Sue Gardiner, 'Let's Talk About Abstraction', *Art News New Zealand*, Winter 2012, p. 89.
24 On Mrkusich and Kandinsky, see Michael Dunn, 'Notes on Development: Painting 1946–1954', in *Milan Mrkusich: Paintings 1946–1972*, exhibition catalogue, Auckland City Art Gallery, 1972, pp. 8–9; and Alexa M Johnston, 'Milan Mrkusich: Pioneer Modernist', in *New Zealand Home & Building: The Newstalk 1ZB 1950s Show*, exhibition catalogue, Auckland City Art Gallery, 1992, pp. 46–55.
25 Gilles Deleuze, *The Logic of Sense*, Columbia University Press, New York, 1990, pp. 100–1.
26 We are grateful to Nicholas Croggon who alerted us to MoMA's 2014 *Gauguin: Metamorphoses*, in which we have no sense of the coincidence or reciprocality between Gauguin and Tahiti, insofar as all that is of interest are the 'metamorphoses' Gauguin wreaks upon the 'native' culture.
27 See on this Terry Smith, *What is Contemporary Art?*, University of Chicago Press, 2009, pp. 4–6.
28 Herbert Badham, *A Study of Australian Art*, Currawong Publishing, Sydney, 1949, p. 146.
29 Wassily Kandinsky and Franz Marc, 'Almanac: Der Blaue Reiter', in *The Blaue Reiter Almanac*, Thames & Hudson, London, 1974, p. 251.

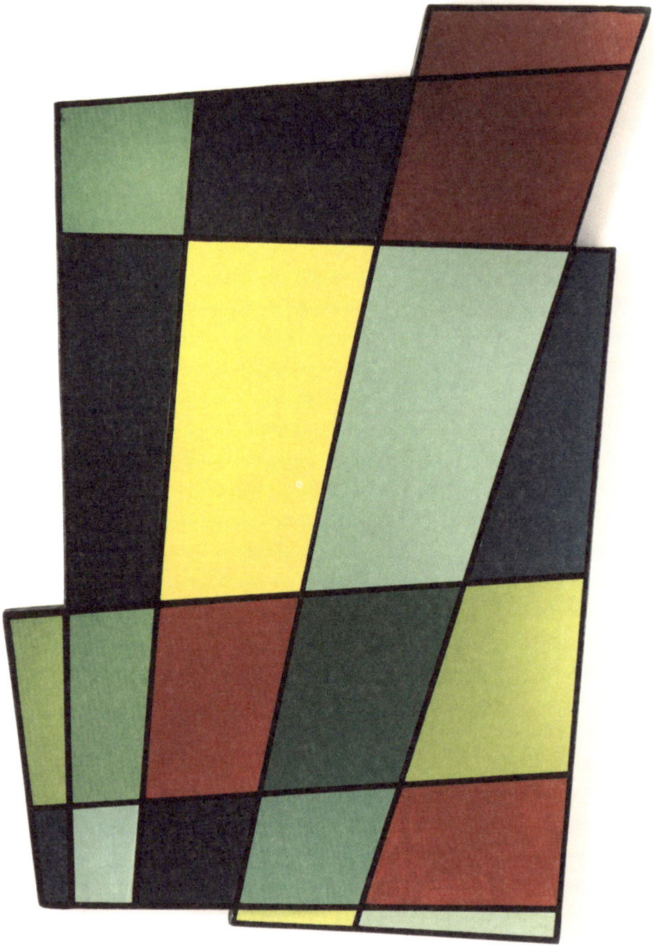

9.1 Juan Melé
Marco recortado no. 2 (Irregular frame no. 2), 1946

Madí and Mary Webb
Australia and South America

Looking at the famous map, *The world at the time of the Surrealists* (see p. 88), published in a special issue of the Belgian magazine *Variétés* dedicated to 'surrealism in 1929', we are struck by the fact that two of the biggest continents are equally diminished and distorted. Australia is smaller than New Guinea and South America is smaller than Mexico. They both lie below the equator. Indeed, every land mass beneath the wavering line of the equator on the map is reduced or inverted in relative scale: Australia is smaller than many Pacific islands, New Zealand is unmoored and floating deep in the South Pacific, and South America is reduced to Peru and Tierra del Fuego. The map is undoubtedly an expression of a surrealist anti-nationalism. As the well-known 1925 group surrealist manifesto 'The Revolution First and Always' declared:

> Even more than patriotism—which is a quite commonplace sort of hysteria, though emptier and shorter-lived than most—we are disgusted by the idea of belonging to a country at all, which is the most bestial and least philosophic of the concepts to which we are all subjected …[1]

But, despite this, their iconoclasm is deeply Eurocentric in its prejudice against the south. For all of surrealist leader André Breton's interest in and collecting of so-called primitive art from Oceania, in the most literal sense of the word, his is still a profoundly Eurocentric view of the world.

We might compare the well-known surrealist map to one drawn in 1936 by the Uruguayan artist Joaquín Torres-García, *América invertida* (*Inverted America*), reproduced in the journal *Círculo y quadrado* (*Circle and Square*). In it the usual orientation of the world is inverted so that the continent of South America is turned upside down and placed largely above the equator, with the rest of the world left out. Torres-García was seventeen years old when in 1891 his family moved from

Montevideo to Barcelona, where in his late twenties he worked with Antoni Gaudí on his Basílica de la Sagrada Família (Basilica of the Holy Family). From there he moved to New York in 1920, returned to Europe in 1922, moved to France in 1924 and settled finally in Paris in 1926. There, by chance, at the exhibition of the German Friedrich Vordemberge-Gildewart in 1929, he met the tireless advocate of abstraction, the Belgian poet, art historian and artist Michel Seuphor, and together the two formed the short-lived avant-garde artist group Cercle et Carré (Circle and Square), which held its first and only exhibition in 1930 and published a short-lived but influential eponymous magazine.

Disenchanted with the Parisian hothouse and its artistic chauvinism, Torres-García moved to Madrid in 1932 before returning to Montevideo after an absence of some thirty-four years. In 1935 he founded La Asociación de arte constructivo (AAC) and the year after published the first number of *Círculo y Cuadrado*, directly translating into Spanish the name of the group he had not long before founded in France. In 1943 he established his influential art school and workshop Taller Torres-García in Montevideo and the following year published his manifesto *Universalismo constructive* (*Universal constructivism*), just five years before his death in 1949, aged seventy-five. In one of the essays

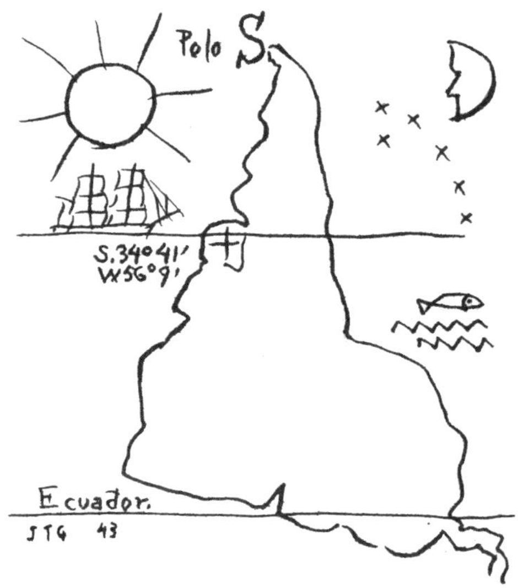

9.2 Joaquín Torres-García
América invertida (*Inverted America*), 1943

in his manifesto, 'The School of the South', originally delivered as a lecture in 1935 not long after his return, Torres-García writes (and his words serve as a perfect description of the map he would make the following year):

> I have said School of the South; because in reality our north is the South. There must not be north, for us, except in opposition to our South. Therefore we now turn the map upside down, and then we have a true idea of our position, and not as the rest of the world wishes. The point of America, from now on, forever, insistently points to the South, our North.[2]

* * *

Now at first it might seem difficult to relate this map to Australia. Indeed, we must acknowledge that the direct historical connections between Australia and South America are few, and any attempt to generalise will suffer from a lack of examples. Almost inevitably, however, transnational exchanges between countries of the South continue to emerge. Only recently we have discovered that one of Torres-García's first students following his return to Uruguay, the highly regarded Rosa Acle, lived in Melbourne for more than seven years, having arrived there in 1940. Acle had first studied with Torres-García in 1934, was a founding member of the AAC in Montevideo the following year and had her abstract art regularly reproduced in *Círculo y Cuadrado* before moving to Paris in 1939, from where she made her way to Australia. When she returned to Uruguay in 1947, she left all of her artwork here and the possibility that there exists a small trove of undiscovered Acle paintings from the 1940s in Melbourne is as remarkable as it is tantalising. Of course, in recent years, cultural theorists here and elsewhere, picking up on Torres-García's ideas, have begun to polemicise for some notion of the 'South' as opposed to a North, but for us their arguments seem too hypothetical or even wishful. Or too much an effect of the present, the taking-up of something that occurred only recently as part of a wider globalism or a spreading out of the centres of world art. In this essay, however, we wish to pursue a particular historical connection between Australia and South America that, although it might appear tenuous, marginal and perhaps of little consequence, nonetheless points to the longevity of our pre-globalist global exchanges. The sudden rise into prominence of the abstract art of Latin America in Europe but particularly in North America since the turn of this century has allowed previously unseen connections to become apparent. It has occurred to such an extent that the work of many Latin American constructive and post-constructive artists—a number of whom we will discuss here—is now incorporated into the über-narrative of the Museum of Modern Art. In the view of American art historian, curator and artist Robert Storr:

> The belated awakening of the North American public to the actual diversity of art issuing from cultures south of the US border is one of the major events of the era.[3]

This history of abstraction has also been the subject of a continued line of investigation by one of Australia's most prominent contemporary artists, the Chilean-born Juan Davila, who has drawn on it repeatedly throughout his career, which is surprising perhaps for such an avowedly representational painter. We would argue that Davila's work not only evidences a present-day connection between Australia and South America, but also makes available a historical connection between the two continents that took place in the past.

We need to acknowledge a kind of paradox or complication here. Davila has always been explicit about labelling and acknowledging his historical sources—this is his postmodernism, and it chiefly concerns Australia's and America's modernisms. However, the key to seeing that his work has always been about South America has been hidden, though nevertheless present from the beginning. In other words, Davila has always been showing us this connection in plain sight, but unlabelled. We say this is because it truly is the key to his work,

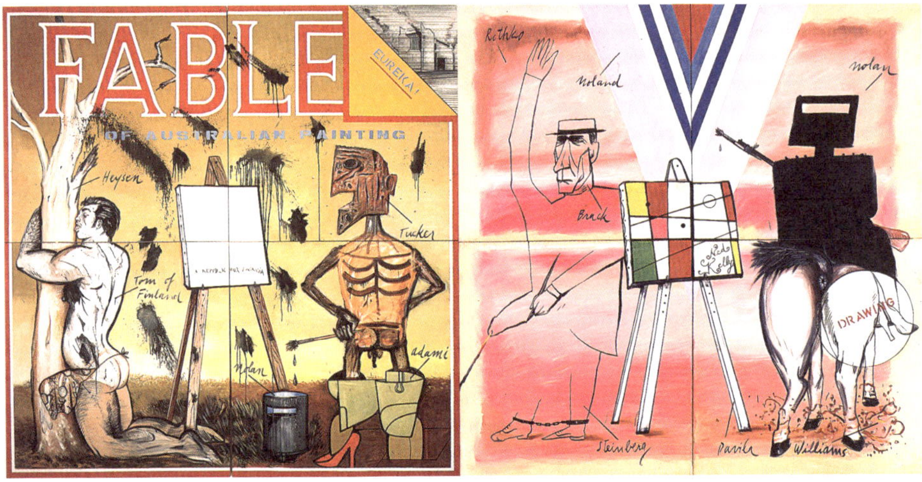

9.3 Juan Davila
Fable of Australian painting (panel 1 and 2), 1983

and perhaps, like his unconscious, he does not want it revealed or even cannot reveal it because it is too close to him. In his panoramic multi-panelled work of 1982 *Fable of Australian painting*, Davila offers us several 'scenes' from the history of Australian painting, each featuring—in a precursor to his later Courbet-derived 'studios'—an image of an artist painting. In the first panel, an Albert Tucker–like Antipodean paints a Tom of Finland–style male hunk humping a spindly gum tree. In the second panel, Nolan's Ned Kelly paints a hawk-faced man by John Brack. In the third panel, a hysterical-looking part-human-part-animal Arthur Boyd paints the elongated figure from Russell Drysdale's *Man feeding his dogs* (1941). And in the fourth and final panel, an amorphous Jedd Garet paints William Dobell's Joshua Smith, who at the same time is seemingly being castrated by a dog. Although each of Davila's painters stands before his subject, what ends up on his easel appears to bear little relationship to what is before him. In the first panel, before Tom of Finland we have a blank canvas with 'A Republic for Australia' written along the bottom; in the third panel, before the man feeding his dogs we have a pound sign; in the fourth panel, before Joshua Smith we have a David Aspden colour-field abstract; and in the second panel, before the Brack we have a strange painting made up of irregular multicoloured squares and rectangles.

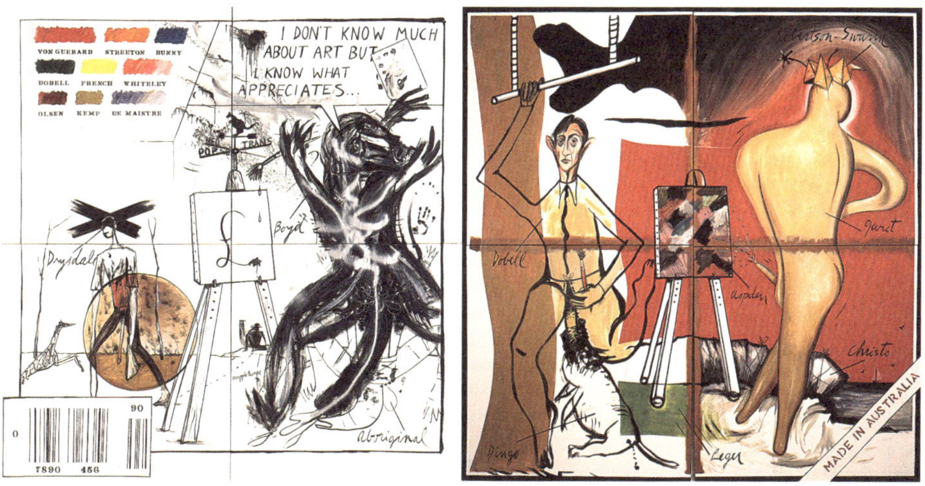

9.4 Juan Davila
Fable of Australian painting (panel 3 and 4), 1983

And, significantly, while almost all the details of these panels (the painter, his subject and frequently his easel) are labelled after their artistic sources, this curious multicoloured patchwork is named, in an apparently autobiographical touch, and against the attack upon authorship of the rest of *Fable*, 'Davila'.

Indeed, if we look closely, we can find this motif throughout any number of Davila's other works, almost like a watermark or, indeed, an artist's signature. We see it, for example, towards the left centre of *The barricade* (1989), at the centre of *Bottle* (1993), at the centre of *Modern ex-voto* (1994) and making up the horse in the two versions of *The Liberator, Simón Bolívar* (1993 and 1994). We have variants of it in *Monogram* (1989) and *Mexicanismo* (1990), and it is behind the design of the political poster *Woomera* (2002). It also forms the underlying grid-like armature and right-hand framing panel in his enormous *Wuthering heights I* (1990), which was shown as part of the exhibition *Transcontinental: Nine Latin American Artists* in Manchester in 1990. The art historian Guy Brett, writing in the catalogue for the 2006 retrospective of Davila held at the Museum of Contemporary Art in Sydney, identified no fewer than fifteen artists whose work Davila was playing on there, including some seven South American artists; but even he was unable to see the real source for this image.[4]

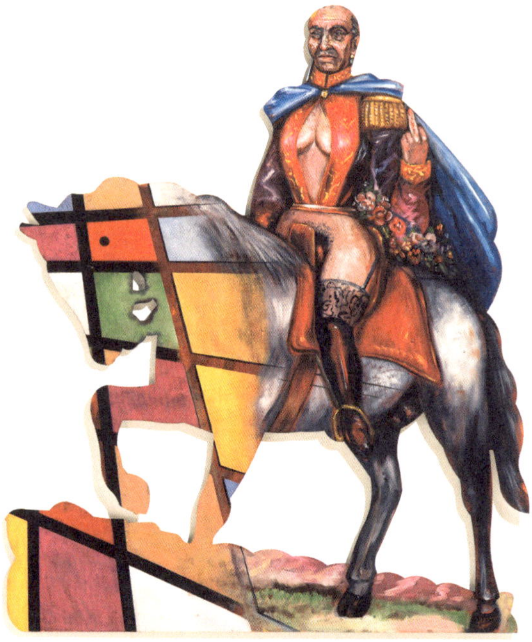

9.5 Juan Davila
The Liberator, Simón Bolívar, 1994

The work that Davila has been using for more than three decades is, in fact, *Marco recortado no. 2* (*Irregular frame no. 2*), painted in 1946 by the Argentinian Juan Melé. The previous year, Melé had co-founded the artists group Asociación Arte Concreto-Invención alongside Tomàs Maldonado, Alfredo Hlito, Raúl Lozza and Lidy Prati. Their activities intersected but also broke with those of Madí, the other Buenos Aires–based group of abstract artists led by Gyula Kosice, Diyi Laañ and Carmelo Arden Quin, among others, which formed in the year Melé painted his *Marco recortado no. 2*. Davila even named a whole work *Madí* (1991), made up of the group's characteristic irregular dynamic frame, around an assemblage on which he hung and mounted various paintings and other objects (a religious calendar, toilet-wall graffiti, black smears of paint). But most crucially for us—and the detail on which we will base our own argument—Davila also incongruously painted an upside-down shred of the Australian flag there. What exactly does Davila mean by making a connection between Australia and this obscure-in-Australia but globally recognised avant-garde movement? And what, we might further speculate, does he make of the fact that any such connection is unknown to us? What might he think is the contemporary political equivalent of this ignorance? How does this blindness, this unwillingness on the part of art historians over the period of the writing of Australian art history to consider these kinds of connections, manifest itself in another, though perhaps equivalent, manner in contemporary Australian social reality?

To begin to answer these questions, let us return to Torres-García's map. As we saw in his manifesto, Torres-García may have been polemical in arguing against Europe's exclusion of South America and for the inversion of the North and the South. But like most polemicists, even those Southernists in Australia today arguing against our provincialism, he did not understand that history had already realised his ambitions. For if it was true that Torres-García founded his Taller, his workshop school, in 1943 to produce South American artists able to engage in, if not lead, contemporary world art, it is also true that by 1948 the Uruguayan and Argentine artists of the Madí group had already shown their work in a room of their own at the Salon des Réalités Nouvelles at the Musée National d'Art Moderne in Paris.

The Réalités Nouvelles, as the association was known, had started in 1947, directly carrying on the role of Abstraction-Création, the longest lasting umbrella group for abstract artists in Paris in the 1930s, an organisation that had in turn grown out of the collapse of Torres-García and Seuphor's Cercle et Carré and the implosion of Theo van Doesburg's Art Concret. Undoubtedly, the most important contribution of the Madí artists was their foregrounding of the irregular frame or shaped canvas as a problem in the history of painting, part of what Argentine painter and writer César Paternosto calls their 'radical removal of the acquired traditions of geometrical abstraction'.[5] It was these South Americans who first broke with the right-angle in painting and began to explore the possibility of the shaped support, and not such North Americans as Frank Stella and Kenneth Noland, as we in the Anglosphere have come to understand.

The Madí group itself, following the pioneering efforts of Torres-García, was officially brought together in Buenos Aires in 1946 by the Hungarian-Argentinian artist and poet Gyula Kosice and Uruguayans Carmelo Arden Quin and Rhod Rothfuss. Of course, as with many significant art movements, the story behind the formation of this group of abstract artists is contested. Kosice claimed that the name of the movement was derived from the republican motto in the Spanish civil war of the 1930s: 'Madrí, Madrí, no pasarán' ('Madrid, Madrid, they will not pass'), that is, the forces of the fascist Franco will not take Madrid. For his part, Arden Quin asserted that the name of the group was an acronym of his complete name: CarMelo Alveo ArDen QuInn. The name of the group is most commonly understood, however, as deriving from the acronym for Movimiento, Abstracción, Dimensión, Invención (Movement, Abstraction, Dimension, Invention). Like the word Dada, whatever its origins, Madí gave its name to an expansive practice, characterised by both a

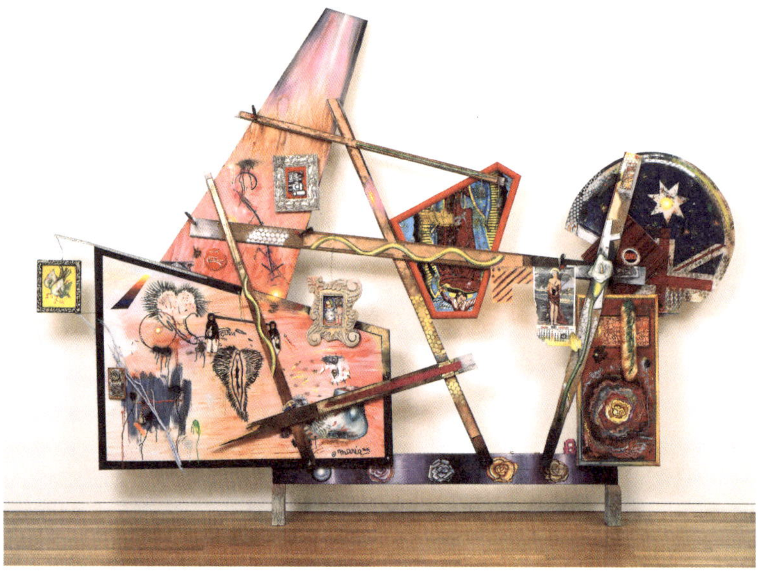

9.6 Juan Davila
Madí, 1991

playfulness and a politics, whose legacy is still relevant and, indeed, under whose name there are still artists exhibiting into the twenty-first century, including such foundational figures as Arden Quin and his fellow Uruguayan Volf Roitman.

In its first exhibition catalogue, in 1946, Madí declared itself a universal art movement, and it translated its chief essays into both French and English. Under the leadership of Arden Quin, Kosice and Rothfuss, the following year the artists began publishing the bilingual, Spanish-French *Arte Madí universal*, which continued until 1954. However, not long after its first issue, the group split and divided itself between a group headed by Arden Quin, which included the German-born Argentine Martín Blaszko, and a group headed by Kosice, which included the Argentinian Laañ. With his wide connections in Europe, Torres-García, who was eventually to take Arden Quin's side, had already been instrumental in the organisation of abstract artists in Paris in the late 1920s and early 1930s. Certainly, his bumping into Seuphor at Vordemberge-Gildewart's exhibition at Galerie Povolozky in Paris in 1929 can be seen as a pivotal moment in the formation of a united bloc of abstract artists against surrealism in France. This meeting typified, in its bringing together of the Uruguyan with the Belgian, German and Polish, the international character of abstract art between the wars in France—an internationalism that was to re-emerge in Paris in the years following the war, with (to take just one expression of it) the 1948 exhibition of the Madí artists in the Salon des Réalités Nouvelles. Indeed, the group quickly went on to gather members from outside South America, as the Réalités Nouvelles did outside France, and like Madí is still running today.

In 1992, French artist Roger Neyrat, a member of Madí from the late 1940s, recalled the Madí workshops of the early 1950s in Paris in his essay 'De la creación del Centre d'Etudes et de Recherches MADÍ' ('On the creation of the Madí Centre for Studies and Research'), published in the catalogue for the exhibition *Arden-Quin—Roitman*, held in Paris in 1995. The Centre was attached, as Neyrat remembers it, to French painter Marcelle Saint-Omer's large studio overlooking the Montparnasse cemetery. On the walls each member hung the particular thing they were working on and at the entrance was installed a strange poem-object by Arden Quin, a transparent plexiglass cube on which was inscribed the line: '*Tout visiteur naît d'un éclat* (*Every visitor is born out of a thunderclap*)'. For Neyrat, it was a 'formidable optical manifesto', and at the Centre the group also showed films, held dinners and organised lectures.[6] According to Neyrat, with studios open all week and artists always being present, the Centre had a constant stream of visitors: curators and art historians, representatives from both the better-known and less well known galleries, and 'famous artists came to see others less important than themselves—Georges Vantongerloo, Herbin, Marcelle Cahn, Marie [*sic*] Webb, Michel Seuphor … Vieira da Silva, César Domela … Calder'.[7]

Now we come to the speculative part of our brief history and our attempt to think what Davila might mean by including the upside-down Australian flag as part of his sculpture *Madí*. Incredibly, among the 'famous artists' recalled by Neyrat is Mary Webb, a Sydney-born painter and collage artist who moved to Paris in 1949, was represented there by Galerie Collette Allendy for most of the 1950s and showed as a *sociétaire* with the Réalités Nouvelles from 1950 until 1956. A founding member of the Club international féminin, she was awarded the Medaille d'argent de la Ville de Paris in 1958, shortly before her death aged fifty-seven. In the immediate aftermath of her passing, Seuphor, author of the monumental *Dictionary of Abstract Painting* (1957), wrote to Webb's friend and colleague Grace Crowley in Sydney, finishing his letter by expressing the hope that 'a few paintings of Mary Webb will now enter the museums and collections of Australia'. However, it would take nearly two decades for her work to be acquired by the National Gallery of Australia, and more than five decades before it was actually put on display, when in 2012 her work was purchased by the Queensland Art Gallery and the Art Gallery of New South Wales, where it rightly now hangs besides that of her contemporaries Crowley and Ralph Balson. And perhaps the first Australian with whom the avant-garde artists of South America intersected was JW Power. Power had been essential to the formation of Abstraction-Création in the early 1930s, the group that, as we say, was the immediate forerunner to the Salon des Réalités Nouvelles. It was in Abstraction-Création's annual *cahier* that Power's work could be seen alongside reproductions of works by other members of the group, such as the Argentinians Juan Del Prete in 1933 and Lucio Fontana in 1935.

In other words, we might say that Davila 'drapes' the Australian flag over his *Madí* in order to remind us that, beyond Davila himself, there has always been a connection between Australia and South America as fellow continents of the South. Because, as mariners from the Old World well knew, the route to the New World went around Cape Horn as much as around the Cape of Good Hope. Indeed, many of the nineteenth-century relationships between the two continents occurred as a result of scientific and economic exchanges taking place along this route. The greatest of our so-called travel artists, Augustus Earle, first left England for America in 1818 before moving to Chile in 1820 and settling in Rio de Janeiro, where in 1824 he painted his well-known *Gate of Pernambuco, Brazil, with new negroes*, the year before he arrived in Hobart. Back in England in 1830 he accepted the following year the position of artist supernumerary on the *Beagle*, which had in fact already left Plymouth. During its stopover at Rio in 1832, Earle left the expedition due to ill-health; his position was taken by Conrad Martens, who went on to work in Sydney and Brisbane, producing his topographic and deep geological images of Sydney Harbour, undoubtedly influenced by his experience on the *Beagle* and contact with

Darwin's emerging theories of evolution. The Swiss artist Louis Buvelot moved to Brazil from Lausanne in 1835 and was established as an artist there by 1840. He returned to Switzerland in 1852 with his French wife, having held the favour of Emperor Dom Pedro II, the last king of Brazil. In 1864, after his wife's death, he moved to Melbourne, where his work influenced the Heidelberg School painters.

That same year, through the botanical exchanges carried on by the shipping industry between South America and Australia, the superintendent of the Botanical Gardens in Brisbane was able to acquire and plant the first jacaranda in that city. These South American native trees have become the self-chosen emblem of Brisbane, brightly colouring its suburbs, the progeny of that first specimen seeded in 1864, which finally blew over in a cyclone in 1976. The original was taken as a subject by Brisbane's first professional artist, English-born Godfrey Rivers, whose painting *Under the jacaranda* (1903) was acquired by the Trustees of the Queensland Art Gallery almost immediately after its first showing.[8] (The year after, Rivers would attempt to duplicate his success with a painting of a red-leafed poinciana from Madagascar, which when it entered the Gallery in 1941 became known as *An alien in Australia*, a title that in some ways could also apply to this much-loved painting of the jacaranda.)

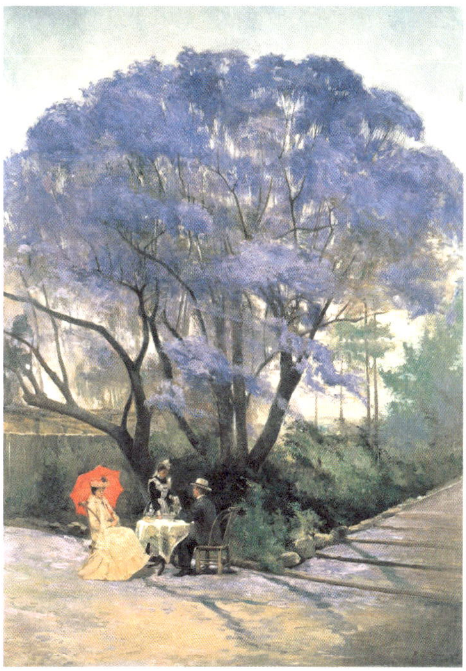

9.7 Godfrey Rivers
Under the jacaranda, 1903

And there was perhaps no stranger exchange between the two continents in the nineteenth century than that set in motion in 1893 when a large group of Australians set sail from Sydney to establish in the mountains of Paraguay a so-called New Australia. Led by ex-Labour journalist William Lane, this utopian community of some 238 adults and children, including the writer Mary Gilmore, was based on the principles of communism, although only for a 'brotherhood of English-speaking whites'. It lasted only a little over a year before internal division led to the departure of Lane in 1894 to found another colony, with the entire enterprise dissolved by the Paraguayan government and each settler given a small parcel of land. It is an echo, even in its failure and even with its—to us—flawed ideals, that comes back constantly throughout our history of another kind of Australia. It can be detected in such novels as Michael Wilding's *The Paraguayan Experiment* (1985), in the historical accounts of Gavin Souter, and even in such popular-culture references as the band Redgum's 1980 theme album *Virgin Ground* and the Weddings Parties Anything song 'Drifted Away' (1990), both of which are based on the New Australia experiment. Today some 2000 descendants of the original colony still live in Paraguay.

Between the wars and after World War II a whole series of Australian artists lived, studied and showed either in South America or with South Americans, imagining it both close-up and from far away. Around 1920 in Paris, JW Power, deciding finally to become an artist, enrolled in the class of the Brazilian Pedro Araújo. Araújo had previously taken over responsibility for the Académie Ranson in 1917, following then-Director Maurice Denis's call-up to the army. Not long afterwards, however, he opened his own school, with the classes becoming renowned for their teaching based on geometry. Power studied with Araújo for about two years before going on to study with Fernand Léger in 1924. This, incidentally, was a path through Paris also taken at the same time by a number of Norwegian artists, in particular, Charlotte Wankel, Raghnild Keyser and Raghnild Kaarbo, as well as the French artist Marcelle Cahn. Power, who owned Araújo's *Breton scene* (n.d.), published his influential book *Éléments de la Construction Picturale* (*The Elements of Pictorial Construction*) in 1932, and acknowledged his debt in a letter that year, writing that 'my own researches extend backwards for about 10 years. I was introduced to the subject by Senhor Pedro Araújo'.[9]

Then perhaps in a more 'nationalist' vein, we might think of Melbourne-based art teacher George Bell, who during a 1934 trip to London paints his vaguely exoticising *Study for Argentina* in London and after his return to Melbourne his *Argentina* in 1937. (In fact, both are portraits of a model at London's Grosvenor School.) From the grandiosity of their titles alone, it is hard not to think of them as clumsy attempts to create an allegorical figure for Argentina itself, as 'Marianne' is for France, the feminine embodiment of the national spirit of a land he had never visited. And we might compare this to a trip that Margaret Preston took around South America in 1937, visiting among other countries Brazil, Chile, Argentina and Uruguay, looking for instances of public or community art serving what she called a 'constructive nationalism'.[10] Here perhaps, if Preston appears to be looking outside of Australia to tell her what Australia is, she is nevertheless only seeing these other cultures through the lens of a parallel nationalism.

But perhaps the most remarkable appearance of Australian artists in South America at mid-century occurred in 1938 when James Cant, Eric Smith and Geoffrey Graham were part of the exhibition *Pintores Ingleses no Segundo Salão de Maio* (*English Painters at the Second Salon of May*) in São Paulo, Brazil. A small, nine-person show of the English Surrealists, beside the Australians it included works by John Banting, WS Haile, Charles Howard, Roland Penrose, Ceri Richards and Julian Trevelyan. Organised by the remarkable artist and architect Flávio de Carvalho in conjunction with the London Gallery, in the view of the writer, curator and art critic Paulo Mendes de Almeida it was "the second in chronological order but in quality the best of the three [*Salãos*]".[11] It was, indeed, this sequence of three annual exhibitions from 1937 until 1939 that could be said to have led to the creation of modern Brazilian art. What is remarkable, in particular, is that the two collages shown in *Pintores Ingleses* were the first to be seen in Brazil. And, of course, all three Australians were known for their work in this classic avant-garde medium, with Cant and Smith's work from around this time being referred to by Herta Wescher in her classic text on the subject, *Collage* (1968).[12] Is it too much to say then that collage in Brazil began with the work of Australians? Like the hitherto hidden presence of Australian artists in the Armory Show in North America in 1913, Australian artists were also to be found in the foundational exhibitions of South American art, as unrecognised by Australians as they were by Brazilians.

Then, in 1948, after the war, the Viennese émigré and future Australian architect Harry Seidler spent two months working for Oscar Niemeyer in his office in Rio de Janeiro, an influence that can be seen in Seidler's work in Australia from the 1950s on. As well, the so-called Dunera boys continued to travel throughout the world after their time here. For two years from 1948, for example, the photographer Henry Talbot, who had trained at the Reimann School, Berlin and Royal Melbourne Institute of Technology, went to live with his parents in Bolivia before returning to Melbourne in 1950. Six years later he co-founded with his old German friend the photographic business that eventually became Helmut Newton & Henry Talbot Pty Ltd. 1950 was also the year that the Viennese Fred Schonbach moved to Brazil, where he spent nearly ten years doing numerous commercial jobs, including designing the cover for the great Argentine writer Jorge Luis Borges's *La muerte y la brújula* (*Death and the Compass*) in 1951, before eventually emigrating again in 1959, this time to North America, where he settled in Washington DC for forty years before finally retiring to Vancouver, Canada.

The same year as Schonbach did the cover for Borges—proving that at least for Australian artists the compass pointed to South America—the inaugural Bienal de São Paulo opened. Only the second such biennale after Venice and the first in the southern hemisphere, it was the exhibition at which the Swiss artist Max Bill famously won the prize for sculpture. Australian art debuted a decade later when in 1961 a small group of abstract painters was selected through the offices of the New South Wales Contemporary Art Society, and included, for instance, Stanislaus Rapotec, Carl Plate and Elwyn Lynn. A decade later still, Gunter Christmann and David Aspden showed in 1971, and they were followed, among others, by Jan Senbergs in 1973, Dick Watkins in 1985 and Mutlu Çerkez in 1998. The next biennial to be established after São Paulo was that of Sydney in 1973.[13] Both art exhibitions—perhaps we can say this now following the injunction of Torres-García—can be understood as seeking to contest the hegemony of the northern hemisphere and the authority of its apparatuses of recognition.

Artists too sought perhaps more directly to overcome this hegemony. Davila's Chilean colleague, the conceptual artist Eugenio Dittborn, was a constant presence in Australia from 1984 until 1990, holding a series of exhibitions around the country devoted to his 'Airmail paintings': paintings on paper incorporating collage and printmaking, which were folded and sent around the world.[14] In 2012 a number of his airmail paintings sent to Davila from 1984 were the subject of an exhibition at the gallery Alexander and Bonin in New York. As the catalogue makes clear, undoubtedly part of Dittborn's motivation, as well as finding a way to work under the dictatorship of Augusto Pinochet, was dispelling the illusion of any distance between Chile and the rest of the world. Or in the words of the catalogue, 'compressing' this distance by at once putting it inside the object and showing that it does not really exist. How could we say this about Dittborn's mail art and not think—and this is precisely again that compression of time of which the catalogue speaks—of the instantaneity of the internet to come? As it says:

> Distance—both the literal distance over which the works travel, and the distance across time that separates imagery from its original context—is folded and compressed into the matrix of each painting.[15]

Do we not find a such a compression of the time and space that 'separates the image from its original context' in the work of the contemporary Melbourne-based painter Diena Georgetti and her remarkable *Compass* (2017)—and, indeed, we can think back here to Schonbach and Borges in which she lays Bill's *Composition* (1965) on top of a turned-sideways version of the Brazilian Ivan Serpa's *Amazonia* (1970)? For all of the dangers of the art-historical sin of pseudomorphism, Georgetti is seeking consciously to produce the kind of connection that we might see also in the relationship between Serpa and the New Zealand painter Gordon Walters, although in that case the two artists worked independently and were unaware of each other.[16] In fact, for her part, Georgetti has been quoted as saying 'I want to make paintings without conditioned standards, that can be of any time, place, genre or age'[17]—which is to say she understands herself as a kind of medium of transmission between seperated cultures, or even a postal worker who puts otherwise unconnected places in touch with each other. To conclude here, do we not see a similar 'compression' in Davila's *Fable of Australian painting* in putting Melé's *Marco recortado* (*Irregular frame*) among so many images of Australian art? And in his failure to signpost it explicitly, is not Davila compressing the space between Melé and himself? For an artist who so clearly makes evident the distance between himself and his sources, is it not revealing that in all his Melé works he keeps a kind of secret close to his chest? Is not, in effect,

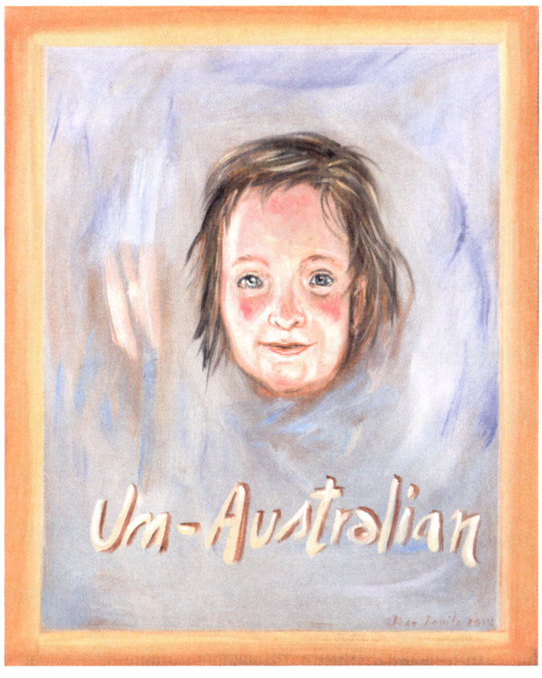

9.8 Juan Davila
Un-Australian, 2014

this continual quoting from Melé autobiographical? What would be at stake in identifying yourself in Australia as Juan Melé? And thereby to understand yourself as written out of the existing constructions of Australian art and culture in the way we have suggested? Is not the answer to be found in the image *Woomera* (2002), given silently, implicitly, in the particular way art (even one as discursive as Davila's) gives answers? The same question arises when we stand before Davila's *Un-Australian* (2014), an image of a young girl distressed and crying. At first, we might think she is a refugee—this work is one of three that includes *Detained* (2014) and *Die elsewhere* (2014). However, isn't she in fact a blue-eyed blonde, a shorthand for 'Australian' identity? What would be at stake here in identifying the 'Australian' as the UnAustralian? How do Davila's art and the historical genealogies he constructs connect us to the cultures of South America in a way that dispossesses us of our Australian identity, making us in effect Un-Australian or somehow as rootless and in between places as the refugee? For in these works Davila is asking us to re-imagine both who we are today and who we have been. To think about not only the contentious present-day politics of our so-called boat people but also the apparently objective dispassionate facts of our art history in the past. As Davila writes of *Fable of Australian painting*:

> The coincidence between the imperial ideology and the present economic rationalism has produced a linear visual representation as our art history, a sort of comic strip. We as artists can mock the dependence of our art history, as I have done in this Fable. It does not alter past ills or propose an Australian national identity. It aims to create a flicker of a doubt but no revisionism.[18]

In this text, Davila is neither playing on the stereotypes of Australian identity nor attempting simply to revise or rewrite them as in postcolonialism, as though they would then go away. Something like this was at stake in the exhibition *Vibration, Vibração, Vibración: Latin American Kinetic Art of the 1960s and '70s*, shown at the University of Sydney Art Gallery in 2012, which included the work of Julio Le Parc, Carlos Cruz-Diez, Jesús Rafael Soto, and Lucio Fontana.[19] Mostly bought in Paris for the University of Sydney's Power Collection by curator Gordon Thompson in 1967, a time when South American artists were enjoying considerable acclaim, particularly through the agency of Denise René, whose gallery had been a bastion of abstract art since opening in 1944, these works were funded by the bequest of JW Power, whose will was written in 1940 in occupied Jersey during the dark days of World War II. In it, he directed that the money be spent 'to make available to the people of Australia the latest ideas and theories in the plastic arts by means of lectures and teaching and by the purchase of the most recent contemporary art of the world'.[20] It was an instruction that eventually led to the formation of the Power Institute of Fine Arts at the University of Sydney, the Power Studio in the Cité Internationale des Arts in Paris and the extensive collection that formed the basis of the Museum of Contemporary Art in Sydney. In this way, didn't Power also found a School of the South, like Torres-García? Wasn't Power, when he was writing his will, changing reality by drawing a new map? Didn't Power, like Davila, propose a new Fable of Australian Art—or rather, as we would say, a certain Fable of UnAustralian Art?

An earlier version of this text was delivered as a lecture at The University of Queensland Art Museum, 26 June 2015.

—

1 Louis Aragon, Antonin Artaud, André Breton, Max Ernst, Robert Desnos et al., 'The Revolution First and Always', in ed. Mary Ann Caws, *Surrealism*, Phaidon, London, 2004, p. 210.

2 Joaquin Torres-García, 'The School of the South' (originally delivered as a lecture in 1935, published as Lesson 30 in *Universalismo Constructivo: Cóntribución a la Unificación del Arte y la Cultura de América)*, reprinted in *El Taller Torres-García: The School of the South and Its Legacy*, ed. Mari Carmen Ramírez, exhibition catalogue, Archer M Huntington Art Gallery, University of Texas Press, Austin, 1992, p. 53.

3 Robert Storr, 'Abstraction's Miraculous Perennial', in *Carmen Herrera*, exhibition catalogue, Lisson Gallery, New York, 2016, p. 23. This century, South American abstract art has been the subject of such exhibitions in North America and Europe as *Abstract Art from the Río de la Plata: Buenos Aires and Montevideo, 1933–1953* at the Americas Society, New York, in 2001; *Dimensions of Constructive Art in Brazil: The Adolpho Leirner Collection* at the Museum of Fine Arts, Houston, in 2007; *Constructive Spirit: Abstract Art in South and North America, 1920s–50s* at the Newark Museum, New Jersey, in 2010; *Geometry Beyond Limits: Latin American Contemporary Art* at the Maison de l'Amérique latine, Paris, in 2010; *Cold America: Geometric Abstraction in Latin America (1934–1973)* at Fundación Juan March, Madrid, in 2011; as well as in the numerous exhibitions supported by the Cisneros Collection and Foundation, such as those in Cambridge, Massachusetts, in 2001; in Austin, Texas, in 2007; and in London, England, in 2014. Perhaps the clearest example of this rethinking of the canon on the basis of South American art is the 2018 MoMA exhibition *Epic Abstraction: Pollock to Herrera*, which concluded with the Cuban-American abstractionist Carmen Herrera, who had shown alongside Mary Webb in 1950 and 1952 at the Salon des Réalités Nouvelles when she was living in Paris (where she met Breton) and was the subject of a late career-defining retrospective at the Whitney Museum in 2016.

4 See Guy Brett, 'Nothing Has Been Settled', in *Juan Davila*, Miengunyah Press, Melbourne, 2006, p. 244, fn. 37. On this exhibition see also Paul Allatson, 'Juan Davila: Queering the Trans-Pacific South', *Artlink*, vol. 27, no. 2, June 2007, pp. 16–20.

5 César Paternosto, 'Irregular Frame/Shaped Canvas: Anticipations, Inheritances, Borrowings', in *Cold America: Geometric Abstraction in Latin America (1934–1973)*, ed. María Amalia García, exhibition catalogue, Fundación Juan March, Madrid, 2011, pp. 33–4.

6 Roger Neyrat, cited in Maria Lluïsa Borràs, 'Madí in Paris in the 1950s', in *Arte Madí*, exhibition catalogue, Museo Nacional Centro de Arte Reina Sofía, Madrid, 1997, p. 298.

7 Ibid., p. 298.

8 Glenn R Cooke, 'Godrey Rivers' *Under the Jacarandah*', *Artlines*, issue 3, 2012, pp. 22–5.

9 JW Power, *Éléments de la Construction Picturale*, Antoine Roche, Paris, 1932, p. 5.

10 Deborah Edwards, *Margaret Preston*, Art Gallery of New South Wales, Sydney, 2005, p. 166.

11 Paulo Mendes de Almeida, 'De Anita ao Museu. São Paulo: Cons. Estadual de Cultura-Imprensa Oficial do Estado', 1961, p. 41. Cited in Renata Gomes Cardoso, 'Os Salões de Maio e a crítica de arte: modernismo, surrealismo e abstração', *Pós*, Belo Horizonte, vol. 5, no. 10, November 2015, p. 135.

12 Herta Wescher, *Collage*, Harry N Abrams, New York, 1968, p. 246.

13 On perhaps another 'Australian' presence in South America, see the well-known Butterfly Chair or BKF Chair, designed by architects Antonio Bonet, Juan Kurchan and Jorge Ferrari Hardoy working with Le Corbusier's studio in Buenos Aires in 1938 under the collective name Grupo Austral[es].

14 Since the 1980s, artists have continued to come to Australia from South America. From Colombia has come the installation artist Fernanda Cardoso, and from Brazil has come the photographer Vanilla Neto, who reminds us so much of the indefatigable globe-trotting travel photographer EB Gibbes, who in 1911 alone took photographs in Brazil, Argentina, Chile and Peru.

15 Press release, gallery Alexander and Bonin, New York, 2012, np.

16 See Rex Butler and ADS Donaldson, 'Gordon Walters: *Les années décisives*, 1946–1953', in *Gordon Walters: New Vision*, ed. Zara Stanhope et al., exhibition catalogue, Auckland Art Gallery Toi o Tāmaki, 2017, p. 142.

17 Sara Savage, 'Diena Georgetti – Art and Artifice', *Vault*, 19, Melbourne, 2017, p. 45.

18 *Juan Davila*, p. 97. It is notable that in recent years the Spanish-speaking world has also increasingly recognised Davila. There was the retrospective *Juan Davila: Imagen Residual/After Image*, at Centro Matucana 100 in Santiago, Chile, in 2016; and *Juan Davila: Painting and Ambiguity* at Museo

de Arte Contemporáneo de Castilla y León in León, Spain, in 2018.

19 *Vibration, Vibração, Vibración: Latin American Kinetic Art of the 1960s and '70s*, ed. Susan Best, exhibition catalogue, University of Sydney Art Gallery, 2012.

20 On the Power Bequest, see the website of the Power Institute Foundation for Art and Visual Culture, University of Sydney, http://sydney.edu.au/arts/power/about/index.shtml.

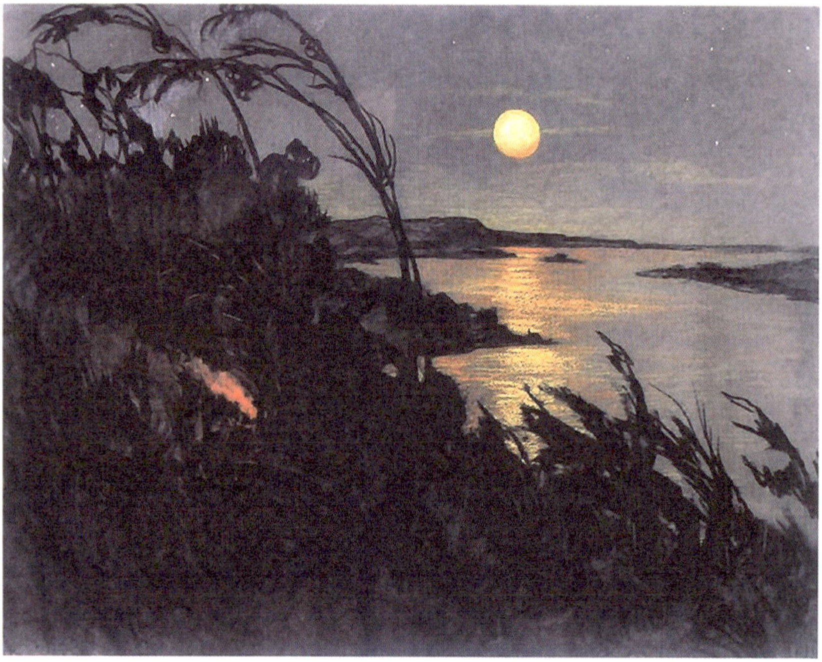

10.1 Stanisław Ignacy Witkiewicz (Witkacy)
Australian landscape, 1918

All the World's Australias

Am I or is Australia far away?
—Ben Vautier, Biennale of Sydney, 1990[1]

One of us was reading the British novelist Zadie Smith's *Swing Time* (2016), about two mixed-race women (the unnamed narrator and Tracey) who as girls had shared a love of dancing to jazz. They drift apart, but by novel's end find themselves together again, with the hip globe-trotting narrator abandoning her career helping African children for a charity foundation in order to support her once-friend who is now living with three fatherless children in a council tenement. But the thing that was interesting about it for us is that the reason the narrator flies around the world from Paris to London to New York is that she works as the personal assistant for a world-famous popstar obviously based on Kylie Minogue, helping her in the charity for children that she runs in Africa.[2] And then the idea struck us: wouldn't it be interesting somehow to compile a list of all the references to Australia and Australian things in world literature? How did all of the world's writers see Australia? What did they want from it? What purposes did their references serve? In Smith's book—but this is a complex question of literary criticism—the narrator works for an *Australian* singer because both are in a sense 'outsiders' in British society; and it has an element of autobiography because we guess that the teenage Smith was a fan of Kylie (or maybe of *Neighbours*). And off the top of our heads, we have always liked the reference to a 'few hectares in Queensland' in Jorge Luis Borges's story 'The Aleph'[3] (it has even been suggested that he actually visited Melbourne in 1938).[4] We also note the fact that the convict Abel Magwitch in Dickens's *Great Expectations* is deported to Australia (a fact that Peter Carey uses to write a whole alternative novel based on his character, in *Jack Maggs*). Indeed, the New Zealand author Ian Wedde has done something similar with the mentions of New Zealand in Herman Melville's *Moby-Dick* in his novel *Symmes Hole*.

Melville describes Australia there as 'That great America on the other side of the sphere'.[5] And who couldn't like English songwriter Kate Bush's 'The Dreaming' (1982), which is about the destruction of Indigenous Country due to uranium mining, beginning and ending with a didgeridoo drone and featuring the prominent British bird-impersonator Percy Edwards playing a sheep?

But beyond listing just a few of the myriad ways in which Australia has been understood by world culture, what would such an exercise demonstrate? Of course, famously in the thinking of Australian culture, we find many (typically European) preconceptions about the place. European cultures project themselves upon it, do not see it as it is, but only through their own eyes. This is the well-known hypothesis of Bernard Smith in his *European Vision and the South Pacific, 1768–1850* and even the argument of the *Colony* exhibition at the National Gallery of Victoria in 2018.[6] This hypothesis reciprocally allows for a moment when Australia is seen 'properly'. This can be either the Heidelberg School (Bernard Smith again) or, miraculously, the moment the First Fleet sailed through Sydney Heads, grasping the uncanny 'distance' and 'unfinishedness' of the land (Paul Carter in 'Encounters').[7] And thereafter it is a matter of sending this 'true' Australia across the globe to challenge how Europeans see themselves and it (Smith again and the postcolonial revisions that followed him). But all of these argue from the position of their being a 'true' Australia: either a particular place that is depicted accurately or not, or an empty space from where we can speak the truth of other representations. Both claim either to speak for Australia or that no one can speak for Australia (which is still ultimately to speak for Australia). Both argue for the possibility of a distinctively Australian art: either as some particular place or national characteristic able to be illustrated (accurately or not), or as an emptiness from where all misrepresentations can be diagnosed. (For Smith, romanticism, which arises as the effect of the contact of Europe with its colonies, is in effect one of these misrepresentations.[8])

But can all of this be thought another way? From a world where there is no distance between countries, where there is no truth and even no place from which to diagnose the lack of truth ('The truth is not the truth!'). From a position of immanence. A newly flat world. A post-natural and a post-national world. What is called, in shorthand, 'the contemporary'. This is what we have previously described as a history of Australian art written from the outside in and not the inside out (but really, the whole distinction between inside and outside no longer applies). It would be a history in which Australia is not somewhere or nowhere but *everywhere*. It would be an Australia that is no longer usable or diagnosable as a trope or symptom, that is, qualitatively (because what anymore could it be compared to?), but rather aggregative or quantitative. It would be an Australia that exists—as on the internet or Instagram—only because it continues to be mentioned, continues to be 'liked'. So what follows is another history of Australian art, following our earlier gestured-to literary one. It would be an Australian art not done by 'Australian' artists (even emigrants and immigrants) and in a way not even done of Australia (few of the artists we speak of have even visited the country). It is a history of Australian art 'after' the history of Australian art, running parallel to that which existed 'before' the history of Australian art (after all, those pre-colonial imagined maps were not done by Australian artists and were not of Australia). But this equivalence is precisely what we saw on the top floor of the *Colony* exhibition, *Frontier Wars*, where a number of the works by contemporary Indigenous artists were not done in Australia, not done of (then) Australians and in a way not even done by 'Australian' artists.[9] So what would be the meaning of our imagined exhibition? What is it of? Who is it for? Here all the complex questions of the future of art history in the contemporary are raised. But we would say that it is no longer a question of understanding, nor perhaps even of overstanding, but rather just of standing. We are ourselves standing in or among the very thing we wish to speak of.

Let us imagine, then, this exhibition; let's call it *All the World's Australias*. After all the European-drawn maps of Australia, including particularly those by the Dutch, British and French, we would start the show with the Belgian artist Théo van Rysselberghe's series of eucalyptus paintings, dating from 1905 to 1912, from which we select *Eucalyptus on the road to Bormes* (1911). Van Rysselberghe had moved to Paris in 1897, working in a broadly neo-impressionist style, but also spending much time on the southern coast of France, where these paintings were made. These are the eucalypts that Napoléon had brought back for Josephine at the Château de Malmaison on the Seine, which soon spread through the warmer parts of Europe.

Van Rysselberghe was a friend of Paul Signac. They both did work for the Parisian anarchist magazine *Temps nouveaux*, and, like van Rysselberghe, Signac painted in the south of France, where the eucalyptus thrived after its introduction. It is he who paints for us the pointillist gumtree in, for instance, *The eucalyptus, Antibes* (1913).

We then include Piet Mondrian's series of eucalyptus paintings from 1912. After seeing the work of Cézanne, Picasso and Braque in Amsterdam in 1911, he moved to Paris the following year, so the first work in our sequence is done in a more conventional manner, leading to the last where his subject has become fully cubist. Now in the Museo Nacional Thyssen-Bornemisza in Madrid, it was called *The eucalyptus tree* when shown at the Sidney Janis Gallery in New York in 1949 after Mondrian's death, because in 1939 he had sent a photo of the work to his friend Ben Nicholson with that title handwritten on the back.

And the final member of our International Gumtree School is the Italian Futurist Giacomo Balla's *Iridescent interpenetration no. 5—eucalyptus* of 1914. It could well be based on Balla's encounter with the eucalyptus when he went to France for the 1912 *Futurist Exhibition* mounted in Paris. Notice the beautiful hazy menthol atmosphere of the work, fully the equivalent of the Heidelberg School, and the predominance of blue and yellow, the colours that allow the nationalist reading of Ian Burn's abstracts of the mid-1960s and that he identifies in turn as characterising the landscapes of Sidney Nolan and Fred Williams.

We then have the much-travelled (America, Britain) French etcher and illustrator Jean-Émile Laboureur, who enlisted in the British army during World War I. Hence his typically cubist image of the typical Australasian soldier, *ANZACs* (1919–1922). Perhaps as a pendant to this we would show in this exhibition, admittedly out of chronological sequence, the Turkish artist Köken Ergun's video work *Heroes* (2018), commissioned by the Australian War Memorial in Canberra and Sydney's Artspace, whose subject is what Ergun calls the 'tourism of martyrdom' on the Gallipoli Peninsula in Turkey.

Next we have an array of Polish artist Stanisław Ignacy Witkiewicz's (aka Witkacy) *Australian landscapes* (1918, see p. 226), which now hang in numerous

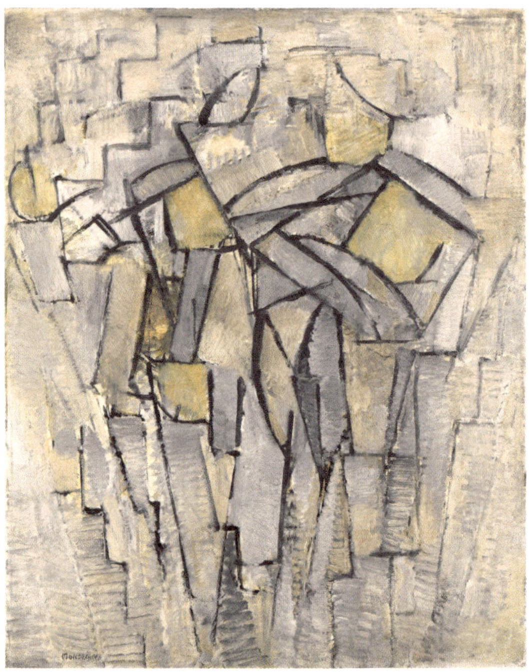

10.2 Piet Mondrian
Composition n. XIII/
Composition 2, 1913

Polish art galleries. Witkacy was the subject of the Sydney artist John Gillies' film or 'cinematic séance in 23 scenes', *Witkacy and Malinowski* (2017–18), about the legendary argument between the artist and the great Polish anthropologist Bronisław Malinowski while they were together on a train from Brisbane to Toowoomba as World War I broke out, and based in part on Witkacy's take on the incident in his play *The crazy Locomotive* (1923).

Then we might include Romanian sculptor Constantin Brâncuși's *Mlle Pogány* (1913), one of his most important works, which we could say retrospectively becomes a sculpture of postwar Australian immigration when Margit Pogany, one of his favourite models, arrives impoverished in Melbourne in 1949 and soon after tries to sell her bronze to the National Gallery of Victoria, which hesitates before it is quickly acquired by the Museum of Modern Art in New York, where it can be seen today.

This retrospective reading of work is what we are tempted to say also of *Painterly musical construction* (1918) by the radical Russian abstractionist Mikhail Matyushin (recently shown at Documenta 14), which somehow points for us towards the paintings that emerged from Papunya in the early 1970s. And likewise, it is Western Desert painting that we are reminded of first of all when

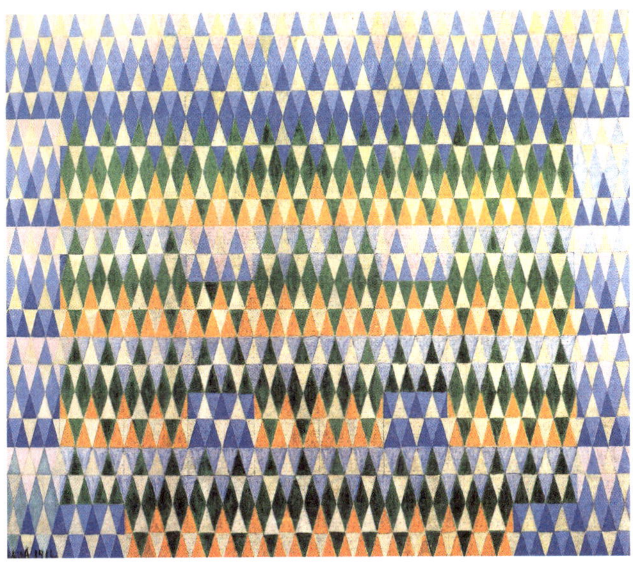

10.3 Giacomo Balla
Iridescent interpenetration no. 5 – eucalyptus, 1914

we see the paintings of the American artist Peter Young. Young's *Number 29, 1968* (1968) was acquired by the National Gallery of Australia in 1975 and with its shifting dotted forms and its aerial perspective, we feel sure it was bought because of its perceived stylistic affinities with the Aboriginal painting that was then emerging from Central Australia. And Young's painting recalls for us the remarkable Vance Kirkland, who in the 1960s and '70s produced his large series known as the 'dot paintings', made of swirling fields of painted spots. Like Young, he produced almost psychedelic cosmologies such as his *Conception of space mysteries* (1974), now held in the Kirkland Museum in Denver. Both Kirkland's and Young's works have been discussed in relation to pointilism (although in Young's 2007 exhibition catalogue the curator Klaus Kertess rather unfortunately titles his essay 'Tribe of One'[10]), but for us the real comparison is with Western Desert painting. (And there are complex questions of isomorphism too with the work of New Zealander Gordon Walters.)

It is notable, as well, that while the famous map *The world at the time of the Surrealists* (see p. 88) miniaturised Australia while vastly expanding the Pacific Islands, André Breton himself had several objects of Indigenous Australian culture in his bureau at home—he called it his 'workshop'—a wall of which is now

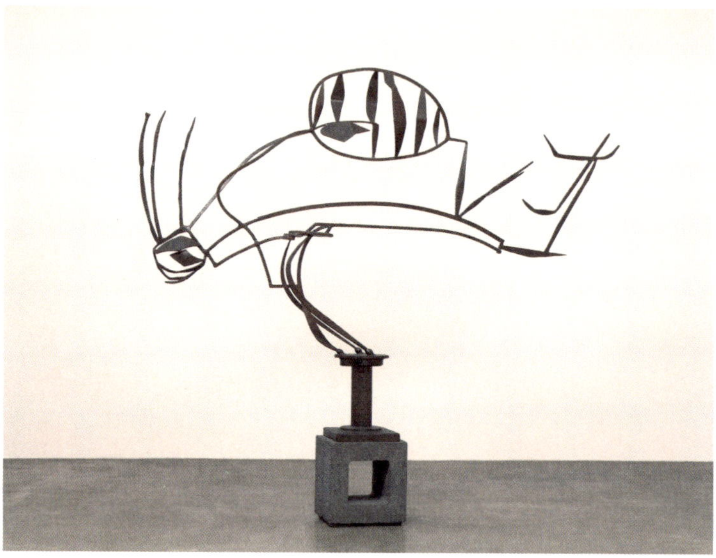

10.4 David Smith
Australia, 1951

installed in the Centre Pompidou in Paris (see p. 90). His collection included four engraved boomerangs, a churinga, as well as a bark painting from Arnhem Land given to him by the Czech artist and art historian Karel Kupka. The question raised here is: is Breton's collection a mere collection, or a surrealist work of art?

Alongside Breton's 'appropriation' of Aboriginal culture, we would have in our exhibition New Zealander Len Lye's animated film *Tusalava* (1929), inspired in part by the Aboriginal rock carvings he had studied around the Hawkesbury River, the collection of Indigenous art at the Australian Museum and his reading of Freud's *Totem and Taboo* when he was living in Sydney in the 1920s. Along the same lines we include the work of another New Zealander, Gordon Walters's *Untitled* (1956), inspired by his own reading and the collection of Indigenous art at the Australian Museum, as well as by his trips to rock art sites around the fringes of Sydney, which he often visited when he was living there in the late 1940s.

Next in the exhibition we would include three different sculptures by American artists with the word 'Australia' in them. The first is David Smith's skeletal X-ray steel sculpture of 1951, *Australia*, said perhaps to have been inspired by the Arnhem Land *rarrk* painting included in the 1941 MoMA show

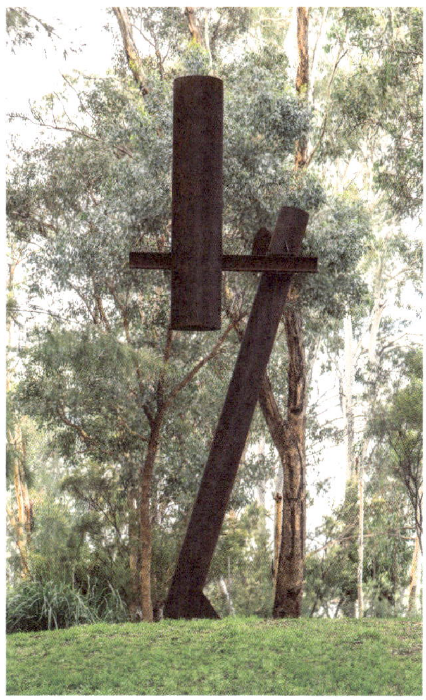

10.5 Richard Stankiewicz
Australia no. 15, 1969

Art of Australia 1788–1941, that toured America for four years and whose catalogue had been given to him by his friend Clement Greenberg. Then there is Richard Stankiewicz's *Australia no. 15* (1969), the outcome of a trip here that year to visit the relatives of his wife. Through his Australian friend the sculptor Robert Klippel, whom he had met when Klippel was teaching in America, he was encouraged to turn this into a longer working holiday and later showed the entire sequence of fifteen welded steel sculptures, all entitled *Australia*, at Watters Gallery in Sydney. Finally, we include Anne Truitt's minimalist vertical wooden sculpture *Australian spring* (1972), with its Nolan-esque high blue horizon line. Truitt did similar-looking works entitled *Antipode* (1980) and *Australian solstice* (1982) on both sides of a trip she took to Australia in 1981.

We would also include the Texan Forrest Bess's *The hermaphrodite* (1957). Bess was a kind of insider 'outsider' artist, being represented by the Betty Parsons Gallery for twenty years, while living alone near a lake outside Bay City, Texas. After reading an article on Aboriginal ceremonial initiations in the journal *Sexology*, he decided in the late 1950s to perform surgery on himself, becoming a kind of pseudo-hermaphrodite; and his painting is clearly reminiscent of Aboriginal culture, although this is rarely mentioned in accounts of it.

10.6 Anne Truitt
Australian spring, 1972

The next painting in our exhibition is by the German Dunera artist Hein Heckroth. His surrealistic and scenographic *Australia* (1941) was made in a detention camp in Hay. Heckroth later went on to become an influential set designer, first in England and then in Hollywood in the 1950s, known for pioneering the magical, fantastic and highly artificial look of such films as *The Red Shoes* (for which he won an Academy Award) and *The Tales of Hoffman*.

Then we would include a pair of collages by two German artists, each from near the end of their lives. When Kurt Schwitters finished his *Out of the dark* (1943), he was living in exile in London, and the work features a torn-up label from a box of Tasmanian apples. Typically Schwitters, the work points to the wartime paradox that the most unimaginable luxury was also an everyday thing. Next to it we have Hans Richter's *Pro contra variation* (1972), which uses a torn-up article about a medical emergency in Brisbane as its single real-world element. The pairing of these artists places their 'Australian' works at the centre of the avant-garde.

Then—in a parallel with the French surrealists' fascination with Pacific and Indigenous cultures between the wars—we have German artists fascinated with Pacific and Indigenous cultures after the war. The first of these is Klaus Rinke, then a professor at the Kunstakademie Düsseldorf, who initially came to Australia for the Mildura Sculpture Triennial of 1976, and subsequently made several return trips for four months at a time. He participated in *European Dialogue: The Third Biennial of Sydney* in 1979 and presented *Klaus Rinke from Germany* at the Art of Man Gallery in Sydney in 1980, all the while continuing to work on his 'vast and amorphous' *Australian diary*, made up of more than 800 enormous works on paper that feature biomorphic imagery and the outlines of human figures—he often calls the work his 'pre-embryonic' diary—that are his response particularly to the Indigenous cultures he became familiar with on his numerous trips to Central Australia. The art historian David Galloway has described *Australian diary* in a catalogue essay for their exhibition at the RMIT Gallery in Melbourne in 2008 as 'one of the greatest and most seminal suites of drawings produced in the twentieth century'.[11] Notably, Rinke was included in an exhibition of contemporary Australian art, *D'un autre continent: L'Australie; Le rêve et le réel* (*From another continent: Australia; the dream and reality*) at the Musée d'Art Moderne de la Ville de Paris in 1983, where his work could be seen alongside a large ground painting by twelve Warlpiri artists from Lajamanu.

Rinke was followed to Australia by his great contemporary and fellow professor in Düsseldorf Joseph Beuys, who came to Canberra in 1982 to install his *Stripes from the house of the shaman 1964–72* (1980) for the opening of the National Gallery of Australia. Rejecting the gallery's initial hanging suggestion, Beuys instead designed a kind of gate or arch, from which he could unfurl his 'stripes'. Built without nails but instead using wooden wedges, it was made from second-hand lumber he sourced from a junk yard near Canberra, as Beuys preferred curved timber over straight, choosing it because he said it 'remembers the tree'.[12] It was while he was in Australia that he must have acquired the boomerang he used in the work we would show, *Untitled (Bumerang mit Spiegel)* (*Boomerang with mirror*) (1982), a wall sculpture incorporating a boomerang from which is hung a broken mirror, the two connected by knotted string. At once the two sides of an exchange, each of these objects also 'returns': the boomerang to its thrower and the mirror to the one who looks.

And the presence of the boomerang in Beuys's work reminds us of all those artists who have used it or have imagined its potential target the kangaroo in their work. We include, therefore, the German artist Hans Grundig's etching of kangaroos resting *Warten* (Waiting) (1935), the English John Skeaping's ceramic Wedgwood figure *Kangaroo* (1927) and the American Alexander Calder's kinetic sculpture *Kangaroo* (c. 1926–31). Alongside them, we include such boomerang artists as Calder again with his *Red boomerang* (1961) and the German-American painter Charline von Heyl, who this century extended this line with her *Boomerang (Aboriginal sin)* (2017). And, following these, we would find a place for the Soviet artist Valdimir Lebedev's lithograph *Okhota* (*The hunt*) (1925), which brings the two 'schools' together.

In 1981, the year before Beuys visited Canberra, Sigmar Polke was moving through Australia, an experience that led to a whole sequence of works. Perhaps the most arresting of these is the one we would show, his ten luminescent Cibachromes collectively called *Untitled* (1992), produced by exposing photographic paper to uranium that he—somehow—acquired in Australia and manage to smuggle into Germany, where he kept it in a lead box in his studio for the rest of his life. It has typically been our flora and fauna that have been used to signify Australia, but in this case it is our geology, reminding us that this was the subject too of Eugene von Guérard's craggy *North-east view from the northern top of Mount Kosciusko* (1863). We would also present Polke's films from his travels through Arnhem Land, Tasmania and Papua New Guinea in 1980–81, which have come to attention since his retrospectives at MoMA and at the Museum Ludwig in Cologne in 2014. Of course, in his trips through Papua New Guinea, he was only following such German artists as Max Pechstein and Emil Nolde, who worked in the Equatorial Pacific before World War I.

This move from geology to water reminds us of the photographs of Martin Kippenberger bedecked as a kind of pirate sailing past the Sydney Opera House, his costume a handkerchief on his head, which in turn reminds us of the surfing imagery that fills the artist's book *The Beatles in Australia* (2011) by Johannes Wohnseifer, Kippenberger's final assistant.

We would include as well the London School painter Michael Andrews's *Near Malu Kata evening, Katajuta (The Olgas)* (1986), sold recently in London for about $2.5 million, based on a trip to Australia in 1983. When first shown at the Anthony d'Offay Gallery in London in 1986 as one of five, the series was entitled *Rock of ages cleft for me*, a reference to Andrews's Methodist upbringing and his belief that this gave him a supposed spiritual affinity with the traditional owners of Uluru. In fact, the work reminds us of a washed-out pastiche of Drysdale's, Nolan's and Williams's outbacks, in a replay of that original taking-up of Australia in London in the early 1960s, with Kenneth Clark and Bryan Robertson and such shows as *Recent Australian Painting* at the Whitechapel and *Australian Painting: Colonial, Impressionist, Contemporary* at the Tate Gallery.

It is well known that the American conceptual artist Sol LeWitt borrowed heavily from the Utopia painter Emily Kngwarreye when making his wall work for the exhibition *Your Mind Is Exactly at that Line* at the Art Gallery of New South Wales in 2014, even to the extent that people did not recognise the work as LeWitt's. The American effectively abandoned his own rigid style for the flowing lines of Australian women's desert painting, and indeed was a passionate collector of Kngwarreye's art.

Beside the elegance of LeWitt's work, we would show the more forthright and graphic work of the Sydney-born Norwegian artist Bjarne Melgaard, whose expressionist paintings in particular have made him a superstar of contemporary art. Like Kippenberger with his frog, Melgaard has created for himself an animalian double in his work, in his case choosing a platypus. (American artist Julian Schnabel has also painted not only *Australia* but *The migration of the duck-billed platypus to Australia*, both of 1986, which only serves to remind us that, more than a century before Schnabel, Dante Gabriel Rossetti and the whole Pre-Raphaelite gang adored wombats and lovingly presented them in their work.[13]) In so repeatedly painting the platypus we feel sure Melgaard is identifying with Australia, and we are certain that anyone in Norway would know that he was born in Australia, just as we are confident that nobody in Australia would be aware that for decades Melgaard has been celebrating our fauna as much as himself in such works as *Sissy platypus* (2009).

Finally, we would include London artist Mark Leckey's large blow-up plastic replica of *Felix the Cat* (2013), featuring the great predecessor to Mickey Mouse, and the character Walt Disney imitated to make his famous rodent. Felix was originally created by the Australian Pat Sullivan, who coincidentally worked next door to Duchamp in the Lincoln Arcade Building at Broadway and Sixty-Third Street in New York, where Duchamp also had a studio in 1915 and 1916 (hence we think of the appropriateness of Leckey's readymade). Indeed, a revolving Felix doll on a gramophone, accompanied by his famous theme music, was the first image to be transmitted on American television in 1928.[14] (And we for our part have always been a fan of 'Tas', the Tasmanian Devil often introduced as the 'Wonder from Down Under', in Warner Brothers cartoons.)

What has all of this been to show? Put simply, that *anyone* can make Australian art. That it is not an exclusive category, that it does not require the artist to be somehow 'Australian', the possessor of a particular national character or sensibility (and, conversely, it is to imply that Australian artists have been able to make French art, British art, American art, German art, Japanese art …). But doesn't this raise, in a manner common in artistic debates today, the issue of who has the right to make Australian art, the question of cultural appropriation or speaking for others? Of course artists from other cultures *can* make Australian art, but do they have the *right* to do so? At this point, we return to Zadie Smith. At a literary festival in Colombia in early 2019, she was asked to speak against the possibility of a non-black novelist representing black characters in their work. To this she replied:

> If someone says to me, 'A black girl would never say that', I'm saying: 'How can you possibly know?' The problem with that argument is it assumes the possibility of total knowledge of humans.[15]

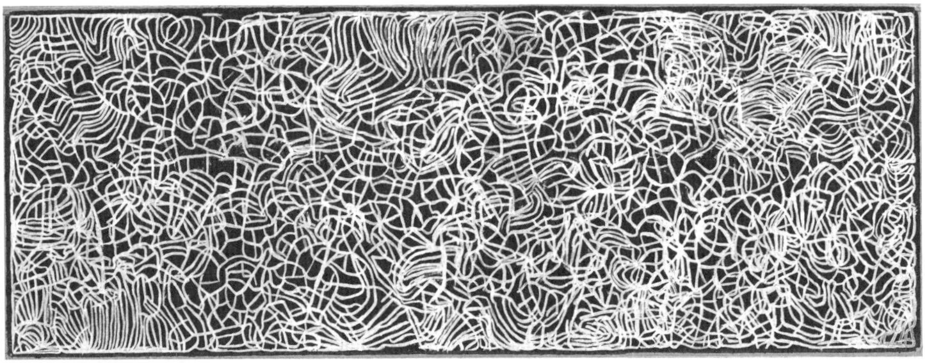

10.7 Emily Kngwarreye
Anwerlarr anganenty (Big yam dreaming), 1995

It is much easier to speak as a black woman for the right of others to represent black women, just as it is perhaps easier for us as Australians to speak for the right of others to make Australian art. And it is true that we *do* speak as Australians here and undoubtedly largely *to* Australians. But in principle—and, as we have tried to demonstrate, in historical fact—it is absolutely possible for others to make Australian art. Artists from other countries (and our own artists living overseas) have made work that is just as 'Australian' as that made by Australian artists living here. It is not anything like an identity or moral question but, as Smith goes on to argue, an *aesthetic* question as to what counts as successful art—and for us what counts as Australian art. In speaking of the fundamental 'irresponsibility' of art, Smith goes on to say:

> We are asked to be consistent as humans over great swathes of time. People are searching through social media [for any inconsistencies]. But everyone is changing all the time … It's a responsibility to be as open as you possibly can to the world as an aesthetic object.[16]

To conclude, we ask: what is the appropriate art-historical method to capture this fundamental 'irresponsibility' of art, the fact that it crosses all borders, all identities,

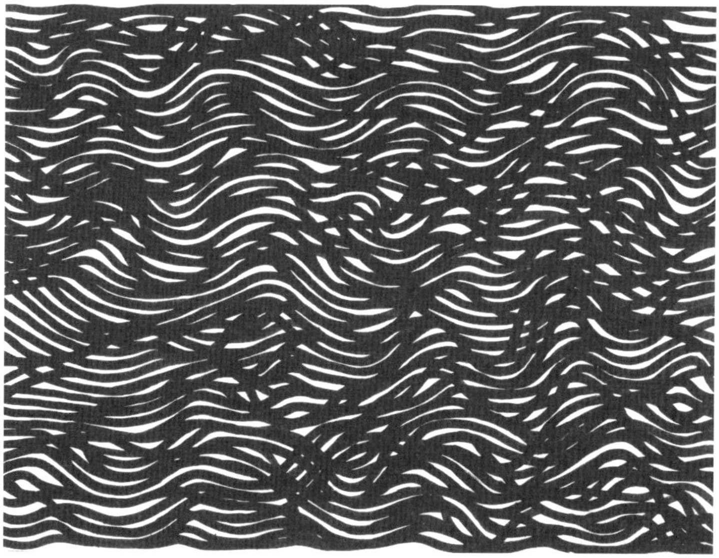

10.8 Sol LeWitt
Tangled bands, 2002

all the limits that art history has attempted to impose on it? How do we not suppose in advance what counts as 'Australian', while nevertheless still wanting, beyond the endless dispersion of the world, to speak of a certain 'Australia'?

An earlier version of this text was delivered as a paper at the Art Association of Australia and New Zealand Annual Conference in Melbourne in 2018.

—

1 The screenprinted text work *Am I or is Australia far away?* by the French artist Ben Vautier can be seen today as part of the interior environment created by the German artist Rosemarie Tröckel for the restaurant in Malkasten, Dusseldorf. Founded in 1848, Malkasten (Painters box) is an artists' association of which Eugene von Guérard was a member following his studies at the Kunstakademie Düsseldorf, before he came to Australia.

2 Zadie Smith, *Swing Time*, Random House, New York, 2016.

3 Jorge Luis Borges, 'The Aleph', in *Collected Fictions*, Penguin, UK, 1999, p. 277.

4 Guy Rundle, 'A Surreal Visitor', *The Age*, 22 April 2002, www.theage.com.au/articles/2002/04/22/1019233309914.html. It was subsequently revealed that Rundle's article was a hoax, but we entirely approve of the words with which he concludes: 'Fictional conjunctions of authors can bring new life to old work. An unremarkable and over-familiar city [Melbourne] can be seen anew through the eyes of a mysterious visitor'.

5 Herman Melville, *Moby-Dick, or The Whale*, Vintage Books, New York, 1991, p. 140.

6 *Colony: Australia 1770–1861 / Frontier Wars*, eds. Cathy Leahy and Judith Ryan, exhibition catalogue, National Gallery of Victoria, Melbourne, 2018.

7 Paul Carter, 'Encounters', *Fleeting Encounters: Pictures & Chronicles of the First Fleet*, ed. Peter Emmett, exhibition catalogue, Historic Houses Trust of New South Wales, Sydney, 1995, pp. 13–18.

8 See on this Paul Foss, 'Theatrum nondum cognitorum', in eds. Peter Botsman, Chris Burns and Peter Hutchings, *The Foreign Bodies Papers*, Local Consumption Publications, Sydney, 1981, especially the passage where Foss writes: 'Everything is sucked into the void to be re-emitted back through the stratosphere to help map the territories of the rest of the globe' (p. 35).

9 We are referring here to Brook Andrew's suite of screenprints *Gun-metal grey* (2007), which draw on the archives of the Royal Anthropological Institute in London, the Pitt Rivers Museum at Oxford University and the Museum of Archaeology and Anthropology at Cambridge University.

10 Klaus Kertess, 'Tribe of One', *Peter Young: Paintings 1963–1980*, PARC Foundation, New York, 2007, np.

11 David Galloway, 'The Passionate Pilgrimage of Klaus Rinke', in *Klaus Rinke: Recent Drawings; Rhine-Ruhr-Danube-Loire-Pacific Connection-re-Australia*, ed. Suzanne Davies, exhibition catalogue, RMIT Gallery, Melbourne, 2008, p. 11.

12 As recalled by Ben Taylor in 'Joseph Beuys was here, 1982', National Gallery of Australia, www.medium.com/national-gallery-of-australia/joseph-beuys-was-here-1982-91524802da18.

13 See on this Angus Trumble, '"O Uommibatto": How the Pre-Raphaelites Became Obsessed with the Wombat', *The Public Domain Review*, January 2019.

14 Although this is not quite the place for it, we cannot help adding here that Disney also owed something to another Antipodean artist. Roger Horrocks in his biography of Len Lye points out that Disney repeatedly showed Lye's films to the animators working on *Fantasia* (1940) and writes 'In *Fantasia* the coloured silhouettes of orchestral players were reminiscent of *Rainbow Dance*, and the coloured sandstorm in the "Rite of Spring" sequence matched the storm in *The Birth of the Robot*' (*Len Lye: A Biography*, Auckland University Press, Auckland, 2001, p. 146). And we for our part cannot overlook the resemblance between the sequence featuring Bach's *Toccata* and *Fugue* and Lye's *Tusalava* (1929).

15 Claire Armistead, '"Identity Is a Pain in the Arse": Zadie Smith on Political Correctness', *Guardian*, 3 February 2019, www.theguardian.com/books/2019/feb/02/zadie-smith-political-correctness-hay-cartagena.

16 Ibid.

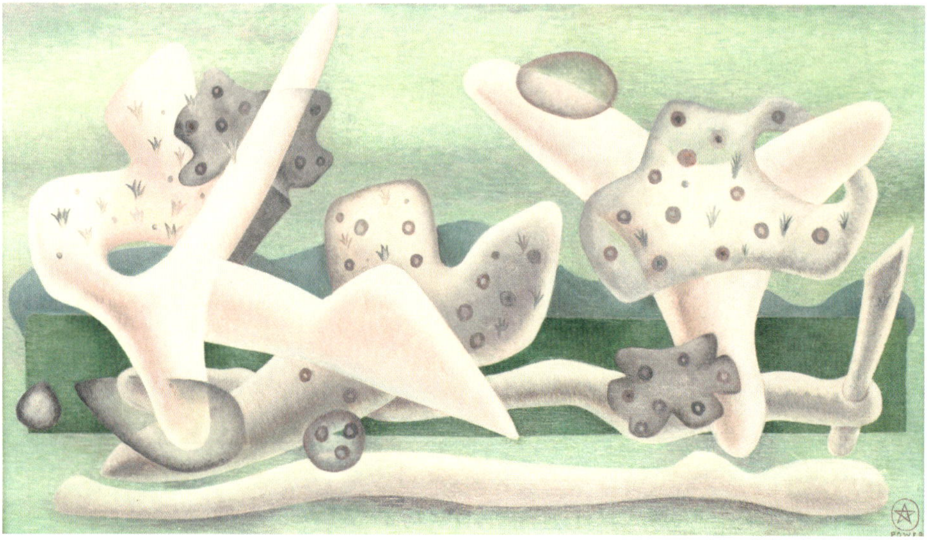

11.1 JW Power

Marine, c. 1933

Epilogue
There Is No Provincialism Solution

Before we conclude, a reprise. In 1896 Henri Matisse was at a crossroads. Despite many attempts, he had been unable to break with the pictorial formulae inherited from his great predecessor Jean-Baptiste-Siméon Chardin. Almost in despair, Matisse left Paris and made his way to Belle-Île off the coast of Brittany. There he introduced himself to the Australian painter John Russell, who went on to show him his particular way of working with unmixed colour. For the future Fauve, it was a breakthrough: 'Russell was my teacher, and Russell explained colour theory to me'.[1]

* * *

For the launch of the new publication *frieze d/e*, an offshoot of the London-based *frieze* magazine for the German-language market, the new editor Jennifer Allen wrote an online editorial entitled 'The Provincialism Solution'. In her editorial Allen makes much of the new global situation of art today, the way the centres of artistic interest are now much more spread out than they previously were. She begins by saying that *frieze d/e* will reflect this new globalism:

> *frieze d/e* is a bi-lingual magazine focusing on contemporary art in Austria, Germany and Switzerland: on what is going on not only in Vienna, Berlin or Zurich, but also in places like Salzburg, Dresden or Winterthur.[2]

Allen goes on to offer a brief history of provincialism, noting that the term was coined—or at least was popularised—some time in the 1690s, when all those living outside Paris or the royal court at Versailles were deemed 'provincial'. (In his 1690 dictionary, Antoine Furetière observed that the term derived from the ancient Romans, who used it to refer to all conquered territories outside Italy.)

As proof of the global interest of the new *frieze d/e*, Allen quotes from the essay 'The Provincialism Problem', originally published in America in 1974 in *Artforum* by the Australian art historian Terry Smith.

Smith's article—now well known outside Australia and a frequent topic of discussion in Australian art circles since it was published—takes up the relationship of Australian art in the early 1970s to that made in New York, which he describes as 'an attitude of subservience to an externally imposed hierarchy of values'.[3] That is, he diagnoses what he sees as Australia's sense of cultural inferiority and the feeling of Australian artists that their work will not count, will be of no value, unless it is seen in New York or seen somehow to manifest the values of the most recent art made there.

He points to what he calls the 'complex history of the Australian expatriates', in which Australian artists wishing to be part of metropolitan art visit New York in order to learn what artists there are doing (and Smith undoubtedly has in mind the example of a number of artists of his generation who did indeed go to New York). There they absorb the latest styles or at least make plausible imitations of the latest styles. But, argues Smith, when they return to Australia, having at no point been in on the 'early innovative struggles' and lacking the proper critical context for their understanding, their work soon runs aground. They can then return to the centre to attempt to re-establish contact, but at some point the connection is broken and their project comes to an end.

It is not that, for Smith, much of American art is not also provincial in relation to that made in New York. As he admits, only a small amount of the art made there actually counts—he mentions, for example, Stella's black paintings of the late 1950s, Judd's sculptures of 1965–66 and LeWitt's framework structures of 1966–67. It is a constantly updated sequence—no single artist definitively belongs to the canon—and the metropolitan continually casts everything outside of it into a provincial relationship.

'Can this provincial bind be overcome?', Smith asks towards the end of his article. As he says, the provincial artist cannot choose but to be provincial. They either compete with the artists of the centre—against whom they must lose—or refuse to; but then this refusal can be seen only as a form of willed exoticism, and in that sense merely another form of response. Smith tentatively puts forward at a certain point a suggestion that is not followed up and that he later appears to reject: 'It seems that nothing but a shuffling of standards [between centre and periphery] can go on until, by some miracle, the local artworld becomes a metropolitan centre'.

In Australian art and art history, there have been a number of responses to Smith's essay. At first there was the postmodern parody of it, in which artists by appropriating well-known images from overseas appeared consciously to play out their provincialism and thus in a way to outwit it. Then there was the postcolonial attempt to value the hybridity of the Australian image, the particular mix of the local and international that could be said to define the 'Australian'. Finally, there was the attempt to argue—as with Allen—that the conditions for provincialism no longer exist, that the new 'global' situation does away with the centre, or at least that the centres of artistic interest are more widely dispersed than before.

But all of these responses, essentially critical of provincialism, still take place on the basis that provincialism *once* existed. Whether provincialism is parodied, used positively or seen to be historically surpassed, it is not denied that provincialism did once exist. If each response puts forward its own provincialism 'solution', it is not denied that there was at least once a 'problem'. Thus the premises of Smith's argument are left essentially intact; nothing challenges them, for provincialism precisely lives on through its own denial, refuting the argument that it no longer exists.

What can it actually mean to say, on the contrary, that provincialism *never* existed? Or, at least, that at no time was it the only possible explanation of events? That provincialism was the outcome of a modernism—and moreover an *American* modernism—that from the perspective of today seems less and less like the hegemonic movement that Smith speaks of and more like merely one version among many others?

For underlying the argument of provincialism is the modernist notion of the avant-garde succession of styles. Smith uses the words 'style' and 'competing styles' no fewer than ten times in his essay. It is what lies behind his idea that the metropolitan centre of art in New York is unlocatable. It is exactly this that defines the dilemma of the provinces: that the centre against which the province is defined cannot be found; that by the time metropolitan style is identified it is already too late, is already in a way only a copy. It is to show that the logic of provincialism is exactly *transferential*, the assumption of a certain art-historical method.

But what if this linear version of art history was not true, not only now but even back then? For looking back at the twentieth century we see not a single river but a vast delta of alternatives; not simply the old New York story of formalist reduction and its aftermath, but the exploration of colour, popular culture, feminism, queer, different forms of sociality, Indigenous art, multimedia, forms of realism, etc. All of these have their own trajectories—and it is this that constitutes the true history of the present, how we must understand how we got to where we are today.

In reality, artists were never subservient to the power of the centre. Art was never defined by styles, but rather by ideas. Artists' 'subservience' was just a projection by critics—modernist or modernist-influenced—and was never the actual reality of artists working in their studios. Artists from different cultures, from different languages and from different *arrondissements* have always sought out the work that interested them, no matter the apparent disparity in power between them and their model.

And it is from this perspective that we can see, from where we stand, the presence of Australian artists working throughout the world, and certainly in major 'metropolitan' cultures, throughout the twentieth century. If not in the imagined New York art world Smith speaks of—in fact an empty set—then they were in all kinds of positions, in all kinds of places. Even if they were not part of modernist history (although they often were), they participated in all kinds of other artistic movements that today seem more and more like the actual history of the present.

In our studies, we have revealed the presence of four Australians (Charles Conder, Derwent Lees, Frank Nankivell and Francis McComas) in the famous Armory Show of 1913. We have recounted the career of Martin Lewis, who showed Edward Hopper how to etch, which led to Hopper's celebrated and iconic American paintings. We have pointed out that the painter of the famous celestial mural in New York's Grand Central Station—a mural Smith that must have walked under as he composed 'The Provincialism Problem'—was an Australian: Charles Basing. We have noted too the connection between the Australian professor of art at the University of Washington, Ambrose Patterson, and the most well known of the North West Painters, Mark Tobey, who together helped found the art scene in Seattle. (Patterson, incidentally, had previously studied in Paris with, among others, the American James Whistler at his short-lived Académie Carmen.)

This is to begin to say, of course, that we also find Australasians in that other arguable metropolitan centre, Paris. There was first of all the New Zealander Frances Hodgkins, who when she taught at the Académie Colarossi became the first woman to teach at a Parisian art school. There was the Australian Rupert Bunny, who along with Patterson was a founding member of the Salon d'Automne in 1903. There was an artist colony of Australians and New Zealanders at Étaples on the Picardy coast from the 1880s until World War II; and at Belle-Île the Australian John Russell, years before he met Matisse, had built his own house and painted the island's rugged coast beside his friend Claude Monet.

Many of these artists have not featured in the traditional accounts of Australian art, based on the formation of a national identity, because they lived for long periods outside the country. But part of what we would call an 'UnAustralian' tradition, that is, a non-nationalist history of Australian art, is that these expatriates are the true precursors to the artists of today. And it is to make the point that Smith's notion of 'an attitude of subservience to an externally imposed hierarchy of cultural values' is not the case: Australian artists were never 'external' to anything, but actually helped form this apparent 'hierarchy'.

In fact, against both Smith's modernism and the postmodernism that arose in opposition to it, the art world was never decentred or the centre was never empty. Rather, from the perspective of today we can see that the centres of art are everywhere. All cities, all places where art is made, are centres. Indeed, every centre of art is the centre of many artworlds, is part of the story of art from many places. That 'shuffling of standards' that must go on until, 'by some miracle, the local artworld becomes a metropolitan centre' has already happened all around the world.

The globalised artworld in which there are many centres of artistic interest—not only Salzburg, Dresden and Winterthur but also Lagos, Guangzhou and Papunya—has been the case not just since 1970 but since at least the late nineteenth century. It is not American modernism that is the story of the twentieth century but transnationalism. We might say of the series of exhibitions undertaken by the Centre Pompidou soon after its opening—*Paris–New York* (1977), *Paris–Berlin* (1978) and *Paris–Moscow* (1979)—that they were an attempt to reassert Euro-American art history at the time of its decline, but this would not be all. At least since the beginning of the twentieth century this capital-city-to-capital-city model has been outmoded altogether as a way of thinking about art.

In this sense it is not even a question of a 'provincialism solution', as though there were a problem that no longer applied. Rather, we would say that the real 'solution' is that provincialism has not existed for at least a century (and maybe not ever). There is no solution because there is no problem. For us, this is a new way of understanding Australian art: not as distant and isolated, *apart from* the world, but as close, belonging, *a part of* the world. (Equally, it is a new way of understanding French or American art not as central and definitive but as dispersed and open to redefinition.)

In fact, if there is a new history of world art to be written, it would not be the simple ecumenical joining of everything, an impossible task that could never be finished. Rather, as we have tried to do in our 'UnAustralian' art history, it would be a matter of starting in one place and seeing how the rest of the world is inseparable from it. What we can see is that Australian art *is* in the rest of the world and the rest of the world *is* in Australian art. After all, in some ways Musée du quai Branly with its roof by Lena Nyadbi is Australian, while the Sydney suburb of La Perouse (or Guriwal, on Dharawal land), which houses the important Indigenous community of the Eora and Yuin nations, is named after the French explorer who established a camp there while navigating the world in 1788.

* * *

In 1931 Auguste Herbin was at a crossroads. Despite the consensus reached in Paris on the part of many non-figurative artists, abstraction had been unable to form a common front against surrealism. Frustrated by infighting in the Salon des Surindépendants and by the failure of van Doesburg's Art Concret and Michel Seuphor's and Joaquín Torres-García's Cercle et Carré, Herbin called the Australian artist JW Power to Paris from England. With Power's support, the newly formed group Abstraction-Création brought together the abstract artists from around the world then assembled in Paris. Through its gallery and annual *cahier*, Abstraction-Création guaranteed, in the words of Swiss art historian Willy Rotzler, that abstraction would become 'a legitimate form of artistic expression that had been publicised all over the globe'.[4]

An earlier version of this text was published in *May* (Paris), no. 8, February 2012.

—

1 Hilary Spurling, 'The unknown Matisse ...', *Book Talk,* ABC Radio National, 5 August 2005, www.abc.net.au/radionational/programs/booktalk/the-unknown-matisse/3627290.

2 Jennifer Allen, 'The Provincialism Solution: Does the Art World Still Have a Centre?', *Frieze.com*, 28 April 2011, www.frieze.com/article/provincialism-solution.

3 Terry Smith, 'The Provincialism Problem', *Artforum*, vol. 13, no. 1, September 1974, p. 55. All further quotes from this essay.

4 Willy Rotzler, *Constructive Concepts: A History of Constructive Art from Cubism to the Present*, ABC Verlag, Zurich, 1988, p. 170.

Other 'UnAustralian art' essays by Rex Butler and ADS Donaldson

'A Short History of UnAustralian art', ed. Ian North, *Visual Animals: Crossovers, Evolution and New Aesthetics*, Contemporary Art Centre of South Australia, Adelaide, 2007.

'Stay, Go, or Come: A History of Australian Art, 1920–40', *Australian and New Zealand Journal of Art*, vol. 9, no. 1–2, 2008–09.

'French, Floral and Female: A History of UnAustralian Art 1900–1930', *Emaj*, vol. 5, 2010.

'Douglas Cooper and Australian Art History', *Broadsheet*, vol. 39, no. 2, 2010.

'Bernard Smith's Real Choice: Surrealism or Abstraction?', *Eyeline*, no. 78–79, 2013.

'Alice or Taos: Two Sides of the Same Coin', *Art Monthly Australia*, no. 282, August 2015.

'I Am, You Are, We Are All Australian', *Broadsheet*, vol. 44, no. 1, 2015.

'Len Lye as a "Sydney" Artist', eds. Paul Brobbel, Wystan Curnow and Roger Horrocks, *The Long Dream of Waking: New Perspectives on Len Lye*, Canterbury University Press, Christchurch, 2017.

'Gordon Walters: *Les années décisives*, 1946–1953', *Gordon Walters: New Vision*, eds. Lucy Hammonds, Julia Waites and Laurence Simmons, exhibition catalogue, Auckland Art Gallery Toi o Tāmaki, 2017.

'Was Australian Art Ever Provincial? A Response to Terry Smith's "The Provincialism Problem: Then and Now"', *Artmargins Online*, 16 September 2017.

'*The Field* at 50', *Broadsheet*, vol. 46, no. 3, 2017.

'Ludwig Hirschfeld-Mack, *Untitled (abstract composition in red, yellow and blue)*, 1960', Monash University Museum of Art, 2017.

'A Chain of Ponds: On German and Australian Artistic Interactions', eds. Benjamin Nickl, Irina Herrschner and Elżbieta M Goździak, *German-Australian Encounters and Cultural Transfers: Global Dynamics in Transnational Lands*, Springer, Singapore, 2018.

'Marcel and Felix: An Australian Rendezvous', ed. Edward Colless, *Apostrophe Duchamp*, A + A Publishing, Victorian College of the Arts, Melbourne, 2018.

'The UnAustralian Artworld', *Discipline*, no. 6, 2019.

'Duchamp and Australia: In Opposition', *Artlink*, vol. 40, no. 1, 2020.

'She-Oak and Sunlight: Australian Impressionism', *MeMO Review*, 5 June 2021

'1968–1982: From Australian Painting to UnAustralian Art', eds. David Homewood and Paris Lettau, *Ends of Painting: Art in the 1960s and 1970s*, Power Publications, 2022.

List of illustrations

3.1, p. 56
Armory Show poster, 1913
Paper, 71 × 56 cm
Elmer Livingston MacRae papers related to the Association of American Painters and Sculptors, 1899-c. 2013
Courtesy the Archives of American Art, Smithsonian Institution, Washington

3.2, p. 61
An overhead installation view of Gallery A at the Armory Show, New York, 1913
Sepia photographic print, 19 × 24 cm
Walt Kuhn Family papers and Armory Show records, 1859-1984
Courtesy the Archives of American Art, Smithsonian Institution, Washington

3.3, p. 63
Charles Basing, View of the ceiling of Grand Central Station, New York, 1913
Image author's own

3.4, p. 65
Armory Show artists and members of the press at the beefsteak dinner given by the Association of American Painters and Sculptors, New York, 8 March 1913
Photographer: Percy Rainford
Walt Kuhn Family papers and Armory Show records, 1859-1984
Archives of American Art, Smithsonian Institution, Washington DC

3.5, p. 67
Flyer for a stag party given by the Penguin Club honouring Horace Brodzky, March 1923
Courtesy the Archives of American Art, Smithsonian Institution, Washington DC

3.6, p. 69
Pat Sullivan in his studio, New York, 1922
Photograph
Browning Photography Studio, New York

3.7, p. 73
Richard Hayley Lever presenting *Mayflower* to President Calvin Coolidge in the Rose Garden at the White House, Washington DC, 1925
Courtesy the Archives of American Art, Smithsonian Institution, Washington

3.8, p. 75
Martin Lewis, *Relics (speakeasy corner)*, 1928
Drypoint, plate 30.5 × 25.4 cm; sheet 45.1 × 35.6 cm
The Metropolitan Museum of Art, New York
Acquired through the Harris Brisbane Dick Fund, 1929

3.9, p. 77
Mary Cecil Allen, *The Mirror of the Passing World*, 1928
W.W. Norton & Company, New York

3.10, p. 77
Mary Cecil Allen, *Painters of the Modern Mind*, 1929
W.W. Norton & Company, New York

3.11, p. 81
Margaret Cilento, *Abstract expression*, 1947
Hard-ground etching, printed in black ink with heavy plate-tone, from one plate, second print from original plate without re-inking (plate inverted)
Plate mark, 13 × 17.6 cm, on irregular sheet, 16.8 × 25.4 cm
National Gallery of Australia, Canberra
Acquired through the Gordon Darling Australasian Print Fund, 1994
© National Gallery of Australia

4.1, p. 88
Le monde au temps des surrealistes (*The world at the time of the surrealists*), in *Variete*, Hors Serie, Giugno, 1929, pp. 26-7
Museum of Modern Art (MoMA), New York
Digital Image © 2021, The Museum of Modern Art/Scala, Florence
© Photo SCALA, Florence

4.2, p. 90
The second room of André Breton's apartment, reconstructed at the Centre Pompidou, Paris.
© Successió Miró / ADAGP © ADAGP, Paris © Association Marcel Duchamp / ADAGP, Paris © Succession Picasso - Gestion droits d'auteur © Alberto Gironella Photo © Centre Pompidou, MNAM-CCI, Dist. RMN-Grand Palais / Image Centre Pompidou, MNAM-CCI

4.3, p. 92
Len Lye, film stills from *Tusalava*, 1929
Photogram
Image courtesy Govett-Brewster Art Gallery/Len Lye Centre

4.4, p. 94
English Surrealist Group members Roland Penrose, Julian Trevelyan, Geoffrey Graham and James Cant protest Spanish War neutrality in McWilliam's Chamberlain masks, May Day, London, 1938

4.5, p. 95
James Cant, *Merchants of death*, 1938
Oil on canvas, 102 × 122 cm; frame, 114 × 135.3 × 5.2 cm
Art Gallery of South Australia, Adelaide
Bequest of Dora Chapman, 1995

4.6, p. 98
James Cant, *Objects in a landscape*, 1936
Oil on canvas, 121.8 × 96.5 cm
National Gallery of Australia, Canberra
Acquired 1995

4.7, p. 99
Peter Purves Smith, *New York*, c. 1936
Oil on canvas, 76.2 × 50.8 cm; frame, 90.5 × 65 × 3.2 cm
Art Gallery of New South Wales, Sydney
Acquired 1960

4.8, p. 100
Herbert McClintock, *Dawnbreakers*, 1939
Oil on canvas on hardboard, 50.7 × 74.5 cm; frame, 67 × 90.7 × 5.2 cm
Art Gallery of New South Wales, Sydney
Acquired 1969
© Estate of Herbert McClintock

4.9, p. 102
Ivor Francis, *Schizophrenia*, 1943
Oil on canvas, 82.5 × 62.2 cm; frame, 106 × 84.5 × 5 cm
Art Gallery of South Australia, Adelaide
Acquired through the Elder Bequest Fund, 1945
© Art Gallery of South Australia

4.10, p. 103
Klaus Friedeberger, *Camp dream*, 1943
Drawing brush and gouache on wove paper, 30 × 25.2 cm
National Gallery of Australia, Canberra
Purchased with the assistance of James Agapitos OAM and Ray Wilson OAM, 2007

4.11, p. 104
Vera Rudner, *Sacrilege*, 1948
Oil on cardboard, 36.5 × 28.5 cm; frame, 51.7 × 44 × 7 cm
National Gallery of Australia, Canberra
Acquired with the assistance of James Agapitos OAM and Ray Wilson OAM, 2007

4.12, p. 106
Mary Cockburn Mercer, *Birth of Venus*, 1941
Oil on canvas, 65 × 72.3 cm
Image courtesy Sotheby's
© Estate of Mary Cockburn Mercer

4.13, p. 107
Dušan Marek, *Equator*, 1948
Oil on board, 121.7 × 91.2 cm; frame, 126.5 × 96 × 5.5 cm
Art Gallery of South Australia, Adelaide
Acquired through the South Australian Government Grant, 1972
© Art Gallery of South Australia

4.14, p. 108
Robert Klippel and James Gleeson, *No. 35 Madame Sophie Sesostoris (a Pre-Raphaelite satire)*, 1947-8
Beech and various woods, painted in oil
49.5 × 10 × 10 cm
Art Gallery of New South Wales, Sydney
Gift of James Gleeson and Robert Klippel, 1970
© Gleeson/O'Keefe Foundation

5.1, p. 114
Installation view of the inner hall and drawing room of Mortimer Menpes's London house at Cadogan Gardens, London, c. 1899
Image courtesy The Victorian Web and George P. Landow

5.2, p. 117
Charles Conder, *9 by 5 Impression Exhibition* catalogue cover, 1889
Photo-lithograph and letterpress on hand-made paper, 17.7 × 21.6 cm
Image courtesy the National Gallery of Victoria, Melbourne

5.3, p. 118
George Rose, *Seoul*, 1904
Photograph, 24 × 29.9 cm
Image courtesy Alamy

5.4, p. 120
Rupert Bunny, *Mme Sada Yacco, Le Shogun (scène de la folie)*, c. 1907
Previously known as *The Geisha Girl*
Oil on canvas, 160 × 118.2 cm
The Stuartholme-Behan Collection of Australian Art, The University of Queensland, Brisbane
Image: Carl Warner
Reproduced courtesy the artist's estate

5.5, p. 121
Rupert Bunny, *Madame Melba*, 1901-2
Oil on canvas, 245.5 × 153 cm
National Gallery of Victoria, Melbourne
Acquired through The Art Foundation of Victoria with the assistance of Henry Krongold CBE and Dinah Krongold, Founder Benefactors, 1980

5.6, p. 122
Martin Lewis, *Street booth, Tokyo, New Year's Eve*, 1927
Drypoint, printed in black ink on cream wove paper
Platemark, 35.5 × 26.5 cm; sheet, 42.3 × 33.6 cm
Art Gallery of New South Wales, Sydney
Acquired through the Australian Prints, Drawings and Watercolours Benefactors' Fund, 2007
© Estate of Martin Lewis

5.7, p. 123
William Hardy Wilson, *City of Kurrajong*, 1951
French crayon, 52.6 × 41.7 cm
National Library of Australia, Canberra

5.8, p. 125
Iri and Toshi Maruki, *The Hiroshima panels*, 1950-52
Installation view, National Gallery of Victoria, Melbourne, 1958
Photo: Mark Strizic

6.1, p. 128
Henri Gaudier-Brzeska, *Horace Brodzky*, c. 1913
Bronze, 69.4 × 51.5 × 34.5 cm
Tate Britain, London
Presented by the Trustees of the Chantrey Bequest, 1957

6.2, p. 132
Raj Nagi, *Portrait of Anthony Martin Fernando*, 2007
Oil on canvas, 184 × 112 cm
National Museum of Australia, Canberra
Image courtesy the artist

6.3, p. 134
Sidney Nolan, *Carcass*, 1953
Oil and enamel paint on composition board, 91.4 × 121.5 cm
National Gallery of Victoria, Melbourne
Acquired through The Art Foundation of Victoria with the assistance of the National Australia Bank Limited, Honorary Life Benefactor, 1995
© The Artist's Estate, All Rights Reserved / Bridgeman Images

6.4, p. 136
William Orpen, *Group associated with the New English Art Club*, c. 1904
Left to right: Legros, Rodin, Steer, Tonks, Brown, Rothenstein, John, Conder, probably MacColl
Pencil, black chalk (or charcoal), pen, ink and watercolour
22.5 × 41.5 cm
National Portrait Gallery, London
Acquired 1995
© National Portrait Gallery, London

6.5, p. 138
Richard Hayley Lever, *Winter, St Ives*, c. 1914
Oil on canvas, 101.8 × 127 cm; frame, 120 × 145.4 × 8.6 cm
Brooklyn Museum, New York
Acquired through the Caroline H. Polheumus Fund, 15.279
Image: Brooklyn Museum

6.6, p. 140
Frances Hodgkins in the Wharf Studio, St Ives, Cornwall, 1918
Sepia-toned photograph print, 6.4 × 9.8 cm
E H McCormick Papers, E H McCormick Research Library,
Auckland Art Gallery Toi o Tāmaki
Gift of Linda Gill, 2015

6.7, p. 144
Dorrit Black, *Nocturne, Wynyard Square*, 1932
Linocut, printed in black ink from one block, on

thin ivory laid mulberry paper
Blockmark, 22.6 × 15 cm; sheet
25.3 × 17.2 cm
Art Gallery of New South Wales, Sydney
Acquired 1976

6.8, p. 145
Horace Brodzky, *Expulsion*, 1914
Linocut printed in black ink on ivory wove paper
Blockmark, 26 × 16.3 cm; sheet (irreg.),
33 × 24.3 cm
Art Gallery of New South Wales, Sydney
Acquired through funds provided by the
Australian Prints, Drawings and Watercolours
Benefactors' Fund, 2003
© Estate of Horace Brodzky

6.9, p. 147
Roy de Maistre, *Conflict*, 1932
Oil on canvas, 112 × 86.5 cm;
frame 116.7 × 91.8 × 7 cm
Art Gallery of New South Wales, Sydney
Acquired 1960
© Roy de Maistre Estate

6.10, p. 148
Roy de Maistre, *Patrick White*, 1939
Oil on canvas, 76.4 × 50.7 cm; frame,
91.3 × 65.7 × 5.5 cm
Art Gallery of New South Wales, Sydney
Gift of the sitter's niece, Miss Frances Peck, 1972
© Roy de Maistre Estate

6.11, p. 154
Germaine Greer and Vivian Stanshall of the Bonzo
Dog Doo-Dah Band on the cover of *Oz Magazine*,
Issue 19, 1969
Image courtesy *Oz Magazine*

6.12, p. 156
Raymond McIntyre, *Self portrait*, 1915
Oil on wood panel, 40.8 × 51.5 cm
Museum of New Zealand Te Papa
Tongarewa, Wellington
Gift of the New Zealand Academy of Fine Arts, 1941

7.1, p. 160
Ludwig Hirschfeld-Mack, *Desolation, Internment Camp, Orange, NSW*, 1941
Woodcut, printed in black ink on thin ivory
wove paper
Blockmark, 21.6 × 13.5 cm; sheet, 33.6 × 21 cm
Art Gallery of New South Wales, Sydney
Gift of Olive Hirschfeld, the artist's widow, 1970
© Reproduced with permission

7.2, p. 164
Bertram Mackennal, *Circe*, 1893
Bronze, 58 × 22 × 26 cm
National Gallery of Australia, Canberra
Bequest of Dr Donald R Sheumack, 1990

7.3, p. 166
Frank Hinder, *Tribute to Kandinsky*, 1938
Drawing in watercolour over drawing in black
pencil, on paper
25.6 × 21.5 cm
National Gallery of Australia, Canberra
Acquired 1981
© National Gallery of Australia

7.4, p. 168
Ludwig Hirschfeld-Mack, *The world to come*, 1940
Pencil, watercolour on ivory wove paper, varnish
Image/sheet, 17.7 × 24.8 cm; sheet, 28.9 × 39 cm
Art Gallery of New South Wales, Sydney
Gift of Olive Hirschfeld, the artist's widow, 1970
© Reproduced with permission

7.5, p. 169
Emil Nolde, *Head of a South Sea Islander*, 1913-4
Watercolour, 48 × 35 cm; 77 × 62 × 3.5 cm frame
Art Gallery of New South Wales, Sydney
Acquired 1989
© Nolde Stiftung Seebüll

7.6, p. 172
Violet Teague, *Boy with a palette*, 1911
Oil on canvas, 175.5 × 108.5 cm;
184.5 × 117.5 × 65 cm frame
National Gallery of Australia, Canberra
Gift of U. S. Teague, 1976
© Violet Teague Archive, courtesy Felicity Druce

7.7, p. 173
Theo Scharf, *Promenade*, from the 'Night in a city', c. 1923
Etching and drypoint on paper
Platemark, 10.2 × 8.2 cm; sheet, 32 × 23.6 cm
National Gallery of Australia, Canberra
Acquired 1982
© The Estate of Theo Scharf

7.8, p. 175
Hein Heckroth, *Australia*, 1941
Oil on hardboard, 47 × 59 cm, 65 × 78.5 × 2.7 cm
National Gallery of Australia, Canberra
Acquired with the assistance of James Agapitos OAM and Ray Wilson OAM, 2007
Courtesy the National Gallery of Australia

7.9, p. 176
Photograph of Alan Moore drawing SS concentration camp guards at Bergen-Belsen, 1945
Courtesy Australian War Memorial, Canberra

7.10, p. 177
Colin Colahan, *Collaborators in the lion's cage in Antwerp*, 1944
Oil on wood, 45.8 × 38 cm, 62 × 54.5 × 4.5 cm frame
Courtesy the Australian War Memorial, Canberra

7.11, p. 182
EO Hoppé and an unknown young woman at Hermannsburg Lutheran Mission Station, Central Australia, 1930
Photograph
Courtesy the EO Hoppé Estate Collection

7.12, p. 183
Tracy Moffatt, *Self portrait*, 1999
Hand-coloured gelatin silver photograph, edition 10/10, 33.5 × 22 cm
The University of Queensland, Brisbane
Acquired 2005
Courtesy the artist and Roslyn Oxley9 Gallery, Sydney
Image: Carl Warner
© Tracey Moffatt

8.1, p. 188
Painting from the Pacific: Japan, America, Australia, New Zealand, May 1961
Image Courtesy of the E.H. McCormick Research Library, Auckland Art Gallery Toi o Tāmaki

8.2, p. 194
Frank Hinder, *Taos landscape*, 1934
Watercolour, ink, pencil, collage on heavy white paper
13.1 × 12.9 cm
Art Gallery of New South Wales, Sydney
Gift of the artist 1981
© Estate of Frank Hinder

8.3, p. 195
Grace Crowley, *Mirmande*, 1928
Oil on canvas, 81 × 100.5 cm; frame, 98.3 × 115.3 7.2 cm
Art Gallery of South Australia, Adelaide
Bequest of Grace Crowley, 1981
© Art Gallery of South Australia

8.4, p. 196
Ralph Balson, *Painting*, 1941
Oil on paperboard, 78.7 × 63.5 cm; frame, 89.0 × 74.0 × 3.0 cm
Art Gallery of New South Wales, Sydney
Acquired 1965
© Ralph Balson Estate

8.5, p. 198
Milan Mrkusich, *City lights*, 1955
Oil on cotton on board, 76.2 × 92.4 cm
Auckland Art Gallery Toi o Tāmaki, Auckland
Acquired 1989
© Estate of Milan Mrkusich

8.6, p. 199
Ralph Balson, *Constructive painting*, 1954
Oil on composition board, 83.5 × 108.5 cm
Art Gallery of South Australia, Adelaide
Acquired through a South Australian Government Grant, 1974
© Ralph Balson Estate

8.7, p. 200
Grace Crowley, *Abstract painting*, 1950
Oil on hardboard, 59.5 × 74.5 cm; frame, 65.5 × 80.4 × 2 cm
Art Gallery of New South Wales, Sydney
Foundation purchase, 2019
© Grace Crowley Estate

8.8, p. 201
John McLaughlin, *Untitled*, 1948
Oil on board, 60 × 45 cm
Image courtesy Esther Bear Gallery, Santa Barbara

9.1, p. 206
Juan Melé, *Marco recortado no. 2* (*Irregular frame no. 2*), 1946
Oil on masonite, 67 × 46 cm
Museum of Modern Art, New York
Image courtesy Moderna Museet, Stockholm

9.2, p. 208
Joaquín Torres-García, *América invertida*, 1943
Ink on paper, 22.1 × 16 cm
Museo Torres García, Montevideo
© Sucesión Joaquín Torres-García, Montevideo, 2015

9.3, p. 210
Juan Davila, *Fable of Australian painting*, (panel 1 and 2), 1983
Oil on canvas, 274 × 1096 cm
Image courtesy Museum of Contemporary Art, Sydney and Kalli Rolfe Contemporary Art, Melbourne

9.4, p. 211
Juan Davila, *Fable of Australian painting*, (panel 3 and 4), 1983
Oil on canvas, 274 × 1096 cm
Image courtesy Museum of Contemporary Art, Sydney and Kalli Rolfe Contemporary Art, Melbourne

9.5, p. 212
Juan Davila, *The Liberator, Simón Bolívar*, 1994
Oil on canvas on metal, (irreg.), 125 × 98 cm
Image courtesy the artist
© Juan Davila

9.6, p. 214
Juan Davila, *Madí*, 1991
Oil, enamel and collage on wood and canvas
292 × 430 cm
Image courtesy the artist and Kalli Rolfe Contemporary Art, Melbourne
© Juan Davila

9.7, p. 217
Godfrey Rivers, *Under the jacaranda*, 1903
Oil on canvas, 143.4 × 107.2 cm
Queensland Art Gallery, Brisbane
Acquired 1903

9.8, p. 221
Juan Davila, *Un-Australian*, 2014
Oil on canvas, 60 × 50 cm
Image courtesy of the artist and Kalli Rolfe Contemporary Art, Melbourne
© Juan Davila

10.1, p. 226
Stanisław Ignacy Witkiewicz (Witkacy), *Australian landscape*, 1918
Pastel, crayon, charcoal, cardboard, 51.5 × 65.5 cm
Adam Mickiewicz Museum of Literature, Warsaw

10.2, p. 230
Piet Mondrian, *Composition n. XIII/ Composition 2*, 1913
Oil on canvas, 79.5 × 63.5 cm
Museo Nacional Thyssen-Bornemisza, Madrid and Scala, Florence
© Mondrian/Holtzman Trust

10.3, p. 231
Giacomo Balla, *Iridescent interpenetration no. 5 – eucalyptus*, 1914
Oil on canvas, 101 × 120 cm
Private Collection

10.4, p. 232
David Smith, *Australia*, 1951
Painted steel on cinder-block base
202 × 274 × 41 cm; cinder-block base, 44.5 × 42.5 × 38.7 cm
Museum of Modern Art (MoMA), New York
Digital Image © 2021, The Museum of Modern Art/Scala, Florence
© Photo SCALA, Florence

10.5, p. 233
Richard Stankiewicz, *Australia no. 15*, 1969
Steel, 539 × 200 × 115 cm
National Gallery of Australia, Canberra
Acquired 1975

10.6, p. 234
Anne Truitt, *Australian spring*, 1972
Wood, paint, 182.8 × 70 × 70 cm
Walker Art Centre, Minneapolis
Gift of Mrs. Helen B. Stern, 1973
© Anne Truitt
Image courtesy Bridgeman Images

10.7, p. 238
Emily Kngwarreye, *Anwerlarr anganenty (Big yam dreaming)*, 1995
Synthetic polymer paint on canvas, 291.1 × 801.8 cm

National Gallery of Victoria, Melbourne
Presented through The Art Foundation of Victoria by Donald and Janet Holt and family, Governors, 1995

10.8, p. 239

Sol LeWitt, *Tangled bands*, 2002
Gouache on paper
Sheet, 154.3 × 170.8 cm; frame, 167 × 182.5 × 5 cm
Art Gallery of New South Wales, Sydney
John Kaldor Family Collection

11.1, p. 242

JW Power, *Marine*, c. 1933
Oil on canvas, 50.8 × 89.3 cm; frame, 67.4 × 105.6 × 7 cm
Chau Chak Wing Museum, Sydney
Mrs Edith Power Bequest, 1961
Image courtesy Chau Chak Wing and the University of Sydney

Index

B

UnAustralian Art
Ten Essays on Transnational
Art History

Rex Butler and ADS Donaldson

POWER PUBLICATIONS

First published in Australia in 2022
by Power Publications

Power Publications
Power Institute Foundation
for Art and Visual Culture
University of Sydney
NSW 2006 Australia
www.powerpublications.com.au

Copyediting: Belinda Nemec
Proofreading: Evie Franzidis
Design: Elle Williams Studio

ISBN: 978-0-909952-10-5

A catalogue record for this book is available from the National Library of Australia.

Front cover:
Diena Georgetti, *Compass*, 2017
acrylic on canvas, custom frame,
79.30 x 52.00 x 4.80 cm
Photo: Sofia Freeman/The Commercial, © the artist, courtesy The Commercial, Sydney

Back cover:
Friedrich Schonbach, cover for Jorge Luis Borges's *La Muerte y La Brujula* (*Death and the Compass*), Emecé Editores, Buenos Aires, 1951. Graphic designer Jorge Laquinandi. Courtesy the Schonbach family, with thanks to Seumas Spark.